# Contributors

Kayla F. Bernheim, Ph.D., Livingston County Counseling Services, Mt. Morris, New York

Dalen S. Cole, M. A., New York, New York

Stephen A. Cole, M.D., A.M., New York Veterans Administration, New York, New York

Stephanie Fitzgerald, R.N., M.S., Center for Rehabilitation Research and Training in Mental Health, Boston University, Boston, Massachusetts

Agnes B. Hatfield, Ph.D., Department of Human Development, College of Education, University of Maryland, College Park, Maryland

Hal Jung, M.S., Counseling and Family Services, Inc., Medford, Massachusetts

Harriet P. Lefley, Ph.D., Office of Transcultural Education and Research, Department of Psychiatry, University of Miami, Miami, Florida

Evelyn M. McElroy, R.N., Ph.D., School of Nursing, University of Maryland, Baltimore, Maryland

LeRoy Spaniol, Center for Rehabilitation Research and Training in Mental Health, Boston University, Boston, Massachusetts

Kenneth G. Terkelsen, M.D., Cornell University Medical Center, New York, New York

Anthony M. Zipple, M.S., C.A.G.S., Center for Rehabilitation Research and Training in Mental Health, Boston University, Boston, Massachusetts

# Preface

The need for this book has grown out of the recent upsurge of interest in providing services to families coping with a mentally ill relative. With changes in treatment philosophy that favor community care over institutionalization, many more psychiatrically disturbed people now live with or near their families. While the degree to which families are necessarily involved was overlooked for a long period of time, there is now wide recognition that families can play a significant role in the patient's recovery and integration into the community. As a consequence, a variety of programs are being created with the purpose of helping these families deal more effectively with their disturbed relative. What is disquieting about this new interest in families of the mentally ill, however, is the degree to which the focus is on techniques to be employed in changing the family and how little discussion goes on about the need for professionals to understand the families they hope to change. Logic would appear to dictate that without a comprehensive understanding of the profoundly difficult task faced by these families, sound technique is unlikely. The focus of this book, then, is the family and how it experiences the tragedy of mental illness in a loved one. We hope our book will serve as an impetus to many more efforts on the part of researchers to comprehend the deeply human problems that arise as a consequence of mental illness.

One might argue that the current fascination with technique does not preclude a real effort on the part of practitioners to enter the complex world of these families. This may be true, but some research plus our own active involvement in the family self-help groups of the National Alliance for the Mentally Ill reveals that many families feel poorly understood by those whose job it is to help them. As we have gotten to know hundreds of families on an informal and nonprofessional basis, we have found a surprising degree of alienation from the mental health profession. Although there is much professional enthusiasm about new family treatments, families by and large do not share that enthusiasm.

This book starts with some assumptions that differ from those of other works on families. We believe that to be successful with families, professionals must know mental illness from the perspective of the family. Professionals must enhance their role-taking capacities and walk in the shoes of the family for a while. It is also our assumption that the quality of life and the well-being of all the members of the family are important. It is distressing to see how willing the mental health profession is to assign responsibilities for care to families with little apparent concern for what happens to these families in the process. This probably would not occur if there were appropriate understanding of the anguish families suffer. We hope our approach will create an interest in and desire for more empathic understanding.

Finally, our book does not start with the assumption that there is something wrong with a family that has a mentally ill member or that there is something unusual about difficulty in coping. We believe that families experience mental illness in ways that any of us experience catastrophic events in our lives. There is necessarily a great deal of floundering, with considerable trial and error as one travels uncharted waters, but what is amazing is how well human beings prevail. Inability to see families of the mentally ill in these positive ways has contributed to their present alienation.

In this volume we have brought together a professionally diverse group of people whose mission was to focus on the family experience and to find a theoretical orientation that would help us to understand mental illness from a family perspective. We were fortunate in having writers from the disciplines of psychology, education, nursing, psychiatry, and rehabilitation. In Section I of our book, we examine the family experience both historically and cross-culturally and we note that families' distress depends upon the responsibility they must bear for direct care and the amount and kind of assistance the society provides. The distress also varies with the meaning society assigns to this disorder and especially the prevailing assumption of etiology. Both the devil theory of our Calvinist forefathers and the family interaction explanations that came later in psychiatry made Western society, and especially America, a difficult place in which to deal with mental illness. An examination of current family theories leads to the conclusion that they all tend to be deficient in some ways and that they

.have not enlarged our understanding of families. What is called for, then, is a paradigm shift. An exploration of the theory of coping and adaptation in Chapters 3 and 4 points to the possibility that this conceptual framework may serve the function that we need. It can provide the kind of comprehensive explanation of both the subjective experience and the objective burdens of mental illness that have been so sorely lacking. It can also explain what human beings need in order to succeed in a difficult adaptive struggle and thus pave the way for new thinking about practice with families.

In Section II, we move from the general theory of coping and adaptation to its application in understanding families as they come to grips with mental illness in a relative. The behavioral manifestations of mental illness are presented as they affect the environmental demands that families face. Research showing families' perceptions of their needs and what they perceive as helpful in coping are discussed. Included in the section are two chapters that capture the subjective experience of families in a sensitive way.

Finally, in Section III, several writers direct the readers' attention to the implications of coping and adaptation theory to research and practice issues. We are led to understand that mental health professionals and families often differ in their perceptions of family needs and problems and they also differ in their evaluations of the mental health services that families are given. This information is important in the light of growing family consumer strength that makes it incumbent upon us to pay attention to consumer preferences. In Section III, models of family practice appropriate to adaptation theory are reviewed. This, of course, leads to the next relevant question about how practitioners are to be appropriately trained.

The concluding chapter opens up some new issues for research and, it is hoped, will serve to provide a challenge to mental health professionals to pose the right questions that will lead to better understanding of the families we are committed to serve.

Agnes B. Hatfield
Harriet P. Lefley

# Contents

# I

# IN SEARCH OF
# NEW PERSPECTIVES

# Families as Caregivers: A Historical Perspective

*Agnes B. Hatfield*

Developments in the field of mental health in the past decade have produced a marked upsurge of interest in families of persons with a chronic mental illness. With the movement away from institutional care in favor of providing care in the community, families are increasingly involved in the lives of their disabled relatives and are often themselves in the role of primary caregiver. This has required that professionals work with families in new and different ways; the good of the patient has necessitated that an effective collaborative relationship exist between the two. This is a relationship that does not develop easily. Why this is so, we think, can best be understood through a historical overview of the treatment of mental illness in this country as it has affected the relatives closest to the disturbed individual. The purpose of this chapter is to present that overview.

It will be demonstrated that the meaning of mental illness to the family and the way that family members are affected is now, and historically has been, the result of (1) where the ill person lives and who is charged with responsibility for his or her care, (2) the meaning of the illness to the family and especially the way in which that meaning is influenced by prevailing theories of etiology, and (3) the degree of understanding, compassion, and support given to affected families and the skill and appropriateness of help offered by the community.

Agnes B. Hatfield. Department of Human Development, College of Education, University of Maryland, College Park, Maryland.

## THE LOCUS OF CARE

Because mental illness has always been such a baffling disorder, producing behavior that is bizarre, disruptive, and sometimes even violent, family life is invariably disturbed when the ill person is located close to home. Society's view of where the patient should live has been marked by a series of sharp reversals in philosophy. Originally families were the sole source of care and the community took little responsibility; then a movement toward institutional care removed most patients from the home in the 19th and early 20th centuries; and finally, in another sharp reversal in the 1950s, home and community were once again the favored place and patients were rapidly deinstitutionalized. Each of these shifts in treatment philosophy had a profound, but rarely acknowledged, effect on the family.

### The Colonial Period

In the 17th century, the mentally ill received little attention from society. Neither the cultural nor material conditions of that period made it possible for a system of care to be considered at that time (Deutsch, 1949). Families were on their own without the mitigating effects of medication, physicians, or support services. Social history has little to say about the effect on the family, but one can well imagine that it was devastating. Since the family as a unit was necessarily very strong during colonial times, one can imagine the typical family straining to accommodate the disordered member with great cost to other members, for the only alternative would be an extrusion from the family with full knowledge that the most harsh and inhumane conditions in the outside world were in store for the person. Sometimes families chose other atrocious alternatives, such as locking people in cellars or attics, or placing them in chains. It is easy to judge these caretakers harshly from the perspective of the 20th century, but they may not have had other alternatives if the family were to survive.

It must have been an incredible hardship on the family to have an unproductive and economically dependent person in a household, in which mere survival in an alien and inhospitable land was at stake. In addition, the suffering of mentally ill persons must surely have been aggravated by the dominant ideology of the times, which deemed mental disturbance to be a natural consequence of a stern, unbending Providence meting out justice to the wicked and deserving (Deutsch, 1949).

## The Emergence of Hospital Care

In the latter part of the 18th century, progressive forces began moving to the fore with a promise of change in the concept of care. Not the least of the accomplishments of this period was the establishment of the first general hospital in America—the Pennsylvania Hospital—where among other classes of ill people to be given care were those suffering from mental illnesses. Although, as Deutsch (1949) notes, the treatment was barbaric, the important fact was that for the first time in American history, a public institution was receiving the mentally ill for the purposes of attempting to cure them. From the standpoint of most patients and relatives of the time, this event was irrelevant, for few could be accommodated. At best only the few in which the families had resources were admitted.

To Virginia belongs the distinction of having erected the first American asylum exclusively for the mentally ill. It was opened in 1773 in Williamsburg, then the capital of the colony. Its purpose was to confine in an asylum those ill who were wandering around and terrifying others, in order to avoid using jails for that purpose. By the first quarter of the 19th century, special institutions for the "insane" were established in eight states. While this was considered a great stride forward, the vast majority of the disturbed could not be accommodated, and life did not change much. At best many wound up in almshouses and poorhouses, where they were thrown in with the other unfortunate poor (Deutsch, 1949).

It was not until the appearance of Dorothea Dix on the national scene that public facilities were proposed for all states (Talbott, 1978). The intent was to provide humane, benign, and enlightened care. The facilities, however, were designed to provide asylum and thus were located outside large population centers and at great distances from the patients' families and other community ties. While the locus of care was in the state hospital, families were afforded respite from the inordinate demands of providing an accommodation in the home setting. However, a decision to put a person away in a hospital was stressful in itself, for the usual expectation was that he or she would be there for life. Some families, no doubt, abandoned their relative, but others tried to maintain regular contact even though it may have been frightening to approach the vast hospital grounds, enter the large forbidding brick building, and get past the keepers of the asylum with their huge rings of keys. Then what they often saw in terms of neglect and inhumane treatment must have deeply saddened them. No wonder some families abandoned their relatives in an attempt to get beyond their pain.

## Movement toward Deinstitutionalization

By 1955, the trend toward increasing admission to state mental hospitals had peaked; since that time there has been a steady decrease in hospital census nationally. This decrease marked the beginning of a movement that came to be known as "deinstitutionalization," an organized effort to move those with severe and chronic mental illnesses from hospitals to the community. Talbott (1978) characterized this trend toward deinstitutionalization as "the most important single development in the delivery of mental health services by state mental hospitals in recent years" (p. 32).

Why a 75-year-old trend toward hospital care that had been considered better than what a community could provide rather suddenly reversed itself is an interesting story in itself. Most important ever in the history of institutional psychiatry was the discovery in the 1950s of effective psychopharmacological agents for treating psychosis. Medications had a dramatic effect on some patients and made it possible for them to be free of restraints and locked doors and to move about freely. For many, although they were not fully well, confinement in the hospital was not longer necessary (Talbott, 1978).

An additional factor in accelerating the movement away from hospital care was a philosophy current in American thought that gave increasing emphasis to the civil rights of patients. As a result of several landmark civil rights decisions it became difficult to hospitalize persons against their will in most states unless there was clear evidence of dangerousness and incapacity to function in the community.

Finally, there was a growing feeling that large impersonal institutions were antitherapeutic, and that many patients suffered as much from the side effects of hospitalization as they did from the mental illnesses themselves. People were much better off, it was thought, being treated in their own communities where they had natural ties. Bachrach (1978) noted that there was an underlying assumption that (1) community care is a good thing for most patients, (2) communities not only can, but are willing to, assume responsibility and leadership in care, and (3) functions performed by hospitals can be performed equally well—or better—in the community. In other words, according to Bachrach (1976), the basic concept of deinstitutionalization involved both (1) the eschewal of traditional institutional settings (primarily state hospitals) for the care of the mentally ill, and (2) the concurrent expansion of community-based service for the treatment of these individuals.

The first goal, movement away from hospitals, occurred with considerable optimism and zeal and proceeded at a rapid rate until the peak population of 558,992 nationally in 1955 was reduced to 193,436 by 1976. In two decades, hospital census had been decreased by two thirds.

Unfortunately the early optimism was short-lived; the whole deinstitutionalization movement was plagued with a great array of problems. To begin with, there was a gross underestimation of the complexity of such a massive movement. There was a lack of initial planning and no clarity as to what level of government (city, county, state or federal was to assume responsibility. Millions of dollars were allocated by the federal government, but little of it seemed to flow to the patient in a useful manner (Bachrach, 1976; Lamb, 1982; Talbott, 1978).

Bachrach (1976) has reviewed the literature on deinstitutionalization and has summarized the problems that were identified. Many mental health professionals resisted working with chronic patients; patients were inadequately prepared for community living; the disadvantaged and minority populations were not understood; there was an inadequate range of services; there was fragmentation and lack of coordination; treatment was inaccessible; there was resistance from communities; and there was severe stress on families. Clearly the full intent of deinstitutionalization was not achieved. While the hospital census was reduced, replacement with alternate types of community care did not occur.

The whole problem has become even more complicated with the identification of a subgroup of the mentally ill population that has come to be known as "the young adult chronic patient" (Bachrach, 1982; Pepper, Ryglewicz, & Kirshner, 1982). These patients show persistent and severe impairments in psychological and social functioning, and no one feels entirely successful in treating them. Sometimes called "the uninstitutionalized generation," they are the first generation of mentally ill persons who have had short-stay hospitalizations or who in times of crisis have been diverted to resources other than institutions. These mostly young persons, ages 18 to 35, have been the beneficiaries of the patient's rights movements and new philosophies of community care, but, unfortunately, have not fared well. Although seriously disturbed, they do not like to define themselves as mental patients and do not use mental health resources appropriately. Some of them are drug and alcohol abusers, some wander from place to place, and some wind up in the criminal justice system. Many try to separate from their families and become independent only to fall back on the family doorstep, seeking support, shelter, and sustenance.

It was difficult to find a statistic that revealed exactly how many former patients were living at home until 1978 (25 years after the beginning of the movement toward deinstitutionalization). At a conference on the chronic mental patient, sponsored by the American Psychiatric Association, Minkoff (1978) reported that a high percentage of discharged patients, probably as many as 65%, went home to live. Generally about 35-40% returned to spouses, 35-40% to parents, and 20-25% live in structured environments, boarding homes, or single rooms.

Drawing from data of the national reporting program of the Division of Biometry and Epidemiology of the National Institute of Mental Health, Goldman (1982) found national data indicating that in 1975, 73% of mental patients admitted to general hospitals were living with the family before admission. Sixty-five percent of the never married were living with family, and almost half of the separated and divorced were living with a family member. However, 1970 survey data of public hospitals showed only 58% lived with families. Goldman explained this discrepancy on the fact that state and county hospitals admit a smaller percentage of those applying who live at home and have families. Goldman accepted 58-73% as a rough estimate of those living at home and assumed Minkoff's estimate of 65% to be fairly accurate. He estimated that about 1 million persons return home, and that at least 25% of these are severely disturbed. Goldman concluded that relationships between the severely disturbed and their families have been altered dramatically since World War II.

In the words of McFarlane (1983a), "in the nearly ubiquitous absence of structured community residences, the caring agent has become the family of origin" (p. 11). McFarlane reported that in one state, New York, in fiscal 1980-1981, 51% of all dischargees from state hospitals were sent to live with family members. Of those patients with stays of less than 3 months, 80% of those released went home for care. In fact, there had been a steady decrease over the past 6 years in the number of patients discharged to alternate residences. With the federal government reducing money for community services and for Social Security disability payments to the chronically mentally ill, McFarlane predicts that there will be no reduction in families as de facto caregivers in the near future. In other words, the family has become the replacement for the ward staff.

It is a matter of considerable consternation and concern that over a period of nearly 3 decades of deinstitutionalization, mental health professionals were so oblivious to what it might mean for families to replace the ward staff without the training and resources ordinarily available in the hospital. It has only been in the last 2 or 3 years that we have been hearing such vigorous statements as Goldman's (1982) comment that "a problem of this magnitude, potentially involving a million families of discharged mental patients and more than half million chronically disabled adults living with spouses in the community, calls for wide scale public health intervention" (p. 558).

Other equally alarming statements have been coming to the fore of late, which raises the question as to what has been the focus of the professions in relation to families. Presumably they have not been bringing resources to bear in supporting families in this onerous task. Caesar (1980) insists it is time to reassess the results of the movement toward community care in terms of its effects on the actual lives of the mentally disabled and their loved ones. In the process of blocking the warehousing of the nondangerous, writes Caesar, "we have consigned many persons to lives of quiet desperation, have destroyed the mental and emotional health of those who love and care for them, and destroyed families—to the ultimate detriment and even destruction of the disabled person" (p. 315).

## THEORIES OF ETIOLOGY

A review of the history of mental illness as it relates to families indicates that the resources of society and the attention of professionals was focused on the issues of etiology. The importance of helping these families in a concrete way or finding alternative types of care was not central in their thinking.

Although Freud and his colleagues considered schizophrenia as having constitutional and organic origins, as did Kraeplin before them, it was apparently Freud's emphasis on the importance of early experience in shaping human behavior that led to an interest in parental behavior as a factor in the development of psychiatric disorder. American psychiatry, according to an analysis by Beels and McFarlane (1982), was characterized by radical environmentalism in the period following World War II. There was considerable optimism that most problems of adults could be explained in terms of child rearing and family environment. Not the least of the problems to be given considerable attention was schizophrenia and its presumed etiology in the family from which the person came.

### The Schizophrenogenic Mother

The family interaction paradigm was first given serious attention in 1948, when Fromm-Reichmann published her theory of the schizophre-

nogenic mother. According to her theory, the origins of the schizophrenic reaction pattern lay in infantile relations with the mother, who
unconsciously conveyed her feelings of rejection to her child. These
mothers, according to Fromm-Reichmann, were cold and distant. Their
lack of warmth and affection impeded the development of the necessary psychological and social skills. The catch phrase "schizophrenogenic mother" caught on and may have had a strong influence on the
plethora of interactionist theories that dominated the field in the next 3
decades.

Hirsch and Leff (1975) reviewed several studies in an attempt to
establish the prevalence of schizophrenogenic mothers, but could not,
in spite of the popularity of the theory, find any supporting evidence
for it. The concept of the schizophrenogenic mother has been weakened
by the test of the time—few theorists use it any longer.

## The Double Bind Hypothesis

Bateson began his project as a general investigation of the nature of
communication and eventually became intrigued with the unique style
of communication of schizophrenics. The observation that schizophrenics consistently mislabel in communication led Bateson to deduce that
they must have grown up in a situation in which they were receiving
conflicting messages from their families. Hence the attention in the
schizophrenic disorder shifted from the individual to the whole family.

The double bind is a special type of learning context from which
the growing child cannot escape. A double bind occurs for individuals
when they receive two or more messages that are incompatible on
different levels of communication. The relationship is such that the
recipients of the communication feel that it is essential to understand
the message and failure to respond to the ambiguities is met by con-
demnation that places these people in an intolerable situation. Given
the loading of incongruent messages that requires the children to deny
certain important aspects of reality, they eventually behave as if they
have lost the ability to discriminate, that is, they manifest schizophrenic behavior. Thus schizophrenia is redefined as a specific pattern
of communication that is learned, rather than an illness of the mind
(Bateson, Jackson, Haley, & Weakland, 1956).

However, essentially none of the contentions mentioned have been
subjected to any type of experimental or systematic testing (Hirsch &
Leff, 1975). Direct observations, tape recordings, and films of families
in group discussions with therapists are used to provide illustrations
of deviant communication, but until recently no experimental tech-

niques have been used to test the double bind hypothesis. Present evidence indicates that double bind communication is no more prevalent in families of schizophrenics than in other families.

## Marital Schism and Skew

The theories of Lidz and his co-workers (Lidz, Fleck, & Cornelison, 1965) grew out of psychoanalytic tradition and were first based on the intensive study of 17 families. Their formulations have the flavor of psychoanalytic thinking, but as applied to the family rather than the individual as the unit of analysis. In their view, all schizophrenics come from families in which there is severe emotional strife. One or both parents are extremely egocentric and display communication styles that reflect this self-centeredness, and this familial disturbance is considered to be a precursor to the severe disturbance of thinking in the offspring.

The term "marital schism" is used to describe a state of chronic discord and disequilibrium in which the personality disturbances of the partners are so severe that they are forced to pursue their own needs while ignoring the needs of others. "Marital skew" refers to a way of achieving relative equilibrium but only by one partner yielding to the abnormalities and eccentricities of the other, which then dominate the family so that no conflict is apparent.

Mothers tend to be impervious to their children's needs, to be too restrictive or insufficiently firm, and they tend to live their lives through their children. Fathers tend to be insecure in their masculinity, in need of constant bolstering to their self-esteem, and are often mildly paranoid. These families have unclear sexual and generational boundaries and are often seductive toward their children. Such abnormal environments predispose their offspring toward irrationality in behavior and distortions in thinking.

Hirsch and Leff (1975) point out that Lidz and co-workers, in the introduction to their work, disclaim scientific exactitude and consider it an exploratory effort that others will eventually test. Despite these disclaimers, however, the researchers present their findings and conclusions as sound and established theory. The investigators were all psychoanalytically oriented and employed no control groups. Given the absence of confirmatory evidence for this theory, it is unfortunate that it continues to be propounded, for it generates guilt and blame in the parents and augments the already painful experience that the family is undergoing. This iatrogenic anguish generated by the professional can cause depression, divorce, and even suicide (Torrey, 1983).

## Hierarchical Incongruity

Haley (1980) and Madanes (1981) feel that defining the aberrant behavior of young people as schizophrenic is not useful. They prefer the adjectives "mad," "eccentric," or "problematic" and see these persons as being in the same category of other misbehaving youth such as delinquents, drug addicts, and cultists. They reject the possibility of a genetic or organic basis of the disorder and feel that the etiology is in the present rather than the past.

What lies behind the eccentric behavior that others call mental illness is an effort on the part of the young person to hold the family together. Basic to the problem, they speculate, are the parents' marital difficulties, which make it difficult for their grown offspring to leave home. Strange alliances develop within the family that cause the authority of one parent to be undermined; the child, then, begins to assume dominance by displaying symptoms. The disorganized behavior is a reflection of the disorganization in the family.

The goal of treatment is to keep the patient out of the hospital and to overcome his or her propensity for failure. In addition, the goal is to move the person toward work and independence. Here the families are very much involved, the therapist joins with the family to create a new power structure with the parents in charge. Parents are required to exact obedience from their offspring; they must essentially push the child into normal behavior. Haley and Madanes believe the patient can choose to behave like a normal person. Medication is reduced or discouraged and hospitalization is used sparingly because it relieves the family of the problem and does not force them to solve it. What this type of family treatment might mean for the family may be judged by one of Madane's more extreme recommendations: In the case of such an event as potential suicide, the therapist decides (and it is to be hoped takes ultimate responsibility for the consequences) whether to hospitalize the patient or to force the family to institute a 24-hour suicide watch. "This," she notes, "usually tests the limits of the parents' patience and helps them take a firm stand in demanding normal behavior from this youth" (p. 135).

## Transactional Thought Disorder

Wynne (1978) and his collaborators see disordered communication as the core problem of families with mentally ill relatives. These families' verbal transactions are chacterized by fragmentation, disjunctive quality, and blurring of attention and meaning. They fail to acknowledge each other, are easily distracted, and lack closure. Even verbalizations that might appear normal to a casual observer, in their family context are revealed to be a thought disorder like that found in most disorganized schizophrenic persons. Believing that the formal aspects of communication are relatively stable, these researchers think that they have found a trait that predates hospitalization of the schizophrenic family member. The schizophrenic's disturbed behavior, such as identity confusion, disturbed perception and communication, is to an extent derived by internalizing the family's social organization and its way of deriving meaning. Wynne acknowledges that schizophrenics may show extreme response patterns, that is, they may have stimulus sensitivity, a tendency to augment or reduce stimulation, and display other psychophysiological disturbances. These he hypothesizes may be genetically predetermined.

Beels and MacFarlane (1982) are critical of the kind of treatment that has grown out of communication theory. They feel it has aggravated guilt feelings and has not provided the kinds of practical help families require; it does not deal with an array of problems associated with feeling stigmatized, or with families' confusion at seeing a loved one schizophrenic.

Terkelsen (1983) reviewed a number of studies relating to family communication disorders and found alternative way of explaining them. He concluded that communication aberrations could be explained as an adaptive response to two therapist attributes: (1) failure to absolve the family of causal responsibility, and (2) failure to inform the family about the nature of mental illness. Many of the responses picked up in the clinic were not ongoing attributes of the family, but were responses of a beleaguered family to an accusatory authority.

## Biological and Genetic Explanations

It is thought by some scientists that mental illness is basically a brain disease (or more likely many diseases) that may be structural or functional in nature. Torrey (1983) reports on autopsies done in various parts of the world that indicated some of the following abnormalities: decrease in the number of neurones; degenerated or swollen brain cells; enlargement of ventricles and atrophy of brain substance; and differences in the corpus callosum, which carries information from one half of the brain to the other.

Even more impressive, according to Torrey, are the functional abnormalities found in schizophrenia. Electrical impulses by which the brain sends messages have been found to be abnormal. With new technology it has been possible to demonstrate different measures of oxygen and glucose use in some schizophrenics. Attention also has been focused in the past decade on neurotransmitters, including dopamine, serotonin, and norepenephrine.

There is a consensus among most schizophrenia experts that genetics plays a role in mental illness, but there is not full agreement as to just what its role is. It is generally thought that the disease itself is not inherited but that what is inherited is a predisposition to react to environmental influences in a special way that leads to a mental disorder. The precipitant causes, then, Torrey speculates, may be dietary factors, environmental contaminants, or stress. Other genetic theorists hypothesize that what is inherited is a specific defect in the brain, such as the sensory-processing mechanisms of the limbic system or of the brain centers that integrate communication.

Once the person has the disorder, one might assume that its etiology is of no significance to the family that takes on caregiving responsibilities; the problems of coping and management are equally difficult no matter what the assumed cause. In part that is true, but families feel much more anguish and guilt if they are told that family organization or child-rearing practices caused the problem than if they believe it is a disease process or genetic influence over which they had no control. In addition, the type of treatment of patient and/or family varies according to the assumed etiology. Some forms of treatment are much more harsh and disruptive than others; some are much more responsive to the needs that families identify.

### Stress Theories

Practitioners in this country have been strongly influenced by the work of Brown, Birley, and Wing (1972) followed by that of Vaughn and Leff (1981) and their contention that the level of expressed emotion (EE) in a family can influence the course of mental illness in a member. In these research studies, the family caregivers are rated on their level of EE at the time of the patient's hospitalization; they are given a composite score based on the number of critical comments, tone of voice, and emotional overinvolvement. The behavior in the clinic is presumed representative of the family's general attitude at home. In families with high EE relapse rate was 56%, whereas the rate of relapse was only 21% for those with low EE.

Usually, stress theorists assume a genetic predisposition (diathesis) in addition to stress, the so-called diathesis–stress theory. The stress theories have gained widespread popularity in this country, but so far the amount of solid research with controls for the complex variables involved is limited. By and large, the theories have led to more practical kinds of help to families, the so-called psychoeducational approaches, which appear to better meet the needs of families. To a large extent, the stress theorists absolve families of being causative in the illness but they do say or imply that families are a factor in perpetuating it. They require that families undertake a fairly rigorous kind of training so that they can become effective caregivers, with effective caregiving defined primarily as preventing relapse and rehospitalization. McFarlane (1983a) contrasts the old way of working with families as trying to make the family normal whereas "the new may require the emergence of somewhat abnormal family processes, such as keeping emotion at a low level, artificially simplifying communication, and establishing age-inappropriate parental control over the patient" (p. 10).

The bulk of the research work on families of the mentally ill during the past several decades has focused on the influence of the family on the patient, but there has also been a significant interest in the burden of a psychiatric illness on those around him or her.

## CONSEQUENCES OF MENTAL ILLNESS TO THE FAMILY

One of the earliest reported studies of the consequences of mental illness for the patient's family was undertaken by Clausen and his co-workers in 1952 (Clausen & Yarrow, 1955). Noting that studies of parents and other family members made prior to that time had been limited to tracing the etiology of the illness, Clausen and his colleagues saw the need to gather systematic data on what happens when mental illness does occur. They saw the need to know a kin's perception of behavior as it becomes more deviant, cultural modes of defining and dealing with mental illness, how different types of people respond to deviance, how morale and cohesiveness are maintained in the family, and the way role structures are forced to change. For this inquiry, 33 families in which the husband was the patient were selected.

Early findings of the Clausen and Yarrow studies were reported in several articles published in the *Journal of Social Issues* in 1955. The authors reported that the social and psychological situations of these families and their mechanisms of adjustment in many ways parallel the dynamics of minority groups. These families were characterized by feelings of underprivilege and marginality. They displayed hypersensitivity to the fact of mental illness and a need to conceal it (Clausen & Yarrow, 1955).

In 1953, Freeman and Simmons undertook a study under the sponsorship of the National Institute of Mental Health's Professional Services Branch to learn about the community experience of former patients. Using semidirected interviews, case-study approaches, and cross-sectional studies, the researchers found a wide range of performance levels in those who remained in the community. Rehospitalization did occur, and a study of the reasons for rehospitalization gave some indication of what families found most burdensome. Low-level performance and passive behavior were not factors in return to hospitals, nor were unemployment or neglect of household duties. Bizarre symptoms were frequently given as reasons, and, for male patients, hitting and hurting others, damaging property, and drinking were behaviors that families could not tolerate (Freeman & Simmons, 1963).

In England, where home care was rapidly gaining favor, Grad and Sainsbury (1963) were concerned about the effect that discharged patients might have on the families they live with. They concluded from a study of 410 cases that families do indeed pay a high price and that those who already have personal or health problems pay the highest price (Grad & Sainsbury, 1963).

In 1974, Creer and Wing, also from England, published *Schizophrenia at Home*, a monograph reporting the study of 80 families in England. In the preface they make clear their purpose: "We think that, as with other chronically handicapping conditions, the close relatives have a store of experience and knowledge which it is of utmost importance to tap, since no system of community care can work fairly and effectively without the relatives' full cooperation" (p. iii). Thus the authors set about gathering data on their 80 families through extensive interviews in their own homes.

 The sources of difficulty reported by the families were many and diverse: uncertainty as to how to deal with the patient's inactivity, confusion about the unpredicability of behavior, and long-term worries about the patient's future in the light of his or her inability to cope with life and to manage independently. The relatives, noted Creer and Wing, tended to live in a permanently anxiety-provoking situation. In addition, there was frequent guilt, depression, disappointment, and frustration or anger at the insoluble nature of the problem. The authors saw these as not abnormal or pathological but simply as a reaction to a confusing, incomprehensible, distressing, and apparently unmodifiable situation.

In an attempt to achieve more clarity about family burden, Hoenig and Hamilton (1966) suggested the need to discriminate between the objective and the subjective burdens involved in providing care. They applied the concept of "objective burden" to describe the adverse effects on the household of such things as heavy financial costs, the effect on health, and the intrusion and disruption of the lives of family members. The "subjective burden" was defined as the sense of loss, grief, guilt, and anxiety due to the abnormal behavior in a member.

Doll (1976) considered it important to carry the idea of subjective burden further and he substituted the words "affective burden." To determine the level of affective burden, Doll developed a modified form of the incomplete sentence test and used it in an interview situation with 125 relatives of disturbed individuals. The interviewed sample was 60% white and 40% black, with 76% in the lower socioeconomic class according to the Hollingshead Scale.

Sixty percent of the patients were rated as performing poorly by their relatives. Three fourths of the protocols indicated that the patient continued to be a problem to the family. Families came across as ambivalent in their feelings, having a sense of concern and caring mixed with resentment and anger. "Much of the time the feelings of helplessness, permanent entrapment," Doll wrote, "came across as a *leitmotif* throughout an overall protocol" (1976, p. 184). He concludes from his study that such factors as social class or closeness of relationship do not affect the extent of subjective burden. In a sweeping statement, the author declared that the burdens of caring for the mentally ill are universal, with no respect for differences in social class, education, age, or the sex of the respondent. Burdens are significantly and consistently related to the psychiatric condition of the patient. There was a trend for an increase in hospitalization to be related to a lack of sympathy and to feelings of being trapped. Families put up with a great deal of deviant behavior, but at a price.

> The paradox of the enlightened move towards a community care system is that, rather than simplifying and humanizing the treatment process, it has immeasurably complicated it. Rather than removing treatment to a more civilized and benign setting, it sends the problems home, which may have devastating consequences for the patient, for his family, and ultimately for the community mental health movement. (Doll, 1976, p. 185).

A second aspect of the study (Thompson, Doll, & Lefton, 1977) was an assessment of the objective burden for the family. This was operationalized as the disruptions former patients have on a family's everyday life or the extent of interference with the functional tasks of the household. The authors reported that a third of their sample said that their daily lives were disrupted by the patient's return. The less their kin's symptoms were under control, the more likely the objective burden was rated high. Single caregivers suffered most.

A comprehensive review of the research on family burden was reported by Kreisman and Joy (1974), who concluded that the whole problem had been inadequately assessed, that mental illness had a profound effect on the family, and that the mental health profession has not responded adequately to family needs. Families, the authors were convinced, were highly stressed due to the episodic eruptions and ambiguous nature of the illness, which requires continuous adjustment of those around the afflicted persons. The need to shift roles and provide constant care without respite placed great strain on the family.

Two writers of the mid-1970s questioned the wisdom of caring for patients at home, arguing that levels of stress are invariably too high. Dincin (1975) felt it was best for adult patients to live away from home, for there is too much pain on both sides. Parents run out of emotional strength to cope. Often they are afraid of their adult disturbed child and cede control of the family to him. Arnoff (1975) observed that there was evidence to indicate that people can be treated in the community, but that due attention has not been given to costs to the family, siblings, and offspring. He concluded that benefits for the patient can no longer suffice as a determinant of policy, that we need to abandon the individual patient model in favor of a more extensive, complex systems model.

The emergence of the self-help movement for families of mentally ill persons in the late 1970s provided a new source of information about family burden and stress and new urging that attention be paid to the problems faced by families. It offered a readily available pool of families who had considerable investment in conveying the realities of mental illness in the home to whomever was willing to listen. Hatfield (1978) surveyed families of one such group, the Schizophrenia Association of Greater Washington, in which 57% of the families responding had a mentally ill relative living at home. Many of these patients were reported as displaying psychiatric disturbances of considerable severity; over a third had threatened suicide, and four had succeeded. Families reported living in constant tension, always on guard, apprehensive about what was going to happen next. They worried about the neglect of their other children and the difficulties these children had in understanding a sibling's bizarre behavior. Marriages suffered, and families felt keenly the loss of time and energy for their own lives.

Holden and Lewine (1982) studied 203 members of seven family self-help groups affiliated with the National Alliance for the Mentally Ill and confirmed the finding that the lives of families were adversely affected by the fact of mental illness. Health problems were seen as stress related; most frequently mentioned were depression, insomnia, hypertension, heart attack, and alcoholism.

There is still much to be learned about the way mental illness affects the family. The currently available research has been primarily concerned with parents of chronically mentally ill young adults, usually of the middle and upper middle classes, in urban and suburban locations. We need to know about other population groups and other relationships—siblings, spouses, and children of mentally ill persons. Later chapters of this book should add to our understanding and pave the way for new research efforts.

## The Responsiveness of Practitioners

How well the affected family manages under the exigencies of mental illness has depended, in part, on the kinds and qualities of services designed to help them. The nature of these services is dependent upon the particular theoretical framework that defines the mental illness, explains its etiology, and projects the kind of treatment of patient and/ or family that is congruent with the reigning ideology.

During the period of radical environmentalism described earlier, which attributed adult problems, including mental illness, to the character of family life, there was only one clear choice. The disturbed patient must be separated from the noxious environment, and he must be given intensive treatment to undo the harm done. Hospitalization served that purpose well. Patients were thought to be receiving benign care in a situation well insulated from the family. The family, in effect, was ignored or rejected. There was little sympathy or concern for a beleaguered family that may have struggled valiantly to stave off institutionalization.

It was such later theories as those of Lidz, Bateson, Haley, and Wynne, less concerned about the individual pathology of its members and more concerned about family interaction patterns, that was the impetus for the rapidly growing field of family therapy in the 1960s and 1970s. An array of approaches to family treatment were developed and enthusiastically offered to the public with considerable optimism as to their efficacy. Although all felt that the key to major disturbances lay in family dynamics, there were considerable differences as to the specific nature of family pathology and what the course of treatment should be. Some made the object of treatment to be the clarification of communication, some tried to improve emotional contact between members, and others encouraged members to express inhibited feelings. Some therapists attempted to liberate the patient from his role as scapegoat or victim; others tried to work through marital problems that were causing their offspring to be schizophrenic. (Beels & McFarlane, 1982).

What were the consquences of these various therapies for patients and families? No one really knows for sure, for few comprehensive outcome studies were ever done. There are, however, a growing number of skeptics. Beels and McFarlane (1982) saw these treatments as reinforcing guilt while failing to give families the specific kinds of help needed. More than they needed insight into the structure and dynamics of family life, there families needed help with their sense of being different and isolated, of being stigmatized by neighbors and relatives. They needed help with the practical problems of day-to-day living with a disturbed relative in order to overcome the sense of chaos that seemed to be threatening their own sanity, and the treatment that they underwent, noted the authors, may have only made things worse.

Krauss and Slavinsky (1982) feel that family therapy is inappropriate for most psychiatric patients and their families, a contention supported by a number of observations. Recapitulation of earlier family experiences and uncovering of family dynamics can in itself become disruptive, so that it is maladaptive. It is certain to increase the amount of expressed emotion that is thought by some to aggravate the condition of schizophrenic persons. In addition, family therapy locates the problem in the family unit; participating in family therapy requires an admission of ownership of the disease by all of its members. Krauss and Slavinsky noted that families tend to reject the modality and are often uncooperative and resistant. Many therapists have unresolved feelings of blame and anger toward families, and these are revealed in treatment sessions. Finally, the sheer numbers of families who need assistance make traditional family therapy impractical.

McFarlane (1983a) pointed out the irony of a situation for families in which one segment of the mental health community judged families to be responsible for their relative's illness, and another segment considered them so competent that they should assume total responsibility for their care. Although the first generation of family therapists were confident about the direction in which they were going, younger therapists were claiming less effective results. They began seeing families in a different light—as confused and perplexed, guilt ridden, and often exhausted. Some therapists began discovering that their accusatory stance was exaggerated by the patient's difficulties. Family theory did not seem to be working.

Additional concerns have been expressed by Heinrichs and Carpenter (1983) who criticized family therapists for acting as though schizophrenia was a homogeneous disorder rather than a heterogeneous collection of illnesses with possibly many etiologies. The theories, they said, were speculative and unproven.

The practices associated with diagnoses and treatment obscured an appreciation of the strengths of people, the positive forces that could be mobilized to help the patient (E. Goldstein, 1981). A focus on family deficit fails to identify the adaptive capacities of people and reduces the chances of bringing families into a good collaborative relationship with the patient's treatment team.

It is important, at this point, to note that the views of families and what kinds of help are useful to them have all been observations of clinicians. What should be evident are the limitations inherent in observations that are made in the artificial social climate of the clinic or office. There the therapist controls the situation, manipulates the participants, and limits the options for response. He or she judges the outcome and determines what the needs of the family are. It was the contention of Hatfield (1979) that families might have a different view of their needs and what kinds of services were helpful. In her study, families revealed that they most frequently sought friends, relatives, and individual therapy (in that order) for support and help. Friends (84%) and relatives (73%) significantly outweighed therapy (55%) in their perceived value to the caregiver. There families listed as the help they most needed:

- Assistance in understanding the patient's symptoms
- Specific suggestions for coping with patient's behavior
- Opportunities to relate to persons with similar experiences
- Substitute care for family respite
- A different living situation for the patient

Holden and Lewine (1982) went further in their study that attempted to assess families' evaluations of mental health practitioners. Families reported dissatisfaction with the nature and level of involvement. Many reported that their involvement with professionals left them feeling guilty and defensive. Not enough assistance was provided in basic information and management. Many professionals were vague and evasive when families pressed them for answers. These researchers concluded that their findings presented a challenge to professionals to reevaluate the level and nature of contacts with families. Attitudinal and behavioral changes on the part of practitioners may be necessary as prerequisites to establishing good working relationships with families. The formation of such an alliance, they affirm, is a first step toward easing the burden and increasing their effectiveness as caretakers.

In order to assess further the needs of families and their perception of a professional's responsiveness to these needs, Hatfield (1983) surveyed 138 members of the National Alliance for the Mentally Ill. Respondents were asked what needs had brought them to the practitioner's office and what needs they felt the practitioner had addressed. The five most important goals of families were:

1. Reduction of anxiety about the patient ($N = 92$)
2. Understanding appropriate expectations ($N = 88$)

3. Learning to motivate patients to do more (N = 86)
4. Learning about the nature of mental illness (N = 81)
5. Assistance during times of crisis (N = 80)

In this study, there were no statistically significant relationships found between what families identified as their needs and what they identified as the focus of attention in therapy.

Some feel that this rather bleak picture of family dissatisfaction may be beginning to change with the advent of a new generation of practitioner that comes closer to addressing the needs identified above. Most of these professionals are associated with the stress theories that have grown out of the work of Brown et al. (1972). They recognize that  the current trend toward community care has brought families into the picture as primary caregivers. Thus their primary goal is to help families become effective caregivers so that their relative does not relapse and return to the hospital. To this end, there are a great number and variety of family approaches being developed, and in many cases considerable effort is going into measuring outcome. Although most findings are not in yet, many of the approaches are now being reported in the literature.

As a part of a large research project on the efficacy of various kinds of treatment of patients and families, Anderson (1983) developed a comprehensive psychoeducational program for families of schizophrenic persons. Phase I of the program is entitled "Connecting with the Family" and involves establishing an alliance with it by showing empathy for its dilemmas and acknowledging its needs as well as those of the patient. Phase II brings families into a daylong survival-skills workshop that provides basic information about the nature of mental illness and strategies for managing it. Phase III consists of highly structured individual sessions in which the family is taught how to apply what has been learned and how to work through the problems that arise. The project has been operating for slightly over 3 years, has involved 33 patients and their families, and, at the time of reporting, had no relapses.

Unique to the research of M. Goldstein and Kopeikin (1981) was their focus on patient and family during the first 6 weeks following hospital discharge. Their crisis-oriented program provided psychopharmacological treatment with injectable phenothiazine, and psychosocial treatment of family and patient in six structured weekly sessions. A first step was to explore the subjective experience of both patients and their relatives at the time of the last episode in order to provide a shared understanding of what went on. Then an effort was made to understand what precipitated the relapse. Subsequent sessions emphasized the identification of stressors for the patient, stress avoidance, and coping strategies. In their study of nearly 100 patients, the authors found the most efficacious treatment to be a combination of family therapy and adequate medication. No person relapsed during the 6-week period of the program. However, the effects of aftercare dissipated over time, and no effects could be discerned 3 to 6 years later. The authors concluded that the period of treatment should be extended and should move beyond crisis-oriented therapy to that of relationship restructuring.

Falloon, Boyd, McGill, Strang, and Moss (1981) have experimented with a program consisting of maintenance on neuroleptics, education of family about mental illness, and training in communication and problem-solving skills. A unique feature of this program, thought to contribute to its success, was holding sessions in the family home. A controlled outcome study of 40 patients and their families was undertaken in which half were assigned to family therapy and half to a regular individual clinic-based supportive-therapy approach. Although the study has not been completed, preliminary findings indicate a substantial reduction in relapse rates. This was attributed to the significantly more consistent compliance with medication. Falloon *et al.* also reported that families had lowered their level of expressed emotion and handled crises better, and that patients seemed to be making better social adjustment and to be less of a burden to their families.

An emphasis on relatives' support groups is characteristic of the treatment procedures of Leff, Kuipers, and Berkowitz (1983), which have as their goals educating the family about mental illness and teaching coping strategies in order to reduce the level of EE. Relatives' groups were thought to be effective in that persons with low EE would serve as good models and could teach management skills to the others—all in a very low-cost way. In addition, the groups countered a sense of loneliness. Patients were excluded so as to provide a safety valve for high-EE relatives. Twenty-four persons (12 in an experimental and 12 in a control group) comprised the group under study. Leff and his colleagues reported that all experimental subjects had shifted to low EE in the course of treatment, the rate of relapse was reduced, and patients were beginning to separate from their families.

The idea of multiple family groups favored by Beels and McFarlane (1982) grew out of early observation that there was a natural tendency for families on hospital wards to cluster and share experiences. Although McFarlane (1983b) explains this phenomenon, rather strangely, in terms of traditional family interaction theory and communication theory, with their implications of family pathology, the fact is that people have always found it useful to share their dilemmas with others in the same boat. This is the foundation for hundreds of self-help groups dealing with a wide range of human problems and is not unique to families with schizophrenic patients. In any case, Beels and McFarlane assemble four to eight families, including the patient, and two or three therapists in groups that meet on a regular basis. A number of advantages are seen for the multiple-group approach. It is possible to slow down—all families do not feel under pressure to come up with a problem each session. The group serves as a support system and can move on as an advocacy group. Professionals deal more realistically and honestly with families, as they are outnumbered in the group. To date no data has been collected on this approach.

If one judges the worth of a theory by the degree to which it has generated wide-ranging experimentation and research, then stress theory has really made its mark, for a host of projects are being reported. Although these newer approaches are usually called "family therapy," their proponents tend to stress the educational activity that goes on. The similarity lies in their emphasis on patient stress, the source of which they see in the level of expressed emotion of family members. The goal is to reduce this source of stress so that the patient is not overwhelmed by it.

One's immediate reaction to these approaches is that they are, indeed, responsive to the needs of families as these families have identified them. Thus there has seemed to be considerable forward movement in the past decade. However, a more thorough exploration leaves one less sanguine about the full impact of these newer developments. The difficulties that some therapists project in engaging families (Anderson, 1983) and in overcoming their resistance to treatment (Beels & McFarlane, 1982) suggests that it may be useful to raise further questions.

A closer reading of the literature brings to light some interesting contradictions that could impede work with families. As one example, there is some confusion about the word *family* in family therapy or treatment. Whose well-being is of concern in these approaches? In terms of stated goals or measured outcomes, only the well-being of one of its members, the patient, is given real attention. Families are charged with one responsibility and that is preventing relapse of the patient, and if relapse occurs, they may be blamed for contributing to the illness or of perpetuating it. This creates a serious bind for the family that ultimately must take responsibility for the well-being of all its members; they may not be able to meet all the practitioner's expectations for attention to the one member of the family. In addition, the focus seems to be on the behavior of the family—usually parents—even though patients are affected by many other complexities beyond the family. Most glaring is the failure on the part of family therapy researchers to make any effort to assess the effects of their strategies on the well-being of other members.

There is another interesting contradiction that looms large in the literature. Proponents of newer approaches frequently call for collaborative relations between families and professionals. "Collaboration" is usually defined as a cooperative relationship between two parties on mutually agreed upon goals and procedures. For example, McFarlane and Beels (1983) speak of families as "working allies" of mental health professionals and of the need for a "common philosophy, language, and set of expectations." But just what this would entail seems to have been missed as these therapists proceed to describe an elaborate "decision-tree model" that makes no provision for involving the family. They write as though all choices of treatment are made for the family, and eventually fairly coercive treatments would be given to families that did not meet the professionals' assessment of appropriate behavior. The goals of a common philosophy, language, and set of expectations, however desirable they may be, are probably not apparent in any current treatment philosophy.

At this point it seems important to ask just how much is really new in the new family therapies. It is probably truly new that practitioners are giving more basic and relevant information and that they are striving to provide more practical coping strategies. Beyond that, much of the thinking and language seems to be mired down in older theories that have presumably been discredited. Like older theories, they have taken very complex interactions of a family in its attempt to meet a serious crisis and determined that the major deficit is in the family— usually the parents. The deficits still frequently carry the old labels "enmeshment," "communication deviance," "isolation," "learned helplessness," "overinvolvement," and others. It appears that the newer therapists, almost all with their roots and training in psychoanalytic and family systems thinking, have not really moved that far. The potential for blame and guilt are still there and the focus is only on deficit; the strengths of families and the heroic lengths to which they go to maintain themselves through crisis after crisis is only mentioned in passing, if at all.

Somewhat rare in the literature are approaches to working with the family that have a primary focus on the family itself. Of interest is the work of Bernheim (1982) and her description of supportive family counseling. She characterizes her work as different from traditional family therapy in that families' disturbing behaviors are not seen as evidences of underlying pathology, but rather as responses to difficulties in dealing with schizophrenic behaviors and attempts to cope with a confusing situation, including the negative and accusatory attitudes of mental health professionals. Her basic assumption is that it is physically and emotionally stressful to live with mental illness and that chronic stress reduces one's capacity to cope successfully. The goals, then, become clear: Reduce the sense of helplessness and build self-esteem; provide information and develop management skills; recognize that others in the family have needs also. Developing an alliance with these families requires overcoming their negative expectations growing out of prior experiences with professionals—expectations of coercion and attention to only the patient's needs. It involves dispelling erroneous notions about mental illness and the family that too often cause the family to protect itself through emotional withdrawal, superficial compliance, and stubbornness.

Atwood and Williams (1978) use supportive family counseling for relatives of schizophrenic patients. Atwood's basic philosophy and approach has much in common with that of Bernheim. She too is critical of professionals who see the family as "sick," and believe that having schizophrenia is *prima facie* evidence that something is grossly wrong with the family. She is concerned that many professionals bring to the clinic their own unresolved problems and that they often side with the patient.

Inherent in Atwood's approach is legitimizing the relatives' role as "significant others," validating the problem as defined by the family, and affirming the problem's manageability. Opportunities to share problems and support each other are provided through the multiple-family approach.

## SUMMARY

That mental illness has always been a dreadful experience for those who have suffered from it, is beyond question. What has gone unrecognized through the years is how much their families have also been affected. Several factors have made a difference. First, the objective burden is invariably heavier when families do direct caregiving or maintain the individual close to home. We are now in a period in which patients live in the community, often with their families, much as in the pre-asylum days, and the stresses for families are tremendous. Second, the degree of subjective, or emotional, burden depends upon the meaning the illness has for the family. Many factors determine this meaning as will be demonstrated in later chapters. In this chapter, we have pointed out that the beliefs about etiology once espoused by clergymen and now by mental health professionals have historically added to the family's anguish about the mental illness. For over 4 decades, one family trait after another has been brought forth and vigorously supported as the cause of mental illness. Over time, these beliefs have lost their credibility, but in the meantime many families have been devastated by iatrogenic guilt. Third, how well families can manage depends upon the adequacy of community supports available to them. There is an emerging interest in giving support to families. The success of these new efforts will depend upon the degree to which professionals are able to understand the family experience from a family perspective and to meet the needs that families identify.

## REFERENCES

Anderson, C. M. (1983). A psychoeducational program for families of patients with schizophrenia. In W. R. McFarlane (Ed.), Family therapy in schizophrenia (pp. 99-116). New York: Guilford.

Arnoff, F. N. (1975). Social consequences of policy toward mental illness. Science, 188, 1277-1281.

Atwood, N., & Williams, M. E. (1978). Group support for the families of the mentally ill. Schizophrenia Bulletin, 4, 415-425.

Bachrach, L. L. (1976). De-institutionalization: An analytic review and sociological perspective. Rockville, MD: National Institute of Mental Health.

Bachrach, L. L. (1978). A conceptual approach to de-institutionalization. Hospital and Community Psychiatry, 29, 573-578.

Bachrach, L. L. (1982). Young adult chronic patients: An analytical review of the literature. Hospital and Community Psychiatry, 33, 189-197.

Bateson, G., Jackson, D., Haley, J., & Weakland, J. (1956). Toward a theory of schizophrenia. Behavioral Science, 1, 251-264.

Beels, C. C., & McFarlane, W. R. (1982). Family treatments of schizophrenia: Background and state of the art. Hospital and Community Psychiatry, 33, 541-549.

Bernheim, K. (1982). Supportive family counseling. Schizophrenia Bulletin, 8, 634-640.

Brown, G. W., Birley, J. L. T., & Wing, J. K. (1972). Influence of family life on the course of schizophrenic disorders: A replication. British Journal of Psychiatry, 121, 241-258.

Caesar, B. (1980). Preserving the family: A brief for limited commitment of nondangerous mentally ill persons. Journal of Marital and Family Therapy, 6, 309-319.

Clausen, J., & Yarrow, M. R. (Eds.). (1955). The impact of mental illness on the family [special issue]. Journal of Social Issues, 11(4).

Creer, C., & Wing, J. K. (1974). Schizophrenia at home. London: Institute of Psychiatry.

Deutsch, A. (1949). The mentally ill in America. New York: Columbia University Press.

Dincin, J. (1975). Psychiatric rehabilitation. Schizophrenia Bulletin, Summer Issue, No. 13, 131-147.

Doll, W. (1976). Family coping with the mentally ill: An unanticipated problem of deinstitutionalization. Hospital and Community Psychiatry, 27, 183-185.

Falloon, I. R. H., Boyd, J. L., McGill, C. W., Strang, J. S., & Moss, H. B. (1981). Family management training in the community care of schizophrenia. In M. J. Goldstein (Ed.), New developments in interventions with families of schizophrenics (New

Directions for Mental Health Services, No. 12, pp. 61-78). San Francisco: Jossey-Bass.

Freeman, H. E., & Simmons, O. G. (1963). *The mental patient comes home.* New York: Wiley.

Fromm-Reichmann, F. (1948). Notes on the development of treatment of schizophrenics by psychoanalytic psychotherapy. *Psychiatry, 11,* 263-273.

Goldman, H. H. (1982). Mental illness and family burden: A public health perspective. *Hospital and Community Psychiatry, 33,* 557-560.

Goldstein, E. G. (1981). Promoting competence in families of psychiatric patients. In A. N. Maluccio (Ed.), *Promoting competence in clients* (pp. 317-342). New York: Free Press.

Goldstein, M. J., & Kopeiken, H. S. (1981). Short- and long-term effects of combining drug and family therapy. In M. J. Goldstein (Ed.), *New developments in interventions with families of schizophrenics* (New Directions for Mental Health Services, No. 12, pp. 5-26). San Francisco: Jossey-Bass.

Grad, J., & Sainsbury, P. (1963). Mental illness and the family. *Lancet, 1,* 544-547.

Haley, J. (1980). *Leaving home: The therapy of disturbed young people.* New York: McGraw-Hill.

Hatfield, A. B. (1978). Psychological costs of schizophrenia to the family. *Social Work, 23,* 355-359.

Hatfield, A. B. (1979). Help-seeking behavior in families of schizophrenics. *American Journal of Community Psychiatry, 7,* 563-569.

Hatfield, A. B. (1983). What families want of family therapists. In W. R. McFarlane (Ed.), *Family therapy in schizophrenia* (pp. 41-68). New York: Guilford.

Heinrichs, D. W., & Carpenter, W. T. (1983). The coordination of family therapy with other treatment modalities for schizophrenia. In W. R. McFarlane (Ed.), *Family therapy in schizophrenia* (pp. 267-288) New York: Guilford.

Hirsch, S. R., & Leff, J. P. (1975). *Abnormalities in parents of schizophrenics.* London: Oxford University Press.

Hoenig, J., & Hamilton, M. W. (1966). The schizophrenic patient in the community and his effect on the household. *International Journal of Social Psychiatry, 12,* 165-176.

Holden, D. F., & Lewine, R. R. J. (1982). How families evaluate mental health professionals, resources, and effects of illness. *Schizophrenia Bulletin, 8,* 626-633.

Krauss, J. B., & Slavinsky, A. T. (1982). *The chronically ill psychiatric patient in the community.* Boston: Blackwell.

Kreisman, D. E., & Joy, V. D. (1974). Family response to the mental illness of a relative: A review of the literature. *Schizophrenia Bulletin, 1*(10), 34-57.

Lamb, H. R. (1982). *Treating the long-term mentally ill.* San Francisco: Jossey-Bass.

Leff, J., Kuipers, L., & Berkowitz, R. (1983). Intervention in families of schizophrenics and its effect on relapse rate. In W. R. McFarlane (Ed.), *Family therapy in schizophrenia* (pp. 173-188). New York: Guilford.

Lidz, T., Fleck, S., & Cornelison, A. R. (1965). *Schizophrenia and the family.* New York: International Universities Press.

Madanes, C. (1981). *Strategic family therapy.* San Francisco: Jossey-Bass.

McFarlane, W. R. (1983a). Introduction. In W. R. McFarlane (Ed.), *Family therapy in schizophrenia.* New York: Guilford.

McFarlane, W. R. (1983b). Multiple family therapy in schizophrenia. In W. R. McFarlane (Ed.), *Family therapy in schizophrenia* (pp. 141-172). New York: Guilford.

McFarlane, W. R., & Beels, C. C. (1983). A decision-tree model for integrating family therapies for schizophrenia. In W. R. McFarlane (Ed.). *Family therapy in schizophrenia* (pp. 325-336). New York: Guilford.

Minkoff, K. (1978). A map of the chronic mental patient. In J. A. Talbott (Ed.), *The chronic mental patient* (11-37). Washington, DC: American Psychiatric Association.

Pepper, B., Ryglewicz, H., & Kirshner, M. (1982). The uninstitutionalized generation: A new breed of psychiatric patient. In B. Pepper & H. Ryglewicz (Eds.), *The young adult chronic patient* (pp. 3-14). San Francisco: Jossey-Bass.

Talbott, J. (1978). *The death of the asylum.* New York: Grune & Stratton.

Terkelson, K. G. (1983). Schizophrenia and the family: II. Adverse effect of family therapy. *Family Process, 22,* 191-200.

Thompson, E., Doll, W., & Lefton, M. (1977, April). *Some affective dimensions of familial coping with the mentally ill.* Paper presented at the 54th Annual Meeting of the American Orthopsychiatric Association, New York.

Torrey, E. F. (1983). *Surviving schizophrenia: A family manual.* Harper & Row.

Vaughn, C. E., & Leff, J. P. (1981). Patterns of emotional response in relatives of schizophrenic patients. *Schizophrenia Bulletin, 7,* 43-44.

Wynne, L. C. (1978). Family relationships and communications. Concluding comments. In L. C. Wynne, R. M. Cromwell, & S. Matthysse (Eds.), *The nature of schizophrenia* (pp. 534-541). New York: Wiley.

# Culture and Mental Illness: The Family Role

*Harriet P. Lefley*

Over the past quarter century, there have been profound changes in the Western world with respect to perception and treatment of the mentally ill.[1] The deinstitutionalization movement has arisen from a number of converging historical currents. First were the symptom-reducing neuroleptics that have enabled many patients to regain levels of contact and functioning previously unattainable, thereby accelerating the closing of hospital wards. Second was the recognition that underfunded and poorly staffed asylums tended to kill rather than cure the human spirit, and that long-term custodial care could result in increased dependency and dysfunction. Concomitantly, long-needed reforms in affirmation of patients' civil rights, together with a search for less costly alternatives to hospital care, fueled an unlikely alliance between civil libertarians and fiscal conservatives in seeking least-restrictive (and, it was hoped, less costly) environments. Meanwhile, the 1963 community mental health centers legislation had gradually generated a network of neighborhood services that, although still inadequate, held forth the promise of community support systems to replace institutional care.

Thus, in the broad cyclical pattern so often characteristic of social change, the movement for deinstitutionalization has removed the men-

Harriet P. Lefley. Office of Transcultural Education and Research, Department of Psychiatry, University of Miami, Miami, Florida.

[1]The "West" is used throughout this chapter in its anthropologic rather than geographic sense, that is, as representative of the modern, industrial world, as opposed to traditional preindustrial cultures.

tally ill from the asylums so compassionately developed by the 19th-century reformers, and once more has returned them to community care. There are differences, of course, between then and now. On the positive side are the availability of antipsychotic medications, community treatment programs (where they exist), and legal recognition of civil rights. On the negative side are inadequate services, often vastly inferior to those in the hospital; totally inadequate housing arrangements; legal constraints and hospital admission criteria that too often may relegate the needy to life on the streets; and extensive family burden (Doll, 1976; Hatfield, 1978).

Today it is estimated that about 65% of patients discharged from mental hospitals return to live with their families (Goldman, 1982). Prior to this, the fate of the chronically ill was typically sealed behind hospital walls. The patient was doomed, but the family survived. The aching dilemma of families with particularly difficult relatives is exemplified in the words of one of the subjects in Creer and Wing's (1974) study of families of schizophrenics in England: "You can put him in a back ward for the rest of his days and then you have written him off; his life is finished. Or you can have him at home, and then you have to accept that you will have to alter your whole life. You will never be free again" (p. 66). While most families do not verbalize their burden in such strong terms, even when they do there is evidence of an unwillingness to abandon even the most severely disruptive mentally ill relatives (Doll, 1976). Yet the statement above tends to confirm the prediction of two noted sociologists, made over 30 years ago, that changes in family structure in the Western world would make it almost impossible to care for physically or psychologically disabled family members at home. Parsons and Fox (1952) maintained that nuclear family structure has little margin for "shock absorption," since there are at most two adults to take roles of major responsibility in the home. Illness of the father-husband has an immediate disruptive effect, economically and emotionally. The wife-mother's illness may be even more devastating, since there is a critical point at which expectancies and tolerances change when the wife has multiple hospitalizations or long-term disability. When a husband or child is ill, households usually continue to function even though the wife-mother may be overburdened with multiple breadwinning and caretaking roles. When she is the one who is ill, however, the husband-father can cope for a short time only and then is forced to make other arrangements for the continuing functioning of the household. A permanent caretaker-substitute for the wife-mother tends to further isolate and make her marginal in the family constellation, leaving her without role or function and severely diminishing her feelings of self-worth. This is particularly true for the psychiatrically disabled wife-mother with a history of multiple hospitalizations.

Extending Parsons and Fox's model, Anthony (1970) went on to describe the life-situational strains, the illness solution, and the illness impact for the father-husband, wife-mother, and child-sibling as they affected each family member and the total family equilibrium.

Surprisingly, Anthony found similar processes of coping and adaptation in families with mentally ill and physically ill (tuberculous) members, with a period of disruption followed by reintegration or disintegration, depending on the family's premorbid adjustment, social and cultural level, and severity of the patient's illness. The disorder, encapsulation, and dynamics of regeneration that he described were, however, related to the demands placed by the patient's illness on "the precariously balanced, emotionally charged system of the modern urban family" (p. 138).

## ARE PERCEPTIONS OF FAMILIES TRANSCULTURAL?

How typical is this situation around the world? How do families cope in other cultures, where hospitals are few and many individuals with psychotic disorders are kept at home? How does family and kinship structure affect coping capability? What are the relationships between families and mental health professionals in other cultures? Are relatives viewed as hindrances or as helpers? What is the family's role in the healing process? And to what extent are family members perceived as malevolent influences from whom the patient should be removed?

While the universality of the major psychoses is indisputable (Leff, 1981), the literature that informs our knowledge of mental illness is largely produced in the Western countries. Writings on the family have primarily dealt with pathogenesis, not with coping. The earlier psychoanalytic approaches focused on unearthing historical materials and avoiding family-therapist alliances, while the later family therapy literature focused essentially on disturbed family systems, principally on the function of the psychotic symptoms in the family economy (Hoffman, 1981).

The unanimity of Western mental health professionals in seeing family psychopathology, despite their pronounced failure to establish a firm empirical base (Blakar, 1980), is in rather sharp contrast to the benign picture of families that emerges from the cross-cultural literature. In nonindustrial societies, families may travel long distances to bring a patient for psychiatric care, often waiting out the long hospitalization period in close proximity to the clinic (Bell, 1982). Here the family is often seen as a supportive asset (Jegede, 1981), or may even be engaged in a therapeutic role (Lambo, 1966). In the Philippines, family members who stay with their relatives within the hospital setting are called "watchers." Higginbotham (1979) has reported an effort by the Department of Psychiatry Unit of the University of Santo Tomas that, by conducting family discussion and education groups with the "watchers," seemed to replicate some of the psychoeducational interventions that American families are asking for today (see Goldstein, 1981).

Predating Western deinstitutionalization by many years, Lambo (1966) started the ARO village system in Nigeria in 1954. Here psychiatric patients live with a relative in a traditional village that is close to the mental clinic. Treatment is organically related to village life, combining native healing rituals with psychotropic medication and group therapy. Recently, the psychiatric village system has been extended to Senegal (Collomb, 1978). Jegede (1981) has pointed out that with treatment ranging from a few weeks to a year or more, it is difficult to get relatives to stay away from wage-earning occupations for prolonged periods of time, and has recommended a salary structure for relatives of psychotics requiring long-term stay. Creating income-producing occupations for natural support systems is an important concept for mental health service delivery and highlights the significance attached to relatives in patient care.

Lambo's emphasis on the community's role in healing is similar to the therapeutic aspects of "community ethos" in China, described as an integral component of their aftercare services for the mentally disabled (Sidel & Sidel, 1972). Both systems involve natural support networks, such as relatives, as much as possible.

Although the cross-cultural literature is sparse in references to family coping and involvement in patient care, there are increasing indications from cross-cultural research that many of the etiological speculations and case reports of disturbed family dynamics simply do not hold up in global perspective.

Assumptions of familial culpability affect the coping capabilities of relatives by diverting energies that could better be applied to more constructive modes of adaptation. Many families learn of their supposed culpability by reading books on the major psychotic disorders to obtain more understanding of their relative's illness—information rarely received from professionals. For others, psychological information on "crazymaking" families trickles down through the popular media. The conventional wisdom of our culture has thus for many years informed families, parents in particular, that they are somehow to blame, generating great psychic expenditures in guilt, self-recrimination, fantasies of altered life scenarios, and searches for psychotherapeutic cures. These etiological assumptions also color not only professional and patient attitudes toward family members, but selective societal investments in different therapeutic modalities. The questions of universality of etiology, symptoms, treatment, and family role thus are integrally related to the aggregate of energies and strengths available to caring relatives in coping with the cumulative stress of mental illness in the family.

## PARENTING AND PSYCHOSIS: SOME QUESTIONS FROM CROSS-CULTURAL RESEARCH

A joke commonly heard among psychologists is that all our known laws of behavior are drawn from two sources: the white rat, and the white middle-class college sophomore. For those, however, whose lives bear the social consequences of research performed on restricted populations, such findings are no joke. Almost all research on families of the mentally ill—predominantly limited to the schizophrenias—has been conducted on Western populations, primarily on middle-class, Caucasian subjects with intact families (Sanua, 1982). Although the majority of studies have been done in the United States, few blacks, Hispanics, Asian-Americans, or Native Americans are represented. There have been few replications outside of the United States, and these are mostly U.S.-British studies that are essentially cross-national rather than cross-cultural (Vaughn et al., 1982). The international literature, of course, has its share of comparative case studies, anecdotal material, and other types of nonblind research, mostly produced by Western-trained psychodynamically oriented individual or family therapists whose patients and families seem to confirm their expectations regardless of cultural setting.[2] Rigorously controlled replications,

[2]The studies conducted by Alanen and his associates (1966) in Finland, are examples of nonblind, clinical interview research. Although he used normal control groups, clinical ratings were administered by those who knew which family members were related to schizophrenics and those whose relatives were normal. This type of research has been criticized by Hirsch and Leff (1975), among others, for failing to supply reliable scientific evidence to support its conclusions. Frank (1965), in a comprehensive review of the literature, suggested that observers on both sides of the Atlantic who found evidence of schizophrenogenic mothers were reflecting a perceptual set attributable to their shared academic training and consequent expectations of psychopathology. Parker (1982) has also commented on this phenomenon.

however—the only type of research that would permit truly ethical researchers to make universal (transcultural) statements about pa- tient-family relationships—are almost nonexistent. In two different categories of robustly designed, controlled family studies, one U.S. project has confirmed earlier findings in Great Britain (Vaughn et al., 1982), while an exceptionally rigorous British replication has produced completely different results from the original findings in the United States. (Hirsch & Leff, 1975). In addition, some of the longitudinal findings beginning to appear, although not specifically on family rela- tionships, strongly suggest that early parent-child interactions are almost incidental to whether or not psychotic breakdown appears in adolescence or early adulthood. Rigorous research in other countries, in point of fact, often reveals that children separated from potentially schizophrenogenic parents are more likely to develop the disorder than those who have been in daily interaction with such parents. A case in point are the follow-up findings of a collaborative National Institute of Mental Health (NIMH)-Israeli schizophrenia study begun in 1965. The research focused on 100 children, 50 high-risk subjects with schizo- phrenic parents and 50 matched controls with nonschizophrenic par- ents. Within each experimental and control group were 25 children raised by their parents in home environments, and 25 raised on an Israeli communal settlement, a kibbutz. At that time, kibbutz-reared children lived communally with their peers, were raised by a profes- sional caregiver, and spent relatively little time with their parents. "Thus, it was reasoned, schizophrenic symptoms found in a kibbutz- raised child more likely would be attributable to genetic factors rather than to the environment produced by a 'schizophrenogenic' parent." (Sargent, 1982, p. 4). When the study began, the average age of the children was 11. From enormous quantities of data, researchers doing blind analysis found two clearly discernible groups. Children of schizo- phrenics, regardless of where they were raised, showed more symp- toms of maladjustment and soft neurological signs than did the control children. In 1981, when the children were in their middle to late 20s, an astonishing finding was made. The results were "completely opposite to what was expected" according to Allan Mirsky, chief of the Labora- tory of Psychology and Psychopathology at NIMH (Wolinsky, 1982, p. 9). The hypotheses had been first, that limited contact with a schizo- phrenic parent might prevent development of the disorder in an at-risk child, and second, that the kibbutz, with its supportive atmosphere and enlightened child rearing by professional caregivers, would produce more stable individuals. Indeed, kibbutz-reared individuals are con- sidered among the most psychologically well-adjusted and productive individuals in Israel. Reports on the current study, however, indicated that the most psychopathology was found in the experimental kibbutz-raised sample. Of the 23 kibbutz-reared children of schizophrenics found in the follow-up study, a total of 16, or 70%, showed signs of mental illness, while only 29% of those raised at home were assigned a DSM III diagnosis. Of the controls, none had schizophrenia and only one raised on a kibbutz had an affective disorder. According to an interview with Mirsky, "The study says something interesting about schizophrenia, that it might not be so bad to grow up with your mother, even if she's mentally ill" (Wolinski, 1982, p. 9).

In another type of rigorous research, the Copenhagen High-Risk Project, a longitudinal study with children of schizophrenic mothers conducted in Denmark, a team of researchers headed by Sarnoff Mednick and Fini Schulsinger found that most of those who developed schizophrenia, unlike the others, had been separated from their parents or substitute parents early in life (Schulsinger, 1976).

Because there has been a great deal of conceptual confusion with respect to the influence of familial factors, it is important to discriminate between environmental variables that are reputed to *cause* severe psychotic disorder, and those that may trigger or exacerbate an already existing condition. The expressed emotion studies are a case in point.

## THE EXPRESSED EMOTION STUDIES: CULTURAL CONSIDERATIONS

In recent years, a number of studies have tended to confirm findings that first began to emerge over 20 years ago at the Medical Research Council's Social Psychiatry Unit in London. Called expressed emotion (EE) studies, they focused on the discovery that psychiatric patients who returned to live with families who expressed a high level of criticism and emotional overinvolvement, tended to relapse and need rehospitalization more frequently than those from families low in EE (Brown, Monck, Carstairs, & Wing, 1962).

Standardized interview procedures at intake revealed that at 9-month follow-up, 58% of the patients from high-EE families had relapsed, as opposed to only 16% from low-EE families (Brown, Birley, & Wing, 1972). The findings were replicated in another study (Vaughn & Leff, 1976) and again in a 2-year follow-up (Leff & Vaughn, 1981). The findings were further replicated in a United States sample at Camarillo/UCLA Mental Health Clinical Research Center for the Study of Schizophrenia (Vaughn, et al., 1982).

Based on the consistency of the EE findings, Falloon and his colleagues at the University of Southern California have developed a 2-year program that involves "(1) maintenance on neuroleptic medications, using the lowest dosages feasible in order to maximize compliance; (2) education of the family and social network about the nature and management of schizophrenia, so that family members can more readily provide a caring, supportive milieu and encourage treatment compliance; (3) family training in effective verbal and nonverbal communication of emotions; in particular, the appropriate expression of dissatisfaction and concern, in order to reduce hostile criticism and overinvolvement; and (4) family training in effective problem-solving skills in order to lessen the impact of stressful life events and reduce the general level of tension in the home" (Falloon, Boyd, McGill, Strang, & Moss, 1981, p. 63). Emphasizing knowledge about schizophrenia; application of behavioral paradigms such as positive reinforcement, shaping, modeling, extinction; and the development of communication skills and problem-solving strategies, Falloon and his colleagues reported encouraging results in a 9-month follow-up, with only one (5%) of a family-treated group manifesting exacerbation of symptoms as compared with 44% of a matched clinic-based treatment control group. A similar psychosocial program was developed by Berkowitz, Kuipers, Eberlein-Fries, and Leff (1981) in London, with particular attention being paid to discussion of relatives' feelings. These authors have a good discussion of whether the disease model actually confers the sick role, as has been claimed by antilabeling theorists, and argue for mental health education for promotion of cognitive mastery and consistency (see also Anderson, Hogarty, & Reiss, 1981).

*Expressed Emotion and Stimulation: Psychophysiological Arousal with Relatives and Nonrelatives*

With respect to the EE studies, Snyder and Liberman (1981) have noted:

> An increase or reappearance of symptoms in a person biologically vulnerable to schizophrenia can be conceptualized as an outcome of the balance or interactions between the amount of life stressors and the problem-solving skills of the individual. Either too much of an environmental change or stressor—such as a harshly critical relative with whom the schizophrenic individual is emotionally overinvolved—or too little in the way of coping and problem-solving skills— as in the case of a person who responds to familial overprotectiveness or criticism with social withdrawal—can lead to symptomatic flareups. (p. 53)

Since relatives are usually the most constant elements in a patient's life, it is natural to highlight overstimulation in the family setting as conducive to a patient's relapse. However, there is considerable evidence suggesting that neurophysiological arousal signs might also be detected in interactions with *nonrelatives*. As may be seen below, this might very well occur in the ambience of foster homes, Veterans Administration (VA) day treatment centers, or even—perhaps especially—in the psychotherapeutic chamber.

The EE research highlights an important area that is functionally related to a whole other area of research—that on hyperarousal and stimulus thresholds. The premise is basically that "if some schizophrenics have a core deficit with inability to filter out vast amounts of stimuli, then an overload of activity in the environment could lead to relapse" (Linn, 1981, p. 44). In a study of 150 different foster homes for VA psychiatric patients, Linn, Klett, and Caffey (1980) found that certain characteristics of homes were related to the social functioning, mood, overall activity, and overall adjustment of patients. "*More activity* in the homes (higher degree of sponsor-initiated leisure activities) related to *patient improvement for nonschizophrenics* and *deterioration for schizophrenic patients*. Likewise, *more intense supervision* (either by sponsor or hospital) was associated with *deterioration in schizophrenics* but *improvement in nonschizophrenics*" (Linn, 1981, p. 43; italics mine). In a study of 10 VA day treatment centers for aftercare patients, Linn, Caffey, Klett, Hogarty, and Lamb (1979) found that good outcome was associated with more part-time staff, recreational therapy, and a nonthreatening environment, while centers with poor outcome had more professional (psychologist and social worker) staff hours, group therapy, and a high-patient-turnover treatment philosophy. These findings are in accord with the cautions of May, Tuma, and Dixon (1976) that a high degree of stimulus input and role diffusion may be toxic for schizophrenic individuals who have deficits in perception, attention, and information processing. The EE investigators themselves have stated:

> In our view, the relatives' EE represents one form of environmental stress, and results concerning its impact on relapse patterns permit one to make predictions about the possible impact of other, similar kinds of stress on patients who are unattached. If certain persons are prone to episodes of schizophrenia because of some underlying psychobiologic vulnerability, then related difficulties in processing complex stimuli and handling social relationships are likely to create problems for such persons in a variety of environments, e.g., a hostel or board and care home, the work place, or certain therapeutic settings. (Vaughn, Snyder, Jones, Freeman, & Falloon, 1984, p. 1177)

## EE, Families, and Culture

Several lines of evidence suggest that such precipitants of relapse may be related to cultural differences in attitudes and behavior toward the psychiatrically aberrant individual. First of all, high EE itself seems to be a culture-bound phenomenon in terms of its salience and relative distribution. Arieti (1981), for example, has pointed out the Brown, Birley, and Wing group worked almost exclusively with patients from an Anglo-Saxon environment, and "what is considered overinvolvement in that milieu may be the usual state of affairs in Italian and Jewish families" (p. 282). In replicating the British studies on a U.S. population in Los Angeles, California, Vaughn et al. (1982) pointed out that

> there were some notable differences between the English and California subjects. In London, a majority of the families were rated low on EE, while in the California sample only one-third of the families were rated low on EE. Ratings of hostility were also significantly more common in the California families. Thus, while cultural differences may produce differing distributions of high vs. low EE in families containing a schizophrenic member, the pattern of high EE retains its predictive significance cross-culturally. (p. 426)

The U.S. replication that was finally reported, however, restricted subjects (Ss) to Anglo-American ethnic origin, since pilot work in the British studies "had suggested that there were considerable variations by ethnic group in relatives' response styles and levels of EE. One could not analyze the data for different ethnic groups together, nor could one generalize from one set of results to the other" (Vaughn, et al., 1984, p. 1170).

The authors are nevertheless correct in pointing out the generalizability of high EE as a stressful factor across cultures. However, the interesting point in this study, confirmed in other cultural analyses, is that high EE seems to be far more prevalent in Western, urban settings than in other less stressful societies.

Several studies of EE in other cultural settings bear this out. A recent study of EE in a predominantly inner-city American setting among subjects from a lower socioeconomic status indicated that the level of family expressed emotion was higher than that reported in previous studies, but a higher cutoff point for criticalness had to be used. Rather interestingly, although 67% of the subjects were black, the black subgroup did not demonstrate a significant correlation between emotion and relapse at any cutoff point. In addition, the authors noted that "many of the questions in the Camberwell Family Inventory asking about family life in terms of routines, patterns, and task distributions were irrelevant to the life-styles of inner city families" (Moline, Singh, Morris, & Meltzer, 1985, p. 1080).

In the same general Los Angeles milieu studied by Vaughn and her associates, Marvin Karno and his associates found it quite difficult to find high EE relatives among Mexican-American families. Preliminary findings found very minimal critical comments, and when they were made, they were associated with the illness itself rather than with the patient.

> An examination of the various adaptation and coping mechanisms utilized by families of schizophrenic patients reveals some consistent patterns. In general, it can be said that Mexican Americans respond to schizophrenic family members with a great deal of tolerance and acceptance. . . . Many family members develop modes of communication that are calming, soothing, warm and patient toward the ill family member. A remarkable degree of respect and sensitivity for the patient's feelings and preferences are often evident. (Jenkins, 1981, p. 9)

In the same paper, Jenkins, a research collaborator in Karno's project, points out several other coping strategies used by the families: guarding and protecting ill family members from the stigma of mental illness by explaining their behavior in a positive, albeit defensive light; taking a nonreactive stance toward patient irritability; and avoiding labeling by instructing other family members to act "as if nothing were wrong" (p. 11), and the like.

In sum, the preliminary findings of this study over a 2-year period indicated that Mexican-American families reacted with great sadness rather than anger, and with tolerance rather than hostility, to schizophrenic members. This was attributed both by Jenkins (1981) and by Karno (1982) to three major factors: (1) acceptance of schizophrenia as a legitimate illness; (2) high willingness to tolerate deviant behavior; (3) strong social and economic support networks available to family members that allow for sharing and buffering the problem.

Similar preliminary findings have come from the application of the EE paradigm in Chandigarh, Northern India, where 90% of the families were reported as low EE in a World Health Organization (WHO) study (see Day, 1982). Leff (1981) has reported that in the same international study there seem to be similarities in U.S.-U.K. comparisons (Rochester, New York, and London). "However, very few of the relatives of the Chandigarh patients showed the high levels of criticism and overinvolvement encountered in many of the relatives in the West. These preliminary data indicate that the Northern Indian relatives are considerably more accepting of schizophrenia developing in a family member than relatives in London and Rochester" (p. 157).

These findings on EE distribution may, in turn, be related to the relatively low incidence of hospitalization found among Mexican-Americans, and on another level, to the findings that emerged from the *International Pilot Study of Schizophrenia* (IPSS) conducted under the auspices of the WHO (1973, 1979).

### The International Pilot Study of Schizophrenia: Family Implications

The IPSS was a transcultural psychiatric investigation originally intended to determine whether the same symptom clusters would be similarly diagnosed by psychiatrists in widely dispersed areas of the globe. The study took place in nine countries: Colombia, Czechoslovakia, Denmark, India, Nigeria, Taiwan, Soviet Union, United Kingdom, and United States. Using the same interviewing tool with careful translation procedures, and uniform training of psychiatrists, a total of 1202 patients were included from the nine centers, with 77.5% receiving a diagnosis of schizophrenia by the research psychiatrists. Despite some differences in symptom profiles (which included 27 clusters, or units of analysis, including such items as auditory hallucinations, flatness of affect, and the like) it was evident that psychiatrists around the world could generally agree on diagnostic screening criteria for schizophrenia, particularly in their usage of Schneider's first-rank symptoms (Leff, 1981).

The diagnostic uniformity finding was considered by many to be confirmation of a universally recognized disease entity, confirming a biogenic model of schizophrenia. However, cultural differences were found in outcome studies conducted 2 and 5 years later. Specifically, it became highly evident that despite the fact that schizophrenics had poorer outcomes than other diagnostic groups, the course and history of the illness was more benign in the developing countries than in more technologically advanced societies. Good outcome figures, many of them remissions, ranged from 58% in Nigeria, 51% in India, to 6% in Denmark and 7% in Moscow. These findings were in good accord with earlier or concurrent studies from Mauritius (Murphy & Raman, 1971) and Sri Lanka (Waxler, 1979), which showed complete recovery from the initial episode with no recurrence in 59% and 40% of the cases, respectively, after a minimum of 5 years follow-up.

A 10-year follow-up study was done of 133 Chinese schizophrenic patients in Hong Kong by Lo and Lo (1977), who were able to determine nature, course, and outcome of the illness for 80 patients. Diagnostic criteria for this group were the standard textbook symptoms used in the West. Congruent with the WHO data, follow-up evaluation of these

Chinese patients indicated that 65% had full and lasting remission or showed little or no deterioration among those who had some relapse. Factors associated with favorable prognosis included acute onset, shorter duration of illness, female sex, presence of symptom groups other than emotional or volitional disturbance, and *the presence of a supportive relative.*

A number of psychocultural factors have been highlighted in explanation of these findings. Leff (1981) has suggested that the two main variables are the attitudes of the patient's family and the relative ease with which symptomatic patients can be reintegrated into society. These are functionally related to Waxler's (1974, 1979) "social labeling" perspective, which holds that societal definitions of cause and resultant expectations determine the course and history of mental illness. In most non-Western cultures "where beliefs about mental illness center on supernatural causation, where the person is not held responsible for his illness, where his 'self' remains unchanged, he can shed the sick role quickly and easily. In contrast, where psychiatric illnesses are believed to involve personality change and personal responsibility, the sick person receives many messages that something is seriously wrong with his self; his self-perception and behavior may conform to these messages and his illness may have long duration" (Waxler, 1974, p. 379). This communications hypothesis may also be subsumed under the "low stress–high support" combination that many commentators believe differentiates the developing from the developed nations and provides the major explanatory paradigm (Mosher & Keith, 1981).

Leff (1981) has emphasized the low stress component, attributing this largely to the ability of the extended family system to dilute the deleterious effects of high EE.

> Family life in developing countries has a different quality from that in the West. Whereas the typical Western family is nuclear, with high social contact between the members and highly charged emotional relationships, the traditional family in a developing country is characteristically extended, with several generations sharing the same household. In such a family with a large number of members, individuals are likely to spend less time with one particular person than in a nuclear family, and emotional relationships tend to be diluted. It is possible that the lower levels of emotion and of social contact in extended families are beneficial to patients suffering from schizophrenia. (p. 156)

While Leff attaches a negative (absence) interpretation—reduction of interactional stressors—to the influence of extended family systems, these networks also offer more positive (presence) opportunities for the supportive environment that Liem and Liem (1978) and Caplan (1981) found central to successful coping. More specifically, the developing countries offer greater availability of meaningful work, and unburdened love. First, for patients the less technologically advanced societies provide occupational choices and roles that may be adapted to realistic expectancies of performance, do not inflict stimulus overload, and yet do not necessarily represent an insult to former levels of aspiration. Thus, in agrarian societies a patient may be returned to village life with totally flexible role demands geared to his level of productivity. Moreover, there are no artificially created jobs, as in many Western vocational rehabilitation projects, nor demeaning occupational choices that the patient recognizes as below his or her level of competence. In the developing countries, former college students are rarely reduced to dish-washing or floor-mopping tasks that further diminish their already low self-esteem simply because their cognitive deficit precludes career choices at a higher technological level. Rather, the patient performs with others in normative occupational roles.

Estroff (1981) has described the built-in double binding effects of a mental health system that offers unrewarding "job training" to individuals who recognize the dead-end, make-work nature of these efforts while they are told they are being trained to return to independent functioning in the community. We must bear in mind that the social labeling perspective extends to the patients as much as to the society in which they were enculturated, and that such masquerades serve to further diminish an already eroded self-concept.

The second point is that the extended kinships networks of developing countries provide a quantitatively larger support system to the patient and family that assists in both physical and psychological survival. One of the reasons for the dilution of expressed emotion is undoubtedly the diffusion of the burden of the nuclear family unit. The importance of this cannot be emphasized strongly enough. By spreading around the burden of housing, caretaking, and attention giving, the family is much more able to sustain low EE, genuine concern, and greater tolerance of aberrant behavior.

The coping resources of both patient and family are thus strengthened in a pattern of circular reinforcement. Realistic, low-expectancy, but normative occupational roles tend to give the patient a niche in society, enhancing his or her self-esteem and reducing dependency on the nuclear family. The family, freed of the nagging burdens of support and attention is able to respond with unhampered caring. In developing countries, low EE may be culturally congruent, but is also may be a coping mechanism that is possible only under conditions that are free of the intolerable strains so often found in Western nuclear family systems.

*Schizophrenia and Socioeconomic Status: The Family Matrix*

A consistent finding in the cross-cultural literature is that the incidence of schizophrenia seems to be significantly higher among people of lower socioeconomic status (SES), including those in the United States (Dohrenwend *et al.*, 1980). This finding provides support for the diathesis–stress position, and is in good accord with the hyperarousal hypothesis because of the higher degree of stress-inducing conditions in lower SES life. This does not necessarily mean that the true prevalence of schizophrenia is higher among lower SES groups. The hyperarousal hypothesis does, however, suggest that the emergence (incidence) of psychotic behavior in sufficiently disturbing form to be brought to official or extrafamilial attention should be correlated with a commensurate degree of aversive stimulation in the environment.

In a study conducted during the 1960s in Puerto Rico, Rogler and Hollingshead (1965) investigated three questions in families where one of the spouses was schizophrenic: (1) Do the life histories of persons who develop schizophrenia differ from those of persons who are not schizophrenic? (2) When and under what conditions do persons who become schizophrenic exhibit the symptoms? and (3) What effect does schizophrenia have on the family? Comparing carefully matched groups of 20 families of schizophrenics with 20 families without the disease, all of the lowest socioeconomic class, the authors found that persons who were schizophrenic did not differ in childhood, youth, or early adult histories from the mentally healthy controls. However, in the year before the onset of schizophrenia, there were more economic, social, and physical problems in the families of the sick spouses, and as the stresses began to increase, the subjects began to demonstrate behavior defined as *locura* (crazy). The study indicated that the extended family structure aids the family in adapting to the disorder, but wives are better able to cope with sick husbands than vice versa.

Rogler and Hollingshead's landmark study indicated strongly that there was little difference between families of schizophrenics and families of "normals" in lower socioeconomic groups in Puerto Rico. Similar findings among black families in an urban ghetto were reported by Verinis (1976). Thus, while the cumulative impact of stressful conditions may trigger breakdown among the biologically vulnerable, there appears to be no discernible difference in family interaction patterns among those with mentally ill and non-mentally ill members in lower-income groups.

Is there an interaction between minority status and SES in the epidemiology of mental illness? Despite variation in child-rearing practices among various ethnic groups (McGoldrick, Pearce, & Giordano, 1982) there seems to be little relationship between this variable and the distribution of major psychotic disorders, SES-controlled, among cultural groups in the United States. Thus, the differences in hospitalization for mental illness, with median income held constant, among Italians, Irish, and Jews seem to be negligible when compared with the rates for the black population (Rabkin & Struening, 1976), which appear more related to the stressors of historical discrimination than to poverty alone.

As Sanua (1982) has pointed out, few studies of families and psychopathology have dealt with the social and cultural system. Almost all research subjects have been white, middle-class, and from two-parent families. It is very difficult to reconcile such etiological concepts as marital schism and skew, cross-sex parental influences, the contradictory differences in maternal-paternal communication deviance, and the hothouse symbiotic relationships cited in the literature, with the hard realities of epidemiological data. These clearly show that in the highest prevalence areas for severe mental disorder (poor urban communities), mother-father families have the lowest risk, those headed by mother and another adult have varying risk, while loosely organized multichild mother-alone families with little parent-child communication have the highest risk (Kellam, Ensminger, & Turner, 1977). Family intactness may be an independent correlate of such variables as economic deprivation and second-class citizenship, which in turn are correlated with epidemiological patterns of mental illness. However, if, as has been frequently suggested by some sociogenic theorists, family intactness is directly related and antecedent to the prevalence of mental disorder, the single-head-of-household structure should theoretically result in fewer conflicting messages from principal adult figures in the family. Here again the issue of values comes through, because the research conclusions derive from culture-bound assumptions that schizophrenia emerges from the dynamics of two-parent nuclear family structure, while epidemiology suggests otherwise. Rather, the data on distribution tend to support the hypothesis that an external social stress factor, which may very well be manifested in more turbulent relations in the family, may help trigger breakdown in the vulnerable individual who cannot tolerate stimulus overload.

## WESTERN VALUES AND ATTRIBUTION
## OF RESPONSIBILITY

American culture, according to anthropologist Francis Hsu (1972) is based on the core values of self-reliance and profound fear of dependency. This notion is supported by corresponding research in the area of locus of control (e.g., Rotter, 1966), which demonstrated that people socialized in the mainstream system typically believe in internal rather than external locus of control—the contemporary analogues of free will versus determinism. Middle-class whites are much more likely to subscribe to this than blacks and others who feel alienated from the primary sources of societal power (Gore & Rotter, 1971). This belief that people can manipulate and control their own destinies is in good accord with Kluckhohn and Strodtbeck's (1961) demonstration that the value orientation of mastery over nature differentiates mainstream Americans from the subjugation or harmony values expressed by other cultures.

There is a substantive difference, however, between mastery as a coping strategy, which connotes competence and control (White, 1974), and mastery as a construct, which implies that human agency can cause and cure all human events. When people are socialized in a value system that sees almost all problems as capable of human resolution, it is only logical to infer that those that are not readily soluble are attributable either to irreversible fate (a minor percentage) or to human deficiency. Psychological or developmental problems that cannot be attributed to known external causes—faulty genes, birth trauma, anatomic or biochemical anomalies, or other discordancies in human development—must therefore be attributed either to the afflicted persons themselves or to those who reared them.

With respect to the patients, our core value of fear of dependency is extremely evident in our traditional approaches to institutional, day treatment, and rehabilitative care. High-expectancy objectives are built into many program models, with the expressed aim of returning the patient to independent living in the community (although many patients indeed have no such history to which to return). Western thinking is linear and goal-oriented. Our terms for service imply linguistically our cultural expectations of linear progress: "transitional," "half-way," "step-level," and the like.

The frequent reports of anxiety and unwillingness to leave transitional community care (e.g., Wing, 1975), suggests that in many cases this orientation asks far too much of many patients, and may exacerbate precisely those feelings of anxiety and apartness that are central to their illness. As a matter of policy, the "transitional" model also imposes a built-in impermanence in the lives of people who may require long-term stability in order to remain intact.

With respect to families, the search for human causation has had massive impact on the attitudes of mental health professionals, impeding the flow of information and support that might normally accrue to people whose loved ones are severely disabled.

Several years ago, Frances Culbertson, former president of the International Council of Psychologists, took her colleagues to task for becoming victims of "mind-set and groupthink" in their attitudes toward parents of autistic children, because of the problem-family model extant at that time (Culbertson, 1977, p. 63). Therapists who hold to theoretical positions implicating the family etiologically "engage in shared stereotypes . . . develop rationalizations to account for anyone viewing a problem differently . . . develop illusions . . . that experts in the area know best what is proper, right, and appropriate, not listening to or ignoring parents' complaints and inquiries" (p. 65).

Contemporary social psychological theories, particularly attribution models, offer a rich vein of explanation for the myth of unanimity and invulnerability that Culbertson claims characterizes mental health professionals with false etiological assumptions (Culbertson, 1977).

While a discussion of attribution is beyond the scope of this chapter, cognitive consistency theories would predict that if one believes in family causation of mental illness, then socializing agents should be perceived as bad or defective persons and that any characteristics that conflict with this view should be rationalized as deceptions or perceptual failures on the part of the therapist. Thus, in all the years of research on schizophrenogenic families, researchers have shown almost no interest in investigating those families—a substantial portion of the variance in their own studies—who produce severely disordered offspring but do not show communication deviance, marital schism or skew, double binding, scapegoating, pseudomutuality, or any of the other malevolent etiological characteristics that they by rights should have. Nor has there been significant interest in investigating the nonschizophrenic children of parents who do show these characteristics. The Danish researcher Rolv M. Blakar (personal communication, 1983) described a case of a family whose blindly scored communication deviance protocols indicated that they might be parents of a schizophrenic offspring (as indeed they were), but who nevertheless were parents of 11 other children, not one of whom was schizophrenic.

Arieti (1981) was one of the first to acknowledge that patients dramatically transform experience, and has commented on his colleagues' eager willingness to believe (and probably reinforce) that emphasis on negative maternal characteristics that is common in psychoanalytic therapy of schizophrenics. He has equated the therapists' naïveté with Freud's early mistaken acceptance of neurotic patients' fantasies about being sexually assaulted by their parents. Similarly, there is a procrustean attempt in some books, purporting to demonstrate the etiological threads that lead to decompensation, to fit portraits of mothers into the mold of schizophrenogenesis while ignoring their positive behavior and totally avoiding the question of specificity. Thus, anthropologist Nancy Scheper-Hughes, commenting on fellow anthropologists Reynolds and Farberow's (1981) home portrait of the mother of a schizophrenic, points out about the mother and son, Jewel and Chuck: "There are a great many negative, anxious, fearful and ambivalent mothers in the world, like Jewel, but there are very few sons as sick and disturbed as Chuck" (Scheper-Hughes, 1982, p. 8). The question of why this child and not others; the total inadequacy of the notion of scapegoating as an explanatory device; and the wildly disproportionate fit proposed between stimulus and response in most of the literature, including the more sophisticated studies on communication deviance, all leave psychogenic explanations extremely wanting. Most important, since almost all researchers rely on basic diathesis, these efforts tend to confound the law of parsimony without bridging the psychocultural gap.

## ETIOLOGICAL THEORIES AND CULTURALLY NORMATIVE BEHAVIOR

Anthropologists have long been in the forefront of those maintaining that "mental illness" may be functionally and conceptually related to a culture's defining criteria for appropriate and deviant behavior (see Benedict, 1934). It thus seems paradoxical that a major etiological theory of schizophrenia, the double bind, should have been promulgated by one of the most noted anthropologists and his associates (Bateson, Jackson, Haley, & Weakland, 1956), while it is a psychiatrist who takes them to task by noting that "double-bind situations are a characteristic of life, not of schizophrenia. . . . Culture itself exposes the individual to many double-bind situations. . ." (Arieti, 1974, p. 99). We may note that Bateson, who himself had written of double binding cultural styles, was not alluding to the broad, malevolent social forces that place individuals in a dual-tension situation from which there is no escape. Lake (1982), for example, has used Bateson's double bind concept to describe how young Native Americans are torn between two worlds, with resulting despair that often leads to violence, substance abuse, or suicide. But the initial conceptualization of the double bind in schizophrenia was strictly psychological. It focused on a parenting style that was spontaneously malignant, embedded in no cultural context and responsive to no external pressures.

While cultural child-rearing practices may or may not be directly related to adult modal personality—an issue that has waxed and waned in culture and personality theory—the notion that discrete socialization practices may be etiologically implicated in the major psychotic disorders is questioned by data and observations that find so-called schizophrenogenic behaviors as normative in specific cultures. Consider, for example, the various characteristics and behavioral clusters that have been represented as etiologically significant in schizophrenia. Primary among them, of course, is the old concept of the "schizophrenogenic mother," developed by Fromm-Reichmann (1939) and reinforced by Lidz, Fleck, and Cornelison (1965), among others. These mothers have variously been described as oversolicitous, domineering, intrusive, immature, repressed, overprotective, and possessive, while at the same time unconsciously rejecting their children's needs. Other characteristics include preoccupation with controlling their children's sexuality, and secretiveness and fear of outsiders. Alanen (1966) found such mothers "possessively protective" if the schizophrenic child were male, "inimically protective" if she were female. The specter of the schizophrenogenic mother has undoubtedly affected professional–family relationships in thousands of cases over a long span of time, despite the recognition by Arieti (1981) that no more than 20-25% of the mothers of schizophrenics he has seen in a 20-year period remotely fit this description. The double bind; marital skew and schism (Lidz, Cornelison, Fleck, & Terry, 1957); Laing and Esterson's (1964) concept of "mystification," and "pseudomutuality" and other types of impaired family communication described by Wynne and Singer (1963) have also been prominent in the armamentarium of etiological speculation.

Yet, Scheper-Hughes (1979), commenting on "the parallels between the stereotypic 'schizophrenogenic' mother and the stereotypic rural Irish mother" (p. 158), suggested that cultures may provide parenting norms that encourage or reinforce precisely these maternal behaviors. Double blinding in humor has been described as characteristic of Irish-American Families (McGoldlrick, 1982). Communication deviance among families in rural Ireland has also been cited as typical behavior. Nancy Scheper-Hughes (1979) characterized their conversations in terms of "double-talk, obfuscation, interruption, and non sequiturs," at the same time contesting the notion that "so-called Irish double-speak may create intolerable levels of ambiguity, which can provoke schizophrenia in vulnerable individuals" (p. 82). Rather, she suggested that schizoid or borderline schizophrenic persons are outlawed and labeled abnormal because of their linguistic inadequacies in a highly verbal society. Referring to the work of Scheper-Hughes, McGoldrick (1982) noted that "family therapists may be familiar with this ambiguous and mystifying communication of many Irish-American families" (p. 316).

Guthrie and Bennett's (1971) cross-cultural analysis of "implicit personality theory" demonstrated that cultures may differ in behavioral predicates, in terms of the clusters of behaviors that are assumed to occur jointly to make up the same summary construct. Guthrie (1966) and Lefley (1976), for example, found that mothers in different cultures varied greatly in their conceptual and behavioral approaches to dependency, and that mothers who seemed to be intrusive and overcontrolling in one society were viewed as protective and family-oriented in another. Cultural variables are similarly evident in the interpretation of symptomatic behavior. McGoldrick (1982) has described what seems to be a cultural norm for thought disorder in the "dreaming mode" of the Irish, a mode that values fantasy over objective truth. "We might call this 'denial,' but it is more like the experiencing of separate realities. As part of the acceptance of the dreaming mode, the Irish show a much greater tolerance of nonrealistic thinking and language than do, for example, the Jews, who value correct thought" (p. 315).

In this connection, the separate realities of practitioners of Vodun, Espiritismo, Santeria, and others who literally believe in two worlds should also be noted. Mathewson (1975), describing Haitian psychiatric patients in Miami, cautioned against diagnostic error by noting that it is culturally consonant for Haitians to believe in a visible world inhabited by humans and an invisible world of the dead, spirits, and other supernatural beings. In cultures that attribute a potential for danger and harm to the usage of magic by others, so-called paranoid ideation may also be within the boundaries of what is normal. Standard assessment procedures for hallucinatory behavior similarly must take into account a cognitive system that attributes a communicative function to dreams. These allow the passing of messages to the dreamer from members of the invisible subworld in an interaction perceived as really taking place. Unless an examiner specified waking hours in the context of psychological testing, a Haitian Vodun believer or Puerto Rican Espiritismo believer might very well respond that they indeed heard voices or saw things that others did not, without conveying a pathological hallucinatory experience.

Cultural differences are found in the symptomatology of the major affective disorders (Marsella, 1980) as well as in the schizophrenias.

With respect to the latter, Marsella (1982) has pointed out that although the IPSS findings demonstrated that psychiatrists from different cultures could agree on whether a symptom were present or absent, meanings and implications of symptoms differed. Moreover, there was great cultural variation in the frequency of various types of schizophrenic symptoms. "For example, autism was very high in Denmark, but virtually absent in India and Nigeria and Taipei. Flat affect was very high in England and Czechoslovakia but was only moderately present in Colombia and Nigeria. Delusions of control were very high in Colombia, Taipei and India, but very low in Denmark, Czechoslovakia, and the United States" (Marsella, 1982, p. 372).

With respect to the question of etiology, however, the distribution of symptoms is only a key to the more important questions of their meaning and source. For example, Opler and Singer's (1957) early cross-cultural comparisons described almost bipolar characteristics of Irish and Italian schizophrenics, with the former obsessed with guilt for uncommitted sins and the latter able to act without remorse. McGoldrick (1982) suggested that this may be attributed to different socialization patterns in Irish and Italian Catholicism, with Irish children taught "the myth of badness" (p. 313), that is, the belief that people are bad and deserve to suffer for their sins. In contrast, she stated that Italians tend to externalize responsibility for badness and to limit guilt primarily to violations of family loyalty.

Other characteristics depicted as specifically schizophrenogenic in the literature seem to be fairly normative in other settings. For example, McGoldrick (1982) described considerable social distance between parents and children in Irish families, with the family often designating a good child and a bad one, ignoring characteristics that do not fit the designated role. In addition to this built-in scapegoating mode, she stated that "discipline in Irish families is maintained by ridicule, belittling, and shaming" (p. 323). In contrast to Irish distance, Italian families show "frequent symbiotic-like relationships between parents and children, and Italian families may not achieve the level of differentiation that predominates in the larger culture" (Rotunno & McGoldrick, 1982, p. 357). These authors caution against viewing enmeshment in Italian families as pathogenic, and even suggest that the absence of emotional fusion, being culturally aberrant, might suggest a "buried issue" (Rotunno & McGoldrick, 1982) and therefore should be explored.

These are but a few examples of the more classic (and often seemingly contradictory) antecedent events that have been proposed as etiologically implicated in mental disorder: double binding, communication deviance, scapegoating, rejection, symbiosis, and the like. Are they reflective of genotypic variables that generate phenotypic epidemiological patterns? As noted, ethnic variation in child-rearing practices, when SES is controlled, shows little relationship to the distribution of the major psychotic disorders.

For mental health professionals, it would seem far more important to use this information on cultural differences not to speculate on etiology, but rather to help families to cope. The ahistorical systems approach in contemporary family therapy would seem to lend itself to this purpose. Thus, with families of schizophrenics, it would seem useful, for example, to help families reduce or expand social distance according to the dual criteria of patients' needs and cultural compatibility, or to utilize artifacts such as "the dreaming mode" as a mechanism of translation to explore the parameters of normal and abnormal thought in cultural context.

## IMPLICATIONS FOR TREATMENT

Currently there seems to be a convergence in the ideas of those mental health professionals who are becoming increasingly sensitive to the need for culturally appropriate treatment, and the new psychoeducational school of family therapy (cf. Anderson, Hogarty, & Reiss, 1981). In both instances there is an implicit emphasis on what cross-cultural researchers call the "emic" approach—that is, the outsider must learn to perceive through the eyes of the subject, rather than superimposing his or her own external model of reality. Among psychoeducational therapists, this involves learning the family's experience of the illness, their theories about causes and their view of roles. Rather than observing a putatively maladaptive "system" through the lenses of theory, the therapist helps the family build survival skills within the framework of their expressed needs.

Family therapists who have had to adapt their professional training to deal with diverse cultural groups have long been aware that the typical therapist posture of distancing, nondirectiveness, and noncommunicativeness, is simply maladaptive with cultural groups that emphasize family primacy. Alber Gaw (1982), for example, advised psychiatric residents and other mental health professionals to deal with Chinese patients as follows:

> Family involvement in the management of the patient's problems is natural to Chinese Americans. The psychiatrist should not hesitate to conduct family interviews, to give advice to members of the family as to how to handle the patient's problem, and to obtain feedback through periodic family interviews. If family members become too intrusive and interfere with the patient's treatment, this should be explained

and appropriate limits set. If psychotherapy or psychoanalysis is to be attempted so that the technical requirement of the therapeutic process necessitates minimal or no involvement with family members, the rationale and process of treatment should be carefully explained to both patient and family members. (p. 25)

Gaw's injunctions, of course, are precisely what most American and other Western families ask for: to be involved, to be interviewed and listened to, to be advised about how to handle patients' problems, and to give the professionals feedback on what is happening as a result of their interventions. Further, if family members are to be excluded from contact with the clinician, how human and how *rational* it would be for them to be advised of the reason for their exclusion, rather than being left to founder, resent, and to despair, with the ultimate perception of not receiving help from the so-called helpers (see Hatfield, 1978).

Coping strategies are above all transactional; there is a continuous feedback loop among the major principals in mental illness—the clients, the clinicians, and the caregivers—that influences the coping process. Thus, the dialogue between families and therapists is critical in helping professionals to better understand obstacles and strengths in the patient-family interrelationships, as well as to ventilate concerns that require training in management techniques.

Further implications for treatment come from the importance of social support networks in providing sustenance for the chronically mentally ill. While the concepts of interdependence and human support undergird the psychosocial rehabilitation model, traditional psychiatric approaches still emphasize that patients can only regain individuation when they separate from those on whom they are dependent. Typically these are the very people with whom they have bonds of love and lifetime caring, as well as dependency. While physical separation may indeed be a preferred solution, for families as much as patients, therapeutic goals are frequently geared toward psychological separation as well—again, based on the premise of pathogenesis. The psychoeducational model has a stated goal of retaining families as a primary resource for patients without being sacrificed on the altar of "expedient separation" (Anderson et al., 1981, p. 92).

## CONCLUSIONS

What are the major lessons to be learned from cross-cultural research with respect to family coping? First, it appears evident that, contrary to the Western value system, a social ambience that externalizes causation of mental illness, subscribes to a disease model, views the afflicted individual as sick rather than as a participant agent in his disability, and gears productivity to realistic expectancy levels, results in more benign family relationships and lower rates of hospitalization. Second, societies that stress mutual interdependence, rather than "independent functioning in the community"—the catchphrase of our aftercare movement—appear to provide a more tolerable atmosphere for the severely psychiatrically disabled. Patients do better in societies in which the mental health professionals emphasize family involvement not because of disturbed psychodynamics but because of recognition that it would be culturally incongruent not to involve the family in information and decisions regarding the patient.

In cultures that do not believe in mastery over fate and nature, mastery nonetheless prevails in terms of providing strategies for adapting to this most devastating of human ills. In contrast, Western cultures, whose major value orientation is mastery, often misuse the concept by assigning human causation and thereby seeking sources of blame in the family system. Cultures that use a disease model as an explanatory device seem able to provide more appropriate levels of stimulation than those that view severe mental illness as a "problem in living." Paradoxically, schizophrenics who return to their villages and live for years without psychotherapy and often without neuroleptics, seem to improve at a significantly higher rate than those who have access to the therapeutics of modern Western psychiatry.

Of overwhelming importance is the recognition that large supportive networks mitigate family burden by providing multiple resources for caregiving, attention, economic sharing, and buffering the effects of disruptive behavior. These networks also are often capable of providing occupations for the patient that are appropriate for her or his level of functioning, thereby assuring a productive social role conducive to the maintenance of self-esteem.

In many respects these cross-cultural findings parallel and validate the roles of the family self-help groups that have united under the banner of such organizations as the National Schizophrenia Fellowship in the United Kingdom and the National Alliance for the Mentally Ill in the United States. Many of these groups tend to function as extended kinship networks, offering psychological support and information sharing, and often developing resources that provide occupational roles for some of their disabled members. Some families have banded together to purchase long-term therapeutic group homes, an effort that would be economically unfeasible alone, and to share financial-planning strategies for their relatives' future. The buffering function of the extended family extends not only to sharing problems and pain, but also to offering extra supportive strengths to the patient. Group members frequently get to know the disabled relatives of others, thereby extending the patient's circle of recognition and implicit friendship, and often providing recreational or group events for meeting others in the "real world" outside of the formal mental health system. All of these are normalizing functions that establish a circularity of coping strength for families and patients and for their interactions with each other, with mental health professionals, and with the culture in which they live.

# REFERENCES

Alanen, Y. O. (1966). The family in the pathogenesis of schizophrenic and neurotic disorders. *Acta Psychiatrica Scandinavica*, 42 (Suppl. 189).

Anderson, C. M., Hogarty, G., & Reiss, D. J. (1981). The psychoeducational family treatment of schizophrenia. In M. J. Goldstein (Ed.), *New developments in interventions with families of schizophrenics* (New Directions for Mental Health Services No. 12, pp. 79-94). San Francisco: Jossey-Bass.

Anthony, E. J. (1970). The impact of mental and physical illness on family life. *American Journal of Psychiatry*, 127, 136-143.

Arieti, S. (1974). *Interpretation of schizophrenia* (2nd rev. ed.). New York: Basic Books.

Arieti, S. (1981). The family of the schizophrenic and its participation in the therapeutic task. In S. Arieti & K. H. Brodie (Eds.), *American handbook of psychiatry* (2nd ed., Vol. 7, pp. 271-284). New York: Basic Books.

Bateson, G., Jackson, D. D., Haley, J., & Weakland, J. (1956). Toward a theory of schizophrenia. *Behavioral Science*, 1, 251-264.

Bell, J. (1982). The family in the hospital: Experiences in other countries. In H. Harbin (Ed.), *The psychiatric hospital and the family*. New York: Spectrum.

Benedict, R. (1934). *Patterns of culture*. Boston: Houghton-Mifflin.

Berkowitz, R., Kuipers, L., Eberlein-Fries, R., & Leff, J. (1981). Lowering expressed emotion in relatives of schizophrenics. In M. J. Goldstein (Ed.), *New developments in interventions with families of schizophrenics* (New Directions for Mental Health Services, No. 12, pp. 27-48). San Francisco: Jossey-Bass.

Blakar, R. M. (1980). Psychopathology and familial communication. In M. Brenner (Ed.), *The structure of action* (pp. 211-263). Oxford, UK: Basil Blackwell.

Brown, G. W., Birley, J. L.T., & Wing, J. K. (1972). Influence of family life on the course of schizophrenic disorders: A replication. *British Journal of Psychiatry*, 121, 241-258.

Brown, G. W., Monck, E. M., Carstairs, G. M., & Wing, J. K. (1962). Influence of family life on the course of schizophrenic illness. *British Journal of Preventive Social Medicine*, 16, 55-68.

Caplan, G. (1981). Mastery of stress: Psychosocial aspects. *American Journal of Psychiatry*, 138, 413-420.

Collomb, H. (1978). L'Economie des villages psychiatriques. *Social Science and Medicine*, 12C, 113.

Creer, C., & Wing, J. K. (1974). *Schizophrenia at home*. London: Institute of Psychiatry.

Culbertson, F. M. (1977). The search for help of parents of autistic children or beware of professional "groupthink." *Journal of Clinical Child Psychology*, Winter, 63-65.

Day, R. (1982). Research on the course and outcome of schizophrenia in traditional cultures: Some potential implications for psychiatry in the developed countries. In M. J. Goldstein (Ed.), *Preventive intervention in schizophrenia: Are we ready?* (pp. 197-219). Rockville, MD: National Institute of Mental Health.

Dohrenwend, B. P., Dohrenwend, B. S., Gould, M. S., Link, B., Nuegebauer, R., & Wunsch-Hitzig, R. (1980). *Mental illness in the United States: Epidemiological estimates.* New York: Praeger.

Doll, W. (1976). Family coping with the mentally ill: An unanticipated prolem of deinstitutionalization. *Hospital and Community Psychiatry, 27,* 183-185.

Estroff, S. E. (1981). *Making it crazy: An ethnography of psychiatric clients in an American community.* Berkeley: University of California Press.

Falloon, I. R. H., Boyd, J. L., McGill, C. W., Strang, J. S., & Moss, H. B. (1981). Family management training in the community care of schizophrenia. In M. J. Goldstein (Ed.), *New developments in interventions with families of schizophrenics* (New Directions for Mental Health Services, No. 12, pp. 61-78). San Francisco: Jossey-Bass.

Frank, G. H. (1965). The role of the family in the development of psychopathology. *Psychological Bulletin, 64,* 191-205.

Fromm-Reichmann, F. (1939). Transference problems in schizophrenia. *Psychoanalytic Quarterly, 8,* 412-426.

Gaw, A. (Ed.). (1982). *Cross-cultural psychiatry.* Boston: John Wright-PSG.

Goldman, H. H. (1982). Mental illness and family burden: A public health perspective. *Hospital and Community Psychiatry, 33,* 557-560.

Goldstein, M. J. (1981). Editor's notes. In Goldstein, M. J. (Ed.), *New developments in interventions with families of schizophrenics* (New Directions for Mental Health Services, No. 12). San Francisco: Jossey-Bass.

Gore, P. M., & Rotter, J. B. (1971). A personality correlate of social action. In R. Wilcox (Ed.), *The psychological consequences of being a Black American* (pp. 370-376). New York: Wiley.

Guthrie, G. M. (1966). Structure of maternal attitudes in two cultures. *Journal of Psychology, 62,* 155-165.

Guthrie, G. M., & Bennett, A. B. (1971). Cultural differences in implicit personality theory. *International Journal of Psychology, 6,* 305-312.

Hatfield, A. B. (1978). Psychological costs of schizophrenia to the family. *Social Work, 23,* 355-359.

Higginbotham,, H. N. (1979). *Delivery of mental health services in three developing Asian nations: Feasibility and cultural sensitivity of "modern psychiatry."* Unpublished doctoral dissertation, University of Hawaii.

Hirsch, S. R., & Leff, J. P. (1975). *Abnormalities in parents of schizophrenics.* London: Oxford University Press.

Hoffman, L. (1981). *Foundations of family therapy.* New York: Basic Books.

Hsu, F. L. K. (1972). American core value and national character. In F. L. K. Hsu (Ed.), *Psychological anthropology* (new ed.). Cambridge, MA: Schenkman.

Jegede, R. O. (1981). A study of the role of socio-cultural factors in the treatment of mental illness in Nigeria. *Social Science and Medicine, 15A,* 49-54.

Jenkins, J. A. (1981, December). *The course of schizophrenia among Mexican Americans.* Paper presented at the annual meeting of the American Anthropological Association, Los Angeles, CA.

Karno, M. (1982, October). *The experience of schizophrenia in Mexican American families.* Paper presented at the meeting of the Society for the Study of Psychiatry and Culture, San Miguel Regla, Mexico.

Kellam, S., Ensminger, M., & Turner, R. J. (1977). Family structure and the mental health of children: Concurrent and longitudinal community wide studies. *Archives of General Psychiatry, 34*, 1012-1022.

Kluckhohn, F., & Strodtbeck, F. (1961). *Variations in value orientations.* Evanston: Row Peterson.

Laing, R., & Esterson, A. (1964). *Sanity, madness, and the family.* London: Tavistock.

Lake, R. (1982). A discussion of Native American health problems, needs, and services: With a focus on Northwestern California. *White Cloud Journal, 2*(4), 23-31.

Lambo, T. A. (1966). Patterns of psychiatric care in developing African countries: The Nigerian program. In H. R. David (Ed.), *International trends in mental health.* New York: McGraw-Hill.

Leff, J. (1981). *Psychiatry around the globe: A transcultural view.* New York: Marcel Dekker.

Leff, J. P., & Vaughn, C. E. (1981). The role of maintenance therapy and relatives' expressed emotion in relapse of schizophrenia: A two-year follow-up. *British Journal of Psychiatry, 139*, 102-104.

Lefley, H. P. (1976). Acculturation, childrearing, and self-esteem in two North American Indian tribes. *Ethos, 4*, 385-401.

Lidz, T., Cornelison, A. R., Fleck, S., & Terry, D. (1957). The intrafamilial environment of the schizophrenic patient: II. Marital schism and marital skew. *American Journal of Psychiatry, 114*, 241-248.

Lidz, T., Fleck, S., & Cornelison, A. R. (Eds.). (1965). *Schizophrenia and the family.* New York: International Universities Press.

Liem, R., & Liem, J. (1978). Social class and mental illness reconsidered: The role of economic stress and social support. *Journal of Health and Social Behavior, 19*, 139-156.

Linn, M. W. (1981). Can foster care survive? In R. D. Budson (Ed.), *Issues in community residential care* (New Directions for Mental Health Services, No. 11, pp. 35-47). San Francisco: Jossey-Bass.

Linn, M. W., Caffey, E. M., Klett, C. J., Hogarty, G. E., & Lamb, H. R. (1979). Day treatment and psychotropic drugs in the aftercare of schizophrenic patients. *Archives of General Psychiatry, 36*, 1055-1066.

Linn, M. W., Klett, C. J., & Caffey, E. M. (1980). Foster home characteristics and psychiatric patient outcome. *Archives of General Psychiatry, 37*(2), 129-132.

Lo, W. H., & Lo, T. (1977). A ten-year follow-up study of Chinese schizophrenics in Hong Kong. *British Journal of Psychiatry, 131*, 63-66.

Marsella, A. J. (1980). Depressive experience and disorder across cultures. In H. Triandis & J. Draguns (Eds.), *Handbook of cross-cultural psychology* (Vol. 5: Psychopathology, pp. 237-289). Boston: Allyn & Bacon.

Marsella, A. J. (1982). Culture and mental health: An overview. In A. J. Marsella & G. M. White (Eds.), *Cultural conceptions of mental health and therapy* (pp. 359-388). Dordrecht, Holland: D. Reidel.

Mathewson, M. A. (1975). Is crazy Anglo crazy Haitian? *Psychiatric Annals, 5*(8), 79-85.

May, P. R. A., Tuma, A. H., & Dixon, W. J. (1976). Schizophrenia: A followup study of results of treatment. *Archives of General Psychiatry, 33*(4), 474-478.

McGoldrick, M. (1982). Irish families. In M. McGoldrick, J. K. Pearce, & J. Giordano (Eds.), *Ethnicity and family therapy* (pp. 310-339). New York: Guilford.

McGoldrick, M., Pearce, J. K., & Giordano, J. (Eds.). (1982). *Ethnicity and family therapy.* New York: Guilford.

Moline, R. A., Singh, S., Morris, A., & Meltzer, H. Y. (1985). Family expressed emotion and relapse in schizophrenia in 24 urban American patients. *American Journal of Psychiatry, 142*, 1078-1080.

Mosher, L. R., & Keith, S. J. (1981). Psychosocial treatment: Individual, groups, family, and community support approaches. *Special Report: Schizophrenia, 1980* (DHHS Publication No. [ADM] 81-1064). Washington, DC: U.S. Government Printing Office.

Murphy, H. B. M., & Raman, A. C. (1971). The chronicity of schizophrenia in indigenous tropical peoples. *British Journal of Psychiatry, 118*, 489-497.

Opler, M. K., & Singer, J. L. (1957). Ethnic differences in behavior and psychopathology: Italian and Irish. *International Journal of Social Psychiatry, 1*, 11-17.

Parker, G. (1982). Re-searching the schizophrenogenic mother. *Journal of Nervous and Mental Disease, 170*(8), 452-462.

Parsons, T., & Fox, R. C. (1952). Illness, therapy, and the modern urban American family. *Journal of Social Issues, 8*, 31-44.

Rabkin, J. G., & Struening, E. L. (1976). *Ethnicity, social class, and mental illness* (Working Paper Series, No. 17). New York: Institute on Pluralism and Group Identity.

Reynolds, D., & Farberow, N. L. (1981). *The family shadow: Sources of suicide and schizophrenia*. Berkeley, CA: University of California Press.

Rogler, L. H., & Hollingshead, A. B. (1965). *Trapped: Families and schizophrenia*. New York: Wiley.

Rotter, J. B. (1966). Generalized expectancies for internal versus external control of reinforcement [Whole issue]. *Psychological Monographs, 80*(1).

Rotunno, M., & McGoldrick, M. (1982). Italian families. In M. McGoldrick, J. K. Pearce, & J. Giordano (Eds.), *Ethnicity and family therapy* (pp. 340-363). New York: Guilford.

Sanua, V. (1982). Family studies in psychopathology. In I. Al-Issa (Ed.), *Culture and psychopathology* (pp. 157-180). Baltimore, MD: University Park Press.

Sargent, M. (1982, February 26). NIMH scientist turns detective to conduct Israeli followup study. *ADAMHA News*, pp. 4-5.

Scheper-Hughes, N. (1979). *Saints, scholars and schizophrenics*. Berkeley: University of California Press.

Scheper-Hughes, N. (1982). Anthropologists and the "craziess." *Medical Anthropology Newsletter, 13*, 1-2, 6-11.

Schulsinger, H. (1976). A ten-year follow-up of children of schizophrenic mothers: Clinical assessment. *Acta Psychiatrica Scandinavica, 53*, 371-386.

Sidel, R., & Sidel, V. (1972, March/April). The human services in China. *Social Policy*, pp. 25-34.

Singer, M. T., Wynee, L. C., & Toohey, M. H. (1978). Communication disorders and the families of schizophrenics. In L. C. Wynne, R. L. Cromwell, & S. Matthysse (Eds.), *The nature of schizophrenia: New approaches to research and treatment*. New York: Wiley.

Snyder, K. S., & Liberman, R. P. (1981). Family assessment and intervention with schizophrenics at risk for relapse. In M. J. Goldstein (Ed.), *New developments in interventions with families of schizophrenics* (New Directions for Mental Health Services, No. 12, pp. . San Francisco: Jossey-Bass.

Vaughn, C. E., & Leff, J. P. (1976). The influence of family and social factors on the course of psychiatric illness: A comparison of schizophrenic and depressed neurotic patients. *British Journal of Psychiatry, 129*, 125-137.

Vaughn, C. E., Snyder, K. S., Freeman, W., Jones, S., Falloon, I. R. H., & Lieberman, R. P. (1982). Family factors in schizophrenic relapse: A replication. *Schizophrenia Bulletin, 8*, 425-426.

Vaughn, C. E., Snyder, K. S., Jones, S., Freeman, W., & Falloon, I. R. H. (1984). Family factors in schizophrenic relapse. *Archives of General Psychiatry, 41*, 1169-1177.

Verinis, J. S. (1976). Maternal and child pathology in an urban ghetto. *Journal of Clinical Psychology, 32*, 13-15.

Waxler, N. (1974). Culture and mental illness: A social labelling perspective. *Journal of Nervous and Mental Diseases, 159*(6), 379-395.

Waxler, N. (1979). Is outcome for schizophrenia better in nonindustrial societies? The case of Sri Lanka. *Journal of Nervous and Mental Diseases, 167*, 144-158.

White, R. W. (1974). Strategies of adaptation: An attempt at systematic description. In G. V. Coelho, D. A. Hamburg, & J. E. Adams (Eds.), *Coping and adaptation*. New York: Basic Books.

Wing, J. K. (1975, October). *Planning and evaluating services for chronically handicapped psychiatric patients in the U. K.* Paper presented at the Conference on Alternatives to Mental Hospital Treatment, Madison, WI.

Wolinsky, J. (1982). Israeli schizophrenia study surprises NIMH. *APA Monitor, 13* (11), 9.

World Health Organization. (1973). *The International Pilot Study of Schizophrenia (IPSS)* (Vol. 1). Geneva, Switzerland: Author.

World Health Organization. (1979). *Schizophrenia: An international follow-up study.* Chichester, England: Wiley.

Wynne, L. C., & Singer, M. T. (1963). Thought disorder and family relations of schizophrenics. *Archives of General Psychiatry, 9*, 191-206.

# Coping and Adaptation: A Conceptual Framework for Understanding Families

*Agnes B. Hatfield*

Recognition of the family as a valuable asset in the care of persons with mental illness has brought to the attention of mental health providers the need to support family caregivers in this demanding task. There is new language in the literature that speaks of establishing alliances with families and working with them on the basis of equity and partnership. There is a tendency for current practitioners to criticize earlier models of family therapy that implicated the family in causing or prolonging mental illness and thus alienated them from the mental health profession. There is also a marked trend to favor an educational approach to providing help in which varying emphases are placed on problem-solving communication, information giving, and behavioral management. These seem to address many of the needs that families themselves identify (Hatfield, 1983; Holden & Lewine, 1982) and therefore should bring much family consumer satisfaction.

There has been considerable attention given to psychoeducational treatments or approaches to families (Anderson, 1983; Falloon, Boyd, & McGill, 1984; Vaughn & Leff, 1981). The term "psychoeducation" is rarely defined, but it appears to mean any approach that focuses on information giving and skill development in work with families. Beyond this, psychoeducation takes many forms and varies in length of treatment; which family members are present; where the treatment is provided; and the relative emphasis on communication skills, behavioral management, information giving, problem solving, and a variety

Agnes B. Hatfield. Department of Human Development, College of Education, University of Maryland, College Park, Maryland.

of other factors. Why practitioners do what they do is not always clear because the approach is generally pragmatic and atheoretical.

The closest that the psychoeducation proponents come to theory is the use of a conceptual model, "expressed emotion" (EE), which grew out of the work of British researchers, Brown, Birley, and Wing (1972). It is not a fully developed theory, but, at least in this country, seems to have grown out of early communication and family systems theories. Practitioners of psychoeducation vary considerably in the degree to which they adhere to these earlier theorists.

Essentially, expressed emotion theory says that the level of EE in the family is significant for the well-being of persons with schizophrenia. The level of expressed emotion is inferred from a score on the Camberwell Family Interview taken at the time of hospitalization (Falloon, Boyd, & McGill, 1984). The number of critical comments together with the quality of emotional overinvolvement categorizes families as having high expressed emotion (high EE) or low expressed emotion (low EE). Researchers have been able to demonstrate a relationship between high EE and patient relapse.

The concept of expressed emotion is open to criticism on a number of points. It is in no way a full-blown theory and cannot provide the framework for understanding the full range of complexities of family life with a mentally ill person. It leads researchers and practitioners to focus on limited and negative characteristics of families and does not provide for a more comprehensive and empathic understanding of families. By placing all families in one of two categories (high EE or low EE) it violates a basic premise of human nature, which is that human characteristics occur on a continuum, rather than on two opposite poles. High EE and low EE are seen as labels that once again depict families as "good families" and "bad families"—usually the latter. High EE is associated with relapse, which in the minds of some families and some practitioners implies a causative relationship. While the practice of psychoeducation seems to offer some help to families, it is unfortunate that it is imbedded in a conceptual framework that is full of pitfalls.

What is needed, then, are new ways of viewing families and thinking about them that provide a significant shift from a past that alienated families from professionals. What the times call for is the development of new theory to (1) provide a new perspective on the family experience, (2) guide practical application, and (3) guide research (Glaser & Strauss, 1967). Good theory is necessary for the production of new ideas and for the invention of solutions to new problems. Without a theoretical structure, researchers may be unaware of their own perspectives and may assume that they come to the situation without preconceived biases. We suspect this is what is happening in some of the "new" approaches to families. No one, says Mehabrian (1968), observes without being influenced by what he or she knows, believes, and expects; all observations involves selection and selective attention.

The choice of a theory or conceptual framework is arbitrary. Each calls attention to certain features of a phenomenon to the exclusion of others. Family theories of the past focused on communication, marital discord, disturbed parent-child relationships, or expressed emotion, but understanding of families was limited and families felt alienated. New theory must provide a more comprehensive view of families and lend credence to the family's perspective of what is going on.

There has been considerable development and application of the conceptual framework of coping and adaptation to further the understanding of people undergoing such stressful life events as premature death, Down's syndrome, cystic fibrosis, Alzheimer's disease, and other tragedies in family life. Rarely has this conceptual framework been used to study families facing the tragic consequences of mental illness. Certainly these families face equally significant trauma and adaptational demands.

Basic to any theory are the assumptions with which it begins. Adaptation theory is based on evolutionary concepts that state that it is in the nature of living things to continue to struggle to survive. Human beings are always doing their best to survive physically and psychologically. The best way to interpret family behaviors is to assume that they are the best adaptation the family can make, given the current circumstances it faces.

The main objective of this chapter is to synthesize the work of leading adaptation theorists as they present the basic theory of coping and adaptation. It is expected that the applicability of this theory to understanding families of the mentally ill will then emerge quite clearly. In a major conference on coping and adaptation in Palo Alto, California, in 1969, the focal question was, "What do we typically do in the face of painful elements of experience?" (Grinker, 1974, p. xi). We cite many participants of that conference as we try to understand what families typically do in the face of the trauma of mental illness.

White (1974) considered adaptation to be the master concept under which mastery, coping, and defense are subsumed. "Adaptation," he stated, "is something that is done by living systems in interaction with their environments" (p. 52). It is characteristic of living systems that they do something more than maintain themselves. They have an urge toward mastery of their environment and a desire for autonomy or self-determination. The adequacy of adaptation is a function of the relationship between external demands and a person's resources for dealing with them. It depends upon having relevant information, adequate internal organization, and freedom of action. Satisfactory self-picture or self-esteem must be maintained (White, 1976).

Mechanic (1974) agreed that adaptation is best thought of as the fit between environment and person, but in that definition, he believed, there has been an overemphasis on intrapsychic adjustment or how the person perceives himself in relation to the environment. Psychologists, he believed, have given primary attention to the attitudes the person has about the environment and have failed to place sufficient emphasis on the person's actual capabilities for meeting external demands. This may explain, in part, findings that families of the mentally ill question the various forms of therapy offered them that tend to focus on feelings. What they insist they need is practical information and know-how (Hatfield, 1983; Holden & Lewine, 1982).

Successful personal adaptation, Mechanic has written, has at least three components: (1) The person must have the capabilities and skills to deal with the social and environmental demands placed upon him. (2) Individuals must be adequately motivated to meet these demands without being overwhelmed by anxiety and discomfort. (3) Individuals must have the capabilities to maintain psychological equilibrium to meet external requirements rather than focusing exclusively on painful inner needs. Psychological defense is a significant adaptational strategy but it should not be considered an end in itself. Rather it is a mechanism for diminishing discomfort and distress so that they do not overwhelm the individual and reduce his or her problem-solving efforts.

There is increasing agreement among theoreticians (Lazarus, Averill, & Opton, 1974; Monat & Lazarus, 1977; White, 1974) that the key concept, "coping," is best reserved for those efforts persons make to master conditions of threat, harm, or challenge when the usual strategies are insufficient. In this regard, it is White's (1974) statement that is most often quoted:

> It is clear that we tend to speak of coping when we have in mind a fairly drastic change or problem that defies familiar ways of behaving, requires the production of new behavior, and very likely gives rise to uncomfortable affects like anxiety, despair, guilt, shame or grief, the relief of which forms part of needed adaptation. Coping refers to adaptation under relatively difficult conditions. (pp. 48-49)

A number of writers (Adler, 1982; Bruner & Connolly, 1974; Maluccio, 1981) use the term "competence" to describe the end goal of coping efforts. It is intelligence in its broadest sense; it is *knowing how* to do something as well as *knowing that* something is so. Competence implies action; it means changing the environment as well as adapting to it. It involves selecting relevant information, having a planned course of action, and then initiating a sequence of movements or activities toward the objectives that have been set (Bruner & Connolly, 1974). Adler (1982) defined competence as the capacity to successfully master life events. The adequacy of performance depends upon ability to perform major social roles, maintain an adequate self-concept, manage strong affect, access available resources, manage developmental transitions, and maintain effective cognitive functioning.

Gordon Allport (1961) saw a drive toward competence as inherent in everyone; within all persons is a significant force that struggles to meet and overcome the demands of the environment.

## THE NATURE OF CRISIS

The onset of mental illness in a member invariably produces a state of crisis for that family. The word "crisis" is used for any rapid change or type of encounter that is significantly outside that person's usual range of experience. The term has been used for any new, intensive, rapidly changing, sudden or unexpected event (Appley & Trumbull, 1977). This sudden change or encounter provides the individual with a "no exit challenge" and might involve loss of a person or loss of an ideal (Hansell, 1976). In a crisis, habitual problem-solving activities are not adequate to the task. As a result, there is a rise in tension, helplessness, cognitive confusion, and a strong need to discharge tension (Rapoport, 1965). Healthy crisis resolution requires cognitive perception of the situation, management of affect, and the emergence of patterns of seeking help for feelings and problem solving.

Hirschowitz (1976) prefers the term "transition states" to "crisis" because he feels the term "crisis" has been taken over by the clinical community and inappropriately used in therapeutic approaches. When service is conceived as treatment, there is a risk that the psychological concomitants of transition states will be viewed as pathological. Hirschowitz views the symptoms of psychological stress as an expectable part of adaptation, for transition from an old role to a new one places heavy environmental demands on the person. Persons are required to modify their identity, images, and roles and face significant strangeness and inescapability. A state of transition aptly characterizes family caregivers of persons with mental illness as they shift their identity from that of a typical "normal" family to one with difficult, special, and stigmatizing problems. Just what that means to them will be elucidated in subsequent chapters.

According to Hirschowitz, transition is marked by pattern disruption in all systems—psychological, physiological, and interpersonal. Habitual patterns of control, organization, and equilibrium become labored and difficult. Interactions have a grasping, awkward quality, with new role requirements only dimly perceived. Cognitive operations may become paralyzed, with a narrowing of perception and a tendency to look back with grief, anger, resentment, and guilt. Under high levels of stress and anxiety, the individual is primarily motivated to reduce the pain with defensive reactions. The role of helper would appropriately be to reduce stress and encourage problem solving and natural adaptation.

Hansell (1976) uses the term "being-in-distress" to describe people faced with unusual adaptive challenges. Like other writers, he uses the term "crisis" to designate the rapid change involved in encounter outside one's usual range of experience. Certain regularities occur in crisis situations, Hansell notes, such as the following:

1. The individual shows a narrowed fixed span of attention. There is little scanning of the environment for solutions. There is a sense of pressure that "something must be done."

2. The individual shows "loosening" and "widening" of affectional attachments. Persons report feeling alienated and alone. The usual matrix of friends, family, groups loses its salience. There may be extraordinary activity to form new attachments.

3. There may be a profound loss of moorings or sense of identity. There is difficulty in summoning a defining set of impressions of who one is and what capacities one has.

4. The person-in-distress performs his or her usual social roles in an unsatisfactory way. The usual intricate patterns of behavior decay and become random and unpatterned.

5. The individual experiences an altered state of consciousness in which he or she recalls events in a random fashion.

6. The person-in-distress experiences a drastically reduced ability to make decisions.

7. Individuals-in-distress send signals of distress, which tend to bring forth helping behaviors in others.

Living with high levels of stress over a long period of time has a profound effect on human functioning and quality of life and may lead to somatic illnesses. Monat and Lazarus (1977) identify three ways this might happen. The first is by the creation of major hormonal outpourings that dramatically alter bodily functioning. The second is by engaging in coping activities that are damaging to health. This might include minimal rest, poor diet, or excessive use of tobacco and alcohol. A third way stress might lead to disease is by creating a preoccupation with the source of stress with failure to note and attend to serious health matters that arise.

## ENVIRONMENTAL DEMANDS

A state of crisis occurs, we have noted, when a person's resources for coping are inadequate to meet the demands of the environment. Wrubel, Benner, and Lazarus (1981) have identified the characteristics of situational demands that tax adaptational capacities.

1. *Uniqueness*. These are situations in which persons have no previous experience to provide knowledge and skills and in which the culture offers no patterns for response. For unpredictable events, it is not possible to anticipate events and make preparation. There may be a failure to recognize the uniqueness of adaptational requirements. It is as though persons are going through a kind of culture shock.

2. *Duration and frequency*. The length of time a demand is present influences the amount and degree of stress. Long duration of overload conditions lead to burnout. "Frequency" refers to the repetition of discrete demands, each of which are time limited but regularly repeated. The combination of long duration and frequency has particular potential for undermining people's coping resources. We begin to see why chronic mental illness with its long duration together with its cyclic exacerbation of symptoms creates such havoc among families. Duration is particularly significant when persons see little possibility of changing self or environment. If duration seems indefinite, interminable, persons may succumb to hopelessness.

3. *Pervasiveness*. When the situational demands permeate every corner of experience or when one demand entails a whole series of additional demands, one has the sense that every aspect of one's life is threatened or disturbed, and that there is no refuge.

4. *Ambiguity*. Some situations are highly explicit and structured. Their demands have great clarity, and what are needed and expected is fairly obvious. It is much more difficult when there is confusion and ambiguity—ambiguity in terms of what is going on, what are the appropriate role relationships, and what is the likely outcome.

The Wrubel *et al.* characterizations provide a useful perspective from which to view families coping with mental illness. Later chapters will examine ways in which behaviors associated with mental illness are characterized by their uniqueness and newness in the experiences of the family, the frequency of upsetting episodes and the terribly long duration of the illness, the pervasiveness of disturbance as it affects all aspects of family life, and the many ambiguities associated with the illness. Truly, having a relative with a mental illness is a situation with all the characteristics of extraordinarily heavy situational demand. As this situational demand becomes more precisely understood, the helping profession will be able to offer the kinds of concrete help and support that will increase the likelihood of good outcome.

Throughout our discussion so far, we have assumed that there is a reality that can be labeled "mental illness in a family member"; however it must be recognized that not all persons interpret that kind of reality in the same way. There is always something in addition to the objective reality as seen by an independent observer; there is invariably the mediation of some appraising, perceiving, or interpretative mechanism (Appley & Trumbull, 1977). Mechanic (1974) stated it very succinctly this way, "Students of coping and adaptation would do well to invest greater attention to the question of how men see their environment and their own potencies in meeting the challenge of the environment" (p. 37).

A number of writers have attempted to conceptualize the interpretive function in crisis situations. For example, Lazarus (1977) uses the term "cognitive appraisal" as a key concept in understanding how people react to their environments. This appraisal is determined by the interplay of personality and the environmental stimulus configuration. Differences of appraisal underlie variations of bodily reactions and types of solutions opted for. The coping episode, noted Lazarus and co-workers (1974) is never a static affair, but changes in quality and intensity as a function of new information and of outcomes of previous responses. The individual is continually searching, sifting, and evaluating cues that the situation presents. Some appraisals are accepted while others are rejected. Lazarus identifies three aspects of appraisal.

1. Primary appraisal: There is a judgment that some situational outcomes will be either harmful, beneficial, or irrelevant.
2. Secondary appraisal: This is a perception of a range of coping alternatives through which harm can be mastered.
3. Reappraisal: This involves a change of perception due to changing interpretation of external or internal conditions.

Rapoport (1965) and Appley and Trumbull (1977) utilize the concept of "threat" to explain how people react to hazardous situations. Threat involves an anticipated harm of some kind that has been identified as a potentiality in a situation. The threat of harm results in negatively toned affect, motor-behavioral reactions, alterations in adaptive functioning, poor physiological states, and conflicts. If people see that their well-being or integrity is endangered, they will devote all of their energy to protect it. More specifically, Rapoport (1965) has noted, a threat to need and integrity will be met with anxiety; a threat seen as loss or deprivation is met with depression. If the situation is perceived as a challenge, people will likely mobilize energy to act. Presumably families coping with mental illness do see mental illness as a threat to their needs and integrity and thus they react with anxiety; they also see mental illness as a loss or loss of an ideal and therefore react with grieving and depression. To the extent that families can be helped to see the problems as a challenge, they will be able to mobilize their resources and actively seek solutions.

Janis (1974) feels the amount of ego involvement or the degree to which the threat is relevant to personal goals, decisions, and social commitments determines the kinds of responses the individual makes. Important considerations are (1) the nature of impending danger, (2) the probability that the dangerous event will occur, (3) the severity of loss if it does occur, and (4) the probability of successful coping with whatever happens.

Coping with the stress of mental illness has many similarities to coping with a variety of other highly taxing situations. Typically, the mental health professional has not seen the dilemma of the family in this way. Rather the professional has operated from other points of view that have been at variance from the way families see the illness. This discrepancy in world view has been a stumbling block to good working alliances (Hatfield, 1984). If professionals can come to see how much stress is involved in mental illness, what aspects of the illness situation are especially demanding, and how families put personal meaning on the crises they confront, then professionals will begin designing the kinds of services that are truly responsive to family needs.

## INTRAPSYCHIC PROBLEMS

Such disruptive life events as mental illness in the family have very painful and highly disorganizing consequences for its members. Among the difficult adaptive tasks are coming to terms with the keen disappointment felt as the result of a loved one's inability to fulfill his or her promise in life; restoring the self-esteem that has been undermined by the overwhelming sense of insoluble problems; managing the anxiety for an uncertain future; and surmounting the complex emotional reactions of guilt, grief, anger, and resentment (Hatfield, 1978; Holden & Lewine, 1982). These warrant a fuller exploration.

## Self-Esteem

Goldschmidt (1974) thinks that human beings are quintessentially concerned with the maintenance of self-esteem or a positive self-image, that they are probably pre-programmed toward self-interested, status-oriented behavior that has survival value for themselves. One gets self-esteem from culturally valued successes in life and from the way one is recognized by others. In America the role of parent is highly valued and people expect to get significant ego gratification from raising their children to successful adulthood. One wonders what happens, then, to the self-image of a parent whose child has a mental illness, a highly stigmatizing disorder. The parents' need to be successful in their parental role may never be fulfilled, and they may be dealt one of life's most severe blows, one potentially damaging if there are not ways for them to come to terms with this loss.

In working with persons facing severe adaptational challenges, White (1974) emphasized that self-esteem must be maintained at all costs and enhanced if at all possible. A satisfactory self-picture must be preserved; there must be left intact a sense of competence, an inner assurance that one can do things necessary for a satisfactory life. Loss of a satisfactory self-image leads to anxiety, shame, and guilt.

As people struggle to master new role demands and maintain a sense of adequacy and security, they may also have to struggle with a degree of identity confusion similar to that of adolescence or other periods of significant role change characterized by introspection and questioning: Who am I? Why do I suffer so? What am I to make of my life? How can I ever feel worthwhile again? This may lead to a sense of helplessness, hopelessness, and giving up. For these reasons White (1976) advises, "No adaptive strategy that is careless of self-esteem is likely to be any good" (p. 31).

To maintain or regain a sense of self-esteem depends upon actual success in coping with the problems presented. The support of others—lay and professional—are needed to help one acquire the information and develop the skills necessary for successful mastery. Sharing experiences can lessen the sense of burden and provide role models of others who have surmounted similar turmoil. Personal worth is reinforced by the care and concern exhibited by professional services or the natural network of friends and relatives. They can provide reassurance and take on themselves some of the actual tasks that must be performed.

For persons for whom the role of caregiver to a disabled person provides only modest ego enhancement, it may be important to seek out other socially valued roles. Hansell (1976) insists that all persons need the opportunity to show what they can do successfully, to prove that they can accomplish a task. From such observations as they and others make about performance, they can come to regard themselves with esteem; others can convey value and dignity on them. "Self-esteem," notes Hansell, "breathes oxygen into the painful unchartered journey of meeting an adaptational change" (p. 42).

## Loss and Mourning

"Loss may be defined as a state of being deprived of or being without something one has had" (Peretz, 1970, p. 4). Losses may take many forms, but one of the most profound losses to be experienced by an individual, is, of course, the loss of a significant or valued person. The loss may be total or partial, permanent or temporary. Furthermore, Peretz points out, "the incapacitation of a valued person through acute or chronic illness may result in loss of some aspects of that person, such as a special quality or attribute which provided gratification" (p. 5). This statement serves as a reminder to all of us, that mentally ill persons lose, temporarily or permanently, many of the personality characteristics by which they are identified. Families may go through a highly traumatic sense of loss accompanied by mourning that, because there has not been actual bodily death, goes unrecognized by those around them. The fact that the illness is cyclical, that the familiar personality leaves and returns, in many cases, provides little opportunity for families to complete the mourning of their loss.

Wikler, Wasow, and Hatfield (1981) studied family reaction to mental retardation in a child and concluded that chronic sorrow is not an abnormal response to having a disabled child, but is, rather, a normal reaction to an abnormal situation. This, they reported, has not been obvious to professionals, judging from the literature. They felt that prolonged grief was not necessarily incompatible with coping effectively with the exigencies presented by chronic disability. Presumably, their findings and conclusions would be equally applicable to families who have suffered a loss through mental illness. However, the literature is devoid of any significant discussions of loss and mourning as they relate to mental illness.

Peretz (1970) provides a significant elaboration of the array of emotional reactions that may accompany loss. "The feelings and emotional states aroused by the loss of a loved one," he says, "include mental pain, yearning, anguish, sorrow, dejection, sadness, depression, fear, anxiety, nervousness, agitation, panic, anger, disbelief, denial, shock, numbness, relief, emptiness, and lack of feeling" (p. 13). The individual may have feelings of resentment and anger toward the loved and lost object, but may have trouble accepting these feelings and as a consequence experience guilt and shame.

Guilt feelings are frequently present in the acute stages of grief as people dwell on the past and recall ways they believe they failed the lost of disabled person. Although these omissions may seem trivial and inconsequential to others, they continue to prey upon the mind of the grieving person unless some respected person absolves him or her of responsibility. Unfortunately, in the field of mental illness, many traditional theories and some current ones, implicate the family in causing or contributing to the disorder, thus the professionals of those persuasions have no basis on which to absolve the family. In their care, the dysfunctional guilt and suffering may actually be augmented.

We have culturally provided customs and rituals for easing the pain of those who have lost someone through death; however, there is little institutionalized support or practice that eases the pain of those who suffer a loss as a consequence of mental illness. Perhaps the most hopeful development on the mental health scene, that speaks to this concern, is the rapidly emerging growth of mutual support groups for families of the mentally ill. It is hoped that these families, each of whom has suffered mental illness in their midst, can view each other in nonjudgmental ways, and provide the kind of support that will ease the mourning process.

## FACTORS IN INTRAPSYCHIC COPING

There is considerable individual variability in the way that different persons respond to various situational demands. A number of factors have been thought to account for these variations.

### Personality Factors

Some investigators of the way adaptation is achieved emphasize general coping traits, styles, or dispositions, and assume that an individual will use the same coping style in most stressful situations. These traits or dispositions are considered fairly stable, and attempts have been made to measure them with personality tests (Monat & Lazarus, 1977). This emphasis on personality leads to the use of such traditional terms as "ego strength," "stress tolerance," and "frustration tolerance" as ways to characterize people. Appley and Trumbull (1977) question the use of these concepts, for they argue that, rather than having enduring predispositions, it is more likely that each person has more or less kinds of insulation against certain kinds of stress producers than have others.

The predictability of tests in measuring these personality traits, Monat and Lazarus (1977) point out, depends upon the generalizability of traits being measured and the many factors, both external and internal, that affect a person's reactions. The authors are probably correct in pointing out that there is potential for more understanding in concentrating on the actual active coping strategies that can be observed in a stressful situation, that more accurate inferences can be drawn regarding coping processes observed than can be gained from measures used in a static situation. He acknowledges that these are time consuming and costly but potentially much more fruitful than the dispositional emphasis.

## Mechanisms of Defense

Monat and Lazarus (1977) use the term "palliative" modes of coping to refer to thoughts or actions whose goal it is to relieve the emotional impact of stress. These are the defense mechanisms of denial or diversion of attention, traditionally viewed as pathological or maladaptive, but which can serve a positive function in allowing persons not to be overcome by stress. Their usefulness is greatest on a short-term basis and in situations where there is nothing the person can do temporarily, or where they permit a more hopeful attitude and prevent a person from giving up.

George (1974) also believes that the classical ego-defense mechanisms can be used constructively in the total process of coping with crisis. Defense operations such as withdrawal, denial, and projection need not preclude eventual adaptation. They can serve as tactical, short-term ego supports. Individuals going through a severe crisis situation must have the capabilities of maintaining psychological equilibrium so that they can direct energies and skills to meet external, in contrast to internal, demands. Psychologists have tended to view defense mechanisms as ends in themselves, but it is more reasonable to see them as a set of mechanisms that facilitate continuing performance and mastery. While defense mechanism may cause difficulty if they go too far, many misconceptions about reality may aid in coping and mastery, alleviate pain, and energize involvement (Mechanic, 1974).

Defense mechanisms, in the view of White (1974), may be strategies of adaptation not all that different in kind from other adaptive strategies. Mentally healthy persons probably all use some degree of reality distortion in order to protect themselves from overwhelming anxiety. Like others in the field, White cautions that defensive strategies may cause trouble in the long run if they make no provision for learning anything new about the sources of danger. Closing off the cognitive field is a static solution.

Successful adaptation, Mechanic (1974) thinks does not necessarily require an accurate perception of reality. We all distort to some extent to enhance our self-respect and self-importance, and to maintain our sanity by suppressing our tremendous vulnerability. Reality, notes Mechanic, is, after all, a social construction and to the extent that perceptions are shared and socially reinforced, they may facilitate adaptation irrespective of their objective truth.

Persons confronting a catastrophic event are thought to go through a fairly predictable evolution of emotional reaction. The initial response is apt to be shock, or a stunned disbelief in which the meaning fails to sink in; it involves an isolation of affect that the person may later characterize as numbness. A period of denial often follows as the person tries to escape the truth of the information. Once the reality begins to penetrate, the individual may react with sadness, anger, and anxiety. "The appropriate criterion for evaluating various defensive processes," Mechanic reminds us, "is the extent to which such defenses facilitate coping and mastery" (p. 38).

## Other Determinants

There are probably a multiplicity of other factors that, if they could be identified, would help us understand how people come to cope with disturbing life events. A few of these are discussed below.

### PRIOR EXPERIENCE

When an event is totally novel, individuals are apt to be bewildered and disorganized as they try and reject a number of strategies until they find one that seems to work. The more successful people have been in solving problems presented by earlier events, the more likely it is that they have skills that they can transfer and the more likely it is that they have confidence that they can surmount their difficulties once more. But failure probably also breeds failure and in itself is stressful.

### MEANING OF THE EVENT

One of the most powerful determinants of coping is the meaning the individual assigns to the event. We have already discussed meaning in terms of appraisal and threat, but much more is involved. Most important is the need for persons to come to terms with the apparent randomness and impersonality of an event that is to them so personally catastrophic. People have an inexorable need to know why this tragedy has happened. Whether it is an early death in the family, a serious accident, or a mental breakdown, the anguished cry is always "why?" or "why did this happen to us?" Psychologists often fail to grasp this existential cry for meaning and trivialize it by assuming that individuals are searching in themselves for personal blame. Sometimes individuals are presuming blame, but often, like biblical Job, they are searching for meaning in an existence rent with tragedy. Whether or not people grow or are destroyed by the experience may depend upon the meaning they can see in it. Each must do this in his or her own way. Some may take comfort in certain kinds of religious significance; some may come to live without an answer, without complete understanding and without full control, but not overwhelmed by the event.

## CULTURAL BACKGROUND

Individuals and how they come to adapt to unusual life circumstances must be understood in terms of their sociocultural background. Out of it grow the interests, beliefs, values, and attitudes. That, if well understood, could clarify the distinctive reactions various family members have. Different ethnic groups provide different views of appropriate parent-child interactions, kin networks, the role of the Church, and the role of medical help.

In a well-functioning social system, the individual's problems of adjustment are met by institutional means, Goldschmidt (1974) states: "Culture provides or should provide, institutional means for individual adaptation" (p. 13). He explains the difficulties of ego maintenance by retardates by pointing out that "to be found wanting in mental capacity is the most devastating of all possible stigmata, at least in our culture—indeed, mental competence is very close to what we might call soul" (p. 27). The problems of mental competence present a similar problem to those afflicted with mental illness and to their families who share the stigma. The more a family values intelligence and achievement, which is probably most American families and especially those of middle and upper classes, the more difficult the task of coping.

## ROLES OF INDIVIDUALS

Who in the family is ill or disabled and what roles he or she ordinarily plays makes a difference in how the family adjusts. Others may have more or less difficulty closing ranks and taking over the role of the disabled one. It is difficult to know how to parent an adult child. Children of disabled parents or the spouse of a disabled spouse may find it awkward and difficult to assume a quasi-parental role to some-one functioning poorly. We have no accepted models for these. If the disabled person is a child in the family, his or her order of birth in the family may make a difference, as may the sex of the child, and what these things mean to that particular family.

STAGES OF THE LIFE CYCLE

Each stage of a family's life cycle has its own pattern of organization, its own vulnerabilities, and its own method of coping (Grinker, 1974). The way a family comes to terms with a disability-related crisis may vary according to the developmental stage of the family. This must be understood in order to know the way illness affects the family and the kinds of readjustments that must be made to accommodate the de-mands of the ill person. For example, chronic mental illness—and especially schizophrenia—most often strikes the late adolescent or young adult. This means that a middle-aged or late-middle-aged parent must again resume the parenting role and in some ways live again as he or she did in earlier stages of the life cycle. At the same time he or she may be working and planning and relating to other children and grand-children in ways appropriate to his or her age and stage of life cycle. This produces stresses and creates difficulties in relating to peers. The need for care may go on into the older years when the parent has more physical infirmities and when retirement plans must be made. There is always the worry over who will take over when the immediate family no longer can.

## INTRAPSYCHIC COPING OUTCOMES

Adjustment to catastrophic events does not come quickly—it requires a long period of adaptive struggle and a long search for a basis of acceptance. Lazarus (1977) has noted that people develop a wide vari-ety of coping processes, including preparatory activities, periodic dis-engagements from stressful transactions, and the use of tranquilizers to lower excessive levels of arousal. They practice positive mental attitudes and try to tell themselves that things will work themselves out. They may seek support from loved ones or those they trust; or they may try this or that stress-prevention fad or fashion, such as transcen-dental meditation, yoga, hypnosis, and so on. They may direct their attention away from the source of threat and toward escapist literature or the movies. They cope with loss ultimately by giving up what was previously a central part of their psychological domain. But, notes Lazarus, we still know extremely little about the conditions, both within the person and in the situation, that lead to one or the other coping process. Nor do we know much, he says, about the relative effectiveness of the various coping strategies in regulating emotional status or about the comparative costs in energy or the maladaptive consequences of each form of coping.

One of the advantages of the theory of coping and adaptation is that it brings back into the literature a focus on the strengths of human beings, their persistence, their will to live, the courage behind the heroism that is as much a part of the human potential as the retreats, the evasions, and the petty impulse gratifications that loom so large in current psychotherapy literature. In fact, stressful adaptive struggles lead not only to equilibrium but may also influence growth and development (White, 1974).

The importance of paying attention to people's strengths has also been emphasized by Kiely (1980), who said that "when a definitive stress theory is finally achieved it will need to account for strengths as well as weakness, courage as well as fear, and for psychological growth as well as failure," and further that "the biological rootedness of animal courage is better understood by ethologists and veterinarians than by psychologists and psychiatrists. Splendid examples of 'the courage to be' encountered by individuals in crises have perhaps been more adequately understood by poets, novelists, and philosophers" (p. 103) than by professionals.

The professional's ability to influence the outcome of intrapsychic coping efforts may well depend upon his or her ability to identify the strengths in people. Professionals often need to build an alliance with families of disabled persons in order to implement plans for care. Such alliances can only grow out of a respect for their strengths.


## DIRECT ACTION COPING

Successful personal adaptation, Mechanic (1974) has reminded us, has at least three components: (1) The individual must have the capacity to maintain a state of psychological comfort and equilibrium, (2) he or she must be motivated to meet the demands of the environment, and (3) he or she must have the necessary skills and abilities to meet the exigencies of environmental demands. We turn our attention now from a focus on aspects of intrapsychic coping to factors associated with behavioral solutions to problems. Several writers (Hirschowitz, 1976; Lazarus, Averill, & Opton, 1974; Mechanic, 1974; White, 1974) believe that mental health professionals have been too preoccupied with the way people feel and not enough concerned about what they do. Mechanic notes that "the person-environment fit has usually been considered an attitudinal fit, or how the person perceives himself in relation to the environment—only recently has there been greater emphasis on the issue of whether the person's actual skills are capable of dealing with true external demands."

Caplan (1964) has presented a comprehensive view of what it means to cope effectively. He has come up with the following characteristics of effective coping:

1. Active exploration of reality issues and search for information
2. Free expression of both positive and negative feelings and a tolerance for frustration
3. Active involving of help from others
4. Breaking down problems into manageable bits and working them through one at a time
5. Awareness of fatigue and tendencies toward disorganization, with pacing of efforts and maintenance of as many areas of function as possible
6. Active mastery of feelings where possible and the acceptance of inevitability where not; flexibility and willingness to change
7. Basic trust in oneself and others and basic optimism about outcome (pp. 68-75)

While Caplan has pointed out the importance of various aspects of intrapsychic coping, he has also emphasized the importance of knowledge and information, the availability of a helping network, and a well-developed problem-solving capacity. In addition to these capacities, those caring for highly disturbed persons need to be especially well prepared in skills of communication and behavioral management.

## Knowledge and Information

Cognitive functions are of utmost importance in the outcome of a serious adaptive challenge. This involves the gathering, selection, storage, organization, and manipulation of information. In addition to their importance in problem solving, cognitive processes have instrumental value in determining emotional reaction. Maluccio (1981) feels there should be greater emphasis on the cognitive in coping and problem solving; the use of the intellect has not been fully exploited by mental health practitioners. White (1974) has stressed the importance of having the right amount of information—neither too little nor so much that the person feels overloaded. It should be provided in a straightforward and unconfused manner. There should be recognition that the need for information varies and is progressively modified over time.

In a book entitled *Helping Ourselves: Families and the Human Network*, Howell (1973) insisted that the primary goal of mental health professionals should be teaching. Much of what professionals know, she said, could be taught to lay persons in such a way that they could solve their own problems. Howell expressed faith in the strength and wisdom of families, once they are armed with knowledge, and in their "capabilities for competent, sensible, and healthy self-determination" (p. xii). In her role as physician, Howell observed that too many agencies make families feel more helpless, dependent, and incompetent. She recommended that families insist that experts share their knowledge and skills so that they can conduct their own affairs and can use paid professionals at their convenience and on their own terms.

Krauss and Slavinsky (1982) believe that families of the psychiatrically disabled could benefit from educational services and has recommended that they be made available through local boards of education, churches, or community mental health centers. In 1967, Pasamanick, Scarpetti, and Dinitz reported on a home care program in which families of mentally ill persons were provided with information and knowledge about coping with a mentally ill relative. They predicted that "when a community mental health center emerges, it is safe to assume that 'educating' families will become a vital and integral part of the worker's role" (p. 75).

When families are approached directly to learn what their needs for services are, high among their priorities are such things as understanding the nature of mental illness, knowing appropriate expectations and how to motivate the patient. They need to know about medications and their management and how to obtain services in the community (Hatfield, 1984; Holden & Lewine, 1982).

## Helping Networks

"Even a superficial thrust into anthropological literature," noted Mechanic (1974), "makes clear how interdependent men are even in the most simple of societies and how dependent they are on group solutions" (34). Major stresses are often not amenable to individual solutions; people depend on highly organized cooperative efforts that transcend those of any individual, no matter how well developed his or her personal resources.

Individuals relate to groups in a variety of ways and they may relate to the same group in different ways. Many groups define values and goals and serve as a reference point from which individuals may evaluate themselves, or they may encourage people and help alleviate

anxiety. Even more important is that group organization and cooperation allow for mastery through specialization of function and pooling
of resources and information. As solutions to important problems become more complex, it is less likely that they can be solved by individual initiative. People otherwise well adapted to problem solving may
be unfit, because of their individual orientations, for the kinds of group
co-operation necessary (Mechanic, 1974).

Self-help groups for those coping with a mentally ill relative are
growing in increasing numbers all across the country. Self-help groups
can meet social needs, needs for hope, and needs for support. In self-
help groups, the need for social pretense is reduced because everyone is
facing the same condition (Krauss & Slavinsky, 1982). Information and
knowledge can be exchanged and models of successful coping provided
for those struggling for mastery. Being able to help others has therapeutic value and may help maintain self-esteem when one is temporarily stymied by one's own problem. The support value of self-help
groups, of knowing that others are in the same boat and have found
methods of coping should not be ignored; they can be a sustaining force
in the week-to-week lives of individuals who have assumed the daily
burden of care for a chronically ill family member (Krauss & Slavinsky, 1982).

In studying parents anticipating the death of a child from leukemia,
Friedman, Chodoff, Mason, and Hamburg (1977) found that friends
and relatives sometimes aggravated the parents' distress, but they also
provided significant emotional support in the form of tactful and sympathetic listening and by offering to be of practical service. The major
source of emotional support during periods of hospitalization seemed
to be other parents of similarly afflicted children. Parents learned from
other parents by noting how they coped and thus avoided "going to
pieces" themselves.

How well people cope with a significant challenge in their lives
may also depend upon the availability of appropriate professional
service. Hansell (1976) recommends a kind of service design that increases the likelihood of adaptational success because this focus will
reduce the need for extended intervals of treatment. The work of the
practitioner should involve (1) activating the scanning activities and
overcoming the tendencies to narrow vision and fixate thought, (2) con-
vening fragmenting networks, (3) providing task definitions, (4) assisting socially isolated individuals to form new social affiliations,
(5) facilitating decisions and actions by regulating the pace and focus
of adaptational work, (6) converting less constructive problem solving
into useful adaptive work, (7) converting signals of distress into thera-

peutic plans, (8) diverting individuals from the sick role to which they may have been assigned by some professional services, (9) managing episodes of crisis behavior.

Krauss and Slavinsky stressed the importance of developing an effective working alliance with families that provide shelter and care for persons with chronic mental illnesses on a daily basis. This requires an effective change of information. Families are an important source of data to practitioners who see clients for limited times and under controlled conditions. Families can provide information on symptom patterns, medication compliance, and general community adjustment. Families, in turn, need information concerning the nature of mental illness, available treatment, expected prognosis, and goals for the patient. Further, note Krauss and Slavinsky, the very existence of a collaborative relationship between family and clinician can engender the kind of high positive regard necessary to sustain an ongoing relationship with the chronically ill family member. These authors believe that family therapy is not an effective way to establish a collaborative relationship with families. Examining family dynamics generates high expressed emotion and produces such iatrogenic effects as guilt and anxiety. Locating the problem in the total family may be inappropriate and counterproductive. Families, they note, have learned to reject the modality and are often uncooperative and resistant. To establish an effective working alliance, "families need to hear that clinicians understand how difficult it is to endure certain behaviors day in and day out and to feel that their efforts to retain the patient as a family member are respected" (Krauss & Slavinsky, 1982, p. 261).

To be effective with families of the disabled, Powers and Dell Orto (1980) believe that professionals should listen and observe while suppressing judgment, establish a trusting relationship with the family, learn the meaning of disability to the family, and build self-esteem and give reinforcements for efforts.

The accessibility of a variety of supportive services is key to successful management of patients in the community. Respite must be provided to prevent exhaustion and burnout and crisis-intervention services must be available through home visits, temporary hospitalization, and 24-hour on-call crisis service.

## Skill Development

Coping often involves doing something. It means confronting the inevitable flow of problematic situations and resolving them in such a way that equilibrium can be restored and major personal needs met. People need to know where to direct their efforts and how to manipulate their environment in order to achieve certain predetermined goals. Basically, they need well-developed problem-solving skills that they can apply in a creative manner to each new circumstance. Problem solving, here, is meant to imply "any activity in which both the cognitive representation of prior experience and the components of a current problem situation are reorganized in order to achieve a designated objective (Ausubel, 1968, p. 533).

Sarason (1981) characterized effective problem solvers as reflective rather than impulsive, predisposed to search, to delay gratification, and to be appropriately assertive. Mechanic (1974) believes that effective problem solvers take on tasks they feel they can handle; they seek information and feedback, plan and anticipate problems, and insulate themselves against defeat. They tend to keep their options open and distribute their commitments. People competent in problem solving, noted Gladwin (1967) (1) learn to use a variety of alternative pathways or behavior responses in order to achieve a given goal, (2) have the ability to comprehend a variety of social systems within society and in particular to utilize the resources that they offer, (3) effectively test reality and have a positive, broad, and sophisticated understanding of the world.

A synthesis of the work of a number of writers (Bruner & Connolly, 1974; Harvey, 1966; Meichenbaum, Butler, & Gruson, 1981) gives us the following steps in problem solving: (1) identifying, clarifying, and defining the problem; (2) generating a series of alternative solutions; (3) weighing consequences in terms of their probable success and social acceptability; (4) formulating the plan and initiating the activity; and (5) learning from success and failures.

How does one judge how well one has responded to the adaptational challenge presented? Harvey (1966) said simply, "In the ultimate sense, adaptability means the capacity to behave in ways maximally consonant with the attainment of ends or goals" (p. 6).

## SUMMARY

Mental health professionals are feeling the challenge of meeting the needs of families with mentally ill relatives. Some things have been learned on a pragmatic level about how to help them. However, there has been little by way of adequate theory to guide new explorations and new methodologies. Thus change is slow. In this chapter, we have explored the theory of coping and adaptation in the search for an adequate framework for the task ahead. We believe we have been able to demonstrate that what adaptation theorists have had to offer about the way people in general adapt to difficult life circumstances has considerable application and usefulness in understanding families of the mentally ill.

## REFERENCES

Adler, P. (1982). An analysis of the concept of competence in individuals and social systems. *Community Mental Health Journal, 18,* 34-39.

Allport, G. W. (1961). *Pattern and growth in personality.* New York: Holt, Rinehart & Winston.

Anderson, C. M. (1983). A psychoeducational program for families of patients with schizophrenia. In W. R. McFarlane (Ed.), *Family therapy in schizophrenia* (pp. 99-116). New York: Guilford.

Appley, M. H., & Trumbull, R. (1977). On the concept of psychological stress. In A. Monat & R. S. Lazarus (Eds.), *Stress and coping: An anthology* (pp. 58-66). New York: Columbia University Press.

Ausubel, D. P. (1968). *Educational psychology: A cognitive view.* New York: Holt, Rinehart & Winston.

Brown, G. W., Birley, J. L. T., & Wing, J. K. (1972). Influence of family life on the course of schizophrenic disorders: A replication. *British Journal of Psychiatry, 121,* 241-258.

Bruner, J., & Connolly, K. (1974). Competence: Its nature and nurture. In K. Connolly & J. Bruner (Eds.), *The Growth of Competence* (pp. 309-313). New York: Academic Press.

Caplan, G. (1964). *Principles of preventive psychiatry.* New York: Basic Books.

Falloon, I. R. H., Boyd, J. L., & McGill, C. W. (1984). *Family care of schizophrenia: A problem-solving approach to the treatment of mental illness.* New York: Guilford.

Friedman, S., Chodoff, P., Mason, J., & Hamburg, D. (1977). Behavioral observation of parents anticipating the death of a child. In A. Monat & R. Lazarus, *Stress and coping* (pp. 349-374). New York: Columbia University Press.

George, A. L. (1974). Adaptation to stress in political decision making: The individual, small group, and organizational contexts. In C. V. Coelho, D. A. Hamburg, & J. E. Adams (Eds.), *Coping and adaptation* (pp. 176-248). New York: Basic Books.

Gladwin, T. (1967). Social competence and clinical practice. *Psychiatry, 30,* 30-43.

Glaser, B., & Strauss, A. (1967). *The discovery of grounded theory: Strategies for qualitative research.* Chicago: Aldine.

Goldschmidt, W. (1974). Ethology, ecology, and ethnological realities. In G. V. Coelho, D. A. Hamburg, & J. E. Adams (Eds.), *Coping and adaptation* (pp. 13-31). New York: Basic Books.

Grinker, R. H. Foreward. In G. V. Coelho, D. A. Hamburg, & J. E. Adams (Eds.), *Coping and adaptation* (pp. xi-xiii). New York: Basic Books.

Hansell, H. (1976). *The person-in-distress: On the biosocial dynamics of adaptation.* New York: Human Sciences Press.

Harvey, O. J. (1966). Ends, means, and adaptability. In O. J. Harvey (Ed.), *Experience, structure, and adaptability* (pp. 3-12). New York: Springer.

Hatfield, A. B. (1978). Psychological costs of schizophrenia to the family. *Social Work, 23,* 355-359.

Hatfield, A. B. (1983). What families want of family therapists. In W. R. McFarlane (Ed.), *Family therapy in schizophrenia* (pp. 41-68). New York: Guilford.

Hatfield, A. B. (1984). The family. In J. Talbott (Ed.), *The chronic mental patient: Five years later* (pp. 307-323). New York: Grune & Stratton.

Hirschowitz, R. G. (1976). Groups to help people cope with the tasks of transition. In R. G. Hirschowitz & B. Levy (Eds.), *The changing mental health scene* (pp. 171-188). New York: Spectrum.

Holden, D. F., & Lewine, R. R. J. (1982). How families evaluate mental health professionals, resources, and effects of illness. *Schizophrenia Bulletin, 8*, 626-633.

Howell, M. (1973). *Helping ourselves: Families and the human network.* Boston, MA: Beacon Press.

Janis, I. L. Vigilance and decision making in personal crises. In G. V. Coelho, D. A. Hamburg, & J. E. Adams (Eds.), *Coping and adaptation* (pp. 139-175). New York: Basic Books.

Kiely, W. F. (1980). Coping with severe illness. In P. W. Power & A. E. Dell Orto (Eds.), *Role of the family in the rehabilitation of the physically disabled* (pp. 94-105). Baltimore: University Park Press.

Krauss, J. B., & Slavinsky, A. T. (1982). *The chronically ill psychiatric patient in the community.* Boston: Blackwell.

Lazarus, R. S. (1977). Cognitive and coping processes in emotion. In A. Monat & R. S. Lazarus (Eds.), *Stress and coping* (pp. 145-158). New York: Columbia University Press.

Lazarus, R. S., Averill, J. R., & Opton, E. M. (1974). The psychology of coping: Issues of research and assessment. In G. V. Coelho, D. A. Hamburg, & J. E. Adams, *Coping and adaptation* (pp. 249-315). New York: Basic Books.

Maluccio, A. N. (1981). Competence-oriented social work practice: An ecological approach. In A. N. Maluccio (Ed.), *Promoting competence in clients: A new/old approach to social work practice* (pp. 1-26). New York: Free Press.

Mechanic, D. (1974). Social structure and personal adaptation: Some neglected dimensions. In G. V. Coelho, D. A. Hamburg, & J. E. Adams (Eds.), *Coping and adaptation* (pp. 32-46). New York: Basic Books.

Mehabrian, A. (1968). *An analysis of personality theories.* Englewood Cliffs, NJ: Prentice-Hall.

Meichenbaum, D., Butler, L., & Gruson, L. (1981). Toward a conceptual model of social competence. In J. D. Wine & M. D. Smye (Eds.), *Social competence* (pp. 36-60). New York: Guilford.

Monat, A., & Lazarus, R. (1977). Stress and coping—some current issues and controversies. In A. Monat & R. Lazarus, *Stress and coping* (pp. 1-11). New York: Columbia University Press.

Pasamanick, B., Scarpetti, F., & Dinitz, S. (1967). *Schizophrenics in the community.* New York: Appleton-Century-Crofts.

Peretz, D. (1970). Development, object-relationships, and loss. In B. Schoenberg, A. Carr, D. Peretz, & A. H. Kutscher, *Loss and grief: Psychological management in medical practice* (pp. 3-19). New York: Columbia University Press.

Power, P. W., & Dell Orto, A. E. (1980). Counselor skills and roles with families experiencing varied disabilities or continued adjustment problems. In P. W. Power & A. E. Dell Orton (Eds.), *The role of the family in the rehabilitation of the physically disabled.* (pp. 353-361). Baltimore: University Park Press.

Rapoport, L. (1965). The state of crisis: Some theoretical considerations. In H. J. Parad (Ed.), *Crisis intervention: Selected readings* (pp. 22-31). New York: Family Services Association of America.

Sarason, B. (1981). The dimensions of social competence: Contributions from a variety of research areas. In J. D. Wine & M. D. Smye (Eds.), *Social competence* (pp. 100-124). New York: Guilford.

Vaughn, C. E., & Leff, J. P. (1981). The influence of family and social factors in the course of psychiatric illness. *British Journal of Psychiatry, 139*, 102-104.

White, R. (1974). Strategies of adaptation: An attempt at systematic description. In G. V. Coelho, D. A. Hamburg, & J. E. Adams (Eds.), *Coping and adaptation* (pp. 47-68). New York: Basic Books.

White, R. W. (1976). Strategies of adaptation: An attempt at systematic description. In R. H. Moos (Ed.), *Human adaptation: Coping with life crises* (pp. 17-32). Lexington, MA: D. C. Heath.

Wikler, L., Wasow, M., Hatfield, E. (1981). Chronic sorrow revisited: Parents vs. professional depiction of the adjustment of parents of mentally retarded children. *American Journal of Orthopsychiatry, 51*, 63-70.

Wrubel, J., Benner, P., & Lazarus, R. (1981). Social competence from the perspective of stress and coping. In J. D. Wine & M. D. Smye (Eds.), *Social competence* (pp. 61-99). New York: Guilford.

# Effective Coping:
# A Conceptual Model

*LeRoy Spaniol*
*Hal Jung*

Human beings adapt to their environment in a variety of ways. At the most basic level, the organism biologically matures and adjusts to its environment. During the psychological maturation process, the individual learns different ways of protecting the self from internal and external threat. Examples of internal threats might be one's affect, impulses, and thoughts. Threats from the external world may include pollution, nuclear war, instability in the job market, and problems of other individuals within the environment, to name just a few.

Many of the terms used to describe the adaptation and coping process are similar in meaning. Because of this overlap and the interchangeability by which terms are used, White (1974) has proposed a classification system to differentiate the various terms. To avoid unnecessary confusion, we use White's system in this chapter. In his schema, adaptation is the superordinate concept and is defined as the individual's adjustment to the environment. Individual adjustment is the manner in which the person deals with different life situations—inner-directed and outer-directed psychological processes as well as the range of positive and negative external events. Thus, an individual develops strategies of adaptation to deal with pleasant and unpleasant circumstances that may offer the threat of danger, the hope of meaningful gain, or a condition in between. The strategies involve the individual's reliance on inner mechanisms such as the defenses or on

LeRoy Spaniol. Center for Rehabilitation Research and Training in Mental Health, Boston University, Boston, Massachusetts.

Hal Jung. Counseling and Family Services, Inc., Medford, Massachusetts.

outer-directed strategies such as problem solving or initiation of direct action.

Subsumed under the concept of adaptation are the concepts of mastery, coping, and defenses. They can be diagramed as follows:

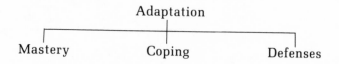

Mastery, according to White, involves any problem that requires cognitive or manipulative complexity but is not charged with anxiety. Mastery implies a surmounting of obstacles to attain success. An example might be family members' acquisition of information about schizophrenia in order to understand better their psychiatrically disabled relative.

Defense mechanisms are defined as those predominantly intrapsychic processes that protect the psyche from danger or attack. Defense mechanisms have an action component that is manifested behaviorally, but the predominant concept emphasizes intrapsychic events. In psychoanalytic literature, defense mechanisms are theorized as processes that protect the ego from overwhelming anxiety, thoughts, affects, and impulses. Examples of defense mechanisms are repression, projection, denial, intellectualization, and isolation. Vaillant (1977) has ordered defenses into a hierarchy ranging from psychotic to healthy modes of adjustment. The limitation of using defenses as a major adaptive style is that the individual learns nothing new about dealing directly with threatening situations. Protection does provide insulation, but it does not promote creative efforts to deal with stressful situations.

Coping is an adaptational mode reserved for situations that require a fairly drastic change or for problems that defy the familiar ways of behaving (White, 1974). It occurs under relatively difficult and anxiety-provoking conditions and requires the production of new behaviors to reduce the threats posed by problem situations.

In keeping with the skills training approach to helping, the focus of the following subsections will be on the concept of coping rather than on mastery and defense mechanisms. The adaptational concept of defense mechanisms is more of an inferred subjective event, and mastery skills are acquired under relatively anxiety-free conditions. But coping skills are acquired in rather difficult situations and such situations are not uncommon for families of the psychiatrically disabled. Thus the study of coping skills can provide insights about the ways in which families learn to deal with their psychiatrically disabled relative.

## COPING VARIABLES

Variables that have an effect on coping outcome can be categorized as internal or external (Caplan, 1981; French, Rogers, & Cobb, 1974; Liem & Liem, 1978; Mechanic, 1974; Murphy, 1974; Pearlin & Schooler, 1978; White, 1974). Internal variables that influence the effectiveness of coping include personality dynamics and problem-solving style. External variables include the physical characteristics of the environment as well as concepts such as social norms and social networks.

### Internal Variables

One of the most ambitious projects on coping stems from the laboratory research efforts of Lazarus, Averill, and Opton (1974), who define coping as "problem-solving efforts made by an individual when the demands she/he faces are highly relevant to her/his welfare (i.e., a situation of considerable jeopardy or promise), and when these demands tax her/his adaptive resources" (pp. 250–251).

Lazarus and his co-workers have identified three major elements in the coping process:

1. The nature of the responses that define coping and from which the coping process is to be inferred. These are assessed through verbal reports, measures of physiological change, nonverbal reactions, and behavior.

2. The situational determinants of these processes, such as the physical environment, social and cultural context, population-demographic characteristics, and the nature of the adaptive problem.

3. The personality determinants of these processes. The differentiation between disposition and coping episode is a major concept in this category. A person's disposition—including attitudes, beliefs, motives, and personality characteristics—creates a tendency to respond in a certain manner, but the authors caution that a tendency toward behaving in a certain manner may not always be manifested.

Another major concept in their understanding of the coping process is "appraisal," a cognitive mediator used to judge whether a particular stimulus is harmful or benign. The appraisal process provides a mechanism to evaluate means of solving a problem and gaining mastery. Appraisal is central to coping and emoting because an individual is presumed to have some control over inner states through this mechanism. Appraisal is further differentiated into three subcategories: primary, secondary, and reappraisal. Primary appraisal is the assessment of the beneficial or harmful effects of a particular event. Secondary appraisal is the perception of the range of available resources to deal with the situation. Reappraisal is the change over time in the original perception of the situation.

These researchers have made some fine distinctions in understanding the coping process by isolating important variables, but their research has been restricted to the laboratory, and, furthermore, has primarily used the medium of film to assess coping processes. Such a laboratory approach, while useful in delineating and isolating variables, is limited in its generalizability. Lazarus (1977) has expressed a need to expand coping research into more natural settings. By doing so, the powerful impact of a real-life stressor could be observed over time and this could supply information that laboratory studies can never hope to achieve.

Although theirs was not a naturalistic study, Pearlin and Schooler (1978) have made a significant contribution to the coping research by studying the coping mechanisms of adults in normative situations. They used exploratory interviews to examine life strains in major social roles, coping repertoires, and emotional stress. They identified three primary coping functions that controlled stress: (1) directly manipulating the environment to reduce the threatening stimulus, (2) perceptually redefining the meaning of the stressor to reduce its threatening properties before it occurs, and (3) managing stress after it has occurred so that it is not overwhelming. They found that the least used coping response was direct manipulation of the environment. They attributed this finding to a number of factors including lack of awareness and/or coping strategies, unwanted side effects resulting from such a coping action, and imperviousness of the stressful situation to manipulation.

In summary, Pearlin and Schooler (1978) arrived at several conclusions:

1. Self-reliance is the ability to solve problems by oneself rather than with outside help. (This finding needs to be interpreted cautiously, however, since the study was not able to determine other important variables related to self-reliance. One such variable would be the availability of supportive resources to the self-reliant individual if these are needed.)

2. Coping responses designed to solve problems and a positive attitude toward outcomes are characteristics of successful marital and parental roles. Adults who are committed to solving their family prob-

lems and are fully involved are the most successfully coping individuals.

3. In the marital and parental areas, both specific coping responses and personality resources—such as self-confidence, esteem, assertiveness—are essential ingredients of successful coping. In the marital area, having effective coping responses is more instrumental to effective coping than having personality resources.

4. Another significant finding is that effectively coping persons exhibit a greater variety and frequency of coping responses.

Because much of the research on internal coping variables has involved families without an identified disabled family member, direct application of such findings can only be inferred. Yet it is important to note that families of the psychiatrically disabled are affected by their appraisal of a situation; their predisposition to respond in certain ways; as well as by their self-esteem, locus of control, and amount of self-denigration. It is clear that one's coping is influenced by cognitive and attitudinal factors. Families who are able to view their ill members in a benevolent or helping perspective would seem more inclined to become successful in their coping. Families who foster a sense of self-esteem and self-responsibility and who make fewer self-deprecatory remarks may find more success in coping.

Pearlin and Schooler's (1978) finding that self-reliance is an important factor in successful coping might be misinterpreted by families to mean that effectively coping persons seek no outside help at all. This view would contradict the studies of Hatfield (1979b), Holden and Lewine (1982), and Kint (1978), which found that families with psychiatrically disabled members have found support groups quite helpful in learning how to cope. It may be that in these studies instances of effective coping involved people who took responsibility—they relied on themselves to do something about the problem rather than waiting helplessly. Thus, Pearlin and Schooler's self-reliance may be extended to mean taking responsibility for oneself by doing something about the problem and not assuming the stance of victim. In any event, the internal factors described in the coping literature do have implications for families with psychiatrically disabled members.

## External Variables

A number of writers have discussed the influence of the environment on the coping process (Caplan, 1981; French et al., 1974; Liem & Liem, 1978; Mechanic, 1974; Murphy, 1974; White, 1974). Whereas the earliest conceptualizations of coping were primarily psychoanalytic and emphasized inner mechanisms, current coping theory recognizes the importance of external factors. These factors include not only physical characteristics of the environment but cultural norms, social institutions, and the nature of the problem situation (Lazarus et al., 1974).

One function of the environment is its relevance as a contextual marker for determining the appropriateness of acquired skills. In a study of the development of the coping process in children, for example, Murphy (1962) noted that coping strategies evolved and changed. Thus, different developmental tasks may require different coping skills. In addition, new coping skills may be dependent on the development of previous coping skills (Spaniol & Lannan, 1984). When the skills required to complete a specific developmental task have not been acquired, individuals may find themselves "stuck" with behaviors that are no longer useful.

Liem and Liem (1978) and Caplan (1981) found environmental support to be a central aspect of successful coping. Environmental support took the form of social networks, understanding spouses, and family ties. The presence of a support environment buffered the impact of stress and contributed to an individual's higher functioning, but it did not necessarily eliminate stress.

Mechanic (1974) asserted that, at the present time, the social and environmental dimension needs more attention if studies of coping are to become meaningful. Liem and Liem (1978) proposed that future research should be directed toward an understanding of the relationship between psychological and social factors related to stress. Furthermore, social factors should not be studied in isolation, but should be analyzed in a comprehensive framework. The authors look at social class in terms of economic stress and social support variables.

The relevance of the environment to coping success cannot be overemphasized. Without proper observance of external factors, a person is only acting blindly and not using the feedback and support available from the environment. Families of the psychiatrically disabled have benefited from assessing the adequacy of their responses to their ill family member. The use of feedback has been as simple as noting the effective stratgies. Families also have discovered the usefulness of an active support and advocacy network, particularly one that includes other families.

## The Limitations of Coping Research

Lazarus and co-workers (1974, p. 257) have found that coping research has been limited by the following problems:

1. The tendency to confuse dispositional variables with response variables. Thus, in studies of coping, a researcher may not necessarily

find the anticipated response even though the individual has a predisposition to behave in the anticipated manner.

2. The tendency to ignore situational determinants. A coping strategy's effectiveness can be understood only in context. A strategy useful in one context may not be useful in another.

3. The parochialism found in coping research. Authorities in the field do little cross-referencing with each other.

4. Lack of adequate empirical support for the theoretical underpinnings of the coping process.

5. Confusion over forms of coping behavior and the descriptive inadequacy of the formal language of coping.

6. Lack of knowledge about the interrelationships and the conditions that bring about coping processes.

Thus the field of coping research is replete with methodological and conceptual problems that limit our ability to understand this vital human activity. But if coping is defined as an individual's innovative responding to threatening situations, a functional beginning has been made. Despite such research and theoretical problems, families of the psychiatrically disabled can profit from current knowledge by making applications when possible to their daily lives.

Two related areas that may further the understanding of the coping process are crisis theory and stress research. Some of the relevant findings from these fields are discussed below.

## CRISIS THEORY LITERATURE

Coping is further clarified when placed in the context of crisis theory (Caplan, 1964; Kalis, 1970), a means of understanding how individuals deal with life transitions and crisis situations. Crisis management is a form of coping behavior; it represents coping under acute, emotionally intense conditions. When a life crisis occurs, an individual is faced with a period of transition that offers an opportunity for either psychological growth or deterioration. The primary goal of crisis intervention is to effect a restoration to the previous level of adequate functioning without engaging in other forms of treatment such as deep exploration of personality dynamics.

Caplan (1964) offered seven characteristics of effective coping under crisis conditions.

1. Active exploration of reality issues and search for information.
2. Free expression of both positive and negative feelings and a tolerance of frustration.

3. Active invoking of help from others.
4. Breaking problems down into manageable bits and working through them one at a time.
5. Awareness of fatigue and tendencies toward disorganization with pacing of efforts and maintenance of control in as many areas of functioning as possible.
6. Active mastery of feelings where possible and acceptance of inevitability where not; flexibility and willingness to change.
7. Basic trust in oneself and others and basic optimism about outcome.

## STRESS RESEARCH LITERATURE

No presentation on coping would be complete without including the role of stress, which serves as the triggering mechanism for adaptive responses. Stress may be defined as "a non-specific physiological and psychological chain of events triggered by a disruption to one's equilibrium or 'homeostasis'" (Adams, 1978, pp. 1-2). Stress and its effects frequently accompany coping behavior. It is the intensity of the stressful event rather than its pleasant or unpleasant nature that determines its impact on the individual (Adams, 1978; Selye, 1974). Lazarus (1977) and Mason (1971) modify this concept by adding that stress is influenced directly by the perception of the stimulus as either benign or harmful and the perception of available resources. The intensity may be important, but so is the perceived nature of the stimulus and the availability of resources. Holmes and Rahe (1967) see stress as a product of the number of life-change units over a period of time. The more change an individual is experiencing, the more that individual is likely to feel stressed. In any case, stress is experienced as a psychological and physiological event.

Selye (1974), a pioneer in the field of stress research, believes that a person has a finite and nonreplenishable amount of energy for adaptive purposes. Each stressful event takes its toll on the individual's resources. Such a view may account for the premature aging that is seen in persons assuming highly stressful occupations.

The physiological chain of events that begins in the hypothalamus and culminates in the various bodily systems with increased heart rate, metabolism, and oxygen consumption has been outlined by McQuade and Aikman (1975). This readiness for action has been labeled the "fight-or-flight" response (Benson, 1975). When an individual is subjected to continuous and severe stress, physiological and psychological dysfunction becomes increasingly likely (Adams, Hayes & Hopson, 1977; Benson, 1975). Over time, stress may cause psychological reactions of depression, irritability, apathy, and changes in eating and sleeping habits (Forbes, 1979). Physiological dysfunction includes hypertension, coronary diseases, ulcers, and dermatitis. Prolonged stress may also lead to "burn-out," a depletion of personal resources to the point of loss of energy to fulfill daily functions (Spaniol & Caputo, 1979; Spaniol & Wells, 1982; Spaniol, 1985). The burden that some families of schizophrenics feel is similar to that of the burned-out individual.

Families of the psychologically disabled can benefit from learning strategies developed to reduce and/or prevent the physical and psychological effects of sustained stress. Physical fitness, relaxation, active problem solving, good nutrition, and an effort to build personally satisfying and fulfilling activities into their lives are some of the strategies families and individuals have adopted to manage the stress related to their psychiatrically disabled relatives.

## FAMILY COPING AND PSYCHIATRIC DISABILITY

Coping theory and research provide us with a perspective for viewing the family as a "reactive/responding" rather than a "causal" agent in relation to schizophrenia. Frequently, as Kreisman and Joy (1974) found in their comprehensive review of the literature, families were considered a major stressor and cause of schizophrenia, as in Fromm-Reichmann's (1984) concept of the "schizophrenogenic" mother. Fortunately, some proponents of this psychoanalytically derived viewpoint have modified their conceptualizations (Arieti, 1974).

The systems-oriented theorists also attributed mental illness to the family. In their conceptualizations, mental illness was a manifestation of the entire family, which was seen as a unit consisting of interacting parts and which operated under a set of rules to mutually determine the behavior of all family members (Bateson, Jackson, Haley, & Weakland, 1956; Bowen, 1960; Lidz, 1958; Wynne, Ryckoff, Day, & Hirsch, 1958). In the pure systems approach, no one individual is blamed for the illness of another family member, but all family members are seen as following implicitly defined rules that regulate the system in a homeostatic manner (Messer, 1970). Homeostasis is maintained even under circumstances involving pathology because the family is locked into this mode of functioning. Although family members are not explicitly blamed, they are implicitly blamed because the model asserts that all members contribute to the pathological condition.

Recent work has considered the family more positively, as a "reactor/responder" (Kreisman & Joy 1974; Spaniol, Jung, Zipple, & Fitzgerald, 1984). A reactor does not cause psychiatric disability, but copes with the disabled family member's behavior in a more or less unskillful way. A responder does not cause psychiatric disability either, but copes with the disabled family member's behavior in a more skillful way. A person whose disposition is to react to stressful events tends to become more stressed and ultimately exhausted. A person who has a disposition to respond to stress tends to feel less stressed and more in control over time. Rather than blaming the family or "benignly" attributing responsibility to them for the psychiatric condition, this viewpoint views the family as reacting/responding to psychiatric disability through coping and adaptation. This change in viewpoint allows a more comprehensive and pragmatic approach to examining family and patient interaction and adaptation. A nonblaming stance broadens the possibilities for helping the family and assists in understanding the family's role in relation to psychiatric disability.

Studies of the family as a reactor/responder to mental illness have pointed to the psychological burden placed on family members (Creer & Wing, 1974; Doll, 1976; Hatfield, 1978, 1979; Kint, 1978; Marcus, 1977; Pringle, 1973; Spaniol et al., 1984). While many of these studies found that families will indeed tolerate a great deal of deviance in their disabled relatives, they experience great emotional stress as they attempt to cope with psychiatric symptomatology. Coping becomes a way of life for these families.

## FAMILY ATTITUDES AND COPING

Coping is influenced by a number of factors, one of which is the attitudes held by family members toward their psychiatrically disabled relative. Attitudes affect the family's behavioral response to the psychiatrically disabled person by creating a family environment that can either increase or decrease adjustment potential. Attitudes can affect interaction by predisposing family members to act in ways that indicate acceptance or rejection of their psychiatrically disabled relative.

The earliest studies of home environments investigated the relationship between family attitudes and the patient, mental illness, hospitals, and tolerance for deviance. These factors were thought to have an effect on outcome, which was globally defined as community tenure (Kreisman & Joy, 1974). Hollingshead and Redlich (1958) concluded from their study that family attitudes determined the decision to hospitalize and also influenced the patient's adjustment to hospitalization.

Researchers hoped that more accepting attitudes as well as increased tolerance for deviance would result in lowered hospitalization rates and increased role performance, but findings have been mixed. In studies dealing with family attitudes toward the patient, mental illness, and hospitals, for example, Freeman and Simmons (1963) found that families of successfully discharged patients accepted their relatives as basically normal people, tended not to blame them, and held a positive attitude toward the hospital. Carstairs (1959) found similar results and identified a "key person," positive attitude, and perception of the patient as nondangerous as important factors. Family members who reported that they were "very pleased" with having the psychiatrically disabled relative at home tended to refrain from using rehospitalization as a coping device (Barrett, Kuriansky, & Gurland, 1972). Not all studies have found a positive correlation between acceptance and community tenure. Kelly (1964) found a nonsignificant difference in family acceptance and community tenure in a group of 65 discharged schizophrenic patients from a psychiatric evaluation project. Family acceptance was not related to exacerbation of symptoms. Other studies have also reported that family members' attitudes toward mental illness are not significantly related to outcome (Davis, Freeman, & Simmons, 1957; Lorei, 1964).

In studies involving outcome and the family's tolerance of deviance, the general finding is that such tolerance is not related to rehospitalization (Angrist, Lefton, Dinitz, & Pasamanick, 1968; Freeman & Simmons, 1963). Tolerance for deviance has been defined as how much deviant behavior the family will tolerate and still keep a patient at home. Contrary to their expected findings, Freeman and Simmons found that the family's higher expectations of the patient resulted in higher role performance. This higher functioning, however, did not relate significantly to the patient's remaining in the community. In a study that assessed family attitudes over an 18-month period, Vannicelli, Washburn, and Scheff (1980) found that family attitudes remained relatively unchanged over time and also showed no relationship to the outcome measure of increased community tenure. Furthermore, they found that attitudes were not affected by the patient's successful functioning. Family members' attitudes held constant despite improvement.

Doll (1976) surveyed 125 relatives of released mental patients and found that family members tolerated a great deal of deviance in their homes. However, this tolerant attitude was upheld at great cost because family members often felt burdened, and so the family environment was one of physical acceptance coupled with emotional rejection. The respondents mentioned that the most disturbing problem was severe psychiatric symptomatology. This finding is similar to the studies by Angrist and co-workers (1963), and by Freeman and Simmons (1963), which pointed to the reappearance of symptoms as the most significant predictor of rehospitalization.

As implied in the Doll (1976) study, an accepting attitude has not always proved to be beneficial to the patient's adjustment, although early notions of successful adjustment suggested that family acceptance was a major factor. The results of a study by Brown, Birley, and Wing (1972) indicate that a return to certain types of "accepting" environments, in this case the overinvolved and overprotective family, was not the best alternative for patient or family. This has been found to be particularly true for moderately to severely disturbed patients. Brown and his associates found a correlation between high expressed emotion (EE) and relapse. The concept of high EE is defined as frequent negative comments indicating criticism, hostility as inferred from nonverbal cues, and emotional overinvolvement. Of these factors, the first was most predictive of relapse.

## A SUGGESTED MODEL FOR EFFECTIVE COPING

The authors would like to suggest a conceptual model for describing the coping process, based on the discussion in the first part of this chapter. A chart describing the overall flow of an ineffective or effective coping process is presented in Figure 1.

For purposes of this model, the authors utilize the definition of "stress" presented by Selye (1974) who defined stress as the nonspecific response of the body to any demand made upon it. It does not matter whether the experience is pleasant or unpleasant. If the experience is intense, it may produce damaging or unpleasant stress. Selye defined unpleasant stress as distress. The stressor or stimulus is anything that causes stress. The cause may be internal or external. Internal stressors may be memories, attitudes, conflicts, unrealistic expectations, or beliefs. External stressors may be positive or negative events such as a job promotion or the loss of a job.

The concept of "appraisal" has been discussed extensively by Lazarus (1977). He defined appraisal as our continuously reevaluated judgments about demands and constraints in ongoing transactions with the environment and options and resources for managing them. The degree to which a person experiences psychological stress is determined by the evaluation of both what is at stake and what coping resources and options are available. Something becomes a stressor only when the mind identifies it as such. Thus, our perception of threat can change

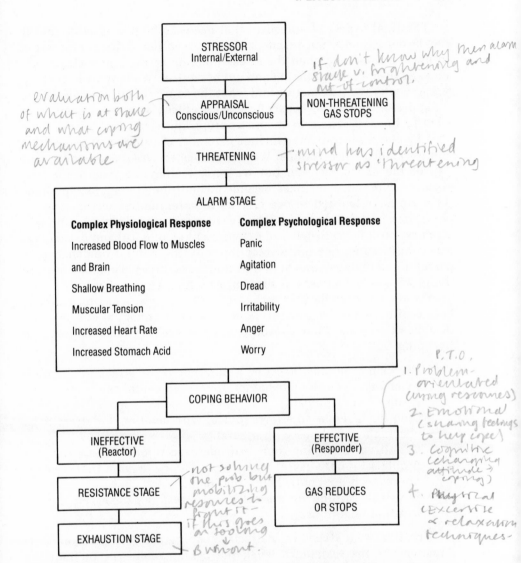

Figure 1. Coping process (general adaptation syndrome). Based upon Lazarus (1977), Selye (1974), Shaffer (1982), and Spaniol (1985).

over time and influence the course of our stress reaction. it is the meanings we place on our experiences from moment to moment that determine our physical and psychological reactions. The importance of the relationship between the mind and the stress reaction is fundamental to managing stress. The mind is the trigger.

The final aspect of appraisal that needs to be discussed is that it may be conscious or unconscious. If our perception of threat represents an unconscious fear, then the stress reaction of the alarm stage may appear especially frightening and out of control. We may be less likely to know why we are reacting and what the source of our scare is. When the appraisal process is conscious, we are at least in a better position to identify the source and to choose appropriate resources.

The alarm reaction may include a number of complex physiological and psychological reactions. We can reduce the frequency and intensity of the alarm reaction but we cannot eliminate it entirely. The alarm reaction may at times become a conditioned response to situations we have learned to perceive as threatening. As we change our perception or develop more adequate resources, our alarm reaction will also need to change. Because of extensive physiological and psychological conditioning, our alarm reaction may lag behind our change in perception and development of additional resources. This may require living with some distress or discomfort while we are changing.

Coping has been defined earlier in this chapter as a person's efforts, both cognitive and behavioral, to manage environmental and internal demands that exceed one's resources. There are four basic approaches to coping.

- Problem oriented: Direct manipulation of the stressful situation by changing our own behavior or environmental conditions (e.g., resource development).
- Emotional: Focused efforts to deal with emotional distress (e.g., sharing our feelings with others).
- Cognitive: Changing our attitude/perception. Redefining the problem in more useful terms (e.g., acknowledging that we cannot or need not control all situations).
- Physical: Minimizing the effects of stress (e.g., exercise and relaxation techniques).

The final two stages in ineffective coping are resistance and exhaustion. At the resistance level, the person mobilizes to fight the stressor and/or the alarm reaction. Resistance implies the person is not solving the problem or coping effectively. If the resistance stage lasts too long, the person may begin to feel depleted. Physical and psychological symptoms may increase during this phase. As the person's physical and psychological resources are depleted, he or she will experience exhaustion. Exhaustion is equivalent to what has commonly become known as "burn-out." On the other hand, if the coping response is effective, the alarm reaction will become reduced or will stop.

## HOW TO COPE MORE EFFECTIVELY

There are some general strategies that are useful in coping with stress. For example, there is an emerging consciousness about the importance of life-style changes. Life-style changes may involve alterations in the physical, emotional, intellectual, environmental, or spiritual areas of our lives. Nutrition and physical fitness are important physical areas of our lives. Nutrition and physical fitness are important physical areas of a person's life-style and proper nutrition and physical fitness can prepare the body to sustain the assault of unwanted stress. The body can feel more energized and the person can feel more capable and competent to deal with his or her internal and external environment.

Emotional areas of life-style change include the development of significant relationships with, or support from, others in our environment who share our concerns. Many families have reached out for this kind of emotional support through the National Alliance for the Mentally Ill or similar organizations. In addition to emotional support, these organizations have also assisted families in becoming involved in direct advocacy or problem solving for their disabled family member. From these groups, families learn new options available to them for coping with mental illness. They are no longer willing to accept blame for the disability of their family member, but they are willing to look at how they might contribute to creating stressful situations within the home, but they are also concerned about the role of society in maintaining the disability.

Environmental areas of life-style change include a new awareness of the risks and options within the environment. Stressors within the living environments of the disabled family members are of particular concern to family members. Where they live, how they live, and the quality of their lives within their chosen environment are practical examples of this concern of family members.

The final area of life-style change is spiritual. There is a growing interest in the development of a meaning in life. Meaning provides a perspective within which the struggles of life can be viewed. Having appreciation for the larger picture, which meaning provides, can increase the ability to be compassionate and understanding. Meaning can help families to integrate the confusing and disorienting impact of their stresses and more quickly resolve them.

In addition to life-style changes there are significant attitudinal shifts occurring in the larger society that are also occurring among family members. There is a growing awareness of individual worth and value. Individuals are important. Family members' potential for personal, organizational, and legislative impact increases as their acknowledgement of their own worth and value increases. Another attitudinal shift is the awareness of relatedness to, and interdependence with, others. People are not alone in experiencing the effects of their life experiences. This is clearly evidenced in the growth of the self-help movement among a wide variety of constituencies over the past decade. Family members are able to reach out for the support of other family members who have had similar life experiences. What they have learned from this type of support has helped family members to cope with daily stresses, solve problems, and advocate for specific reforms.

A final attitudinal shift involves the awareness that problems are solvable and that resources are available or can be made available. At the root of hopelessness is helplessness. As individuals become more "helpful" to themselves and others, they feel more hopeful. This does not mean that changes will come fast but that we can learn to be more in charge of our lives through increased information, skills, and support.

In addition to the life-style changes and attitudinal shifts, there are specific coping strategies that can be useful to family members. One strategy is to understand and control their own responses. They can begin to achieve this through openly discussing their feelings and reactions with other family members and friends. This prevents the buildup of indifference and resentment and is especially useful when dealing with a family member who generates strong feelings. Pacing can also be a useful strategy. For example, families can learn to understand their own daily and monthly rhythms. With this understanding they can begin to structure and focus their activities in a more useful way. When families do not pace themselves, they will find their energy being used up and their strength becoming depleted.

Another personal strategy for families is distancing themselves from situations they cannot or need not assume responsibility for. For example, it may be hard to stop responding to behavior that they find personally distasteful, but that is not harmful to the disabled person or to someone in their environment. This is not to say that they may not choose to respond, but that it may be more useful at times to focus on behaviors that are more harmful or destructive. The judgment involved in their choice of what to respond to and how to respond can be shaped through their interactions with other family members and knowledgeable professionals. The process of learning to distance can be very distressing, and families will find the support of others especially important during this period. The benefit of this strategy is that it becomes more possible to focus their energy in more useful directions.

The ability to distance themselves allows them to gain a new perspective and a new resolve to engage their disabled family member in more important ways.

Some families have found the development of more personal skills very useful. The more serious the problems we have to face, the more skillful the person has to be to manage his or her life adequately. Psychiatric disability makes high demands on families for special knowledge and skills. Since a "cure" is unlikely, families may need additional skills to provide the parenting, nurturing, and training disabled persons need to make their life work for them.

Another useful strategy for family members is to build a fulfilling life for themselves. They are not doing their disabled family member a favor by discounting themselves. It is important to have some challenges and exciting things to do that they naturally enjoy. Focusing on important tasks, directions, and people in their life can be an important source of energy and satisfaction for them. It is important to acknowledge that they cannot take good care of others if they are not taking good care of themselves. Many people find it hard to do things for themselves. Yet, when they are not acting in their own best interest, they are modeling how not to make it to their disabled family members.

The importance of a support group has been mentioned but it bears repeating. Family members should join a peer support group for emotional support, direct problem solving, and advocacy. The group process can help family members to deal directly with their sources of stress, both internal and external. The group process can help family members to face the fear and the pain in their lives rather than deny it or feel victimized by it. Regular meetings can assist family members in talking about painful experiences and looking for personal and organizational solutions.

Another strategy is to develop a more useful philosophy of life. A philosophy that involves personal meanings that support their efforts and one that gives understanding and forgiveness to their limitations can be especially valuable. This development might involve spiritual as well as philosophical aspects. It may contain a belief that enhances their feeling of worth and the worth of others. Rethinking their personal philosophy can also increase their awareness of, and openness to, what is real. Their perceptions are often clouded by their past and by current attitudes and beliefs they need to challenge. What they perceive as real may only be their opinion. The awareness that their perceptions are limited can be distressing but can also loosen their rigidity and open them up to letting their perceptions develop with their experiences and interactions. A more useful personal philosophy can also help them to maintain a flexibility to life and its challenges. It can encourage them to look for options if something doesn't work instead of feeling stuck.

A final strategy is to give themselves the time to make the changes they want and need. If they have not been coping successfully or have been feeling especially stressed, it may require 2 to 3 years of personal effort to turn their lives around. This may seem excessive, but we probably have spent many more years learning to be the way we currently are. Change involves a decision, but it also involves the learning of new behaviors, a great deal of practice, and substantial support. Change that they do not personally choose is virtually impossible. Change that they do choose is merely very difficult.

## REFERENCES

Adams, J. D. (1978). Improving stress management. *Social change: Ideas and applications, 8*(4), 1-12.

Adams, J. D., Hayes, J., & Hopson, B. (1977). *Transition: Understanding and managing person change.* New York: Universe Books.

Angrist, S., Lefton, H., Dintz, S., & Pasamanick, B. (1963). *Women after treatment: A study of former mental patients and their normal neighbors.* New York: Appleton-Century-Crofts.

Arieti, S. (1974). *Interpretation of schizophrenia* (2nd rev. ed.). New York: Basic Books.

Barrett, J. E., Kuriansky, J., & Gurland, B. (1972). Community tenure following emergency discharge. *American Journal of Psychiatry, 128,* 958-964.

Bateson, G., Jackson, D., Haley, J., & Weakland, J. (1956). Toward a theory of schizophrenia. *Behavioral Science, 1,* 251-264.

Benson, H. (1975). *The relaxation response.* New York: Morrow.

Bowen, M. (1960). A family concept of schizophrenia. In D. D. Jackson (Ed.), *The etiology of schizophrenia.* New York: Basic Books.

Brown, G. W., Birley, J. L. T., & Wing, J. K. (1972). Influence of family life on the course of schizophrenic disorders: A replication. *British Journal of Psychiatry, 121,* 241-250.

Caplan, G. (1963). *Principles of preventive psychiatry.* New York: Basic Books.

Caplan, G. (1981). Mastery of stress: Psychosocial aspects. *American Journal of Psychiatry, 138,* 413-420.

Carstairs, G. M. (1959). The social limits of eccentricity: An English study. In M. K. Opler (Ed.), *Culture and mental health: Cross-cultural studies.* New York: Macmillan.

Creer, C., & Wing, J. K. (1974). *Schizophrenia at home.* London: Institute of Psychiatry.

Davis, J., Freeman, H. M., & Simmons, O. (1957). Rehospitalization and performance levels of former mental patients. *Social Problems, 5,* 37-44.

Doll, W. (1976). Family coping with the mentally ill: An unanticipated problem of deinstitutionalization. *Hospital and Community Psychiatry, 27,* 183-185.

Forbes, R. (1979). *Life stress.* New York: Doubleday.

Freeman, H. E., & Simmons, O. G. (1963). *The mental patient comes home.* New York: Wiley.

French, J. R., Rogers, W., & Cobb, S. (1974). Adjustment as person-environment fit. In G. V. Coelho, D. A. Hamburg, & J. E. Adams (Eds.), Coping and adaptation. New York: Basic Books.

Fromm-Reichmann, F. (1984). Notes on the development of treatment of schizophrenics by psychoanalytic psychotherapy. Psychiatry, 11, 263-273.

Hatfield, A. B. (1978). Psychological costs of schizophrenia to the family. Social Work, 23, 355-359.

Hatfield, A. B. (1979). Help-seeking behavior in families of schizophrenics. American Journal of Community Psychology, 7, 563-569.

Holden, D. F., & Lewine, R. R. (1982). How families evaluate mental health professionals, resources, and effects of illness. Schizophrenia Bulletin, 8, 626-633.

Hollingshead, A., & Redlich, F. (1958). Social class and mental illness. New York: Wiley.

Holmes, T. H., & Rahe, R. H. (1967). The Social Readjustment Rating Scale. Journal of Psychosomatic Research, 11, 213-218.

Kalis, B. L. (1970). Crisis theory: Its relevance for community psychology and directions for development. In D. Adelson & B. L. Kalis (Eds.), Community psychology and mental health: Perspectives and challenges. Scranton, PA: Chandler.

Kelly, F. (1964). Relatives' attitudes and outcome in schizophrenia. Archives of General Psychiatry, 10, 389-394.

Kint, M. G. (1978). Schizophrenia is a family affair: Problems of families in coping with schizophrenia. Journal of Orthomolecular Psychiatry, 7, 236-246.

Kreisman, D. E., & Joy, V. D. (1974). Family response to the mental illness of a relative: A review of the literature. Schizophrenia Bulletin, 1(10), 34-57.

Lazarus, R. S. (1977). Cognitive and coping processes in emotion. In A. Monat & R. S. Lazarus (Eds.), Stress and coping: An anthology. New York: Columbia University Press.

Lazarus, R. S., Averill, J. R., & Opton, E. M. (1974). The psychology of coping: Issues of research and assessment. In G. V. Coelho, D. A. Hamburg, & J. E. Adams (Eds.), Coping and adaptation. New York: Basic Books.

Lidz, T. (1958). Schizophrenia and the family. Psychiatry, 21, 21-27.

Liem, R., & Liem, J. (1978). Social class and mental illness reconsidered: The role of economic stress and social support. Journal of Health and Social Behavior, 19, 139-156.

Lorei, T. (1964). Prediction of length of stay out of hospital for released psychiatric patients. Journal of Consulting Psychology, 28, 358-363.

Marcus, L. (1977). Patterns of coping in families of psychotic children. American Journal of Orthopsychiatry, 47, 388-399.

Mason, J. W. (1971). A re-evaluation of the concept of non-specificity in stress theory. Journal of Psychiatric Research, 8, 323-333.

McQuade, W., & Aikman, A. (1975). Stress: What it is, what it can do to your health, how to fight back. New York: Bantam.

Mechanic, D. (1974). Social structure and personal adaptation: Some neglected dimensions. In G. V. Coelho, D. A. Hamburg, & J. E. Adams (Eds.), Coping and adaptation. New York: Basic Books.

Messer, A. A. (1970). The individual in his family: An adaptational study. Springfield, IL: Thomas.

Murphy, L. B. (1962). The widening world of childhood: Paths toward mastery. New York: Basic Books.

Murphy, L. B. (1974). Coping, vulnerability, and resilience in childhood. In G. V. Coelho, D. A. Hamburg, & J. E. Adams (Eds.), Coping and adaptation. New York: Basic Books.

Pearlin, L. I., & Schooler, C. (1978). The structure of coping. *Journal of Health and Social Behavior, 19,* 2-21.

Pringle, J. (1973). *Schizophrenia: The family burden.* Surbiton, England: National Schizophrenia Fellowship.

Selye, J. (1974). *Stress without distress.* New York: Signet.

Shaffer, M. (1982). *Life after stress.* New York: Plenum Press.

Spaniol, L. (1985). *Beyond stress management: A holistic approach.* Newton, MA: HSA Publications.

Spaniol, L., & Caputo, J. (1979). *Professional burn-out: A personal survival kit.* Belmont, MA: Human Service Associates.

Spaniol, L., Jung, H., Zipple, A. M., & Fitzgerald, S. (1984). *Families as a central resource in the rehabilitation of the severely psychiatrically disabled: Report of a national survey* (final report). Boston: Boston University, Center for Rehabilitation Research and Training in Mental Health.

Spaniol, L., & Lannan, P. (1984). *Getting unstuck: Moving on after divorce.* New York: Paulist Press.

Spaniol, L., & Wells, J. (1982). *Managing professional stress and burn-out: A step-by-step guide.* Belmont, MA: Human Service Associates.

Vaillant, G. E. (1977). *Adaptation to life.* Boston: Little, Brown.

Vannicelli, M., Washburn, S. L., & Scheff, B. (1980). Family attitudes toward mental illness: Immutable with respect to time, treatment, setting, and outcome. *Journal of Orthopsychiatry, 50*(1), 151-155.

White, R. W. (1974). Strategies of adaptation: An attempt at systematic description. In G. V. Coelho, D. A. Hamburg, & J. E. Adams (Eds.), *Coping and adaptation.* New York: Basic Books.

Wynne, L. C., Ryckoff, I., Day, J., & Hirsch, S. (1958). Pseudomutuality in the family relations of schizophrenics. *Psychiatry, 21,* 205-220.

# II

## HOW FAMILIES COPE WITH MENTAL ILLNESS

# Behavioral Manifestations of Mental Illness

*Harriet P. Lefley*

Mental illnesses are the most baffling of human disorders because they are manifested behaviorally rather than physiologically. This has generated an ideology and a literature, exemplified by the work of writers such as Thomas Szasz (1961), which rejects the validity of psychotic behavior as illness and defines it in terms of societal labeling and function.

The convergence of powerful findings from genetic, biochemical, pharmacologic, neuroradiological, and neuropathological research, and from studies of cognition and perception, have led most experts in the field to agree that the major psychoses are indeed diseases of the brain. Nevertheless, because the specific biological substrates are still unclear, the emphasis continues to be on the control or redirection of aberrant behavior. Moreover, intracultural and cross-cultural variability in the distribution, content and salience of the behavioral correlates of the major disorders, as well as apparent culture-bound syndromes that do not seem to fit a universal diagnostic grid, continue to confuse the issue of what comes under the rubric of mental illness.

This chapter will focus on four basic aspects of the behavioral manifestations of mental illness. The first two, symptomatology and level of functioning, are addressed as conditions that characterize the illnesses and inform their consequences. The latter two aspects are discussed as sequelae of the state of being mentally ill. They include

Harriet P. Lefley. Office of Transcultural Education and Research, Department of Psychiatry, University of Miami, Miami, Florida.

patients' subjective reactions to the experience of being deviant, and their interpersonal coping strategies.

In this model, the essential behavioral features of mental illness are determined by diathesis, although their specific manifestations and perpetuation are subject to environmental forces. The sequelae, involving exogenous mood state, self-concept, and productivity, are largely psychosocially determined. They are behavioral reactions of the mentally ill to societal treatment of the mentally ill.

The discussion then focuses on the questions of purposiveness and volition; these are interrelated but independent issues. "Purposiveness" refers to the functional or symbolic value often ascribed by mental health professionals to the behavioral manifestations of mental illness. Their assumption is that these meanings are not necessarily under conscious control; in fact, they are most likely to be oblique manifestations of repressed or primitive material. "Volitional" aspects, on the other hand, refer to behaviors that can be altered by the patient under appropriate contingencies of reinforcement. Both familial and societal coping with the behavioral manifestations of mental illness are integrally related to volition, since this single issue determines accountability and culpability in law.

## CHARACTERISTIC BEHAVIORS OF MENTAL ILLNESS

### Clinical Symptoms

The clinical manifestations of various types of mental illness are encompassed in several established classificatory systems. Primary among these is the current third edition of the American Psychiatric Association's (1980) *Diagnostic and Statistical Manual of Mental Disorders* (DSM-III). DSM-III has changed some previous clinical categories and has added multiaxial codes that take other behaviors and contextual information into account for diagnostic specificity and treatment planning.

DSM-III criteria for diagnosis of a schizophrenic disorder describe characteristic symptoms involving the content and form of thought, perception, affect, sense of self, motivation, relationship to the external world, and psychomotor behavior. Most families of schizophrenics have observed one or more of the criterion symptoms. These include (1) bizarre delusions, such as being controlled, thought broadcasting, thought insertion, or thought withdrawal; (2) somatic, grandiose, religious, or nihilistic delusions; (3) delusions with persecutory or jealous content; (4) auditory hallucinations; (5) incoherence, marked loosening of associations, markedly illogical thinking, and the like. Also observed have been the prodromal or residual symptoms of social isolation or withdrawal; marked impairment in role functioning; markedly peculiar behavior; marked impairment in personal hygiene and grooming; blunted, flat, or inappropriate affect; digressive or over-elaborate speech; odd or bizarre ideation, and unusual perceptual experiences.

The florid or positive symptoms of schizophrenia often require crisis intervention and hospitalization. It is the negative symptoms, however, such as social isolation and withdrawal, that are more persistent across time and in some ways more demanding of the coping capabilities of families.

In the case of bipolar affective disorders, both manic and depressive episodes pose special problems for families. According to DSM-III, the manic phase can include marked increase in activity; restlessness; talkativeness; flight of ideas with racing thoughts; grandiosity; decreased need for sleep; distractibility, and excessive involvement in activities that have a high potential for painful consequences. Examples are buying sprees, sexual indiscretions, foolish business investments, and reckless driving. In a major depressive episode, at least four of the following behaviors are observed almost constantly for at least 2 weeks: significant change in appetite; insomnia or hypersomnia; psychomotor agitation or retardation; loss of interest or pleasure in usual activities, with diminished sexual drive; loss of energy and fatigue; feelings of worthlessness or inappropriate guilt; diminished ability to think or concentrate; recurrent thoughts of death, suicidal ideation, or suicide attempt.

These symptoms are characteristic of the major disorders but by no means cover the range of aberrant behaviors manifested in daily living. Overwhelming anxiety, as well as obsessive, compulsive, and phobic behaviors are often observed. Of particular concern are abusive or dangerous behaviors, which are discussed further in the section on family coping.

## Level of Functioning

DSM-III notes that "schizophrenia always involves deterioration from a previous level of functioning during some phase of the illness in such areas as work, social relations, and self-care. Family and friends often observe that the person is 'not the same'" (American Psychiatric Association, 1980, p. 181). Even with symptom containment under psychotropic medication, diminished skills and impoverished interpersonal relationships frequently interfere with attainment of an improved level of functioning.

The positive symptoms of schizophrenia and the hypomanic activities of affective disorders, no matter how bizarre, do not seem to have as profound an impact on levels of functioning as the negative symptoms of withdrawal, social isolation, blunted affect, or aloofness. In schizophrenia, acute symptomatology, later onset, clear precipitating events, good premorbid adjustment, and marriage are associated with a good prognosis. Paradoxically, the presence of depression in schizophrenia also is a good prognostic sign (Kaplan & Sadock, 1981). These authors note that "there are five possible outcomes for the schizophrenic patient: full and permanent recovery; full remission, with one or more future relapses; social remission, with personality defect and with the patient either capable of self-care and self-support, or dependent on protection and supervision; stable chronicity; and deterioration to a terminal stage" (p. 332). The last stage is apparently a rare phenomenon among those who have become ill during the last 25 years.

Patients suffering from affective disorders are generally more functional. Indeed, there may be high levels of productivity among those suffering from a mild form of bipolar illness. In contrast to schizophrenia, where exogenous depression is a reality-based feature of the illness and hence a good prognostic sign, the decreased psychophysiological activation of endogenous depression clearly precludes any normal level of functioning.

Nevertheless, prognosis for the affective disorders shows a much better picture than formerly. In contrast to Kraepelin's report of only 33% remission in involutional melancholia, Kaplan and Sadock (1981) state that 50–80% currently recover. Prophylaxis against both unipolar and bipolar disorders is now possible, particularly with the discovery of lithium carbonate, electroshock therapy, and antidepressants. "Without prophylactic treatment, the usual course of recurring episodic affective disorders is a gradual loss of social, economic, and psychological position in society" (Kaplan & Sadock, 1981, p. 369).

Impaired levels of functioning are related to loss of old skills and failure to acquire new ones; thus, they affect productivity, self-concept, and potential for change in the patient. They also add to family burden, perpetuating economic and social dependency. The combination of positive clinical symptoms and low functional levels tends to evoke a powerful psychological reaction in the patient. These reactions are also part of the array of behavioral manifestations of mental illness.

## Subjective Reactions to the Experience of Being Mentally Ill

It has often been pointed out that a person suffering from mental illness is much more than "a schizophrenic" or "a depressive" and should be recognized as such. Each is an individual with personality characteristics, strengths, talents, and a history of accomplishments who happens to be suffering from a particular disorder. By transcending the idea that the diagnosis is the person, it is easier to work more effectively with this individual both as a patient and as a family member. But it is also easier to recognize that during periods of remission or lucidity, a mentally ill person is well able to understand the damage done to her or his life by this terrible disease, and to suffer from its sequelae as much or more than from its actual symptoms.

In an interesting paper, Jeffries (1977) noted the tendency of psychiatrists to view the residual symptoms of schizophrenia as an ongoing disease process rather than as a "stress response syndrome" and suggested that certain symptoms might constitute a reaction to the experience of madness. Altered mind and body images might be part of the reactive neurosis, as well as an agoraphobia based on the idea that "I must not go where people can see me and identify my craziness" (p. 200).

Despite apparent apathy or self-absorption, mentally ill persons are typically extremely sensitive to the environment and to the perceptions of others. One of the most devastating sequelae of mental illness is the reaction to one's own deviance. Many can sometimes see their own "craziness" through others' eyes. Dysfunctional mentally ill persons are acutely aware of their lack of skills, impaired productivity, and poor future prospects. They can see that others of their own age are married, starting families, finalizing career plans, and they are painfully aware of their own deficiencies and the impoverishment of their lives. The sadness of this situation is that the insight is typically enervating rather than energizing. For many of the chronically impaired, the challenge of changing one's life is too threatening to be acted upon.

Another aspect that has been discussed in the literature is the patient's powerful affective response to emergence from chronic withdrawal and abandonment of the patient role. Harris and Bergman (1984) describe four reactions: fear, grief, despair, and anger. Inevitably, there is fearfulness about returning from the protected environment of the hospital to the demands of the outside world. The fear is reinforced by the realities of community reintegration, and particularly by the need to relearn vocational, competitive, and psychosocial coping skills. In this regard, there is grief for the developmental stages that have been missed during the long periods of psychosis and the losses of skill-building and career opportunities. Despair and hopelessness about the future are concomitants of this grief, while anger arises as a realistic response to the pain and deprivations of one's life. Yet the authors see anger as a positive sign, reflecting the patient's reemergence from psychosis into an attempt to cope with the demands of living.

### Defensive Behavioral Strategies

Some of the behavioral manifestations of mental illness represent maladaptive efforts to cope with a life situation of low entitlement and aversive living conditions. Crude manipulation of families, providers, and other patients is one of the defensive strategies sometimes used by patients. Typically this is done unskillfully, because the chronically mentally ill lack the exploitiveness, self-assertiveness, and goal orientation of sociopaths. Nevertheless, a successful manipulation is one of the ways of exerting power by the otherwise powerless. A different type of defensive strategy, with more serious consequences, is a tendency of some young patients to run away in an apparent effort to seek a better life. Some may travel to other cities, hitchhiking or spending their last dollars on bus fare, without any clear notion of where they are going or what they will do on arrival. As in the wandering that sometimes occurs in cases of organic mental disorder, there may be a concurrent clouding of memory, but this appears quite different from psychogenic fugue. In recent times, there have been a considerable number of discharged patients wandering away from board and care homes into depressed downtown areas, ultimately becoming a part of the homeless population.

One of the most perceptive pictures of the world of the mentally ill is given by Estroff (1981) in her description of the life of psychiatric clients in the community. Estroff describes a helping establishment full of contradictions and Catch-22 dynamics that help to keep clients "crazy." In dealing with the establishment, as in dealing with their families, mentally ill persons learn an array of coping strategies to maintain a delicate balance between the dependency they are afraid to relinquish and the autonomy they wish to be ceded by others. There is an inherent double bind in the life condition of the chronically mentally ill, which is only exacerbated by periods of partial remission. Estroff (1981, pp. 189–190) gives a number of rules for "making it crazy," which typically include approach–avoidant components. For example:

"Sincerely try new things, like working, every once in a while; but when you get fired, or quit, prove to yourself and others that you really are sick and cannot manage." Other rules, such as, "Assume that you are going to fail at almost anything except patienthood" are matched with "Assume that if you do not take care of yourself someone else will." The oppressive, self-fulfilling role expectancies of patienthood are reinforced by simply being part of the mental health system. "Do not become too compliant and cooperative with . . . staff, because they will think you are too dependent and will reject you. Or if you really do comply with treatment, then you will either have to get better or get psychotic (just when things are going well so that you can start all over)." In contrast, the criteria Estroff offers for making it *without* craziness involve separation from the helping program; acquiring subsistence by culturally sanctioned means, such as work, apart from disability and special status; minimal contact with psychiatric professionals; and establishment of multiple primary interpersonal and social relationships with normals.

It is interesting that Estroff's description of two clients who were able to return to their parents' homes (one against staff advice) indicated noteworthy progress. Although these may have been selective cases, their "exit from the crazy system" to the world of normals seems to have had salutary effects. This picture is in sharp contrast, of course, to the notion so common in the field that families provide a toxic atmosphere for the returning patient.

## FAMILY COPING WITH BEHAVIORS
## OF MENTAL ILLNESS

In any discussion of family coping, behavioral manifestations of mental illness must be assessed in terms of the reactions they typically evoke in other individuals. Most families have a range of interactional norms within which they operate; these are determined by cultural context, individual temperaments, family size and structure, and the specific family history. Overall, however, there are certain role expectations to which most human beings adhere, inside and outside of the family system.

Parsons's (1951) classic definition of the sick role exempts ill persons from their usual social responsibilities providing three obligations are met: First, they must not be responsible for their condition; second, they must be motivated to get well as soon as possible; and third, they must seek technically competent help so that they can recover. Mentally ill persons rarely fulfill all three requirements; frequently they are perceived as fulfilling none. This perception informs the *dilemma of functional expectancy* that is found not only in families, but among many providers of services to the mentally ill. The dilemma lies in not knowing what types and levels of expectations are appropriate for a particular patient, and how to react when goal behaviors are not fulfilled. Many professionals are less adept than families in setting appropriate behavioral targets, because they must use a normative set of expectancies rather than ipsative (individually normalized) expectancies that implicitly are set by those who know the person well.

## The Behavior-Response Linkage

There are three categories of behavior among the mentally ill that evoke differential response in significant others. The first category involves behaviors that elicit anger, irritability, or exasperation. These behaviors intrude on the lives of others and make extraordinary demands upon family caregivers. In most normal families, they would evoke either high expressed emotion or extreme suppression of affect.

### THREATENING OR ANNOYING BEHAVIORS

*Hostile, Abusive, or Assaultive Behaviors.* Typically reflecting poor impulse control, these behaviors are often related to inadequate or inappropriate medication, a condition that revives hallucinatory or delusional ideation. Hostility may be directed at other family members because of the patient's unwillingness to abide by rules, jealousy of more functional members, perceived obstruction of desires, unfulfilled dependency needs, hypersensitivity to criticism, attributions of intrusiveness, or any number of the usual psychodynamic agendas among family members. In the families of the mentally ill, however, agendas that might long ago have been resolved are frequently kept alive because of the patient's anger and the unremitting abrasive impact of his or her behaviors. Particularly threatening are verbal and physical aggressiveness toward children, who are frequently the targets of paranoid ideation or reminders of a more favored status in the past.

*Mood Swings and Unpredictability.* Mood swings are not exclusive to cyclothymic personalities. They are found in schizophrenics as well as those suffering from affective disorders. While the range from depression to hypomania is not as great, these differing shades of affect add to the unpredictability that many family members find so difficult to deal with. In many severely disordered people, there are fluctuating diurnal rhythms of mood and also of contact with reality—periods of greater clarity and higher functioning, which unfortunately do not persist. Many family members find it difficult to contend with this type of inconsistency. It seems to reinforce the notion that the patient could perform at higher levels if only she or he were willing to try.

*Socially Offensive or Embarrassing Behavior.* In addition to personal abuse, family members must often contend with the patient's acting out toward others. This may generate reluctance to take the patient to a restaurant, theater, or other public place for fear of enduring a scene. The following two case vignettes suggest the type of situations that families often encounter.

> A 17-year-old schizophrenic young man makes clumsy sexual advances to the girlfriends of his 12-year-old sister. The friends are afraid to come to her house and the child is agonized with embarrassment, and in danger of losing her peer group. The parents do not know how to treat the situation or how to instruct the young girl on what she should say to her friends.

> The patient goes up and down the street bumming cigarettes and money from the neighbors. Initially tolerant, they begin to refuse her requests. She becomes increasingly abusive and threatening. The neighbors don't want her living in the neighborhood and begin to ostracize the family.

Many families find themselves in situations in which economics dictate that the adults work, and there is no single caregiver available at all times. Unless they are fortunate enough to have a nearby day-treatment or vocational program (and the patient meets the eligibility criteria, and is willing to go), there is little they can do about monitoring the patient's behavior.

*Amotivation, Parasitism, Refusal to Take Responsibility for Self, Apparent Malingering.* Amotivation has been classified among the negative symptoms of schizophrenia, but there may be a substantive difference between the apathy and anhedonia that appear to be neurologically based, and the lack of motivation that derives from a learned history of failures. Families are constantly frustrated by the self-imposed isolation of the mentally ill family member, who seems willing to spend a lifetime doing nothing in a world in which activity is valued. Efforts to stimulate an interest in performance seem doomed.

Unwilling to take a chance at failure (and perhaps fearing the stimulation of even partial success in task mastery), the patient seems to establish the self-fulfilling inevitability of an empty life.

*Self-Destructive Behaviors.* Rejection of a functional role is one way of being self-destructive. More overt behaviors include refusal to take psychotropic medications, which almost inevitably results in decompensation and the revolving-door syndrome, or conversely, substance abuse, with similar sequelae. In this category, we are differentiating between behaviors that seem to represent a defiant exercise of the will to remain sick, and the type of suicidal behavior that reflects profound hopelessness and despair.

*Behaviors Disturbing to Household Living.* Sociopathic behaviors are not typical of the severely mentally disordered, although occasionally there is stealing of household money to buy cigarettes, food, or soft drinks. As in institutional settings, more functional patients will sometimes steal radios, clothing, or similar items that may be bartered. These are self-perceived survival mechanisms, and are rarely manifestations of aggression toward others. *Poor handling of money* is a typical complaint. Families are often forced to set up elaborate systems for money management in order for the patient to maintain his or her resources until the next check is received. Frequently there is conflict with those whose ahistoricity seems to make it impossible for them to remember their self-inflicted cycles of feast and famine.

*Poor personal hygiene* is a common complaint among family members, particularly failure to bathe and change clothes. *Indifferent housekeeping* may result in dirty rooms, vermin, and additional offensive odors.

*Sleep reversal* is another difficulty encountered by family members with the usual diurnal cycle, especially if they need a full night's sleep. Frequently a mentally ill person will pace up and down all night, sometimes playing the radio or stereo, keeping the family and neighbors awake. The pattern is often difficult to break, resulting in great irritation.

*Property damage*, both deliberate and inadvertent, is a constant irritant. Patients may destroy furniture and other household possessions in conditions of rage or frustration. As is evident in any institutional or programmatic setting, mentally ill people smoke a great deal. Because of the limited and diffused attention of many patients, fire in the household is a distinct danger.

These household disruptions often generate a cycle of events. Family members, few of whom can show the saintlike behavior of constant low expressed emotion (EE), register protest and complaint regarding intrusions on their daily equilibrium. Patients, fragile at best, respond with withdrawal, depression, or come full cycle to the assaultive aggression indicated at the beginning of this section. It is particularly in this area of day-to-day living that the frustrations of coping with the behavioral manifestations of mental illness are most evident. These are the ordinary behaviors that require a specialized knowledge of limit setting and other patient management techniques among family caregivers.

BEHAVIORS INVOLVING LACK OF HUMAN RELATEDNESS

In various types of mental illness, there are symptomatic behaviors that appear to other people as distancing mechanisms that serve to shut off human interaction. The silences of aphasia or alogia, although based on sensory-neural abnormality, are frequently perceived as unwillingness rather than as inability to communicate. Psychodynamic explanations frequently compound the perception of family members that the patient is deliberately withholding herself or himself, or otherwise trying to convey through nonverbal means the message that contact is too painful. For years, the motor restlessness and muscular quivering of akathisia have been interpreted as somatic representations of the patient's inner turmoil, particularly when accompanied by mutism. Conversely, the waxy flexibility found in stuporous catatonia has been psychodynamically interpreted as an extreme reaction in which patients distance themselves from their own body, as well as from putatively damaging others.

It is true that family caregivers often become exasperated with the prolonged silences that frequently punctuate responses to simple questions, and other attentional deficits that interfere with normal communication. It is also apparent that many schizophrenics find external stimulation too arousing, and therefore indeed try to cut off human contact as an adaptive strategy. These distancing mechanisms tend to further alienate family members who are trying to reach out, be supportive, and fulfill their self-image as caring human beings.

The literature on families of the chronically physically handicapped, the mentally retarded, the mentally ill, and other disabled dependent populations shows a commonality of responses. These include changed relationships with other family members, friends, and neighbors; a tendency toward encapsulation; a long-term readjustment in family life style; and sometimes marital and sibling conflict because of the more restricted caregiving role of the wife-mother. In many of these situations, there is sometimes a feeling of being trapped in an intolerable situation without remedy or relief (see Lefley, 1981 for overview). Even among families of the mentally retarded, where familial adjustment must occur relatively early in the child's life, there are recurrent stresses that keep reemerging over time affecting the coping capabilities of the family (Wikler, 1981).

There are, however, substantive differences among these situations. When a physically handicapped person retains an intact personality and, apparent motivation for alternative activities, or when a Down's syndrome child manifests a cheerful disposition and loving devotion to family members, the burden of care is immeasurably lightened. The key issue here is one of rewards. Westermeyer and Pattison (1981), writing of social networks of mentally ill persons in Lao villages, noted that social support seems to be a function of the presence or absence of "symmetrical reciprocity." The years accumulated by the mentally ill persons in giving to others constituted a "social reserve" or "social capital" upon which they were later able to draw assistance (p. 132).

The anthropological notion of instrumental exchange is an extremely important construct in any discussion of caregiving to the mentally ill. By now the phenomenon of burn-out is well-known in the mental health field. Professionals do not receive many rewards in the course of treating the chronically mentally ill. Dealing with chronic patients, perceived as low yield for a heavy investment of time and effort, is related to low job satisfaction and high job turnover (Pines & Maslach, 1978). Family members, whose contact is more constant and whose burn-out is exacerbated by more personal emotional strain, cannot simply resign from their role. For this coping strategy to occur, there must be massive realignment of the entire caregiving situation and an emotional coming-to-terms with the guilt, relief, and revised self-concept that such a move entails.

Lack of human relatedness is thus one of the most devastating manifestations of mental illness for family members with a reasonable need for the rewards of interpersonal relationship. For the sake of both the caregivers and the integrity of the patients, mentally ill persons must be brought to the point of some degree of mutually recognized reciprocity.

BEHAVIORS EVOKING EMPATHIC PAIN IN FAMILY MEMBERS

The previous discussion of the reactions of the mentally ill to their own experience of deviance has indicated that many patients are painfully aware of their own destroyed aspirations and the poverty of their lives. This is particularly the case with those whose achievement levels and self-expectations were relatively high prior to the first breakdown. Within the family constellation, formerly functioning individuals must adapt to loss of role, reduced productivity, decreased self-esteem, and feelings of being a burden to loved ones.

Citing the typical mourning statement of a discharged patient, "I have wasted fourteen years of my life," Harris and Bergman (1984) note: "The comparison between oneself and one's former self can be devastating. The patient must be permitted to grieve for the self that he or she has lost" (p. 32). Family members share the mourning for the lost self that is experienced by their loved one, and also by themselves. In contrast to the professionals, who never knew the premorbid personality, family members typically remember happier times in the life of a child or adolescent who bears little relationship to the dispirited person who bears her or his name today.

The depression, fear, and anxiety experienced by patients who are beginning to return to the world of reality are empathically felt by their parents, wives, and siblings, and sometimes by their children as well. Some theoreticians have postulated that families fear the recovery of their mentally ill members. In some cases they may be partially right, but their rationale—that symptom remission will disturb family equilibrium—seems outrageously wrong. A mystery that requires its own research effort is why so many mental health professionals prefer to see psychopathology and ignore the prosocial elements of interpersonal life: familial bonding, love, sympathy, and empathy. The law of parsimony suggests that fear of the patient getting well is based, not on loss of the glue that binds the dysfunctional family system, but rather on the desire to shield a loved one from known suffering, as he or she confronts the realities of stigma and a second-rate life. The return to reality is the stage during which there is frequent loss of hope for ever attaining the kind of life to which the patient's talents and intelligence entitled him or her. For some, this is the period in which successful suicides occur. Of all the behavioral manifestations of mental illness, this pain is probably the most devastating phenomenon with which families have to cope.

## BEHAVIORAL MEANINGS AND PARSIMONIOUS INTERPRETATIONS

One of the most persistent convictions among mental health professionals is that almost all manifest behavior has a latent meaning that is different from that which is observed. This conviction has been shared with the popular media, and family members are well aware that mental illness is considered a product of "crazymaking" families who inflicted damage without necessarily knowing when, how, and why they did so. Although many families have been able to overcome and relinquish the offender image, the cycle of guilt and inappropriate blame assigned by mental health professionals (Lamb, 1983) still continues to burden the caregiver role. A significant component of this burden is the self-monitoring by some family members of the meanings and intent of their own behavior, as well as that of the patient.

Among behavioral manifestations of mental illness, aggression, withdrawal, dependency, manipulation, and the like are assumed to represent long-standing defensive reactions to aversive familial stimuli. Similarly, the content of hallucinatory and delusional symptoms are assumed to have psychodynamic meanings that reflect the individual's interpersonal history in the dysfunctional family matrix.

Young schizophrenics sometimes manifest aggression toward the mother. The theme reinforces reflexive (knee-jerk) interpretations of maternal overprotection, seduction, intrusiveness, refusal to let go, or conversely, rejection and covert hostility toward an unloved child. The mother is the object of aggression because her behavior, past or present, has earned it. Yet, the quality of life of the mentally ill is so poor that there is surely no need to look for circuitous explanations for negative behavior. Regardless of the level of creature comforts and supportive resources, even the medication-stabilized mentally ill suffer from frustration with their own dysfunction, as well as identity problems generated by social stigma and self-devaluation. Aggression is a common phenomenon among those who feel disenfranchised. On a societal level, it is perceived as a rage reaction to the experience of powerlessness.

Certainly there are few people as powerless as the chronically mentally ill. The schizophrenic and dysfunctional bipolar adult is frequently still locked into the dependency-independence conflict of adolescence. He or she wants individuation, but is unable to function at a more mature level. Anger directed at the mother reflects the conflict of one who wants to move away from the life buoy, but is afraid of drowning. Yet if the parent removes the buoy, the child may indeed drown or else founder so miserably that his or her progress is significantly impeded. In these cases, withdrawal or depression may replace the more proactive aggression. Thus parents are locked into a balancing dilemma that persists far beyond the cutoff time of late adolescence or young adulthood.

It is a mistake to believe, as so many parents are taught to do, that the progress of an adult patient depends on the parent's behavior. Parents can and should set limits on how much of themselves they will give to their offspring. This refers to the behaviors they will tolerate, the time and energy they will invest, and the extent to which they are willing to suppress their own needs as persons. But these limits are for the parents' integrity, not the child's.

Although these statements refer to parent-child relationships, where the dependency trauma is more profound, they apply to the whole family constellation. Family members should not be burdened by the conviction that if only they act differently, the patient's behavior will improve. Sometimes, indeed, external limits and low EE will provide more security for a stimulus-bombarded schizophrenic. But familial coping with mental illness requires a shedding of rescue fantasies that in great part have been nurtured by professionals. It is grandiose for families to believe that they have caused or can cure a phenomenon as awesome as mental illness. They can only try to modify their behavior to make life more comfortable for themselves and their mentally ill relatives.

## VOLITION AND MENTALLY ILL BEHAVIOR

The previous discussion has indicated a gamut of family reactions ranging from anger to pity and empathic pain. As many have noted, family reactions based on a medical model of mental illness are typically more benign than those derived from a model of problems in living (Karno, 1982; Siegler & Osmond, 1974). In any environmental context, there are different societal reactions to antisocial behaviors perceived as biologically based and nonbiologically based. The distinction is also important in law. The former implies behavior that is essentially (1) beyond ordinary volitional controls and (2) a function of severe cognitive impairment. Antisocial behavior that is not medically based, in contrast, implies volition and choice. Thus, assaultive behavior that derives from a florid hallucinatory experience of thought insertion is perceived differently, in law and in treatment, from an assault that is arbitrarily inflicted by a sociopath in the course of theft.

The madness-badness dichotomy is meaningful to those who must deal on a regular basis with behavior that is extremely burdensome. Although it may seem that intolerable behavior requires the same sort of management, regardless of cause, the motivational state of the actor strongly affects how families cope. Alcohol and drug addictions may also be diseases, in terms of physiological response to a particular substance, but initiation of the disease process is under personal control. The same argument applies to substance-induced psychotic states that may result in harm to oneself or others; that is, the actor has the option of abstinence, and therefore is responsible for his or her actions. This option does not, however, usually apply in the case of schizophrenic or manic episodes. While the patient's decision to take medication may have bearing on their occurrence, this is not always or even typically the case. Moreover, the decision to reject medication is frequently a function of mental incompetency.

In coping with aberrant behavior, therefore, the family has fewer options in dealing with psychotic members than with those whose disturbed behavior is perceived as voluntarily induced. With the latter, a range of disciplinary controls can be exercised, varying only in intensity or scope. With the former, ahistoricity on the one hand and dependency on the other preclude the use of forceful punishment or extrusion from a support system required for survival. "Tough love" rarely works with young schizophrenics.

Yet, the mentally ill person is never totally without violition. That is, there are presumably always elements of internal control that can be directed toward healthier ends. The difficulty is in recognizing the boundaries. An example of this problem is found in the John Hinckley case, in which the parents of the would-be presidential assassin were advised by his psychiatrist to demand that the young man fulfill what turned out to be unrealistic goals of independence. Yet there was no apparent reason for either the practitioner or the parents to question the validity of this decision or to predict later events based on the young man's overt behavior. Although young Hinckley's actions obviously were deranged, his level of functioning was higher than that of many schizophrenics, as manifested in his ability to purchase a gun, drive a car, travel to distant cities, and plan the itinerary for a murder. The legal dilemmas of defining insanity (knowing the difference between right and wrong, or dealing with uncontrollable impulse) are not the problems of families or providers. However, the dilemma of defining volition is indeed their problem.

This is what makes the treatment decision so difficult. In the Hinckley case, the father has repeatedly blamed himself in public for failing to recognize the avolitional aspects of his son's behavior, implying that had the son been accepted in his home, the unfortunate historical events would not have occurred. However, there was no way of predicting that the assassination attempt would not have occurred at another time. Nor was there any reason to believe that the attempted murder of a president followed an experience of paternal rejection; the young man had tried it before with another president. Aside from rare cases of patent abuse, familial self-blaming usually has little basis in reality. In one situation, families may regret the imposition of structured demands, while in other cases, such demands are not only warranted but necessary.

In the Hinckley case, the family's recognition that the young man was mentally ill, rather than a simple malingerer or troublemaker, made an enormous difference in their subsequent behavior and life decisions.[1] This case, of course, has had a great impact on both our psychiatric and legal systems. The storm surrounding the verdict of not guilty by reason of insanity (NGRI) has revived the vital issue of a mentally ill person's right to exculpability on grounds of psychopathology versus society's right to hold the mentally ill accountable as responsible human beings.

The American Psychiatric Association (1983), "speaking as citizens as well as psychiatrists" (p. 683), has issued a statement recommending retention of NGRI. "The insanity defense rests upon one of the fundamental premises of the criminal law, that punishment for wrongful deeds should be predicated upon moral culpability. . . . Defendants who lack the ability (the capacity) to rationally control their behavior do not possess free will. They cannot be said to have 'chosen to do wrong'" (p. 683).

The family movement has come out strongly in favor of retaining the insanity defense, and has also been monitoring other changes in mental health law. Both families and mental health professionals have been emphasizing patients' right to the most therapeutic setting as an issue equal in importance to their right to the least restrictive setting, although the latter has been the primary issue in mental health advocacy law.

The balancing of patients' rights and patients' needs highlights the other side of the volitional equation. The insanity defense issue emphasizes a mentally ill person's right to be held not responsible for offenses against society; the patients' rights issue emphasizes a men-

---

[1]In his testimony at his son's trial, Jack Hinckley stated "I am the cause of John's tragedy" because of failure to have recognized the extent of his illness. Undoubtedly the father felt guilty about his perceived rejection of a son who seemed aimless, dependent, and unmotivated. Yet the decision to deny young Hinckley admission to the parental home, with its professional imprimatur, can be interpreted not as rejection, but as a proactive attempt to force independence by withholding the source of dependency. The Hinckleys gave powerful behavioral evidence of nonrejection of their youngest child throughout his trial and in the years afterwards. They left their home in Colorado and moved to Washington to participate in weekly family therapy sessions with their son at St. Elizabeths Hospital. In addition, Jack Hinckley sold Vanderbilt Energy Corp., the oil company he founded over 14 years ago, and using his own money and business acumen, has established the American Mental Health Fund, which he hopes "will do for mental illness what the American Cancer Society has done for cancer." Traveling around the country to raise money for research and public education in mental illness, the Hinckleys have stated in various public speeches, "We are going to bring some good out of this tragedy" (Cuniberti, 1984). In cases as dramatic as these, psychodynamic explanations of compensatory behavior seem completely beside the point.

tally ill person's right to be the *only* one responsible for decisions that may result in offenses against the self, as well as against society. The law thus seems able to sustain bipolar visions of accountability. These are, of course, vital social issues that will ultimately be resolved in the crucible of science, politics, and history. Meanwhile, the unresolved questions of volition, rationality, and accountability in the behaviors of mentally ill persons continue to have profound impact on the emotions and lives of family caregivers.

## POTENTIAL FOR BEHAVIORAL CHANGE

The author is aware that much of this chapter has dealt with behaviors of mental illness in negative terms. Unfortunately, the Laingian fantasies of creativity and growth as aspects of the psychotic experience have not been confirmed in research or in practice. Mental illness as positive experience is a concept alien to most patients and their families. They would rather not have endured it. It is also unfortunate that the hopeful mythology that accompanied deinstitutionalization is now seaming apart, and it is necessary to face the reality that closing hospitals has not eliminated a persistent cohort of the chronically mentally ill. The current attention to treatment modalities for the young adult chronic patient, often never institutionalized, highlights the perpetuity of the behaviors of mental illness (Pepper & Ryglewicz, 1984). For family caregivers, the parameters of these behaviors and the potential for change are questions underlying critical life decisions.

At this point in history, it is difficult to determine the extent to which behavioral manifestations of mental illness can be modified, and indeed, what such changes signify in terms of the underlying disease process itself. There is great variation in the rationales and models for psychodynamic psychotherapies, and almost no hard evidence of sustained efficacy in severe mental illness (Gunderson & Mosher, 1975). The application of family systems theory for schizophrenic patients is not only highly questionable (Leff, 1980) but may indeed be damaging by misinterpreting the meaning of behavior and deflecting from the appropriate target issues.

Behavior therapy seems to offer the most promising techniques, but long-term effects vary considerably. In institutional settings, behavior modification has been valuable in advancing impaired patients from one step level to the next. However, these behavioral changes typically reflect patient cooperation rather than competency, and rarely are at the functional levels required for independent community living. A long-term follow-up of behavior therapy in a state hospital setting indicated surprisingly good activity levels in terms of personal hygiene and household maintenance tasks, although only 28% of the patients had been employed at any time since discharge (Banzett, Liberman, Moore, & Marshall, 1984). The impressive work of Paul and Lentz (1977) similarly indicated that social learning programs were superior to more traditional therapeutic approaches in helping severely impaired institutionalized patients to function in community settings. Yet even these authors noted that "the absolute level of functioning achieved by residents who were able to move to the community was still sufficiently marginal that efforts to develop even more effective programs are clearly called for" (p. 468).

In the case of mental illness, as in mental retardation, there is a great deal of individual variation in capacity for behavioral change. The growing research literature on cerebral ventricular enlargement in a substantial subset of the mentally ill (primarily schizophrenics but including other syndromes as well) suggests that we are now approaching an era of greater ability to assess neuroanatomical correlates of specific types of behaviors. Increased ventricular size, an indicator of brain atrophy, appears to be correlated with (1) failure to stabilize on medications and (2) negative symptoms of schizophrenia, for example, apathy, anhedonia, amotivation, emotional flattening, and decreased attention span (Andreasen, Olsen, Dennert, & Smith, 1982). Levy, Kurtz, and Kling (1984), who had previously found significantly higher Beck Depression Inventory scores in patients with enlarged ventricles, investigated the relationships between suicide attempts and ventricular-brain ratios (VBRs) in 32 schizophrenic patients. Using a VBR cutoff of 8.4% (2 standard deviations about the mean for normal controls), they found that 10 of the 12 patients with VBRs over 8.4% had made suicide attempts, compared with only 2 of the 20 patients below the 8.4% cutoff. During the 6-month follow-up period, there were three severe suicide attempts, and two were successful. All three patients had VBRs over 10.8%. Such findings suggest one reason that external therapeutic modalities may not be uniformly successful with all patients.

While the continuing research on neurological, anatomical, and biochemical substrates may ultimately yield physiological parameters for a continuum of the potential for behavioral change, it is necessary to utilize our existing technologies for improving the lot of chronic patients and their families. Despite reams of theory on the basis for psychotic behaviors in family systems, research has produced no empirical evidence that such behaviors are maintained because of functional value for either the patients or their families. On the contrary, there is every reason to believe that such behaviors are maintained because of learning difficulties or neurological hypersensitivity to aversive stimuli in the environment. Since these conditions can be modified to some extent in all but the most severe cases, the present thinking is that behavioral manifestations of mental illness can be improved for most patients, resulting in a better quality of life for themselves and for their significant others. The comprehensive psychosocial treatment models outlined by Paul & Lentz (1977) and by Anthony (1979), particularly social skills training (Brady, 1984), seem to offer far more promise for change than psychodynamic or traditional family therapy approaches.

## REFERENCES

American Psychiatric Association. (1980). *Diagnostic and statistical manual of mental disorders* (3rd ed.). Washington, DC: Author.

American Psychiatric Association. Insanity Defense Work Group. (1983). American Psychiatric Association statement on the insanity defense. *American Journal of Psychiatry, 140,* 681-688.

Andreasen, N. C., Olsen, S. A., Dennert, J. W., & Smith, M. R. (1982). Ventricular enlargement in schizophrenia: Relationship to positive and negative symptoms. *American Journal of Psychiatry, 139,* 297-302.

Anthony, W. A. (1979). *Principles of psychiatric rehabilitation.* Amherst, MA: Human Resource Development Press.

Banzett, L. K., Liberman, R. P., Moore, J. W., & Marshall, B. D. Jr. (1984). Long-term follow-up of the effects of behavior therapy. *Hospital and Community Psychiatry, 35,* 277-279.

Brady, J. P. (1984). Social skills training for psychiatric patients. I: Concepts, methods, and clinical results. *American Journal of Psychiatry, 141,* 333-340.

Cuniberti, B. (1984, February 23). The Hinckleys go on a crusade. *Miami Herald,* pp. 1C, 3C.

Estroff, S. E. (1981). *Making it crazy: An ethnography of psychiatric clients in an American community.* Berkeley: University of California Press.

Gunderson, J. G., & Mosher, L. R. (Eds.). (1975). *Psychotherapy of schizophrenia.* New York: Jason Aronson.

Harris, M., & Bergman, H. C. (1984). The young adult chronic patient: Affective responses to treatment. In B. Pepper, & H. Ryglewicz (Eds.), *Advances in treating the young adult chronic patient* (pp. 29-35). San Francisco: Jossey-Bass.

Jeffries, J. J. (1977). The trauma of being psychotic: A neglected element in the management of chronic schizophrenia. *Canadian Psychiatric Association Journal, 22,* 199-205.

Kaplan, H. I., & Sadock, B. J. (1981). *Modern synopsis of comprehensive textbook of psychiatry III* (3rd ed.). Baltimore: Williams & Wilkins.

Karno, M. (1982, October). *The experience of schizophrenia in Mexican American families.* Paper presented at the meeting of the Society for the Study of Society and Culture, San Miguel Regla, Mexico.

Lamb, H. R. (1983). Families: Practical help replaces blame. *Hospital and Community Psychiatry, 34,* 893.

Leff, J. P. (1980). Developments in family treatment of schizophrenia. *Advances in Family Psychiatry, 2,* 313-333.

Lefley, H. P. (1981). Social aspects of medicine. In J. J. Braunstein & R. P. Toister (Eds.), *Medical applications of the behavioral sciences* (pp. 195-217). Chicago: Year Book Medical Publishers.

Levy, A. B., Kurtz, N., & Kling, A. S. (1984). Association between cerebral ventricular enlargement and suicide attempts in chronic schizophrenia. *American Journal of Psychiatry, 141,* 438-439.

Parsons, T. (1951). *The social system.* New York: Free Press.

Paul, G. L., & Lentz, R. J. (1977). *Psychosocial treatment of chronic mental patients.* Cambridge, MA: Harvard University Press.

Pepper, B., & Ryglewicz, H. (Eds.). (1984). *Advances in treating the young adult chronic patient.* San Francisco: Jossey-Bass.

Pines, A., & Maslach, C. (1978). Characteristics of staff burnout in mental health settings. *Hospital and Community Psychiatry, 29,* 233-237.

Siegler, M., & Osmond, H. (1974). *Models of madness, models of medicine.* New York: Macmillan.

Szasz, T. (1961). *The myth of mental illness.* New York: Hoeber-Harper.

Westermeyer, J., & Pattison, E. M. (1981). Social networks and mental illness in a peasant society. *Schizophrenia Bulletin, 7,* 125-134.

Wikler, L. (1981). Chronic stresses of families of mentally retarded children. *Family Relations, 30,* 281-288.

# The Meaning of Mental Illness to the Family

*Kenneth G. Terkelsen*

INTERVIEWER: What have you missed most as a result of having a
   mentally ill relative living at home with you?
RESPONDENT: My life.

The appearance of mental illness in a family member is invariably a
disaster for the whole family, a disaster in which all are victims of the
event and its sequelae. No one, and no part of the emotional life of
the family escapes unaffected. Children, siblings, and parents feel the
effects of direct involvement, while grandparents, aunts, uncles, cousins and more remote relations usually learn of the affliction from those
closer in. The illness even reaches those to whom its existence is never
exactly disclosed: kept from direct involvement, they elaborate explanations for the patient's mysterious, erratic inaccessibility, drawing on
gossip if not on fact. The illness touches everyone, affecting attitudes
toward self and toward life, producing symptoms in other members,
altering family structure, influencing life choices, and more.

Despite the pervasiveness of these effects, very little investigative
attention has been paid to the meaning that mental illness has for
relatives. Research into attitudes held by the general public toward the
mentally ill as an impersonal class of citizens indicates that mental
illness is generally regarded as an undesirable attribute (Rabkin,
1972). The relevance of this line of research to the study of attitudes of
actual relatives toward actual family members who are mentally ill is
thrown in doubt by studies indicating that recognition of mental illness is often diminished in those closest to the patient (Mills, 1962;

Kenneth G. Terkelsen. Cornell University Medical Center, New York, New York.

Rose, 1959; Sakamoto, 1969; Schwartz, 1957). In this light, Kreisman and Joy (1974) observed a decade ago that research into attitudes and beliefs of families about their own mentally ill members was nonexistent. The situation has not improved substantially in 10 years.

Within the clinical arena, professional attention is still devoted largely to treating the patient, and family members are relegated to adjunctive roles or regarded as barriers to recovery. Those who reveal their own suffering and injury too extensively are likely to be seen as unduly self-absorbed. So, for the most part, encounters between professionals and family members have not served as the basis of inquiry into the meaning of mental illness. Even the various forms of family therapy have proved uninformative in this regard, so fixed have they been on changing the quality of interaction among family members and raising the patient's level of social adaptation. The current interest in expressed emotion (EE) in relatives of schizophrenics (Falloon, *et al.*, 1982; Vaughn & Leff, 1976) is the contemporary form of this preoccupation. EE is a measure of certain parent behaviors as manifested in one-to-one research interviews and includes (1) the number of comments made by a parent referring in a critical way to any aspect of the patient's behavior, (2) the number of openly hostile comments, and (3) a global estimate of the parent's degree of emotional involvement with the patient. The interviewer asks neutral questions such as, "When did you first notice something different about him?" and "Has the way she looks after herself changed at all?" Direct inquiries about emotional responses such as "How did you feel about that?" are kept to a minimum, and ratings are made on *spontaneous displays* of criticalness, hostility, and emotional involvement. The EE score, the composite of the three separate scores, correlates strongly with relapse rates in schizophrenics (Brown, Birley, & Wing, 1972; Vaughn & Leff, 1976). However, regardless of its place in the study of the course of illness, the EE inquiry is uninformative on the questions addressed here. The research into EE takes us *outward* from the conduct of parents to the patient's clinical status, and *not inward* to the parent's experience of illness.

Indeed, so few formal studies of the meaning of mental illness to family members exist that this chapter could be a catalog of required rather than completed research. Beyond that, what is possible at present is to introduce a conceptual framework to direct future research. The focus of a study on the meaning of mental illness is perturbations in the relative's inner world occurring in connection with illness-related behavior. "Illness-related behavior refers to that part of the patient's conduct, or the conduct of other family members, professionals, or friends, that is a response to the illness in any of its aspects. The primary sources for this inquiry are relatives' personal accounts of internal experiences occurring in connection with illness-related behavior. It will be noted that the object of this inquiry is a key intervening variable between illness-related behavior and coping responses, because, in learning to cope with mental illness, relatives must cope first with those elements of their own experience evoked by illness-related behavior.

Since the meaning attached to mental illness varies as a function of a wide array of modifying factors, the study of personal meanings takes form around the study of modifiers. Variations in the way relatives give meaning to illness arise from five main sources: (1) extent of the relative's involvement in the daily life of the patient; (2) the relative's models of causation, symptoms, and outcomes; (3) the phenomenology and natural history of the illness; (4) the relative's personality and life history, including prior experiences with mental illness; and (5) responses of other persons to the illness and to the patient.

## EXTENT OF RELATIVE'S INVOLVEMENT IN THE DAILY LIFE OF THE PATIENT

The most potent variable in relatives' response to mental illness is the degree of involvement with patient and treatment. Prolonged, intimate exposure to the daily life, personal habits, and preoccupations of a mental patient has a more decisive impact on an observer than occasional, cursory, or stereotyped encounters. Consequently, it is usually the members of the immediate family who experience most directly the extent of incapacitation in the ill person.

### The First Tier of Involvement

Within the immediate family, one member, most often a mother or sister or wife, assumes the role of principal caregiver and is most profoundly affected by the acts and lapses of the patient. This daily caregiver carries the main burden of the illness in the family. Her daily experience may well become restricted to a few illness-related preoccupations. She is there when the patient withdraws from contact with the world outside the family, servicing needs as his or her capacity for self-care diminishes. She thinks about the patient's needs, how to meet them, and how to console the patient when these needs cannot be met. She wonders, more openly and continuously than others, why the illness has been visited upon the family. She reviews her recollections of the patient's early life for clues to its origins. She rereads old letters and reports from teachers and camp counselors, and examines family albums searching faces for early evidence of trouble. She examines her own conduct and that of others—family members, friends, teachers, any others involved with the patient—for clues to its development. She reads articles and listens to programs on mental illness. She talks to other families about their experiences. She visits the patient's doctors, asks questions over and over. What is it? What went wrong? How can I set it right again? She listens to the patient's own life review, trades recollections, follows small bits of evidence down endless blind allies. She absorbs the impact of the patient's fear and frustration at being ill, receives the blame for presumed wrongdoings.

Having recognized more immediately than others the true extent of the patient's impairments, she lives with her heart in her throat when the patient withdraws and refuses contact. When the patient ventures away from the shelter of home, she waits for the phone to ring, and is shot through with fear and relief when the call finally comes. Where are you? Are you all right? What are you doing for money? Who are you staying with? Will you please call again soon? She suffers more acutely than other family members, and in some ways even more than the patient, experiencing with each fluctuation in functioning, and with each return of symptoms the collapse of her hopefulness. She makes the contacts to arrange for readmission to hospital, and goes with the patient when the time comes. She tells the story of relapse to doctors, social workers, and endless others, revealing her discouragements, her frustrations, her private theories of cause and cure, all in the hope that something will turn the illness around and restore the patient's former state of aliveness. She witnesses the impatience and naïveté of over-worked, well-meaning professionals. She takes in their suggestions for modifying family life, and suffers from the implications. Either they took too close an interest, or put too much pressure on, or attended too little to the early evidence of trouble. She sinks in an agony of remorse and self-reproach. Then, so as to prepare for continued service, she redoubles her efforts, cutting herself off still more from life beyond the patient. Her life slides gradually into a constant stream of nursing activities. Relief comes only in the transient evidences of peace of mind in the patient, some enjoyment, some small mastery. Time away from the task is spent thinking about the ill person, about what else can be done. In time, all life outside her preoccupation vanishes. The illness has become her *raison d'être* and she has been reduced to the shadow of her charge.

## The Second Tier of Involvement

Even though a primary caregiver's emotional involvement with the patient may be no greater than that of other members of the family, there are substantial differences in their experience of the illness. By reason of their less intimate exposure to the evidence of incapacity, others are less dominated by the patient's daily routines. Leaving the confines of the home, they put aside illness-related concerns for long stretches of time, during which other interests and necessities absorb them. Two qualitative differences in experience follow from having retained a life apart from the illness. Second-tier relatives may experience less frequent intrusions into the flow of experience when away from the patient. Paradoxically, however, they may experience a more noticeable interruption of their outside interests when some worrisome aspect of the illness inserts itself into consciousness. They may experience wider and more abrupt shifts in felt burden, from extensive dissociation from the patient and disavowal of the illness, to intense and immediate terror, irritation, and despair. As a result, they, more than primary caregivers, may come to dread the illness and the patient, and erect avoidant defenses against involvement. The illness becomes the enemy of a carefully guarded repose. Work, friends, interests away from the household, all take on special importance as they become means of containing the intrusion of illness-related concerns into their daily experience.

Divergences in response to illness between first- and second-tier caregivers threatens the family's preexisting cohesiveness. Just as second-tier members erect barriers against involvement with the patient, they may also develop an aversion to involvement with the primary caregiver. In her single-minded concern with the patient, she may attempt to involve others, even the whole family, in one or another aspect of the caretaking enterprise. She talks to them about the patient, invites their participation, seeks their advice. Others may find such conversation and entreaties just as disruptive as direct confrontations with the patient's illness-related behavior. They may seal themselves off from the primary caregiver. Husband and wife become estranged. Brother grows remote from sister. Child ceases contact with parent. For the primary caregiver, there is no choice but ministering to the patient. For the rest, the option to escape the pressures of the first tier of involvement is viable and often exercised in the service of self-preservation.

## The Third Tier of Involvement

The position of members of the family outside the immediate household differs from that of each previous group. Grown siblings, aunts, uncles, grandparents, cousins, and all other relatives may share with members of the immediate household a generalized interest in the patient's welfare, but often have substantially less direct contact with illness and patient. Like second-tier relatives, they may underplay or disavow the presence of illness and incapacity, regarding the patient as faking or lazy, and claiming that the illness is cured when it is merely in remission. Concern about patient and caregivers may be interspersed with bewilderment and irritation arising from the dissonance in beliefs—their own and those of the primary and secondary caregivers—regarding appropriate responses to illness and patient. They may experience a helplessness deriving from their remoteness from the situation; wonder about their own contributions and obligations; fear that the primary caregiver or second-tier relatives are mishandling the situation; and fantasize about rescuing the patient from excesses or insufficiencies of the primary caregiver. One grandmother, whose 15-year-old severely impaired grandson visited her several times a week, insisted that the problem stemmed from her daughter's attitudes. "He needs more love. She's never happy and that hurts him."

Together with other members of the immediate family, third-tier members may seek to circumscribe the impact of the illness on their own lives. On the other hand, they are not exposed so directly and intensively to the illness, the patient, or the concerns of the primary caregiver. Less subject to these intrusions, they may be more accessible to patient and caregiver, albeit in a less constant fashion than second-tier members.

## LABELING AND MODELING OF ILLNESS BY RELATIVES

Diagnosis is the first step in understanding and treating illness. It is also a potential area of suffering for families. In contemporary Western societies, the diagnostic terms "schizophrenia," "mania," "depression," "personality disorder," "alcoholism," and others have no universally accepted meaning and do not conjure up specific images of circumscribed problems, but rather amorphous images of dreaded outcomes—a back-ward lunatic in a straitjacket, a criminal, a skid-row bum, or funereal images of suicide and murder. It is these images, to which diagnosis is a catalyst, that so deeply frighten relatives, causing them to step onto the path toward recognition of illness in shock and disbelief. Beyond this primal imagery, though, the problem presented to relatives by a psychiatric diagnosis lies in its easy capacity to invade and corrode their sense of history—their images of the family's past and future. Disruption of the meaning of past and future are mediated by the manner in which the relative models cause and outcome of illness.

## The Relative's Model of Etiology

Family members who believe that their relative's illness has *biological* roots are in a very different position from those who regard the illness as arising from interpersonal, and especially intrafamilial interaction. The former may conjure up extreme images of a mentally deficient, palsied idiot, thereby causing the relatives to ignore areas of preserved functioning in the patient. They are likely to experience helplessness in the face of the illness and overvalue professional attention, especially physical treatments and research into physical causes. They may worry that other family members are genetically vulnerable to developing the illness and may experience despair for the patient's future, to the extent that the presumed physical underpinnings of the illness are also perceived as inalterable. However, they are less likely to attribute the illness to misconduct on the part of the family or to experience the patient as lazy or faking, and they are more likely to take useful distance from the patient.

By contrast, relatives who hold an *interpersonal* theory of etiology are at risk for blaming family members, including themselves, for the illness, reasoning that as the family is the source of character, it is also the source of madness. In our time, mothers are most subject to this form of retrospective scrutiny, coming under fire from themselves, other relatives, and the patient, as well as from friends and professionals. However, every member of the family may apply a similar scrutiny to all other members. Mother was too careful. Father was too critical. Sister did not include him enough in her life. Brother did not help enough with schoolwork. Grandfather should have taken more of an interest in him. Aunt might have invited him for weekends. Cousins should have known something was going wrong in the immediate family and responded somehow.

Two especially malevolent consequences follow upon this line of analysis operating within the family. First, members of the family are set against each other as accuser and accused. Very often, in order to preserve the peace, blameful discussion is avoided, and, instead, what develops is a particularly corrosive form of silence, punctuated by vituperative confrontations at moments of crisis. So, over years, though no one is speaking openly or directly about it, each member privately convicts someone, whether it be self or another. The ultimate, extreme implication of this development is that mutual trust and respect among members of the family is extensively degraded. Images of self or other family member as damager, as soul-killer, as evil despoiler of independence and aliveness, intrude into the minds of all family members, competing with and supplanting, to some extent, more benevolent imagery. In some families, a kind of cold war mentality may surface, laying waste many potential moments of nurturance and mutual enjoyment. A son reasons, "if mother did that to my sister, then I must presume she has or will do some similar damage to me." Even more disturbing may be the thought that one has been spared, evoking a further complication in the form of survivor's guilt and raising questions about what stroke of fate or what aspect of character explains the exemption: "What do I have to do to make sure she doesn't do it to me too?"

A second and related adverse effect of the family's own interpersonal theory is that the stream of development is intruded on by acts geared to repair damage to the patient or prevent it in others. Whatever behavior a family member imagines to have been the source of the illness is reversed and this opposing behavior is presented to the patient. Of course, it is possible that such changes will actually be salutory, though more by luck than design. More likely, the changes add nothing to the quality of the patient's life or actually confound his or her own efforts at recovery. For example, if parents come to believe that they gave the patient too much space in the past, they may now hover over him or her, unwittingly blocking development of autonomous action and appropriate self-regulatory behavior.

Reparative motivations may also have effects on other members of the family, including future generations. The parents in the preceding example may hover over their other children. Or a sibling, arriving at the same conclusion, may resolve to hover over her own children years hence. Here the motive is prevention rather than reparation, but the result is the same—interference with the interpersonal processes by which relatives cue to needs in others and respond in timely and appropriate ways.

Interpersonal modeling may interfere with appropriate modification of behavior. Fearing that some past actions may have led to the illness, and acting on the premise that changing is equivalent to having been a damager, a relative may staunchly adhere to this line of action, buffering him- or herself against remorse of unbearable intensity. Ironically, the problem with continuing prior behavior may be related more to interference with flexible present-time cueing than with any direct-past insult arising from the action.

Notwithstanding these untoward developments, relatives holding to an interpersonal view may be less likely to feel hopeless. The illness seems less ominous since it is perceived as alterable, that is, by changing external influences impinging on the patient. One mother remarked, "I was even willing to be wrong if it would make my daughter better!" She had experienced intense guilt and had consistently been involved in attempts to rectify her presumed harmful influence on her daughter, but as long as she retained an interpersonal model of its roots, she would not perceive her daughter as internally wounded or permanently altered. She maintained hope at the expense of guilt.

## The Relative's Model of Prognosis

Most relatives encounter mental illness for the first time with a simplified view of the course the illness will take. One father, looking back on his 26-year-old daughter's first episode of illness at age 21, described sitting in an inpatient multiple-family group, listening to other relatives talk about relapses and remissions. He felt sorry for these other parents and out of place. He was *certain* his daughter would *never* be back in a hospital: although his daughter had always been a rather avoidant person, she was intelligent and had done well through 3½ years of college, and the whole course of her life, except for the 3 days prior to hospitalization were, as he viewed it, incompatible with a future of remissions, relapses, and limited functioning. On the other end of the spectrum are relatives who cannot picture a favorable outcome. Whether because of prior experience with a mentally ill person or prevailing public images of incurability and chronicity, some find it impossible to imagine a future in which their relative is ill-but-recovered. Whereas the former may have a bouyant future-oriented attitude toward the patient and ignore evidence of prolonged, especially subtle or invisible impairments, the latter is at risk of capsizing into irretrievable despair and passivity.

In practice, modeling processes may get very complex. At a given point in time, a particular relative may find that his or her method of internally representing etiology and prognosis draws on several conflicting sources. Preformed attitudes arising from general public attitudes toward mental illness intersect with more informed estimates arising from contemporary research, and with notions evolving from direct contact with a particular mentally ill person, a relative. The latter undergo modification as a function of duration of illness, the specific profile of symptoms to which the relative is a witness, the orientation of others to the illness, the efficacy of treatments, and so on. Moreover, public knowledge and beliefs about mental illness change over time as a function of the availability of new scientific information and the level of public exposure to the mentally ill.

## CONTRIBUTIONS FROM THE PATIENT AND THE ILLNESS

Exposure to various aspects of a mental illness and to its treatment, including the attitudes of patient, relatives, therapists, and others to the illness, all have an effect on the meaning given to the illness at a moment in time.

## Premorbid Personality of the Patient

Unlike professionals, relatives have known an intact, whole person prior to the appearance of illness. Who this person was, in the experience of the relative, heavily influences the relative's experience when the illness finally becomes manifest. So, for example, the parents of a vibrant, charming, academically successful young person will experience an agonizing sense of loss when illness strips these talents away.

> It came as an utter and unbelievable surprise. We are still in a state of shock. We are all grieving for years now. We have watched a young life that was eager, healthy, attractive, with intelligence, humor, and incisive sensitivity into human relationships, waste away, without any friends (when there were so many in the first 20 years), unable to stand any stress, being self-conscious and terrified, and almost never free from voices assailing him and sounds he cannot bear. (Mother of 28-year-old son ill 8 years)

In contrast, parents of a young person who was shy, dependent, overly sensitive, and who always had trouble keeping up in school experienced much less of a sense of loss when their child reached an equivalent level of disability. Some relatives, in this latter situation, report feeling relieved, as though they had been waiting for years "for the other shoe to drop." In the first instance, the illness meant the destruction of a highly valued idealized image of the patient's future, while in the other it constituted a confirmation of pre-existing images of the child as vulnerable or wounded. In between these two extremes, there are numerous possibilities for mixtures of shock and relief, as a function of the profile of the patient's premorbid talents and deficits, as perceived by the relative. Divergent views may develop as the relative recalls conflicting aspects of the patient's premorbid self.

## Specific Illness-Related Behaviors

As described in Chapter 3, the range of variation for behavior related to mental illness is enormous, and it is beyond the scope of this chapter to catalog any significant portion of these behaviors or their meaning to relatives. Certain illness-related behaviors are so commonly present that their generic meaning deserves separate mention here. *Withdrawal* is practically universal and evokes the most varied responses among relatives. For one person withdrawal may represent laziness, while for another it may suggest impending loss of control and disaster. For the former, withdrawal signifies not illness so much as moral terpitude, and appears to call for vigorous, activating interventions. For the latter, withdrawal is very much a sign of illness-related vulnerability, indicating the patient's need for peace and a minimum of performance pressure. In addition, relatives may feel devalued by a withdrawing patient. That is, the patient's avoidance is taken not as a statement about his or her internal state, but rather as a negative evaluation of the observing relative.

*Bizarre conduct, incoherent speech*, and reports from the patient of *unusual perceptions* (i.e., hallucinations) or *unusual beliefs* may evoke fear of or compassion for the patient (or both). These frank departures from ordinary reality, being more easily recognizable as manifestations of illness, may evoke less annoyance or hurt than withdrawal. *Irritable, argumentative, aggressive behavior* lies somewhere between withdrawal and bizarre behavior, much more consistently triggering annoyance, especially if aggression is directed toward members of the family. Aggression may evoke less conflicted responses than withdrawal and less compassionate responses than frankly bizarre behavior.

## Patient's Manifest Sensitivity to the Human Environment

Most mentally ill persons are supersensitive to the manner in which they are treated and the respect they are accorded by family, friends, and others they encounter (Vaughn & Leff, 1976). From the relative's point of view, however, the problem is that this sensitivity is variably evident. Some patients immediately and vigorously demonstrate distress when treated inappropriately. Others conceal their vulnerability by delaying and muting the manifestations of distress. In the former situation, relatives may quickly learn to cue to the patient's specific sensitivities, and even take to "walking on eggshells" in an attempt to forestall periods of hurt and emotional outburst. The illness may come to mean inhibition of specific behaviors in the presence of the patient. In the latter case, however, relatives may never be able to establish meaningful connections between an episode of distress or deterioration and events or interactions with the ill person and so they feel that they are constantly haunted by something unpredictable or whimsical.

## Stage of Illness

Relatives may have little difficulty recognizing an acute deterioration in functioning accompanying bizarre behavior and nonsensical speech as evidence of illness. Their experience at these times is likely to be characterized by sympathy, empathy, and understanding for the patient. But *prior* to the appearance of gross evidence of impairment, and *after* the acute symptoms have subsided (i.e., during prodromal and residual phases), they may not believe the patient has a legitimate claim to the sick role. From the view of the relative, the prodromal period and the phase of remission are often times in which the patient is seen as not ill. During these times, withdrawal, underactivity, seclusiveness, lack of interest in ordinary activities of life are likely to leave relatives feeling taken advantage of, ignored, and disrespected by a person who is manipulating or exaggerating his or her troubles. Very often, the ability to perceive the patient as having a continuing vulnerability, especially when he or she is not blatantly impaired, develops only after repeated experiences of remission and relapse. Thus relatives in the midst of the first period of remission are much more at risk for feeling used than are those in the 3rd or 5th or 10th remission. Early on, resentment of the patient is common during remissions, as are shock and disbelief when the reappearance of manifestly disordered behavior makes it clear that the behavior during a previous prodromal or residual period was illness-related after all.

## Course of Illness

In the absence of broad prior experience, the relative's model of the outcome of illness is often heavily influenced by the patient's present state. One father remarked, "It's how my boy is, is how I feel." Thus when his son was in the throes of a florid, stormy relapse, spending time in jail and subsequently in hospital, this man was continuously depressed, and he was cheerful and jocular when his son started dating and returned to school. Only over the course of 6 years of a relapsing-remitting course did the father begin to assemble a more complicated model, suggesting that he might reasonably expect some degree of fluctuation in his son's functioning. The simplest effects on relatives (although by no means the easiest to accept) are had with illnesses that produce constant deficits or move quickly toward enduring remission. However, the great majority of mental illnesses today run a fluctuating course (Bleuler, 1978). The effect on relatives is similar to that on the prisoner dragged before the firing squad daily only to be given a last minute reprieve. One mother remarked,

> You can't grieve with this illness because you never know what to expect next. Just when you are getting adjusted to the idea she's a permanent hospital patient, she improves. And while you are adjusting to her getting better, she has a setback. You're always wondering, what's next? (Mother of 23-year-old daughter ill 7 years)

The relative's capacity to maintain an image of life as predictable and controllable is challenged by these fluctuations. Some relatives cease going on vacation or making plans to be out with friends, not because they are afraid to leave the patient, but because, after several disruptions, they no longer believe his or her present state will last long enough for them to carry a planned event to completion.

## Patient's Cooperativeness with Treatment

Nothing satisfies therapists or relatives more than an obviously ill patient who is an active agent in his or her own treatment and goes on to full recovery. But the course of illness, and the patient's capacity to be actively and optimistically involved is under constant assault from the various forces of demoralization, loss of insight into existence of illness, the wish to be totally well, and more. It is inevitable, then, in the course of any illness that the patient will reject treatment either explicitly or covertly. Relatives witnessing these lapses in patienthood may experience helplessness about being deceived, mixed with apprehension about relapse, if they regard the person as ill.

> I know that I go up and down disastrously with the changes in her condition, and it is by supreme effort of thought that I maintain some equilibrium, even though she has been sick a long time now. When I hear that she is apart again and refusing treatment, I actually feel sick to the pit of my stomach. I feel a surge of despair with thoughts that if I were dead, I could be out of the whole mess. (Mother of 26-year-old ill 5 years)

On the other hand, regarding the person as recovered may lead to resentment over the rejection of treatment for producing what is seen as an unnecessary period of pessimism, apathy, and dependency. With time, and with the capacity to model a fluctuating course, relatives may become more capable of tolerating periods of inadherence with treatment.

## Incursions into the Family's Mutual Caregiving Patterns

Every routine household function (cooking, cleaning, washing up) that the patient ceases to perform either must be picked up by another member of the family or goes undone. Most families evolve over time a coordinated, implicit set of agreements for collective functioning. Whether household tasks are highly distributed or taken over predominantly by one or two persons, the loss of the patient's contribution to the household is noted, both as a loss of concrete caregiving services and as a failure of the implicit contract between family members. Since these agreements are so important to the continuation of relatives' experience of family mutuality and cohesiveness, this loss can be a significant source of resentment, no matter how extensive the family's recognition of illness. A decline in the patient's employment status may leave relatives with a financial burden accompanied by resentment based not just on current hardship but also on the loss of hoped-for future enjoyments. One wife wrote:

> For years I've looked forward to the day the kids would be grown and I could travel. Now I realize that, with my husband's illness I'll never be able to afford these things. It's like losing a leg! (Wife of 47-year-old man ill 6 years)

For many families, the most devastating effect on daily life is the loss of the patient's affectional responsiveness. In discussing his wife, one relative said, "I can take the mess around the house okay. It's I don't see she cares about us any more is the big hurt." Since the loss of affectional behavior may not be perceived as illness-related, relatives may not describe or experience its effects on them. Perhaps their reticence in this regard derives from the implication that, if the patient no longer cares about them, some essential aspect of what it means to be a family has been lost. The experience of being loved and positively valued, but also the capacity to reciprocate these sensibilities, is deeply challenged. These incursions are often not limited to relationships between relative and patient: the inability to love spreads to involve relationships between others in the family. At least until the family recognizes the patient's difficulty in caring as a manifestation of the illness, an invisible, an unspeakable emotional deadness exists in the family.

## THE RELATIVE'S PERSONALITY AND LIFE HISTORY

In addition to being shaped by variables having to do with proximity to, modeling of, and nature of illness, what mental illness means to a particular member of a family is influenced by certain aspects of that member's orientation to life, including attitudes related to place in the life cycle; response disposition in the face of hardship; and previous experience with mental illness in a family member, friend or self.

### The Relative's Place in the Life Cycle

Mental illness has different meanings for family members of different ages. For those in advanced adulthood it may have limited impact on self-definition and sense of future. For young and middle-aged *adults*, however, illness may substantially alter perceptions of self and one's sense of future. For example, the grown sibling of a newly ill younger brother reported reservations about getting married and related complications in his sense of commitment to his girlfriend of 8 years. He became preoccupied with certain similarities of cognitive style, that is, a tendency to pull back in the face of vigorous emotional interaction. He also became preoccupied with the question whether his brother's illness was genetic in nature, and freely admitted that he wondered whether he might father children similarly affected.

The effects on generational peers is not always so obvious. Young adult cousins of a 24-year-old man ill and currently hospitalized for the third time in 6 years spent whole evenings together reassuring each other that their cousin was *not* ill but only pretending to be ill. They were uniformly unreceptive to the possibility that he really was very ill. Nor did they voice any concerns about their own health. But the topic of his behavior did frequently dominate their conversation.

Parents in early and middle adulthood at onset of an adolescent's mental illness may experience extensive concerns about self and future self. Does this illness mean I am a damaging influence on children? What about the other kids? Can *I* get sick in this way? Will I be a caregiver for the rest of my life? Ordinary age-appropriate experiences of ambivalence toward children are intensified. Confusion about one's identity as an adult, or at least as a *useful* adult, is heightened.

Members of the family who are adolescents when another member becomes ill experience equivalent intensification of ordinary phase-appropriate identity confusion. How often does something like this happen? Is it connected to growing up? Is it worth growing up if this is what happens? Is there any reason that this will *not* happen to me? The resulting cloud of self-doubt may endure well into adulthood. It may influence career choices. One adolescent chose a career in medicine or nursing, while another became a vegetarian and joined an Eastern religious cult church within a year of the first illness of a cousin. It may influence choice of spouse. One college student whose mother was mentally ill in her adolescence selected for boyfriends only those who were entering psychology or psychiatry. She herself later became a social worker. Finally, adolescents may be more likely to experience shame and dread that their peers will discover that they have a mentally ill relative.

For those who are children during the onset of illness, the central issue is the impact of the illness on the child's experience of order, constancy, and nurturance. For a 7-year-old girl whose mother spent

2 years in the hospital, the main question was, "Who'll take care of me?" She developed an extremely close relationship with an older sister, and later placed great emphasis on continuity of involvement with her own children. The illness may also evoke concerns about having caused the illness. One 8-year-old thought that his mother got sick because he never obeyed her immediately and often complained about having to go to bed on time.

## The Relative's Generic Responses to Hardship

Related to place in the life cycle is the relative's internal resourcefulness in coping with various threats represented by the illness. One woman seemed only minimally perturbed by her son's frequent relapses, even though he often brought the family into the public eye with his behavior. Yet another found each of her daughter's periods of disorganization wrenching in the extreme, even though the daughter was well liked and repeatedly recruited a great many caregivers to her aid in a distant state.

Certain differences in the experiences of these two women are more a reflection of enduring personality traits than responses to specific aspects of the illnesses they confronted. The first woman characteristically took a benevolent view of each development in her son's struggle to recover, minimizing signs of trouble until some dramatic event drove home unavoidably that he had relapsed. Only rarely did she appear to lose contact with a vision of a future in which he would be better. Her own sense of self-worth seemed unaffected by the fluctuations in his clinical state. By contrast, the second woman reported minor fluctuations in her daughter's condition, and usually foresaw relapse in advance of the daughter's therapists. Except when the daughter was in full remission and working productively, she experienced a painful loss of all images of a future daughter except that of a demented, institutional inmate. Her own self-worth sank, and would have crashed altogether except that she launched in such moments into a critique of the clinicians for their inability to maintain the daugther in a state of remission. Under similar circumstances of severity, stage, and course of illness, these two women differed strikingly in the degree to which their self-worth and their vision of a better future were challenged by fluctuations in the clinical state of the ill offspring. These and other largely uninvestigated personality variables contribute to an unknown but substantial degree to the relative's experience of illness.

*Prior Experience with Mental Illness in the Family*

Families experiencing mental illness for the first time are in a different position from those with some prior experience. The novice family must construct ways of understanding the patient's behavior and ways of responding, while at the same time securing the patient in a crisis situation, acquiring basic information about treatment facilities, and deciding who to tell and what information to give about the illness and the patient's status. In the veteran family, on the other hand, some members may function as expert informants to the household in which the second illness has developed. This expertise may be a two-edged sword. The course followed by the first-ill member may reassure the immediate family of the second-ill provided the first-ill had a short-lived illness and recovered completely. When the outcome is less optimistic, the course of the first-ill serves as a warning of dreaded possibilities. As a result, relatives of the first-ill may be effectively excluded from the circle of care for the second-ill. In one family, parents staunchly held to the view that their son had a drug problem even though the son had had periods of erratic behavior quite similar to that in a chronically psychotic cousin. They consulted the cousin's psychiatrist about their own son without informing the cousin's parents, and did not discuss the cousin or the cousin's illness until the psychiatrist did.

The appearance of mental illness in a second family member is also a two-edged sword for the immediate family of the first-ill. On the one hand, it may relieve guilt and dissipate blame if the second illness promotes a shift from an interpersonal to a heritable model of etiology. Such was the case for the parents of the severely ill cousin in the previous vignette. On the other hand, members of the family who feel personally immune to illness even after the first illness may become apprehensive after the appearance of a similar illness in another relative. In one family, relatives held that a woman's illness was due to psychological abuse at the hands of her husband, and ignored the possible genetic implications even when the woman's nephew became similarly ill. The second illness threatened to overturn a major explanatory system through which the loyalty bonds to her own parents and siblings were secured.

## THE RELATIVE'S SOCIAL NETWORK

Mental illness is usually experienced as an intrusion into the preexisting life of a family. Given this historical perspective, all of the variables discussed above interact in vastly complex and largely uninvestigated ways to disrupt the social network of each member of the family. Dislocation in the network produces, in turn, a new and usually more restricted and less rewarding definition of one's place in a community.

### The Relative's Natural Network

It has frequently been observed that families of the mentally ill are socially isolated (Beels, 1975). Unfortunately, this aspect of the family's life is usually taken as evidence of social incompetence or seen as a limiting factor in efforts to gain access to the family for purposes of family therapy or other maneuvers to benefit the patient. What has, as a result, been neglected is the mechanisms by which social isolation arises with the appearance of mental illness in a family member. First, as noted in Chapter 2, there is a general tendency for any person in crisis times to narrow the field of interest. Friends and acquaintances, together with many social involvements, drop away in the service of concentrated attention to the new problem. However, relatives of the mentally ill experience a special isolation inasmuch as their problem is both uncommon and feared. One parent remarked,

> There is that terrible sense of isolation we all have felt as individuals. No matter how sympathetic friends are, you still have that sense of being somewhat of a pariah with some hideous problem that makes you a creature to be pitied. That's a terrible role to assume. (Mother of 25-year-old son ill 6 years)

Family members often relate to friends and neighbors through the vehicle of reports about offspring. Adults talk about their children and grandchildren. Adolescents talk about their brothers and sisters. In these encounters, the relatives of the mentally ill are at a disadvantage. If they conceal the truth, they alienate themselves from the inquirer. If they reveal the truth, they risk exposure to embarrassment, pity, and naive encouragement.

> The focus has always been, when you talk to friends, on "is he getting *better*, is he getting *well*?" It's very frustrating to have a mentally ill child, to be faced with a perpetual traumatic situation, and to have well-meaning friends asking, in effect, when it will be over. You know it will never be over, but how can they know that and believe that? (Father of 25-year-old son ill 6 years)

Friends are also at a disadvantage, inasmuch as they have little contact with the ill person in present time, that is, during the period of the illness. Their disbelief and bewilderment is reminiscent of that in relatives, except that in the absence of corrective exposure to the patient, it is not likely to move toward acceptance. Resolution of these tensions between caregiving relatives and their friends commonly takes the form of quiet, mutual avoidance. But while friends move on to new friends, the relatives of the mentally ill stay more and more to themselves. Just as their access to alternate involvements is sealed off by mutual avoidance, so also is their desire for social encounters muted by the anticipation of public humiliations.

Similar processes are at work in relationships even closer to kinship. Take for example the responses of a fiancee of one patient's brother. Raised by an alcoholic father in a modeling environment that attributed mental illness to the influence of parents, this young woman came to regard her future in-laws with suspicion, a development that in turn produced a palpable alienation between her fiance and his parents. Subsequently the couple married and took an interest in the ill brother that arose in part from her wish to rescue the ill brother from his parents, and partly from her husband's desire to alleviate guilt at having isolated himself from his parents. From the point of view of the parents of the ill brother, the illness not only introduced a new burden, but also interrupted a central element in their mutual network—ongoing mutual enjoyment of their successful son and his new wife.

Chains of interaction involving multiple variables acting simultaneously and in sequence give rise over time to an altered, leaner natural network surrounding each relative. Two further interconnected aspects of these network distortions bear on the meaning of the illness. First, the extent of involvement of outsiders with the ill member usually diminishes over time. Second, the balance of caregiving and respite attained for primary caregivers shifts increasingly toward more caregiving. Take for example the situation of a mother who assumes primary caregiver status for a daughter whose illness is regarded by other family members as an endless burden. Suppose the mother is blamed by others in the family for the illness and at the same time is given little support in her caregiver role. For this woman, the balance shifts largely in the direction of caregiving, with little opportunity for meaningful respite. At the same time, under the cumulative weight of her own guilt, blame from others, and the leaden, hopeless specter of decades of disability, she experiences a loss of self-esteem.

Although there is strong, ongoing pressure for diminished involvement with extrafamilial parts of the relative's and the patient's natural networks, some relationships may deepen to unexpected levels of affirmation, support, and mutual respect. A young woman geneticist from a family with no prior experience of mental illness regarded her future brother-in-law's mental illness as a threat to her unborn children. She

turned to colleagues for information about risk factors in mental illness and learned from her future in-laws that the illness arose from an
obstetrical complication and that no one else in the family was affected. The daughter-in-law experienced significant reassurance about
her own future as a mother, while the mother-in-law experienced
herself as a nurturer and mentor in an unexpected part of the next
generation. From the vantage point of the parents, the illness may
actually have opened a significant new relationship in their network.

## The Relative's Illness-Related Network

Very few relatives possess a natural network with sufficient diversity
and density of resources to respond to all needs created by prolonged
caregiving to a mentally ill family member. The limits of the network
become evident when the relative seeks expert guidance in coping with
the illness and its consequences in the life of the family. These encounters open up a new kind of network to the relative, a network in which
membership is tied to the relative's status as a caregiver. Two aspects
of this new network deserve separate emphasis: (1) encounters with
mental health clinicians and (2) encounters with other family caregivers.

### ENCOUNTERS WITH MENTAL HEALTH CLINICIANS

Direct involvement between family and professional caregivers has
increased dramatically in recent years as the mentally ill have moved
from institutional to community care. The encounter has not always
gone well, however. Hatfield (1982) wrote that despite a common
interest in the patient's welfare, professionals and relatives are still
very often worlds apart. Terkelsen (1983) suggested that theories invoking family interaction in the etiology of mental illness produce
misalliances between clinicians and relatives, and wrote of the need to
specifically absolve family members of initial causal responsibility for
the illness as a precondition of meaningful collaboration. Where this
does not take place, relatives may acquire attitudes toward themselves
and the patient that interfere with constructive coping. Left to their
own devices in a culture that holds parents responsible for all developments in children, family members may feel that parental authority is
challenged by the sheer existence of mental illness. Certain hospital
and clinic policies and practices may foster this view. For example,
telling parents that they cannot visit or phone their own child in a
hospital, or insisting that all members come to family therapy sessions,
are practices from which family members may infer that parental
authority is being discredited.

Recent recognition in the professional community of the positive role that family members play in the care and rehabilitation of the mentally ill is leading to a more constructive professional orientation toward the family. Since these changes are occurring more rapidly in some institutions than in others, family members will encounter many discrepancies and disagreements in the next 20 years. For example, parents of a 21-year-old daughter ill 5 years were told not to visit their daughter in her halfway house more than once a week, and under no circumstances to let her sleep at home. A year later the halfway house employed a new social worker recently trained in family therapy. The social worker called the parents in for family therapy sessions, even though the parents had not indicated a desire for such treatment. Two months later, the director of the halfway house told the parents, in front of their daughter, that they should start making plans to take their daughter home soon. When the parents pointed out that this seemed like an abrupt shift from agency policy and all that had gone before, the director replied that things had changed and that they now saw families as being good for patients. To the parents, nothing had changed: despite an apparent shift in orientation toward the family, the agency had not considered the impact of a return home on the parents or on other members of the household. Little respect had been paid to the family's life and welfare apart from their relationship to the ill member.

## ENCOUNTERS WITH OTHER FAMILY CAREGIVERS

That "terrible sense of isolation" described by one parent is overcome for many relatives upon meeting others performing similar roles in other families. Making contact with other persons confronting similar issues can rapidly neutralize years of experiencing the problems of caregiving as if they were unique. That "sense of being a pariah . . . a creature to be pitied" is reduced by being with other caregivers and hearing that others have experienced the same unpleasantness, the same despair, anger, and anxiety. And if the future must be uncertain, at least there are other lives to follow. Successes may serve to inspire those caregivers who have yet to see favorable developments in their ill relative. The failures may forewarn of the tentativeness of recoveries generally, and also console those who are facing failures themselves. In time a composite picture begins to form for the caregiver, representing the range of outcomes. Indeed, there are some who have dreadful outcomes and some others who do amazingly well. But in hearing the stories again and again, relatives may begin to see that, for the most part, patients with prolonged mental illnesses run an uphill-downhill course, and, as a result, to take a more detached view of the advances and declines of their own ill member.

The capacity to endure in the face of a tenacious problem depends on the existence of a community of fellow sufferers who affirm and protect one's sense of worth even when the evidence of the moment is ambiguous or contrary, who share and keep alive a common interest in the midst of a wider society that does not care, who provide counsel and concrete assistance, and who foster a belief in the future when all others fail to do so. For relatives of the mentally ill, making contact with such a community provides a form of support unavailable in the professional sector of their illness-related network. It is a new form of *neighborhood*, in which neighbors are defined not by geography, but rather in terms of need.

What is unclear at this writing is the direction in which caregivers' neighborhoods will develop. In the past decade, there has been a virtual explosion of interest among relatives of the mentally ill in self-help and advocacy groups, with more than 650 having formed in this country. The interest achieved national proportions in 1979 with the formation of the National Alliance for the Mentally Ill. Organizations of this kind are just the beginning, and will be acceptable to only a portion of the totality of caregiving relatives. However, less formal connections are emerging, connections that closely reflect the structure of natural networks except that they are peopled exclusively by caregiving relatives. These neighbors do not convene under the auspices of an organization. They may meet for lunch or talk on the telephone, sharing and passing on the news flowing through the network. To be sure, many of the individuals peopling these invisible networks participate in formal organizational efforts as well, and it may be that the informal networks require their formal counterparts for their inspiration and continuity. What is unknown at this juncture is how all this will evolve. But what is certain is that formal and informal caregiver neighborhoods have great potential as supports for relatives of the mentally ill, and have immense impact on the meaning the illness has for them.

## REFERENCES

Beels, C. C. (1975). Family and social management of schizophrenia. *Schizophrenia Bulletin*, 1(13), 97–118.

Bleuler, M. (1978). *The schizophrenic disorders: Long-term patient and family studies* (S. M. Clemens, trans.). New Haven: Yale University Press.

Brown, G. W., Birley, J. L., & Wing, J. K. (1972). Influence of family life on the course of schizophrenic disorder: A replication. *British Journal of Preventive Social Medicine,* *16,* 55-68.

Falloon, I. R. H., Boyd, J. L., McGill, C. W., Razani, J., Moss, H. B., & Gilderman, A. M. (1982). Family management in the prevention of exacerbation of schizophrenia: A controlled study. *New England Journal of Medicine, 306,* 1437-1440.

Hatfield, A. B. (1982). Therapists and families: Worlds apart. *Hospital and Community Psychiatry, 33,* 513.

Kreisman, D. E., & Joy, V. D. (1974). Family response to the mental illness of a relative: A review of the literature. *Schizophrenia Bulletin,* 1(10), 34-57.

Mills, E. (1962). *Living with mental illness: A study in East London.* London: Routledge & Kegan Paul.

Rabkin, J. (1972). Opinions about mental illness: A review of the literature. *Psychological Bulletin, 77,* 153-171.

Rose, C. (1959). Relatives' attitudes and mental hospitalization. *Mental Hygeine, 43,* 194-203.

Sakamoto, Y. (1969). A study of the attitude of Japanese families of schizophrenics toward their ill members. *Psychotherapy and Psychosomatics, 17,* 365-374.

Schwartz, C. (1957). Perspectives on deviance: Wives' definitions of their husbands' mental illness. *Psychiatry, 20,* 275-291.

Terkelsen, K. G. (1983). Schizophrenia and the family: II. Adverse effects of family therapy. *Family Process, 22,* 191-200.

Vaughn, C. E., & Leff, J. P. (1976). The influence of the family and social factors on the course of psychiatric illness: A comparison of schizophrenic and depressed neurotic patients. *British Journal of Psychiatry, 129,* 125-137.

# The Evolution of Family Responses to Mental Illness through Time

## Kenneth G. Terkelsen

The ways families respond to mental illness vary as a function of time. To some extent, the variation is due to changes in the manifestations of illness and the degree of social and occupational disability attached to the illness; to such treatment-related factors as hospitalization, contact with professionals, and medication effects; and to intercurrent events and developments in the family unrelated to the illness. However, quite aside from these extrinsic factors, the way family members respond to mental illness and to the ill person undergoes its own patterned temporal development, a pattern that transcends individual differences in response disposition.

The purpose of this chapter is to trace this process as it is currently known. Since there are virtually no longitudinal investigations in this area of inquiry, the material for this chapter is derived from personal and clinical longitudinal experience with families. Accordingly, the longitudinal process of coming to terms with mental illness in a family member is represented as a series of phases. The intention in this form of exposition is to paint a picture of phenomena that, in real life, are constantly moving. No family proceeds in a lockstep fashion from one phase to the next and so on. Specifically, in virtually every family, there is great variation of the pace at which individual members move on this path. Recognizing and coming to terms with mental illness in a

Kenneth G. Terkelsen. Cornell University Medical Center, New York, New York.

loved one is a dubious and unredeeming business at best, and profoundly disruptive of the well-being of the family in all instances. In
such matters, where a favorable outcome in the affected person may
take years to attain and is often unattainable, the process by which
family members come to terms with the illness is often characterized
as much be stalemates and reversals as it is by forward movement.
This complexity is reduced in what follows in the service of fostering
for the reader a sense of the movement through time in the family's
responses to evidence of mental illness. It is this sense of movement,
that is of developing competence, that is essential for a full appreciation of the importance of the coping and adaptation perspective in
work with families of the mentally ill.

## PHASE ONE: IGNORING WHAT IS COMING

Although some psychotic episodes emerge literally "out of the blue," it
is typical that mental illness makes itself known to family members
and other intimates through the medium of subtle alterations in the
behavior and life-style of the affected person. Presumably because of
the dread of mental illness in the general population, many family
members react by minimizing these early changes, by ignoring their
significance as predictors of more extensive changes to come. What
will eventually be seen as the first symptoms of illness are initially
seen as normative variations of personality development or responses
to stressful life circumstances. Some family members adopt the attitude that these alterations of behavior will work themselves out in
time ("He'll grow out of it soon enough") or as a result of environmental
changes. Others may move in to find out what is troubling the affected
person, in a more proactive effort to provide assistance, expecting to
"nip it in the bud." Even in the latter circumstance, however, clear
recognition of the illness-related nature of the behavioral alterations is
not common. Typically at this stage of illness, family members approach unusual behavior as manifestations of temporary destabiliza-
tion rather than as the first signs of an enduring condition.

Since the behavioral changes are minimized or normalized or seen
as transient during this first phase, the psychological impact of the
illness is still circumscribed. Emotional reactions are confined to intermittent anxiety and vague feelings that something "might" be seriously
wrong. Often some family members will be overtly concerned about
the changes while others in the family are dismissing that concern and
advising time or a change in circumstance. These differences in re-

sponse occasionally lead to serious conflict regarding the need for a decisive response, but more commonly such disagreements as do arise are no different in intensity from all the other conflicts that are constantly arising and being resolved in the life of the family. None of the undermining of self-image and morale that will emerge later is apparent during this phase. The family as a whole is more or less inaccessible to concern manifested by outsiders, and does not seek, at least not in any consistent way, professional guidance.

## PHASE TWO: THE FIRST SHOCK OF RECOGNITION

Eventually something happens. The adaptive decline or constriction of life-style of the affected person escalates past some invisible threshold of severity sufficiently to trigger major and enduring concern in more than one family member. Indisputable manifestations of mental illness appear and persist and can no longer be minimized, normalized, or regarded as temporary. Or some outside person—a friend of the affected person, a teacher, an employer—makes a compelling case that the manifestations that have been apparent for some time are really of greater significance than has been thought by the family. Or the most concerned member of the family manages to recruit an outside expert to convince the more sanguine relatives as to the seriousness of the situation. By whatever route, the family is for the first time mobilized by recognition of mental illness to a course of action appropriate to the presence of significant infirmity in a family member.

At this juncture, several responses, variously represented in each family, emerge. Some organize to get professional help, making calls and visits to doctors and social workers, to clinics and hospitals. Others redouble earlier efforts to "reach" the affected person, by exhorting him or her to seek help, by trying to engage him or her in discussion in an attempt to find something that is "bothering" the affected person and advising changes in life-style so as to diminish the effect of the offending processes. Still others enjoin the affected person to "pull himself together" or to "get his life back on the tracks." Regardless of whether the family moves toward organized professional help or toward its own or other nonprofessional forms of assistance, the common denominators of this phase are persistent and increasingly urgent help-seeking behavior, intensifying anxiety, and dread of the now more compelling possibility of further worsening of the affected person's social and occupational disabilities and of the appearance of life-threatening behaviors.

## PHASE THREE: STALEMATE

Almost without exception, things do not go well. The affected person is often not as far along in terms of recognizing the implications of the changes in him- or herself and rejects help, whether it be professional intervention or the assistance, interest, and inquiry of family and friends. This recalcitrance, whether it be a further manifestation of the illness or a reflection of the affected person's own need to minimize the significance of the changes, often disrupts the family's help-seeking efforts. Unity around the idea that something serious and enduring is afoot is still quite new, and often collapses at the first signs of reluctance from the affected person. Those who were last to recognize that there is real trouble are the first to change their minds and revert to their earlier stance of normalizing, minimizing, and temporizing. In these circumstances, even those whose recognition endures the affected person's first rebuffs are confused, bewildered, and overcome with a sense of helplessness, so unaccustomed are they to having their efforts to help rejected. Alternatively, the family seeks outside help and is told that the situation is not as serious as they think. Professionals have their own timetable for recognizing illness, leading them to normalize, minimize, and temporize. In addition, professionals may divert attention from the rising evidence of impairment in the affected family member, focusing instead on anxiety and discord among other family members and concluding that it is the family as a whole or some particular members other than the affected person who require professional attention. Finally, whether in response to the attention given by the family or in an active effort to conceal the extent of impairments, the affected person may find her- or himself having less trouble and may even, pull her- or himself together, temporarily improving social and occupation functioning and decreasing displays of overtly disordered behavior.

In the face of these confounding developments, anxiety may increase to panic proportions while conflict between family members comes more and more into the open. Some members find themselves retreating into emotional distance, while others grow increasingly preoccupied with the affected person and lose all concern for self. Other family problems naturally arising in the ordinary course of life are ignored as the problem of the affected person's welfare occupies center stage more and more in the life of the family. In turn, these problems may intensify, since insufficient attention is being paid to them, or may recede as the family collectively and often without very much open discussion finds itself prioritizing and postponing appropriate problem-solving activity. At times, family members find themselves stalled in open and continuing conflict regarding the affected person's problematic behavior, no longer able to ignore, yet unable to act effectively.

## PHASE FOUR: CONTAINING THE IMPLICATIONS OF ILLNESS

Faced with a persistent disparity between evidence of a serious problem and inability to solve that problem, many family members attempt to cope by limiting the implications. Some will retreat from the affected person in order to diminish exposure to the evidence of impairment. Others will revert to minimizing and temporizing. Others, especially if the affected person has "improved" or if professionals have given a minimizing opinion regarding the implications, will conclude that he or she was ill but is "all better now." Still others will conclude that the problem lies outside of the affected person, in the form of drugs, adverse environmental influences, or incompetent professional attention, or that the person suffers from exhaustion or from a physical illness for which there is a cure, albeit not yet applied. Others will conclude that the affected person is not impaired at all, but is faking it or is just being lazy. The common denominator in this phase is the attempt to circumscribe the implications of the decline in functioning. If the affected person does indeed have a problem, it is not necessarily to be regarded as insoluble, not necessarily enduring, and not necessarily arising from any infirmity or vulnerability residing within the affected person himself. He is not sick or ill. He does not have a disease. Or if he does have a disease, it is one that can easily be cured or will resolve the way that a cold or a pneumonia does. During this phase, the notion of an enduring infirmity within the affected person that will not give way to available forms of help is still beyond comprehension. Family members may continue to experience high levels of anxiety, may still be distracted from other problems, and may still experience a diminished interest in their own usual activities and pursuits. But they are still optimistic and hopeful, and they do not yet know about the rage and despair, the shame and guilt that will fill their experience as the problem continues or gets worse.

## PHASE FIVE: TRANSFORMATION TO OFFICIAL PATIENTHOOD

Eventually something very compelling or disastrous occurs. The affected person becomes impaired or out of control to the point where life, his or her own or someone else's is threatened. There is a suicide attempt, an assault, or an arrest for disturbing the peace, some behavior that forces the attention of public authorities onto the affected person and onto the family. The affected person's social status is transformed to that of "patient." He or she is officially identified as a psychiatric patient, as a person with a life-threatening emotional or mental illness. Whether suddenly or in small steps, the family is hit with the full force of the implications: One of the family has a mental infirmity that will not go away. This realization sets in motion the processes detailed in Chapter 6. The meaning of mental illness in the family now spreads throughout virtually every aspect of the family's functioning. Preexisting inclinations to minimize and temporize will continue for some families and for some members in most families, but now these are less efforts to ward off the anxiety regarding the existence of mental illness than they are attempts to fight back its implications.

## PHASE SIX: THE SEARCH FOR CAUSES

Built into the Western orientation to illness is the notion that informed action is predicated on a detailed understanding of the cause or causes of the condition. Thus, as soon as the family accepts the presence of mental illness, the search for causes emerges in full force. The direction of the search depends on the family's preexisting beliefs about the nature of mental illness. Some families look for trouble in the family. Other families seek a biological explanation.

In nearly every family, given the contemporary popular and professional view that mental illness derives in large part from the quality of family life, everyone, or at least those regarded as the functional authorities in the family, experience a rising sense of personal, existential guilt regarding the presence of mental illness in the affected person. Some will cope with guilt by resolving to alter their own conduct and the conduct of the family as a whole, launching a campaign to cleanse the family of its presumed toxicity. They will open themselves to professional help aimed at improving the quality of family interaction, entering into family therapy, multiple-family group therapy, and related encounters with experts in family interaction. Others will cope with guilt by blaming someone or something else. They may agree that the family is a toxic force for the patient, but focus the blame on some other family member's conduct. Thus the effort to cleanse the family becomes, for these, more a form of indictment of the "truly guilty party" than an effort to improve the quality of family life for the patient. And while anxiety may diminish as the family seeks to heal itself, the whole of the family's life is now flooded by guilt, blame, and an endless stream of overt and covert recriminations. If sufficiently intense, and especially if fostered or permitted by professionals, the resulting experiences of remorse and betrayal can permanently disrupt the family's collective sense of competence and health. One member is ill, but the entire family loses its pride and internal cohesiveness in the attempt to find a cure for that one.

For others, the search for causes takes form around a predominantly biological model of mental illness. The behavior of the affected person is thought of as the externally observable manifestations of a disordered brain. The search for causes leads these families to attend seminars and lectures on mental illness, to read about mental illness, to watch for programs on mental illness on radio and television. Their curiosity centers on recent advances in brain anatomy, physiology, and chemistry, as demonstrated by new methods of brain imaging (CT scan, PET scan, BEAM). They seek out the research on the genetics of mental illness or the evidence for nutritional causes and chemical intoxications (vitamin deficiencies, heavy metal poisoning, and so on). They look back to the possibilities of brain injury at birth or during pregnancy. They review the record of the affected person's exposure to childhood viral and bacterial diseases.

The biological orientation to causes often carries with it less in the way of existential guilt than does the interpersonal orientation, inasmuch as the presumed causative forces are generally not perceived by members of the family as under the control of the family. (There are exceptions to this, like the mother who experiences searing remorse at having had a forceps delivery of her son: She regards this action as something she could have averted—so she could have protected her son from that injury and did not do so.) The greater emotional hazard attached to the biological inquiry arises from the current lack of corrective measures for these biological processes. Thus the family that searches for a brain disorder is more susceptible to therapeutic despair than to existential guilt.

Regardless of which direction the search takes, the family is ultimately confounded by the absence of definitive answers and the resulting controversy among professionals regarding the etiology of mental illness. Families cope with the controversy in several ways. In some, a consensus view evolves along interpersonal or biological lines. In other families a multidimensional view evolves in an attempt to integrate information from interpersonal and from biological sources. Quite commonly, the controversy in the field is played out within the family, with some members adopting the interpersonal and others adopting the biological orientation, while still others espouse a multidimensional view. Moreover, the manner in which the family resolves the controversy may change over time, with the addition of new information from the research community, with a change in the behavior of the affected person, and as a result of input from clinicians.

## PHASE SEVEN: THE SEARCH FOR TREATMENT

Once key members of the family have come to accept the presence of mental illness in the affected person, the search for effective treatments commences. The direction this search takes is strongly influenced by three main factors—the family's level of acceptance of the presence of illness, the family's perception of causes, and the profile of treatment services available to the family. Very often members of the family come to terms with the reality of illness at varying rates and under the influence of differing circumstances. For example, the affected person may not have come to terms with the presence of illness at the point in time when others in the family have arrived at a reasonable consensus. Or one key member of the family is still denying the presence of illness while others are looking into available treatments. In still another variation, one member of the family is seeking a treatment based on a biological view while another searches for a treatment based on an interpersonal view of the illness.

Because of the immense variability that is possible in any family regarding the level of recognition and the perception of causality for the family as a whole and for its individual members, the search for treatment is often a conflictual experience for the affected person and for other family members. Especially during the early stages of the search, contact with the professional community serves as much to educate the family regarding the presence and nature of mental illness as it does to provide treatment for the affected person. Furthermore, there is so much diversity of opinion on the contemporary scene regarding effective treatments for mental illness that the family itself and the family in the encounter with the professional community is substantially in chaos regarding what action is to be taken. The situation is made more problematic when, as is usually the case, the professionals are intent on getting on with the treatment of their choice while various family members are still trying to sort out for themselves the nature of the illness and what treatment should be given. In addition, if the affected person does not respond to the treatments that are given, the family's attempts to support those treatments and the involved professionals often falls apart, to be replaced by another round of discussions about the causes of the illness and searches for effective treatments. Thus, far from simply providing a solution to the problem of the affected person's illness, the search for treatment often poses a major challenge to the family's capacity to cope with ambiguity, controversy, and unanticipated outcomes of treatment.

Another part of the challenge encountered by the family in this phase is that treatment for mental illness, especially in its severe forms, takes place in a set of institutional environments most of which are unfamiliar to the family at the outset. Most families have had minimal exposure to hospital settings prior to the onset of illness in the affected person. And even those who are familiar with general hospitals from contacts around an episode of physical illness are not prepared by that prior experience for the institutional policies and practices within the mental health service system. They will often have to learn about involuntary treatment policies, confidentiality of therapist-patient communications, psychotropic medications, psychotherapy, group therapy, family therapy, and family support groups, therapeutic milieus, treatment teams, a multitude of therapeutic disciplines, insurance provisions for the treatment of mental illness, transfers to other units and to other hospitals, and more. Beyond the mental hospital, the family is also confronted with the challenge of learning about other institutions that play important parts in the treatment of mental illness: day hospitals, halfway houses, rehabilitation programs, aftercare clinics, Social Security provisions for the mentally ill, supervised community living programs, and more, each with its own distinctive policies and practices. And through all this learning about the mental health service system, the family is confronted by a panoply of attitudes on the part of staff regarding the place of the family in the illness and in its treatment. Some clinicians will adopt the attitude that the family has a crucial role in treatment and recovery while others will avoid contact and regard the family as a pathogenic force to be avoided by the patient. Others will blame the family while insisting that the family take the patient home as soon as he or she is minimally recovered from the most crippling manifestations of the illness. Very few clinicians will take the time to explain the workings of the institution, leaving family members with the task of learning how to deal with the institutions at the same time that they are learning how to understand the illness.

## PHASE EIGHT: THE COLLAPSE OF OPTIMISM

In all but the mildest of cases, as treatment progresses, it becomes increasingly apparent to the family that the affected person is not returning to his or her previous level of adaptation. Symptoms may recede but typically do not disappear altogether from view. Withdrawal and impairments in social and occupational spheres persist or become more pronounced. Clinicians speak of the patient's need for extended treatment after the period of hospital treatment, perhaps in another hospital, in a residential rehabilitation center, in a day hospital program, or continuing office treatment. The patient comes home or proceeds to a new residence. Weeks go into months as the treatment continues in one form or another. The patient makes some progress, loses ground, regains his or her ability to engage in some activities but not others. Months go into years. The patient suffers a relapse and then another, appearing to worsen and to lose ground with each recurrence. In time, the family's cumulative experience with the illness leads to the conclusion that the illness is not going to simply go away and that the whole family must make some accommodation to prolonged, possibly permanent, incapacitation of the affected person.

Often the hope that the illness will pass and leave the family unaffected, except for memories of unpleasant times, has enabled the family to cope with the burdens of the illness and the loss of vitality in the affected person. To the extent that the hope of cure has played a part in the family's coping repertoire, the chronicity of mental illness constitutes an assault on their ability to continue to support the patient and treatment efforts and to bear the attendant burdens. At the same time, while the family loses its attachment to the hope of cure, it is apparent in most cases that the affected person has evidenced a capacity for some productive activity, ranging from minimal self-care skills to partial employment, and from occasional social contacts to resumption of previous friendships. Thus the picture is complicated. Cure may be out of reach, but some forms of aliveness are attainable. Yet valuing the latter is difficult so long as hope of cure is retained.

The collapse of therapeutic optimism is another challenge serving to activate coping processes in the family. Sometimes favorable developments follow, sometimes not. For example, the patient may come to be seen as a permanent invalid, completely incapable of constructive activity and requiring constant supervision and caretaking. This development may guarantee that the patient has access to the caregiving resources of the family, but it also generates two ongoing risks. First, the family is more in danger of becoming overwhelmed by caregiving tasks to the extent that they perceive the patient as incapable of action in his or her own behalf.

In one family, recently retired parents rotated "coverage" of the house so that their withdrawn and demoralized son was never left home alone. They expressed a fear that he would commit suicide if they went away for even a single day. They served meals in his room since he showed no interest in eating with them or cooking for himself. They cleaned his room. They made sure his car had gas lest he run out of gas on his occasional forays away from home. These parents came for consultation at a point when, having despaired of their son ever doing these things for himself, they were wondering how long they could keep up the sacrifice of their own longed-for retirement years.

A second complication of perceiving the patient as a total invalid is that the patient's own active efforts to recover interests, activities, and involvements may be inhibited.

In the situation noted above, as the parents reduced services, the son began to look after his own needs. When they left dinner for him in the kitchen, he went there to eat. When they told him he could cook for himself, he did so. When they ceased cleaning his room, he took over, reorganizing it to his own preferences.

This young man's capacities for self-care might not ever have emerged had the parents continued on the premise of total invalidism.

As the family faces the prolonged partial incapacity mandated by mental illness, resentments emerge from several sources. The incapacitation of one member requires rearrangements in the ecology of care-giving within the family as a whole. Invariably some of the needs of other members go unmet as more and more attention is devoted to the needs of the patient. Furthermore, the family's collective sense of esprit is damaged by the shame and, in many cases, the guilt that comes with having a mentally ill member. The more socially disruptive behaviors of the patient may lead the family to retreat from some or all ordinary social involvements. Finally, the ill member very often ceases to participate as a reciprocal caregiver, forcing other members to take up his or her household tasks. Each of these deprivations can quite naturally give rise to frustration that increases irritation. The anger may be directed at the patient, although in many families the ordinary social constraints against directing anger at an ill person may inhibit family members from experiencing or expressing it toward the patient. Thus, the irritations may spill into other relationships and be directed at other members of the family.

In addition to excessive concern and resentment, family members may find themselves being repelled by the patient. The patient's behavior may be frightening or offensive and it is likely that family members will witness more of this behavior than outsiders do. Family members may cope with the fear and revulsion rising within themselves by restructuring their lives so as to reduce contact with the patient. Some will move away from the household or even to another area altogether. Others will stay away from the household during the hours the patient is known to be about the house. Still others will avoid direct interaction with the patient even when he or she is in the same room.

Very often these reactions—overconcern, resentment, avoidance—increase in intensity and become a part of the family's emerging set of ordinary coping processes as the hope of complete cure declines under the weight of prolonged incapacitation.

## PHASE NINE: SURRENDERING THE DREAM

Eventually the collapse of optimism sets in motion yet another process: mourning the loss of idealized internal images of the affected member. The idealized internal image is an image of another person held in the minds of his or her family members. It contains part-images consisting of recollections of all past interactions. At the same time, it contains extrapolations or anticipations of what the person will be like in the future. This is a process that occurs in every family and for all family members. When a person becomes mentally ill as an adolescent or young adult, other members have already accumulated a large array of past part-images, on the basis of which they have elaborated projections of future developments. Quite naturally, as in any family, parents, siblings, grandparents dream of the future that is implied by these future projections. Then, as the illness and its effect on the future that is realistically attainable becomes evident, some of these dreams of the affected person's future, these future part-images, come under seige. It is no longer possible to think of the dreams as representations of *believable* futures.

The natural reaction to this development is grief. In its broad features, this process resembles the grief process following the death of a loved one. In this case, the affected person lives on, but the dream of his or her future developments, achievements, and accomplishments begins to die in the minds of family members. Family members experience pangs of sadness and regret as the disparity between what seemed possible and what now seems attainable hits home. Then there are periods of time characterized more by avoidance of the realization of the loss. The mourning process is made up of moments of sadness and moments of aversion alternating at variable intervals over days, weeks, and months. In increments, the future part-image components of the internalized image cease operating as believable futures and assume the role of an ideal representation of what might have been but will not be.

Things are not that simple of course. At least four confounding factors modify the course of mourning the idealized internal images attached to the mentally ill. First, it is often several years before the family comes to realize that the illness is prolonged in nature and that no matter how long they wait, total remission is unlikely. Second, mental illness is typically an *invisible* infirmity. There are no external cues through which the observer can anchor himself to the nature or extent of the limitations imposed by the illness. Family members and others have only their recollections of the affected person's conduct in moments of active illness with which to stay anchored to the realization that there is an illness and that the affected person has some real limitations in functional capacity.

Third, the natural history of mental illness is characterized by a continuous series of fluctuations, small and large, in level of functioning and degree to which symptoms are manifest to others. Commenting on his 20-year follow-up experience with schizophrenics, Manfred Bleuler observed:

> In the course of the years it is not always the same patients who show recovery, improvement, no change, or deterioration. . . . Patients are constantly changing back and forth between states of recovery, improvement, nonimprovement, or deterioration. . . . Easily half to three-quarters of all schizophrenics about ten or more years after onset, attain reasonably stable states that last for many years. [However] even in these states all sorts of minor changes constantly do occur. (1978, pp. 413–414)

Since these fluctuations commonly continue indefinitely, family members can never be quite sure that their dreams of the affected person's future are unrealistic. Indeed, they may not be able to establish any reliable means of anticipating the direction of future developments.

Closely related to the phenomenon of longitudinal variability, a fourth confounding factor is the recursive effect of changing expectations on the affected person's state of well-being. As family members and others take note of impairments, they modify their expectations. The affected person, noting a relief of pressure to perform beyond his or her limits, may ease up and be able to function at a slightly higher level. This improvement may then in turn spark renewed hope for more extensive recovery in family members and others, leading to increased pressure for performance, followed by a deterioration in the affected person's ability to function. The cycle of rising and falling expectations and rising and falling level of function makes some contribution to the variability in course and keeps the family in a state of uncertainty as to what they can realistically expect.

One aspect of the mourning process that deserves special mention has to do with sadness and discouragement emerging in family members at a time when the affected person appears to be improving. Some family theorists have claimed that this sequence is evidence that family members do not want the patient to get better, that they have an investment in the patient being ill. These theorists have missed the crucial part of this reaction: As the patient improves, and then as the rate of improvement slows, the extent of improvement becomes known to the family. Commonly the patient is leveling off in a state that is experienced by the clinicians as substantially better. But the clinicians have rarely known the patient prior to onset of illness. For family members who have known the patient through a lifetime, he or she may appear grossly impaired in comparison with what they remember of his or her capabilities prior to onset of illness. Thus, while clinicians are celebrating what looks to them like recovery, the family is being hit hard by the realization that their loved one is still very far off from his or her former self.

## PHASE TEN: PICKING UP THE PIECES

To the extent that family members effectively mourn the loss of unattainable future part-images of the affected person, the path is laid open for learning to restore some balance in the family's life. This process, which we might call getting the illness in perspective, involves two interdependent processes. First, the family learns to compartmentalize the illness and its attendant concerns so that it is seen as one of an array of challenges in the life of the family, rather than as the only problem or as the central problem. As one father described, "You try to allocate a smaller space for your son as someone who, although not completely beyond your grasp, has his own path to follow." Second, the family discovers or rediscovers activities unrelated to the illness and its concerns, and learns to regard these activities as legitimate foci of involvement.

The way families activate this process of compartmentalization and redirection is changing presently, as a result of changes in professional and societal approaches toward the mentally ill. During the era of asylum care, it was customary for a family faced with mental illness to place the affected person in an institution, anticipating a lifetime of confinement. Through this socially sanctioned vehicle, the family was able to put the illness at a distance and take up other interests and other problems. Now, in the era of community care, it is no longer seen as possible or desirable to arrange for this kind of total compartmentalization. Families are just now in the process of learning how to retain meaningful involvements with the affected person while at the same time preserving or resurrecting the capacity for involvement in other pursuits. At present, the solution is very frequently for one member of the family (the primary caregiver) to specialize in looking after the welfare of the affected person while the rest of the family pursue other interests. In this circumstance, compartmentalization is achieved at the expense of the capacity for redirection in the primary caregiver. Alternatively two or more relatives may "spell" each other, taking turns in looking after the affected person and releasing each other for some respite and relief. Still other families have found that the only way to compartmentalize the illness is to ask for periodic reinstitutionalization of the affected person for short intervals, during which the family gets away for some vacation time. In truth, many families are finding that there is no really good way to bring about meaningful compartmentalization that permits a restoration of balanced family priorities while at the same time providing for the affected person's needs to the satisfaction of all concerned. It is precisely for this reason that families of the mentally ill have become increasingly vocal about the need for the restoration of long-term hospital services, provision of community residences in adequate numbers and increases in funding for day programming and case management services.

## CONCLUSION

The aim of this chapter has been to detail some of the complexities encountered by families and witnessed by professionals as families work their way from a position of naïveté about mental illness to a position of understanding, acceptance, and restored balance. The process is prolonged in nature, due to the vagaries of the condition—its incomprehensibility and its relative invisibility—and to the highly undesirable nature of information about illness in general, and about stigmatizing illnesses in particular. The process is usually characterized by diversity and fluidity of attitudes within and between family members, by dramatic forward strides in understanding and equally dramatic reversals, and always by a wide array of disagreeable emotions. Families faced with unremitting, prolonged, or fluctuating levels of infirmity in an affected member eventually experience a collapse of therapeutic optimism and then the sorrow of letting go of the dreams of unattainable futures. In the present era of community-based care, the aim of many families is to achieve an accommodation through which the welfare of the affected person is brought into balance with the welfare of other family members. Most families favor the move away from total institutions. However, the sought-after balance is hard to discover and harder to maintain. Families burdened by the effort have begun to call attention to the inadequacy of currently available social supports and clinical services. Families that stay committed to their affected relative deserve the understanding, support, and—most of all—the respect of attending professionals. Research on the impact of the struggle to come to terms with mental illness on the family in its other responsibilities and interests is largely a thing of the future.

**REFERENCE**

Bleuler, M. (1978). *The schizophrenic disorders: Long-term patient and family studies.* New Haven: Yale University Press.

# Families as a Resource in the Rehabilitation of the Severely Psychiatrically Disabled

*LeRoy Spaniol*
*Hal Jung*
*Anthony M. Zipple*
*Stephanie Fitzgerald*

## INTRODUCTION

The current trend in the treatment of the severely psychiatrically disabled emphasizes community-based treatment approaches. This has resulted in shorter periods of hospitalization and use of a wide array of aftercare and rehabilitation services. Community-based treatment has also resulted in large numbers of psychiatrically disabled persons returning to their families. A variety of studies have reported that from 25 to 66% of deinstitutionalized patients return to their families (Goldman, 1982; Lamb & Oliphant, 1978; Minkoff, 1979). There are approximately 800,000 severely psychiatrically disabled people living in the community and up to 500,000 of these are living at home (Goldman & Gatozzi, 1981). It is clear that families have become primary caregivers for the severely psychiatrically disabled. However, families frequently do not have the information, skills, or resources to adequately assist their disabled family member (Hatfield, Fierstein, & Johnson, 1982).

Because of the importance of the family and home environment in the rehabilitation of the severely psychiatrically disabled person, means of identifying family needs and strengths, as well as of maximizing the positive influences of the family, need attention from the

LeRoy Spaniol, Anthony M. Zipple, and Stephanie Fitzgerald. Center for Rehabilitation Research and Training in Mental Health, Boston University, Boston, Massachusetts.

Hal Jung. Counseling and Family Services, Inc., Medford, Massachusetts.

mental health and rehabilitation profession. Specifically, families often need additional information, skills, and support to cope with their disabled family members. Moreover, mental health professionals often need additional knowledge and training in order to work more closely and cooperatively with family members (Spaniol, Zipple, & Fitzgerald, 1984; Zipple & Spaniol, 1984)

*Background*

Families have been viewed from different persepctives throughout the history of psychiatric treatment. Frequently, as Kreisman and Joy (1974) found in their comprehensive review of the literature, families were considered a major stressor and cause of schizophrenia, as in Fromm-Reichmann's (1948) concept of the "schizophrenogenic" mother. Fortunately, this psychoanalytically derived viewpoint has been discounted (Arieti, 1974).

The systems-oriented theorists also attributed mental illness to the family. In their conceptualizations, mental illness was a manifestation of the entire family, which was seen as a unit consisting of interacting parts and which operated under a set of rules to mutually determine the behavior of all family members (Bateson, Jackson, Haley, & Weakland, 1956; Bowen, 1960; Hirsch & Leff, 1975; Lidz, 1958; Wynne, Ryckoff, Day, & Hirsch, 1958).

Recent work has considered the family more positively, as a "reactor." The person who is reacting is not causing psychiatric disability but is responding to the ill family member's behavior. Rather than blaming the family or "benignly" attributing responsibility to them for the psychiatric condition, this viewpoint views the family as responding to psychiatric disability through coping and adaptation (Hatfield, 1978, 1979; Kint, 1978).

The family's response to the stresses of living with a psychiatrically disabled family member have been described by a number of researchers (Creer & Wing, 1974; Hatfield, 1978, 1981a; Lamb & Oliphant, 1978). For example, in Hatfield's (1978) survey of 89 caregivers living in the Washington, DC area, the emotional burden of family members was characterized primarily by stress, then anxiety, resentment, grief, and depression. Furthermore, the family's inability to cope resulted in marital strain, disrupted social life, and caused hardships for siblings.

Much of the current literature focuses more on the family's inability to cope than on their effective coping repertoires. A frequently mentioned solution to helping the family cope is the development of alliances with other families (Hatfield et al., 1982; Lamb & Oliphant,

1978; Park & Shapiro, 1976), with supportive networks (Beels, 1978, 1981), or with professionals (Anderson, Hogarty, & Reiss, 1980; Appleton, 1974; Byalin, Jed, & Lehman, 1982; Hatfield, 1979; Kanter & Lin, 1980; Leff, Kuipers, Berkowitz, Eberbein-Vries, & Sturgeon, 1982; Liberman, Wallace, Vaughan, & Snyder, 1979). These alliances are proposed to help families develop a support system that teaches skills, gives information, provides support, promotes advocacy, and builds confidence.

## Families and Mental Health Professionals

Not only must family members learn how to cope with their disabled family member, they must also learn how to cope with mental health professionals. Families have reported that service providers are not always helpful and can be negligent in encouraging families to be part of the treatment process (Appleton, 1974; Hatfield, 1978, 1979; Terkelsen, 1983). As a result, some families rarely turn to professionals for help, but seek support and guidance from self-help groups (Hatfield, 1981b; Straw & Young, 1982). In addition, self-help groups may be able to meet needs such as the desire to share problems with people who are experiencing similar difficulties, to perform advocacy functions, and to receive practical information, all of which professionals are often unable to meet (Killilea, 1976).

Several studies have disclosed the degree of dissatisfaction expressed by families who received professional services (Creer & Wing, 1974; Holden & Lewine, 1982; Wasow, 1980). In the Creer and Wing (1974) study, relatives were most concerned about the lack of information and guidance received from service providers. When they looked to a psychiatrist for practical advice, they received little or none. Furthermore, the survey revealed that social work services were considered unreliable as well as unsympathetic.

## Purpose of the Study

Families are frequently primary caregivers for their disabled family member; are an important resource in that person's rehabilitation; and need information, coping skills, and support in order to adequately assist him or her. Families have also learned many useful coping strategies that can be shared with other family members. While recent approaches to working with families have focused more on their information, skill, and support needs, limited information was available at the inception of this study on their practical needs and their coping strengths. Also, while data had begun to appear supporting the problems families were encountering with mental health professionals, little data was available on how mental health professionals perceived the needs and coping strengths of family members. Thus, the purpose of the overall study was to identify family needs and coping strengths as well as perceptions of mental health professionals. This chapter will focus on the needs portion of the study and the professional perception of family needs.

## METHODS

*Sampling*

FAMILY SURVEYS

A national sample of families was developed from the membership list of the National Alliance for the Mentally Ill (NAMI). NAMI staff members in the Washington, DC central office helped Boston University staff in identifying a sample from their membership list of approximately 6,250 names. A selection procedure known as systematic sampling was used to determine 10% of this population for the needs survey. The initial sample of 625 potential subjects for this survey were each sent a letter from the NAMI requesting their participation in the study. Of these, 187 families agreed to participate. Questionnaires were sent to these families and 140 usable questionnaires were returned, for a response rate of 75% of those who agreed to participate.

The family respondents are not representative of all families of the psychiatrically disabled. Those who responded all belong to the NAMI. Tables 1 and 2 show the demographic characteristics of the family respondents and of the family members with the disability. The family respondents were predominantly white, female, over 50 years of age, highly educated, employed in professional or managerial occupations, and had family incomes of over $25,000. With these limitations in mind, it seems most prudent to consider the respondents as a large and unique group of individuals who were highly motivated to participate in the study.

The family members with the disability were predominantly under 30 years of age, male, well educated, unemployed, hospitalized more than five times, and with a current diagnosis of schizophrenia or paranoid schizophrenia. Their living situations were varied, with over 25% living at home, 15% in a community residence, and 14 to 21% in independent living.

*Table 1.*
Selected Demographic Characteristics (%) of the Family Respondents (N = 140)

| | |
|---|---|
| Age | |
| 21–50 | 21 |
| 51–60 | 45 |
| ≥61 | 34 |
| Sex | |
| Male | 20 |
| Female | 80 |
| Education | |
| College degree or more | 49 |
| Some college | 27 |
| Post-high school technical training | 5 |
| High school or equivalent | 16 |
| Other | 3 |
| Marital status | |
| Married | 76 |
| Divorced-separated | 13 |
| Other | 11 |
| Length of membership in self-help-advocacy group | |
| <1 year | 22 |
| 1–2 years | 29 |
| >2 years | 49 |
| Size of city of residence | |
| ≥100,000 | 46 |
| 50,000–99,000 | 21 |
| <50,000 | 20 |
| Rural | 13 |
| Total family income level | |
| <$15,000 | 16 |
| $15,000–$25,000 | 28 |
| $25,000–$40,000 | 26 |
| >$40,000 | 30 |
| Occupation | |
| Professional | 41 |
| Managerial | 13 |
| Other | 46 |
| Ethnic-racial group | |
| White | 90 |
| Black | 2 |
| Hispanic | 1 |
| Other | 7 |
| Geographical distribution | |
| South | 15 |
| East | 26 |
| Midwest | 23 |
| West | 36 |

*Table 2.*
Selected Demographic Characteristics (%) of the Family
Member with the Disability (N = 140)

| | |
|---|---:|
| Age | |
| <20 | 6 |
| 21–30 | 50 |
| 31–40 | 36 |
| ≥40 | 8 |
| Sex | |
| Male | 70 |
| Female | 30 |
| Education | |
| College degree or more | 16 |
| Some college | 38 |
| Post-high school technical training | 5 |
| High school or equivalent | 29 |
| Other | 12 |
| Employment status | |
| Full time | 5 |
| Part time | 9 |
| Unemployed | 77 |
| Other | 9 |
| Total number of hospitalizations | |
| ≥10 | 21 |
| 5–9 | 30 |
| 2–4 | 40 |
| ≥1 | 9 |
| Current living arrangement | |
| Family home | 34 |
| Mental hospital | 19 |
| Residential home | 17 |
| Independent living | 14 |
| Other | 16 |
| Current diagnosis | |
| Schizophrenia | 46 |
| Paranoid schizophrenia | 23 |
| Manic-depressive | 10 |
| Other | 21 |

PROFESSIONAL SURVEY

The sampling of mental health professionals was developed by randomly selecting one community mental health center from each of the 48 continental states. Each center was invited to participate. Of the 48, 12 (25%) agreed to participate. Centers from each region of the country were represented and there was an even split between rural and urban centers. Each center was asked to provide names of practitioners who worked with families that had psychiatrically disabled members. In all, 245 names were submitted. All 245 were sent questionnaires. Ninety-three subjects or 38% of the professional sample returned usable questionnaires.

The 93 respondents are a sample of community mental health professionals who worked with families and psychiatrically disabled clients and who were motivated to respond to a survey questionnaire. Table 3 summarizes the demographic characteristics of the professional sample. Subjects were young, with 63% age 35 or younger, moderately experienced, with 60% having 6 or more years of mental health experience, and in direct service positions, with 88% having direct service activities as 50% or more of their job. The full range of mental health disciplines were represented, with the most commonly reported disciplines being social work (44%), clinical/counseling psychology (24%), and nursing (11%). The group was well educated, with 74% having at least a master's degree. Fifty-eight percent were female. The professional sample subjects worked in a wide range of settings with outpatient counseling/psychotherapy (38%), consultation or training (29%), and social/vocational rehabilitation settings (13%) being the most common settings.

## Design

This study utilized a survey research design to evaluate the needs and coping strengths of family members and the perceptions of mental health professionals. The choice of this methodology was based on the lack and subsequent need for information from a national sample of families and mental health professionals. The development of the methodology was aided by Dillman's (1978) Total Design Method (TDM), which provided a unique guide to questionnaire construction, mailing, and follow-up procedures, and Berdie and Anderson (1974), who complimented Dillman's approach to questionnaire design and use.

## Instrumentation

The survey instruments were based on models available in the literature and on innovations and modifications made by the researchers. Each survey instrument had both closed and open-ended items. The needs survey and the professional survey shared some items in common for purposes of comparisons. The initial drafts of the instruments were developed by the research staff; these were then reviewed and critiqued by family members, professionals in the field, and other

*Table 3.*
Selected Demographic Characteristics (%) of the
Professional Respondents (N = 93)

| | |
|---|---:|
| Age | |
| <30 | 28 |
| 31–35 | 35 |
| 36–40 | 16 |
| 41–76 | 21 |
| Sex | |
| Female | 58 |
| Male | 42 |
| Educational level | |
| Doctoral degree | 16 |
| Master's degree | 58 |
| Bachelor's degree | 22 |
| Less than bachelor's degree | 4 |
| Mental health experience | |
| <5 years | 40 |
| 6–10 years | 30 |
| 11–15 years | 18 |
| ≥16 years | 12 |
| Mental health discipline | |
| Social work | 44 |
| Clinical/counseling psychology | 24 |
| Nursing | 11 |
| Rehabilitation counseling | 5 |
| Other | 16 |
| Current work setting | |
| Outpatient counseling/psychotherapy | 38 |
| Consultation of training | 29 |
| Social/vocational rehabilitation setting | 13 |
| Inpatient hospital | 8 |
| Day treatment | 5 |
| Crisis intervention | 4 |
| Professional Responsibilities | |
| Direct service | 66 |
| Supervision or management | 6 |
| Both (duties evenly split) | 22 |
| Geographical distribution of the 12 centers | |
| Urban      n = 6 | |
| Rural      n = 6 | |
| | |
| South      n = 2 | |
| East      n = 6 | |
| Midwest      n = 2 | |
| West      n = 2 | |

researchers. The purpose of the review was to evaluate the relevancy of the items to our own research objectives. It was also important that the reviewers were potential users of the data, and individuals who represented the populations assumed to be in need, that is, family members and mental health professionals. The feedback from this process supported the basic approach and content of the instruments. It also resulted in suggestions regarding ambiguous items and unnecessary items that were incorporated into the final draft of the instruments. Following this expert review, a field test of the instruments was carried out. A pilot sample for each instrument was developed. Responses indicated that subjects were able to understand and complete the questionnaire and found the items relevant to their own personal experience. Frequently, additional comments were written into the margins of the questionnaires that indicated that our target audiences were well motivated by the items and, indeed, were eager to communicate with us. No statistical analysis was carried out on the pilots. The results of both expert review and field-testing supported the assumption that the instruments would be relatively stable as well as valid in content vis-à-vis the purpose of the study. In addition, the overall simplicity of the instruments was perceived as minimizing problems concerning their validity (Kerlinger, 1973).

## RESULTS

*Family Needs Survey*

The family needs survey showed that overall dissatisfaction with mental health services was high. Combined very-moderately ratings of overall dissatisfaction were 45%. Specific services by with which family respondents were very-moderately dissatisfied included social rehabilitation (51%), vocational rehabilitation (50%), individual therapy (49%), and drug medication (39%). The only service with which the family respondents were very-moderately satisfied was drug medication (51%).

Of the family respondents, 53% reported that their frequency of contact with mental health professionals was once every 2 months or less. While 51% indicated they were very-moderately dissatisfied with the frequency of contact, 59% of the family respondents indicated they wanted more contact. Family members also rated the level of satisfaction with various professional activities occurring during their contacts, indicating that they were primarily dissatisfied with treatment coordination (50%), practical advice (47%), information about the illness (46%), emotional support (44%), and referral assistance (44%).

Families were most satisfied with the practitioners attitude toward the ill member (55%) and attitude toward the family (45%). When asked to rate their most important areas of need with respect to professional activities, family members identified practical advice (24%), information about the illness (21%), and treatment coordination as most important.

Seventy-eight percent of the family respondents indicated that their disabled family member had been disabled for more than 6 years, 45% had been disabled for more than 10 years. In spite of the length of disability, 58% reported that mental health professionals had not helped them at all to adequately understand their family member's disability. The information given was too vague, too incomplete, or contradictory.

This lack of information is reflected in the responses of families regarding psychopharmacological interventions with their disabled family members. Although 95% of the disabled family members had been on medication within the 12 months preceding the survey, 47% of the family respondents indicated they were not informed about how medication would help their family member; 60% were not informed about the side effects of the medication; 72% were not informed about what to do in case of side effects; 51% were not informed about the reasons for using the particular medication; and 56% were not informed about proper dosage levels. In general, 52% of the family respondents were very-moderately dissatisfied with medication services.

Many family members also reported increases in levels of stress and its resulting symptoms. When asked to identify how symptoms of stress have increased or decreased over the past year, family members indicated the following symptoms had increased: anxiety (58%), frustration (58%), worry (56%), sense of burden (55%), depression (48%), grief (47%), fear (44%), and anger (42%). Symptoms that decreased somewhat included shame/embarrassment (21%), and guilt (18%). Behaviors of the disabled family member that family respondents found most troubling included schizophrenic symptoms (24%), depression (17%), listlessness and low energy (12%), aggressiveness (11%), withdrawal (9%), self-injury (7%), decision-making abilities (6%), and grooming and hygiene (5%).

*Family Needs Survey Comparisons*

Calculations on overall satisfaction with mental health services and a variety of rated items on the need survey were made using *t* tests (Tables 4 & 5). Very and moderately dissatisfied responses were combined to become "dissatisfied" and very and moderately satisfied re-

*Table 4.*
Relationships between Overall Satisfaction with Mental
Health Services and Satisfaction with Specific Services

| Variable | $n^a$ | Mean$^b$ | $t$ | $df$ |
|---|---|---|---|---|
| Drug medication | | | | |
| Dissatisfied | 52 | 2.50 | 5.94*** | 101 |
| Satisfied | 51 | 4.02 | | |
| Individual therapy | | | | |
| Dissatisfied | 48 | 2.00 | 4.62*** | 98 |
| Satisfied | 52 | 3.27 | | |
| Family therapy | | | | |
| Dissatisfied | 33 | 1.88 | 2.83** | 66 |
| Satisfied | 35 | 2.86 | | |
| Group therapy | | | | |
| Dissatisfied | 32 | 2.13 | 2.66** | 59 |
| Satisfied | 29 | 3.07 | | |
| Crises intervention | | | | |
| Dissatisfied | 44 | 2.57 | 2.47* | 72 |
| Satisfied | 30 | 3.43 | | |
| Vocational rehabilitation | | | | |
| Dissatisfied | 38 | 1.76 | 1.83 | 68.7 |
| Satisfied | 39 | 2.36 | | |
| Social rehabilitation | | | | |
| Dissatisfied | 46 | 2.04 | 1.24 | 86 |
| Satisfied | 42 | 2.40 | | |
| Sheltered workshop | | | | |
| Dissatisfied | 29 | 1.97 | 1.08 | 46 |
| Satisfied | 19 | 2.37 | | |
| Hospitalization | | | | |
| Dissatisfied | 42 | 2.52 | 4.92*** | 69 |
| Satisfied | 29 | 4.00 | | |
| Day treatment program | | | | |
| Dissatisfied | 33 | 2.42 | 1.40 | 56 |
| Satisfied | 25 | 2.92 | | |
| Educational services | | | | |
| Dissatisfied | 35 | 2.03 | 1.32 | 57 |
| Satisfied | 24 | 2.50 | | |

$^a$Sample size varies because of missing data.
$^b$The respondent was asked to rate satisfaction with various mental health services on a 5-point scale where 1.0 = very dissatisfied, 2.0 = moderately dissatisfied, 3.0 = neither satisfied nor dissatisfied, 4.0 = moderately satisfied, and 5.0 = very satisfied.
*$p < .05$.
**$p < .01$.
***$p < .001$.

Table 5.
Relationships between Overall Satisfaction with Mental
Health Services and Satisfaction with Professional Activities

| Variable | $n^a$ | Mean$^b$ | t | df |
|---|---|---|---|---|
| Practical advice | | | | |
| Dissatisfied | 51 | 2.04 | 4.16*** | 97 |
| Satisfied | 48 | 3.17 | | |
| Information about illness | | | | |
| Dissatisfied | 50 | 1.45 | 3.80*** | 96 |
| Satisfied | 48 | 3.33 | | |
| Emotional support | | | | |
| Dissatisfied | 47 | 1.49 | 3.72*** | 89 |
| Satisfied | 44 | 3.25 | | |
| Referral to services | | | | |
| Dissatisfied | 49 | 2.04 | 3.67*** | 86 |
| Satisfied | 39 | 3.08 | | |
| Treatment coordination | | | | |
| Dissatisfied | 45 | 1.73 | 3.35** | 69.7 |
| Satisfied | 40 | 2.67 | | |
| Attitude toward family | | | | |
| Dissatisfied | 49 | 2.41 | 4.11*** | 95 |
| Satisfied | 48 | 3.67 | | |
| Attitude toward ill member | | | | |
| Dissatisfied | 52 | 2.90 | 4.29*** | 99 |
| Satisfied | 49 | 4.02 | | |

[a]Sample size varies because of missing data.
[b]The respondent was asked to rate satisfaction with various mental health services on a 5-point scale where 1.0 = very dissatisfied, 2.0 = moderately dissatisfied, 3.0 = neither satisfied nor dissatisfied, 4.0 = moderately satisfied, and 5.0 = very satisfied.
**$p < .01$.
***$p < .001$.

sponses were combined to become "satisfied." "Neither" responses (9%) were not included in this analysis. There were significant differences between the "dissatisfied" and the "satisfied" respondents and the level of satisfaction with a variety of specific mental health services. Those who were generally dissatisfied with mental health services were also dissatisfied with specific services such as drug medication, individual therapy, family therapy, group therapy, crisis intervention, and hospitalization. Those who were generally satisfied with mental health services tended to be also satisfied with specific mental health services. On several items in which there were no significant differences, both the overall dissatisfied and satisfied respondents indicated that they were dissatisfied with specific services such as vocational rehabilitation, social rehabilitation, sheltered workshops, day treatment, and educational services. Thus, even those who were generally satisfied with mental health services still had some measurable level of dissatisfaction with these specific services. In the case of family therapy, even though there was a significant difference between the two groups of respondents, the difference was between a very negative and a less negative response. Thus, both groups of respondents had serious concerns about the usefulness of family therapy. There were also significant differences between the "dissatisfied" and the "satisfied" respondents and the level of satisfaction with a variety of specific professional activities. Those who were generally dissatisfied with mental health services were also dissatisfied with specific professional activities such as practical advice, information about the illness, emotional support, referral to services, treatment coordination, attitude toward the family, and attitude toward the disabled family member. Those who were generally satisfied with mental health services tended to be also satisfied with specific professional activities. Though there was a significant difference between the respondents on treatment coordination, both groups of respondents tended to score the item negatively. Thus, both groups of respondents had serious concerns about treatment coordination.

The researchers also used $t$ tests to analyze the relationship between overall satisfaction and ways in which the family respondents' mental health had been affected over the 12 months prior to the survey. Those who were generally dissatisfied with mental health services felt an increased experience of frustration ($t = 2.13$, $df = 89.1$, $p < .05$) and of anger ($t = 2.07$, $df = 79$, $p < .05$). Their sense of burden also approached a level of significance ($t = 1.80$, $df = 91$, $p > .05$).

*Professional Survey*

Professionals were asked five specific questions in the survey about families who have psychiatrically disabled members, First, respondents were asked to assess the general level of satisfaction that families have with mental health services. Of these, 14% felt that families were moderately dissatisfied, 4% felt that families were neither satisfied nor dissatisfied, and the large majority (82%) believed that families were either moderately or very satisfied with mental health services.

Second, respondents were asked to assess the level of satisfaction that families had with specific mental health services. Respondents reported a low level of dissatisfaction among families. For six of the specific services, including crises intervention (80%), individual therapy (73%), drug medication (69%), day treatment (64%), and vocational rehabilitation (53%), more than half of the respondents believed that families were moderately to very satisfied. Respondents felt that families were moderately to very dissatisfied with family therapy (15%), vocational rehabilitation (17%), and sheltered workshops (13%).

Third, in reply to the question about which of the several specific mental health services represented the most important areas of need, 24% of the respondents listed family therapy as the most important need. Crisis intervention (12%), drug medication (11%), and social rehabilitation (11%), were also frequently reported as the most important need, with 18% of the respondents listing vocational rehabilitation as the second most important need. Family therapy (17%) and group therapy (10%) were also frequent responses.

Fourth, respondents were asked to report their opinion of the level of satisfaction that families had with certain professional activities. For each of the activities listed, the most frequent response was "moderately" to "very satisfied." The only activities that as many as 10% of the respondents reported families as being moderately to very dissatisfied with were treatment coordination (15%), providing information about the illness (11%), and providing practical advice (10%). For six activities, including providing emotional support (78%), referral to appropriate services (77%), attitude toward ill family members (75%), providing practical advice (70%), attitude toward family (70%), and providing information about the illness (69%), more than half of the respondents believed that families were moderately to very satisfied.

Finally, respondents were asked to list the three professional activities that represented the most important areas of need. Nineteen percent listed providing information about the illness as the most important area of need. Providing practical advice (18%), and treatment coordination (17%) were also frequently reported as the most important need. Treatment coordination was listed by 27% of the respondents as the second most important need, with referral to appropriate services (20%) and providing emotional support (19%) also being frequent responses.

*Family Need Survey and Professional*
*Survey Comparisons*

Utilizing $t$ tests, an analysis was made of the relationship between comparable items on the professional survey and the family needs survey. Tables 6 and 7 report results that were significant at $p > .05$. Tests for homogeneity of variances were conducted that indicated that there were significant differences between groups in terms of variance. Therefore, $t$ tests using the separate variance estimate were computed.

*Table 6.*
Comparison between Family and Professional Responses on
Family Satisfaction with Specific Mental Health Services

| Variable | $n^a$ | Mean$^b$ | $t^c$ | $df$ |
|---|---|---|---|---|
| Overall satisfaction | | | | |
| Families | 118 | 2.82 | 6.48*** | 198.16 |
| Professionals | 87 | 3.83 | | |
| Drug medication | | | | |
| Families | 134 | 3.14 | 4.17*** | 211.71 |
| Professionals | 81 | 3.84 | | |
| Individual therapy | | | | |
| Families | 132 | 2.70 | 7.25*** | 214.48 |
| Professionals | 87 | 3.84 | | |
| Family therapy | | | | |
| Families | 88 | 2.49 | 5.43*** | 149.06 |
| Professionals | 68 | 3.57 | | |
| Group therapy | | | | |
| Families | 79 | 2.61 | 6.41*** | 129.93 |
| Professionals | 68 | 3.82 | | |
| Crises intervention | | | | |
| Families | 101 | 2.85 | 7.24*** | 166.02 |
| Professionals | 85 | 4.14 | | |
| Vocational rehabilitation | | | | |
| Families | 99 | 2.05 | 6.51*** | 154.32 |
| Professionals | 62 | 3.32 | | |
| Social rehabilitation | | | | |
| Families | 114 | 2.26 | 9.09*** | 176.95 |
| Professionals | 65 | 3.74 | | |
| Hospitalization | | | | |
| Families | 99 | 3.14 | 3.72*** | 161.97 |
| Professionals | 80 | 3.78 | | |
| Day treatment | | | | |
| Families | 74 | 2.69 | 6.33*** | 122.24 |
| Professionals | 73 | 3.89 | | |
| Educational services | | | | |
| Families | 76 | 2.25 | 6.72*** | 123.98 |
| Professionals | 50 | 3.66 | | |

[a]Sample size varies because of missing data.

[b]The respondent was asked to rate satisfaction with various mental health services on a 5-point scale where 1.0 = very dissatisfied, 2.0 = moderately dissatisfied, 3.0 = neither satisfied nor dissatisfied, 4.0 = moderately satisfied, and 5.0 = very satisfied.

[c]All $t$ values were computed using separate variance estimates due to significant differences in variance between two groups.

***$p < .001$.

*Table 7.*
Comparison between Family and Professional Responses on
Family Satisfaction with Specific Professional Activities

| Variable | $n^a$ | Mean[b] | $t^c$ | df |
|---|---|---|---|---|
| Practical advice | | | | |
| Families | 127 | 2.57 | 7.61*** | 205.83 |
| Professionals | 85 | 3.78 | | |
| Information about illness | | | | |
| Families | 125 | 2.74 | 6.24*** | 207.08 |
| Professionals | 86 | 3.80 | | |
| Emotional support | | | | |
| Families | 119 | 2.60 | 8.16*** | 190.15 |
| Professionals | 89 | 4.02 | | |
| Referral | | | | |
| Families | 115 | 2.57 | 9.42*** | 177.12 |
| Professionals | 86 | 4.05 | | |
| Treatment coordination | | | | |
| Families | 112 | 2.29 | 7.49*** | 194.61 |
| Professionals | 86 | 3.57 | | |
| Attitude toward family | | | | |
| Families | 127 | 3.08 | 5.11*** | 197.28 |
| Professionals | 86 | 3.93 | | |
| Attitude toward ill person | | | | |
| Families | 130 | 3.40 | 3.50*** | 215.20 |
| Professionals | 88 | 3.94 | | |

[a]Sample size varies because of missing data.
[b]The respondent was asked to rate satisfaction with various mental health services on a 5-point scale where 1.0 = very dissatisfied, 2.0 = moderately dissatisfied, 3.0 = neither satisfied nor dissatisfied, 4.0 = moderately satisfied, and 5.0 = very satisfied.
[c]All t values were computed using separate variance estimates due to significant differences in variance between two groups.
***$p < .001$.

The standard deviations were significantly different for the professional and family respondents on virtually all items. Professional responses tended to congregate around the mean, while family responses had a significantly greater variance. Thus, professionals as a group tend to view families similarly, while families as a group do not tend to view professionals similarly. The first item on Table 6 describes the relationship between professional and family responses to overall satisfaction with services and shows that professional and family member perceptions of overall satisfaction are significantly different. Professionals tend to see family members as very to moderately satisfied with mental health services, while family members tend to see themselves as more dissatisfied. With respect to specific services, professionals and family members differ significantly on how they perceive family satisfaction with drug medication, individual therapy, family therapy, group therapy, crisis intervention, vocational rehabilitation, social rehabilitation, hospitalization, day treatment and educational services. That is, professionals consistently view families as being more satisfied than families themselves. With respect to specific professional activities (Table 7), professionals and family members differ significantly on how they perceive family satisfaction with providing practical advice, providing information about the illness, providing emotional support, referral to appropriate services, treatment coordination, attitude toward the family, and attitude toward the ill family member. That is, professionals perceive family members as being more satisfied with specific professional activities than families themselves.

## DISCUSSION

The sample of families surveyed in both the needs and coping surveys is similar in many ways to the samples of other surveys of family members belonging to the NAMI. The membership is primarily made up of white, middle-class families. The respondents tend to be over 50, well educated and employed in managerial and professional positions. They appear to be responsible, solid members of their community. In many ways, this is a unique development for the field of mental health. In the first place, families are finally organizing for support and advocacy for the severely mentally ill. Family members of other types of severely disabled people (e.g., mentally retarded, developmentally disabled) have been extremely effective in influencing legislative, policy, and funding priorities for their disabled family members. Secondly, the family members who are organizing are successful and influential people in their own right. They are people who have achieved career and financial success and who are used to being heard and working for what they want. Because their concerns are real and their vision is clear, they will undoubtedly become a powerful advocating force for their disabled family members.

### Needs Survey

The reported overall dissatisfaction with mental health services was high (45%). The core of the dissatisfaction with services appears to be directed toward social rehabilitation, vocational rehabilitation, individual therapy, and drug/medication management. These needs reflect the primary service concerns of families in the present study and confirm the findings in more geographically limited need studies. Families frequently do not feel supported by these services, the availability of which is limited and the quality harshly criticized. The source of family dissatisfaction appears to be that these services do not provide the kind or quality of support that families need nor do they meet the needs of families as families see them. They often have a content and a process that is not based on how families perceive their needs. The validity of the perceptions of family members is supported by the responses of the professionals, which describe them as viewing the needs of families quite differently.

Even though families were dissatisfied with overall services, they still were strongly interested in more contact with professionals. Families continue to look toward the professional for help, even when they are dissatisfied. It appears that they realize the limitations of the mental health system and mental health professionals but feel that they are often all that they have. Families are willing to work with the professional and the system to improve services and to contribute their own time and skill. However, families want the mental health professional to be the team leader. The specific activities families look to professionals for assistance on are treatment coordination, referral assistance, practical advice, information about the illness, and emotional support. The one service they typically do not want from professionals is therapy for themselves. Families do not want to be seen by professionals as being the problem. They want to be seen as having a problem, that is, a problem in living with a family member who has a severe disability.

Families also express serious dissatisfaction with medication management. They feel that they do not have enough information on proper dosage levels, the reason that particular medications are prescribed, information on how medication is supposed to help, and information on medication side effects. Families frequently express a desire to be better informed but feel ignored or discounted by the mental health professional. The source of this desire for more information by families appears to be their need to deal with the practical problems surrounding medication management for their disabled family member. They are frequently the people who have the responsibility of monitoring their disabled family member's medication, yet do not feel they have sufficient information to do an adequate job. The mental health professional needs to acknowledge the family's de facto role of primary caregiver and provide the family with the medication management assistance the family sees itself as needing.

A final area of concern identified by family respondents was their own subjective level of stress. Even though many family members report having developed strategies to cope with their stress symptoms, they acknowledge that stress management is an ongoing issue. The subjective symptoms reported by families include anxiety, frustration, worry, sense of burden, depression, grief, fear, and anger. The sources of these symptoms appear to be both internal and external. The internal sources include the family's attitudes and coping skills. By "attitudes" the authors mean family beliefs about responsibility for the illness, responsibility for managing particular behaviors, and, in general, responsibility for "managing" their disabled family member's life. By "coping skills" the authors mean both the ability to "handle" difficult situations that arise and the opportunity to call upon proven resources when needed. The external sources of stress are the real problems of caring for a disabled family member and the frustrations of dealing with what family respondents see as a frequently unreceptive and, at times, discounting system.

Attitudes and coping skills are not simple matters to understand and clarify. Several examples may help the reader to understand our meaning. Families can believe they are essentially alone in advocating for their disabled family member. This belief may carry a different stress consequence than the belief that there are other family members who experience similar problems and who are willing to share the advocacy task. Also, a family member who increases his or her options for dealing with specific problems may experience less stress than a family member who feels limited to a coping strategy that has not worked very well. Finally, a family member who is able to distance him- or herself from bizarre behaviors that essentially do not harm anyone may experience less stress than a family member who feels the need to control these behaviors. More useful attitudes and coping skills are learned through experience and the sharing of these experiences with other people. The outstanding success of the family support groups as a source of support for family members appears to be based upon the group's ability to assist families in formulating more useful attitudes and practical coping skills.

## Professional Survey

The results of the survey of mental health professionals suggests two key findings. First, most professionals seem to believe that families who have psychiatrically disabled members are generally satisfied with the mental health services that are currently being provided. Both the very high percentage (82%) of professionals who believe families to be very to moderately satisfied with the overall service system and the large number of specific services that most professionals believed to be satisfactory to families suggest that professionals have a strong belief that families are pleased with the services offered in the mental health system.

Second, and related to the first finding, the large majority of professionals believe that families are very to moderately satisfied with professional activities within these service settings. More than two thirds of professionals surveyed indicated that families were very to moderately satisfied with the activities listed. In short, professionals generally believe that families are both satisfied with services and satisfied with the behavior of professionals within these service settings.

There are two possible explanations for these findings. First, it may be that the respondents are a very narrow sample of professionals and indeed work in settings where services and professional activities are satisfactory to families. However, given the wide geographical distribution of the sample of professionals and the similar distribution of family members who responded, this does not seem likely. What is more likely is that mental health professionals, like most people, firmly believe in the value of their work and in their own personal efficacy within their jobs. As Peters and Waterman (1982) suggest, most people are convinced that they are exceptionally effective in their jobs, even when there is strong evidence to the contrary. It seems likely that the responses of professionals are colored by their belief that consumers are happy with the services being provided.

There are several broad implications that can be drawn from these findings. First, these findings suggest that professionals may not be very willing or able to conduct an unbiased evaluation of family satisfaction. There is a need to do more frequent and honest evaluation of family satisfaction with mental health services. The current scarcity of satisfaction surveys in the literature indicates the degree to which this need is not being met. More hard data on satisfaction may help professionals to modify their views on family perceptions of mental health services.

Second, these findings suggest that professional training tends to support the belief that consumers are satisfied with mental health services. In graduate programs, there is a strong emphasis placed on theory, treatment, and, in some cases, outcome. However, it is assumed that what are being provided to families and consumers are the services they desire and need. Graduate training could include a discussion of how to assess the needs and functional skills of families and how to tailor assistance to individual family needs. This would take a limited amount of professional and family time and energy and would tend to prepare professionals to listen to what families have to say about family needs and the needs of their disabled family member.

Third, there seems to be a lack of acknowledgement among mental health professionals concerning the serious gaps and deficits in the technology of mental health service delivery. The fact that professionals are overwhelmingly of the opinion that families are satisfied with mental health services and professional activities may suggest that professionals are satisfied with the current "state of the art" of mental health technology. Yet, the family respondents clearly want more effective services and more highly skilled service providers. And the skills and services needed by families are often not available among the professionals with whom families have to deal.

### Comparison of Family Need Survey and Professional Survey

It is clear from the comparison of the data that professionals do not see families the same way that families see themselves. Professionals do not appear to be in tune with the actual needs of families or with their level of dissatisfaction with mental health services. The source of this discrepancy is difficult to pinpoint and can only be guessed at. It is the authors' opinion that professionals really don't know what families want or need. They haven't been trained to listen to families and to assess their need from the families' own perspective. Nor are professionals aware of the recent literature reviewing the research on families of the mentally ill. Professionals essentially lack the knowledge and the skills to understand and to work with these families. Fortunately, families have not given up on professionals. Families want professionals to maintain their leadership role and to increase their level of knowledge and skill. The question remains whether the professional will want to make the necessary changes to meet the changing role requirements demanded by families of the severely mentally ill.

What would professionals need to do in order to be more sensitive and responsive to the needs of families. They would need to challenge their own attitudes and beliefs about families. They could learn to view families as primarily reactors to, rather than the cause of, mental illness. They could update their own information and skills for working with families in more practical ways. They could listen to what families are saying and take their perceptions seriously. Finally, professionals could learn to work cooperatively with families. Families are important caregivers and frequently have resources and energy available to utilize for their disabled family member. These resources and this energy are most available when supported by a sensitive mental health professional.

## CONCLUSION

Because of the importance of the family and home environment in the rehabilitation of the severely psychiatrically disabled person, means of identifying family needs and strengths as well as of maximizing the positive influences of the family need attention from the mental health and rehabilitation profession. Mental health administrators, mental health practitioners, and legislators need to listen to what families have to say and to take their concerns seriously. In addition, mental health practitioners need to be open to reviewing and possibly updating their attitudes toward, and practices with, families that include a person with a severe psychiatric disability. Mental health practitioners may need additional knowledge and skills to work more closely and cooperatively with families. The authors hope that this study will encourage other researchers to look at how the family as a resource enhances the rehabilitation of their disabled family member and how enlightened mental health professionals can enhance the family as a source of support.

### ACKNOWLEDGMENT

This chapter was written with the support of National Institute of Handicapped Research Grant No. G008005486.

### REFERENCES

Anderson, C. M., Hogarty, G. E., & Reiss, D. J. (1980). Family treatment of adult schizophrenic patients: A psychoeducational approach. *Schizophrenia Bulletin, 6,* 490-505.

Appleton, W. S. (1974). Mistreatment of patients' families by psychiatrists. *American Journal of Psychiatry, 131,* 655-657.

Arieti, S. (1974). *Interpretation of schizophrenia* (2nd ed.). New York: Basic Books.

Bateson, G., Jackson, D., Haley, J., & Weakland, J. (1956). Toward a theory of schizophrenia. *Behavioral Science, 1,* 251-264.

Beels, C. C. (1978). Social networks, the family and the schizophrenic patient. *Schizophrenia Bulletin, 4,* 512-521.

Beels, C. C. (1981). Social support and schizophrenia. *Schizophrenia Bulletin, 7*(1), 58-72.

Berdie, D. R., & Anderson, J. F. (1974). *Questionnaire design and use.* Metuchen, NJ: Scarecrow Press.

Bowen, M. (1960). A family concept of schizophrenia. In D. D. Jackson (Ed.), *The etiology of schizophrenia.* New York: Basic Books.

Byalin, K., Jed, J., & Lehman, S. (1982). *Family intervention with treatment-refractory chronic schizophrenics.* Paper presented at 20th International Congress of Applied Psychology, Edinburgh, Scotland.

Creer, C., & Wing, J. K. (1974). *Schizophrenia at home.* London: Institute of Psychiatry.

Dillman, D. (1978). *Mail and telephone surveys: The total design method.* New York: Wiley.

Dincin, J., Selleck, W., & Streicker, S. (1978). Restructuring parental attitudes—Working with parents of the adult mentally ill. *Schizophrenia Bulletin, 4,* 597-608.

Fromm-Reichmann, F. (1948). Notes on the development of treatment of schizophrenics by psychoanalytic psychotherapy. *Psychiatry, 11,* 263-273.

Goldman, H. H. (1982). Mental illness and family burden: A public health perspective. *Hospital and Community Psychiatry, 33,* 557-559.

Goldman, H. H., & Gatozzi, A. A. (1981). Defining and counting the chronically mentally ill. *Hospital and Community Psychiatry, 32*(1), 21-27.

Hatfield, A. B. (1978). Psychological costs of schizophrenia to the family. *Social Work, 23,* 355-359.

Hatfield, A. B. (1979). The family as a partner in the treatment of mental illness. *Hospital and Community Psychiatry, 30,* 338-340.

Hatfield, A. B. (1981a). Coping effectiveness in families of the mentally ill: An exploratory study. *Journal of Psychiatric Treatment and Evaluation, 3,* 11-19.

Hatfield, A. B. (1981b). Self-help groups for families of the mentally ill. *Social Work, 26,* 408-413.

Hatfield, A. B., Fierstein, R., & Johnson, D. (1982). Meeting the needs of families of the psychiatrically disabled. *Psychosocial Rehabilitation Journal, 6*(1), 27-40.

Hirsch, S. R., & Leff, J. P. (1975). *Abnormalities in parents of schizophrenics* (Maudsley Monographs No. 22, pp. 99-101). London: Oxford University Press.

Holden, D. F., & Lewine, R. R. J. (1982). Families of schizophrenic individuals: An evaluation of mental health professionals, resources, and the effects of schizophrenia. *Schizophrenia Bulletin, 4,* 626-633.

Kanter, J., & Lin, A. (1980). Facilitating a therapeutic milieu in the families of schizophrenics. *Psychiatry, 43,* 106-119.

Kerlinger, F. N. (1973). *Foundations of behavioral research.* New York: Holt, Rinehart & Winston.

Killelea, M. (1976). Mutual help organizations: Interpretations in the literature. In G. Kaplan & M. Killilea (Eds.), *Support systems and mutual help.* New York: Grune & Stratton.

Kint, M. G. (1978). Schizophrenia is a family affair: Problems of families in coping with schizophrenia. *Journal of Orthomelcular Psychiatry, 7,* 236-246.

Kreisman, D. E., & Joy, V. D. (1974). Family response to the mental illness of a relative: A review of the literature. *Schizophrenia Bulletin, 1*(10), 34-57.

Lamb, R., & Oliphant, E. (1978). Schizophrenia through the eyes of families. *Hospital and Community Psychiatry, 29,* 803-806.

Leff, J., Kuipers, L., Berkowitz, R., Eberbein-Vries, R., & Sturgeon, D. (1982). A controlled trial of social intervention in the families of schizophrenic patients. *British Journal of Psychiatry, 141,* 121-134.

Liberman, R. P., Wallace, C. J., Vaughan, C. E., & Snyder, K. L. (1979, April). *Social and family factors in the course of schizophrenia.* Paper presented at the Conference on Psychotherapy of Schizophrenia: Current Status and New Directions. Yale University School of Medicine. New Haven, CT.

Lidz, T. (1958). Schizophrenia and the family. *Psychiatry, 21,* 21-27.

Minkoff, K. (1979). A map of the chronic mental patient. In J. Talbott (Ed.), *The chronic mental patient* (11-37). Washington, DC: American Psychiatric Association.

Park, C. C., & Shapiro, L. N. (1976). *You are not alone: Understanding and dealing with mental illness.* Boston: Little, Brown.

Peters, T. J., & Waterman, R. H. (1982). *In search of excellence.* New York: Warner Books.

Spaniol, L., Zipple, A. M., & Fitzgerald, S. (1984). How professionals can share power with families: A practical approach to working with families of the mentally ill. *Psychosocial Rehabilitation Journal, 8,* 77–84.

Straw, P., & Young, B. (1982). *Awakenings: A self-help group organization kit.* Washington, DC: National Alliance for the Mentally Ill.

Terkelsen, K. G. (1983). Schizophrenia and the family: II. Adverse effects of family therapy. *Family Process, 22,* 191–200.

Wasow, M. (1980). *Professionals have hurt us—parents of schizophrenics speak out.* Unpublished manuscript. (Available from M. Wasow, Mt. Sinai Medical Center, 950 N. 12th St., PO Box 342, Milwaukee, WI 53201.)

Wynne, L. C., Ryckoff, I., Day, J., & Hirsch, S. (1958). Pseudomutuality in the family relations of schizophrenics. *Psychiatry, 21,* 205–220.

Zipple, A. M., & Spaniol, L. (1984). *Current educational and supportive models of family intervention: A review and suggestions for their use.* Manuscript submitted for publication.

# Social Support and Family Coping

*Agnes B. Hatfield*

It is now generally believed that social support plays a major role in modifying or mitigating the deleterious effects of stress on health. Of key importance in determining the outcome of a crises is the absence or availability of social supports in the environment. People depend on others for justification and affirmation; few can survive without the support of some segment of their fellow humans (Caplan, 1974). How well families do in the face of a severe mental illness may depend to a significant extent on how well their needs for support are met.

Caplan (1974) defines social support systems as attachments between individuals and groups of individuals that promote mastery of emotions, offer guidance, provide feedback, validate identity, and foster competence. People help by sharing tasks; supplying extra resources, such as money, material, and tools; and they give practical advice and information. Almost every social relationship has the potential for giving emotional support. There is potential support based on attachment, such as in the family; through shared interests or similarity of circumstances in the community; or through bonds of loyalty; or through other kinds of investment in another's well-being (Weiss, 1982).

Interest in the self-enhancing potential of social networks has mushroomed among social scientists and mental health professionals, including those whose primary interests are persons with mental ill-

Agnes B. Hatfield. Department of Human Development, College of Education, University of Maryland, College Park, Maryland.

ness and their families (Beels, 1978; Hatfield, 1979; Killilea, 1982; Swenson, 1981). Some writers, Hirsch (1981), for example, caution that we cannot yet be sure whether this is destined to be a fad or a serious contribution to the field. While respecting this caveat, it is worth noting that the interest in social networks has held up well in the last couple of decades and, in fact, the interest is growing, if we can judge by the numerous books and articles that are appearing in print.

Hirsch (1981) favors a definition of social networks "as a personal community that embeds and supports critical social identities" (p. 16). These are particularly important during times of major life changes, when an existing identity structure may be shattered and there is a necessity for rebuilding a more satisfactory identity structure and a community to support it. The onset of mental illness in a family member is a time of major life change in which members of the family are required to build a new identity structure and, predictably, they did create a new community to support it. For many family caregivers, the National Alliance for the Mentally Ill (NAMI) has become their new community, through which they establish identity and receive the needed social supports. This development will be discussed later in this chapter.

Hirschowitz's (1976) concept of persons being in transition is useful in thinking about those who are thrust into the unanticipated role of family caregiver to a seriously disturbed relative. They must abandon old expectations of high-achieving sons and daughters with bright futures and independent lives and accept a harsh new reality of a young person whose energies are taken up in a struggle to cope with a severely handicapping condition. Parents must lay aside their earlier plans for less responsibility and more freedom in their later years and adjust to the realities of long-term caregiving. One mother stated very poignantly what many others have undoubtedly felt, "All my life I have been tied down, and now I don't see any prospect of ever being without a dependent."

Maintaining the old support systems can be very difficult for these families, for their life circumstances have changed so much. Most middle-aged and older parents are relatively free to make their own plans, come and go as they wish, but this is not true for parents who are caring for handicapped children—they may need to make complicated plans just to get out of the house. Thus old social relationships may fade away. When one is out of phase in too many ways with other persons of one's developmental age, social life can be very difficult. If the mentally ill relative is a spouse, there may be a need for an even more radical shift, as old relationships with other couples disintegrate. Families may go through critical periods of loneliness and isolation before their social networks are restructured to meet the new challenges.

## THE NATURAL SUPPORT NETWORK

Personal relationships remain the primary source for caring for people. With our strong tendency to professionalize all human problems, we lose sight of the part played by an array of informal caregivers: family members, friends, neighbors, clergy, co-workers, beauticians, or bartenders, to name a few. In one of his earlier books, Caplan (1963) pointed out that primary relationships "are often the first choice of people in trouble, even before professional caregivers are consulted" (p. 49). A number of other writers have reported findings that family, relatives, and neighbors are as helpful, and sometimes even more helpful than professionals (Froland, Pancoast, Chapman, & Kimboko, 1981; Hatfield, 1978).

Uzoka (1979) has concluded that recent research has effectively made the point that there are more mutually supportive relationships among relatives than the mental health profession has generally recognized. He feels that there has been a tendency for professionals to advance a distorted version of the nuclear family and, in the process, they have inadvertently weakened the bonds between members. Uzoka particularly has drawn attention to professionals' tendencies toward "labeling relationships as dysfunctional simply because they do not fit the practitioner's model. True desire for mutually gratifying contact is labeled as dependency, and the repression or suppression of desire for such contact is equated with psychologically adaptive behavior" (p. 1102). One is struck by the amount of literature on mental illness in which families are labeled as "dysfunctional," "enmeshed," or "symbiotic." This leads us to wonder if by the use of these poorly defined and variously used terms, some professionals may not be inadvertently and unnecessarily disrupting important family bonds.

Caplan (1976) insists that mental health professionals should recognize the fortifying values of natural person-to-person supports and should find ways of working with them. Caplan also believes that families and relatives are more available to each other than conventional wisdom dictates. In fact, they can serve in a wide variety of roles: They can be collectors and disseminators of information about the world; they can serve as feedback and guidance systems about how the outside world reacts to various members' behaviors, and they can do this in an understandable and minimally threatening way; they can serve as sources of ideology and value system when people face novel life situations; they can serve as a source of practical service and concrete aid during times of crisis; they can be a haven for rest and recuperation; they can serve as a control group where appropriate behavior can be required; they can serve as a resource and a validator of identity when persons under stress may be confused about their identity; and they can contribute to emotional mastery through active listening, offering support and love, and permitting grieving. Caplan, like other writers noted in this chapter, feels that psychiatrists exaggerate the pathogenic characteristics of families, and he recommends that a goal of therapy should be to promote family cohesion.

Howell (1973), drawing on her experience as a physician, has expressed considerable faith in the strength and wisdom of families once they are armed with knowledge, and she believes in their "capabilities for competent, sensible and healthy self-determination" (xii). She observed, however, that too many agencies make families feel helpless, dependent, and incompetent. She advised families to develop a wide network of family, friends, and neighbors and suggested that they insist that experts share their knowledge and skills so that families can conduct their own affairs and can utilize paid professionals at their own convenience and on their own terms.

In the Report to the President from the President's Commission on Mental Health (1978), there were considerable references to community supports and the values of social and personal networks as adjuncts to the more formal mental health service system. This is particularly important, noted the report, for those who have severe and chronic mental illnesses. Families, friends, and neighbors are usually the first people to whom persons with emotional disturbances turn. This is even more true in racial and ethnic communities that over the years have necessarily developed strong culturally sensitive networks of support.

The nation can ill afford to waste such a valuable resource, the Report went on to say, and it urged providers of mental health services to "emphasize the strengths of individuals and families and not their weaknesses," and suggested that they "focus on health rather than sickness" (p. 15). The Report recommended that a major effort be made to recognize and strengthen the natural networks to which people belong; identify the potential social supports that formal institutions within the community can provide; improve linkages between community support networks and formal mental health services; and initiate research to increase our knowledge of informal and formal community support systems and networks.

While there appears to be considerable general agreement as to the beneficial effects of natural support networks on those going through crisis, there is less agreement about how these supports actually influence psychological adjustment. While we intuitively accept the importance of interpersonal support, scientists have difficulty pinpointing the mechanisms by which social support exerts its influence (Killilea, 1982). There is need for research on exactly what role supportive people play in mediating stress; there is need to measure the psychological processes involved (Eckenrode & Gore, 1981; Schulberg & Killilea, 1982). Wellman (1981) believes that we have a ways to go to formulate questions in such a way that data can be gathered. Health, he acknowledged, is apparently related to supportive ties, but not all ties are supportive. Personal ties are complex and support-nonsupport dichotomies de-emphasize the multifaceted, often contradictory nature, of ties and networks. We must create an analytic strategy, he advised, that takes into consideration the complexity of ties and networks.

Jenkins (1984) identified two models in the literature that have attempted to explain the psychological value of social networks. One point of view is that social supports have a direct effect on adjustment. It says, in effect, the better supported individuals are, the less psychological distress they will experience, regardless of the level of stress in their lives. The second point of view suggests that social support mediates the relationship between stress and adjustment, that is, it serves as a buffer for the individual. The latter model seems to be getting most attention in research at this time.

A number of researchers have recommended that in order to understand the "stress buffering" functions of social supports, more rigorous and systematic approaches to the measurement of network participation is needed (Eckenrode & Gore, 1981; Jenkins, 1984; Kazak & Marvin, 1984). Social network analysis characterizes systems of support along a number of dimensions, such as size (the number of people included in the network), density (the extent to which people in a network contact each other, and multidimensionality (the number of functions served by the relationship) (Jenkins, 1984).

In general, the larger the social network, the greater the likelihood of successful coping and adaptation. Network density provides a measure of the interrelatedness of the network; high-density networks have many links among members and low-density networks have fewer. High-density networks may foster extreme closeness and a sense of community or they may become groups in which high degrees of consensus stifle independent action. Less dense networks are believed to provide the individual with more diverse coping strategies, thus providing more choice for the individual and the potential for more successful adaptation (Kazak & Marvin, 1984).

"Multidimensionality" refers to the number of functions served by a relationship. If a relationship serves only one function, it is unidimensional, and if it serves more than one function, it is multidimensional. Relationships that serve several functions have greater potential for meeting diverse needs. Other characteristics of network linkages may also be important: Intensity, or how strong the ties are; durability, or the stability of relationships over time; homogeneity, or the degree of similarity of individuals; and reciprocity, or the degree to which individuals are both givers and beneficiaries.

A recent social network analysis study by Kazak and Marvin (1984) of families with children having spina bifida may shed some light on the way supports work for families of other handicapping conditions, including mental illness. The researchers reported that high levels of stress were associated with handicapping conditions, that the stresses appeared to be very appropriate to the situation, and that whole families adapted to stress in ways that were quite functional. They noted, however, that these families' ways of adapting to stress might not always meet the clinicians' preconceived notions as to how families should adapt. These families had highly functional spouse subsystems, that is, husband and wife related to each other and supported each other very well. However, the caregiving role fell mostly to the mother, with the father somewhat of an outsider. The authors felt this might be an adaptive arrangement. Because of the unrelenting financial burden, the father may spend most of his energies on maximizing income, while the mother made most of the decisions and took most direct responsibility for the child and his or her siblings.

Although the size of the extended family network was not unusual, Kuzak and Marvin found, families that had a member suffering from spina bifida had fewer friends. Again, the authors felt that this was adaptive, given the degree of energy needed to care for the child and the limited time these families had to cultivate interests to share with friends. The authors drew several implications from this study for clinicians working with families of handicapped children. Many of these conclusions are applicable to practitioners working with families with mental illness in a member.

1. Clinicians must view family and network differences in terms of their adaptability to the circumstances of that particular family. They should avoid a universal standard of right behavior for all families and not label deviations from this standard as pathological. Families should know that their particular structure may be typical of other such families; realizing this should in itself be stress reducing.

2. One goal in working with families of handicapped children should be to assist the parents, and especially the mother, in identify-

ing and assessing specific sources of parenting stress. "Burn-out" happens frequently, and it then becomes difficult for people to clearly identify the stress they are subjected to.

3. Another goal is for the clinician to help the family identify ways of keeping the extended family involved. The tendency toward a more limited friendship network might be offset by encouraging families to join parent support groups.

The issue of social supports is an important one in the area of mental illness, just as it is in other kinds of life crisis. Therefore a more sophisticated conceptualization of social supports is much to be desired. There is still much to be learned about what transpires in human dialogue and what constitutes help. We need to know more about social supports in relation to specific adaptive challenges (Gottlieb, 1981). We were able to find little research in the literature regarding social supports and families of the mentally ill. Mental illness presents a very special kind of adaptive challenge.

The formation of mutual help groups all across the country has been one adaptive response of families to the demands of mental illnesses. Through the development of mutual support groups, families have created a new community that serves their needs and that forms the basis for an advocacy movement. Most of these mutual support groups are affiliated with an umbrella organization, the National Alliance for the Mentally Ill. We will explore this development next.

## THE ROLE OF SELF-HELP GROUPS

Social scientists are showing considerable interest in the recent flowering of self-help groups in this country. The upsurge of such groups has been especially noticeable since World War II. Borman (1982) estimated that there are over 400 distinct kinds of groups in the United States and Canada, serving an estimated 15 million persons. Organizations of parents of children who are ill or suffering from physical or mental problems were the first to surface. The tendency is to form groups around conditions for which there is no medical cure but in which there is a residue of chronic impairment, and in which problematic medical, social, and psychological effects remain (Gussow, 1976). It is becoming apparent now that medicine is organized in an older model for acute illness; doctors do not always understand the frustration of adaptation to a chronic disability. Mental illness tends to fit the characteristics of a chronic disability, so it is not surprising to find a surge of organizational effort in this area. What is surprising is that it took so long for families with mentally ill relatives to get together.

Undoubtedly the stigma of mental illness is one reason; another may be that the guilt imposed by theories of family etiology kept families overlong in the closet.

Katz and Bender (1976) have defined self-help groups as

> voluntary small group structures for mutual aid in the accomplishment of a specific purpose. They are usually formed by peers who have come together for mutual assistance in satisfying a common need, overcoming a common handicap or life-disrupting problem, and bringing about desired social and/or personal change. The initiators and members of such groups perceive that their needs are not or cannot be met by or through existing social institutions. (p. 9)

Many social scientists agree that the growth of self-help groups is a signal that society's traditional arrangements are not working. The emergence of these groups provides new ways to solve difficult problems of living. What is unique is that they focus on peer support and education and rely less heavily on professionals and agencies. It is more akin to the old concept of neighbor helping neighbor. There is a recognition that professionals are not omnipotent and that the medical community has a limited ability to provide human comfort (Back & Taylor, 1976; Killilea, 1982; Tracy & Gussow, 1976).

Vattano (1972) and Gartner and Riessman (1977) saw the self-help movement as a power-to-the-people movement, a true expression of a democratic ideal that acknowledges individuals' capacity to help one another rather than depend upon professionals. They saw it as linked to the American tradition of volunteerism—it may represent a distrust of bureaucracy and the medical profession's inability to solve all human problems. The self-help concept may eventually become a permanent feature of the mental health system.

Katz (1961) also drew attention to the climate in this country that seems to support a spirit of volunteerism. The organizational-mindedness of Americans was noted as early as 1841 by a noted French visitor, De Tocqueville. Other aspects of American culture also support the concept of self-help. Katz saw these as Americans' tendencies to stress private initiative or a do-it-yourself philosophy, and its abundant economic endowment and humanitarian motives. Katz was impressed by the spontaneous origin of self-help groups, which he believed arise out of the interest and problems of people and are not imposed from the outside—leadership is determined from within.

Gartner and Riessman (1977, p. 7) have identified the following list of features that are critical to self-help groups and that serve to distinguish them from other voluntary organizations:

1. Self-help groups always involve face-to-face interactions.
2. The origin of self-help groups is usually spontaneous (not set up by some outside group).
3. Personal participation is an extremely important ingredient, as bureaucratization is the enemy of self-help organizations.
4. The members agree on and engage in some actions.
5. Typically the groups start from a condition of powerlessness.
6. The groups fill needs for a reference group, a point of connection and identification with others, a base for activity, and a source of ego reinforcement.

There is rather considerable agreement among social scientists as to the ways in which self-help groups benefit their members:

1. Members serve as role models to each other. Role models cannot be provided by physicians—only by those who share the experience. Members note how other people cope with a particular dilemma and begin modeling their own behavior after them. Physicians can offer encouragement, admonition, and advice, but are seldom able to link the prescription to the social milieu. This can only be demonstrated by other persons with the problem (Katz, 1961; Killilea, 1982; Tracy & Gussow, 1976).

2. Help giving is reciprocal and inherently therapeutic. "It is an ancient philosophy which recognizes, develops, and nurtures the strength of people to not only help themselves but also to reach out and help others to help themselves," noted Hess (1982, p. 11). Knowledge gained from one's own experience is highly valued. People who have been recipients of help can be helpers in turn. Experts in a self-help group are simply fellow sufferers who identify with the people they are helping in a reciprocal way (Silverman, 1982). The helpers feel less powerless and more useful. They feel interpersonally competent and satisfied that they are fulfilling the obligations and expectations of mutual support (Killilea, 1982). For these reasons, Silverman (1982) made a strong plea for using the term "mutual help" rather than "self-help", but the latter term seems to predominate in the literature.

3. Opportunities for learning are provided. Adaptation involves learning, noted Silverman (1982) and adaptive strategies are affected by the learning opportunities available. There are few other educational opportunities that are as appropriate to the situation as those found in self-help organizations. People who suffer from transition and crises need information about diagnosis, treatment, ways of coming to terms with loss, and methods of learning new roles. Professional knowledge is necessarily based on an incomplete view of the situation;

outsiders who do not live with the situation on a daily basis do not always understand. Learning from peers means getting information in an understandable form, one easier for the lay person to digest (Silverman, 1982).

Lieberman and Borman (1976) have observed that most self-help groups tend to fit into one of two types: First there are support groups that devote their time to giving service, information, and comfort to their members. Then there are advocacy groups, whose primary mission is to "change something out there." Many groups start out with a support function and over time turn to advocacy. The National Alliance for the Mentally Ill, to be described next, has attempted to maintain both kinds of functions, and has added some additional goals.

## The National Alliance for the Mentally Ill

During the decade of the 1970s, support and advocacy groups of families with mentally ill relatives began forming independently of each other in diverse spots across the country. By a variety of means, these local groups discovered each other's existence and began considering the advantages of pooling their efforts by forming some kind of affiliate relations. This led to a gathering of some one hundred local groups in Madison, Wisconsin, in September 1979 and the formation of the National Alliance for the Mentally Ill (NAMI). Just 6 years later, the NAMI has nearly 500 affiliates in all 50 states, and has a mailing list of 50,000 persons nationwide. With an office and staff in Washington, DC, it has established a presence in the nation's capital, and has become well-known among organizations of mental health professionals. The purposes of the NAMI have been fairly consistent since its inception in 1979 (Hatfield, 1983):

### SUPPORT AND EDUCATION FOR FAMILIES

It was probably the need for support and information that first brought families together and it continues to be a primary reason for members to join local affiliates. Most affiliates with multiple goals make it a point to set aside one or more meetings a month for "emotional support" or "sharing and caring" as these evenings are sometimes called. In addition, considerable support and advice is given by telephone. As has been discussed above, families of the mentally ill find there is no substitute for being able to share feelings and experiences with those who are in the same situations. People no longer feel so alone—they find hope, greater perspectives, and new ideas for handling problems in a spirit of togetherness.

## EDUCATION FOR FAMILIES

Historically, little information of any kind was given to caregiving relatives when the patient left the hospital. Families, however, have a burning desire to know all they can about the strange disorder called mental illness. They learn by inviting knowledgeable professionals to meetings. Professional journal articles are summarized and circulated, members are alerted through newsletters to local lectures and relevant television programs, and some affiliate leaders attend professional meetings and conferences and report back to their members. In the past 3 or 4 years, several books and monographs have been written for the education of families (Bernheim, Lewine, & Beale, 1982; Hatfield, 1982; Torrey, 1983; Vine, 1982; Wasow, 1982). Some of these were written by a relative of a mentally ill person, others by sympathetic professionals. In addition, the office of the NAMI is creating educational pieces for its members.

## EDUCATION OF MENTAL HEALTH PROFESSIONALS

The rapid growth of the family self-help movement in this country reflects, in part, the alienation from mental health professionals felt by many families. Not only do these families share with other families of chronic disorders the frustrations of dealing with a busy medical profession more in tune with providing acute care, but, in addition, families of the mentally ill have found it necessary to combat the accusatory attitude of many service providers. Finally, these families feel that even those with generally positive attitudes toward them, still need a lot of education to fully understand the *real* experience of having a loved one become mentally ill and all the stresses entailed in caring for an ill relative at home. Collaborative efforts can be enhanced as professionals increase their role-taking capacities.

There is evidence that many professionals still do not feel positive toward families. In a recent review of language used by mental health professionals, Hatfield (1984) revealed that there is still frequent negative language used to describe families. Rarely are families seen in a positive light, their strengths recognized, or their heroic efforts to support a deeply disturbed relative acknowledged. The author questioned the degree to which attitudes had really changed.

## ADVOCACY

Families experience mental illness as something catastrophic for them. No patient or family can by itself garner the resources necessary for even minimal care, and, unfortunately, appropriate care is not one of society's priorities. Systems advocacy is going on in many states and localities and on the national level. There is clearly a dire need for supervised housing. Publicly supported hospitals often do not meet standards of optimum care. Only a small percentage of persons, estimated at between 15 and 25%, have access to a constructive day program and the need for case management and crisis care is largely unmet. These are goals of the family movement.

CONSUMER RESPONSIBILITY

Mental illness is a costly disease and families are frustrated and angry when they see themselves paying dearly for a service that did no good. Families are teaching themselves to ask relevant questions about the nature of a service, the length and cost of treatment, and evidence of its efficacy. Practitioners will be required to explain their treatments and their services in clear, jargon-free language and to appropriately use family involvement. Apparently, many families depend on their group's lay referral system, which provides information about which professionals to engage and which ones to avoid.

RESEARCH

Clearly, families feel that ultimate hope lies in research. Members of the NAMI are establishing their own research foundation as a means of affecting the direction that research into mental illness takes. They support increased budgets in Congress for neurological research and for evaluative studies of social programs.

People frequently ask how the NAMI differs from another well-known and older organization, the National Association for Mental Health (NAMH). The two organizations differ in several ways. NAMI used the words "mental illness" in a rather restricted sense to mean a disorder of severe proportions that seriously disables people who have it. Mental illness is considered a real disease, which is biologically caused and for which a cure is not possible at this time. NAMH, on the other hand, equates "mental illness" with "emotional disturbance" and assumes it is on a continuum with the milder upsets that bring people into clinics for help. NAMH has prevention as one of its goals; it apparently believes that improving social and psychological conditions can prevent mental illness. NAMI members argue that prevention is not possible until we know causes.

While both are voluntary organizations, the makeup of the membership differs considerably. In NAMH, membership comes from all segments of society—professional and nonprofessional, with some patients and families of patients. NAMI is made up primarily of families with mentally ill relatives and the leadership roles are held by family members. NAMI has adhered to a fairly classic self-help style as described by Katz and Bender (1976) and Silverman (1982) above. Although these two voluntary organizations are quite different in makeup and philosophy, they tend to coalesce around many issues and this is done both locally and nationally.

## THE RELATIONSHIP BETWEEN FORMAL AND INFORMAL CAREGIVING SYSTEMS

The question now arises as to how informal systems of care, such as family, friends, and self-help groups, can relate to the system of care provided by the mental health profession. Froland et al. (1981) believe that trying to link formal and informal caregiving is like linking two cultures with different belief systems. Informal caregiving is not a one-way activity, they point out, but is a mutual interchange in which there is both giving and receiving of help. Formal caregiving, on the other hand, does not involve reciprocity and it operates under a system of explicit categories for assessing need and eligibility. There is a clash when one style of caregiving seeks the certainty of formal rules and routine procedures and the other seeks the privacy of unspoken rules and spontaneous activity. The authors feel collaboration is possible if there is an understanding of the strengths and weaknesses of each system.

Gartner and Riessman (1977) have examined the relationship between professional and aprofessional practice and have concluded that, although there is considerable difference in their style of caregiving they can effectively work together. Traditionally the professions were characterized by their control of entry into the professions; their colleague, rather than client, orientation in terms of standards; an occupational code of ethics; and a theoretical basis for their professional caregiving. The authors criticized the basis upon which professional power rests. They are especially concerned by what they see as the tendency to be colleague-oriented rather than client-oriented. They feel that the self-help movement acts as a source of pressure toward a consumer orientation and, as such, will result in increased professional accountability.

Borkman (1976) introduced new concepts to characterize the difference in style that have been noted by several writers (e.g., Caplan, 1974; Froland et al., 1981; Lenrow & Burch, 1981). Borkman uses the term "experiential knowledge" for knowledge based on personal experience with a phenomenon. This wisdom tends to be concrete, specific, and commonsensical. It is based on personal experience and is more or less representative of others who have the same problem. There is experiential expertise that refers to the competence or skill one gains from direct and immediate involvement with a difficulty. Professional knowledge requires formal training and appropriate credentials. This knowledge comes from research and theory and leads the professional to see phenomena more objectively and dispassionately.

Borkman defines self-help organizations as organized experiential knowledge. Members pool a great deal of experience and from this they learn how their problems are alike and how they are different from that of others. Because self-help groups are pragmatic and voluntary, there is always a testing of workability of the prevailing ideas. Members drop away if ideas are not useful; the survival of the group depends on developing models of help that members see as relevant.

Tension between professionals and self-help groups may be due to these two competing systems of knowledge. How well the two can collaborate may depend on sensitivity to these diverse ways of looking at things and a mutual respect for the legitimacy of these two points of view.

Lenrow and Burch (1981) have advanced some further explanations about the source of tension between self-help groups and professionals. To begin with, these authors point out, most lay people have a mixture of distrust and respect toward professionals. There seems to be a range of opinions as to just how expert professionals really are. Some people feel they have the answers and they should take charge when problems arise. Others feel that professionals are no more competent than lay people. Many people have a sense of dependence on the professional's perceived power and a resentment about feeling vulnerable to the professional's possible abuse of power. Some lay persons, say Lenrow and Burch, believe professionals are essentially exploitive, being more concerned about their economic interests and privileges than with the well-being of the people they serve.

While lay persons have preconceived ideas about professionals, Lenrow and Burch point out, professionals also have preconceived ideas about lay persons. They may see them "as raw materials to develop in their own image" (p. 236) rather than respecting the self-enhancing characteristics that are peculiar to these groups. Professionals may see lay persons as simplistic, irrational, and/or irresponsible and believe that they need to be regulated by professionals. There are still other professionals who tend to romanticize the knowledge and skill of lay persons. Given these misperceptions on both sides, there is reason to wonder if potentially they can work together. The authors feel that this is, indeed, possible if each of these groups are willing to identify and value the unique resources available to each and then rationally coordinate an exchange of resources.

The authors recognize that there are powerful barriers that mitigate against the development of an effective state of interdependence. One barrier is the strong tendency to believe that expert knowledge is scientifically determined, scarce, and comprehensible to only a few. This justifies a unilateral use of power and a right to decide what is good for the population the professional serves. An uncritical view of science and a failure to recognize its limitations creates an exaggerated view of professional expertise. This view is not something imposed on lay persons; rather it is something they often prefer to believe when they are feeling helpless and vulnerable in the face of difficult problems and overwhelming stress. Also a factor, is that people are taught deference to professional people as children and continue in adulthood to relate to them in compliant and passive ways. These styles of relating are systematically reinforced by the structure of human service settings and training. Bureaucratic arrangements reinforce reliance on hierarchical and impersonal styles of dealing with people.

Despite the institutional, cultural, interpersonal, and intrapsychic obstacles, Lenrow and Burch (1981) believe that it is possible to develop collaborative relationships between lay and professional people. They believe that professionals can become sensitive to the perceptions and priorities of informal caregivers and can solve problems jointly with them. The authors believe that this period of history favors the development of equalitarian attitudes and relationships between professionals and lay persons.

# REFERENCES

Back, K. W., & Taylor, R. C. (1976). Self-help groups: Tool or symbol. *Journal of Applied Behavioral Science, 12,* 295–309.

Beels, C. C. (1978). Social networks, the family, and the schizophrenic patient. *Schizophrenia Bulletin, 4,* 512–520.

Bernheim, K. L., Lewine, R. R. J., & Beale, C. T. (1982). *The caring family.* New York: Random House.

Borkman, T. Experiential knowledge: A new concept for the analysis of self-help groups. *Social Service Review, 50,* 445–456.

Borman, L. D. (1982). Introduction. In L. D. Borman, L. E. Borck, R. Hess, & F. L. Pasquale (Eds.), *Helping people to help themselves* (pp. 3–15). New York: Haworth Press.

Caplan, G. (1963). *Principles of preventive psychiatry.* New York: Basic Books.

Caplan, G. (1974). *Support systems and community mental health.* New York: Behavioral Publications.

Caplan, G. (1976). The family as support system. In G. Caplan & M. Killilea (Eds.), *Support systems and mutual help: Multidisciplinary explorations* (pp. 19–36). New York: Grune & Stratton.

Eckenrode, J., & Gore, S. (1981). Stressful events and social supports: The significance of context. In B. H. Gottlieb (Ed.), *Social networks and social support* (pp. 43-68). Beverly Hills: Sage.

Froland, C., Pancoast, D. L., Chapman, N. J., & Kimboko, P. J. (1981). Linking formal and informal support systems. In B. H. Gottlieb (Ed.), *Social networks and social support* (pp. 259-276). Beverly Hills: Sage.

Gartner, A., & Riessman, F. (1977). *Self-help in the human services*. San Francisco: Jossey-Bass.

Gottlieb, B. H. (1981). Social networks and social supports in community mental health. In B. H. Gottlieb (Ed.), *Social networks and social support* (pp. 11-42). Beverly Hills: Sage.

Gussow, Z. (1976). The role of self-help clubs in adaptation to chronic illness and disability. *Social Science and Medicine, 10,* 407-414.

Hatfield, A. B. (1978). Psychological costs of schizophrenia to the family. *Social Work, 23,* 355-359.

Hatfield, A. B. (1979). Help-seeking behavior in families of schizophrenics. *American Journal of Community Psychology, 7,* 563-569.

Hatfield, A. B. (1982). *Coping with mental illness in the family: A family guide*. Rosslyn, VA: The National Alliance for The Mentally Ill.

Hatfield, A. B. (1983, October 2-7). *Emerging issues of the family self-help movement*. Paper presented at International Symposium on the Future of the Mentally Ill in Society, Hebrew University, Jerusalem, Israel.

Hatfield, A. B. (1984, August 28). *Semantic barriers to collaboration between professionals and families*. Paper presented at the Annual Convention of the American Psychological Association, Toronto, Canada.

Hess, R. (1982). Self-help as a service delivery strategy. In L. D. Borman, L. E. Borck, R. Hess, & F. L. Pasquale (Eds.), *Helping people to help themselves* (pp. 1-2). New York: Haworth.

Hirsch, B. J. (1981). Social networks and the coping process: Creating personal communities. In B. H. Gottlieb (Ed.), *Social networks and social support* (pp. 149-170). Beverly Hills: Sage.

Hirschowitz, R. G. (1976). Groups to help people cope with the tasks of transition. In R. G. Hirschowitz & B. Levy (Eds.). *The changing mental health scene* (pp. 171-188). New York: Spectrum.

Howell, M. (1973). *Helping ourselves: Families and the human network*. Boston, MA: Beacon Press.

Jenkins, S. C. (1984). *Social support and psychological adjustment of families of the chronically mentally disabled*. Unpublished manuscript, University of Maryland.

Katz, A. H. (1961). *Parents of the handicapped-self-organized parents' and relatives' groups for the treatment of ill and handicapped children*. Springfield, IL: Charles C. Thomas.

Katz, A. H., & Bender, E. I. (1976). *The strength in us: Self-help groups in the modern world*. New York: New viewpoints.

Kazak, A. E., & Marvin, R. S. (1984). Differences, difficulties and adaptation: Stress and social networks in families with a handicapped child. *Family Relations, 33,* 67-77.

Killilea, M. (1982). Interaction of crisis theory, coping strategies, and social support systems. In H. C. Schulberg & M. Killilea (Eds.), *The modern practice of community mental health* (pp. 163-214). San Francisco: Jossey-Bass.

Lenrow, P. B., & Burch, R. W. (1981). Mutual aid and professional services—opposing or complimentary? In B. H. Gottlieb (Ed.), *Social networks and social support* (pp. 163-214). Beverly Hills, CA: Sage.

Lieberman, M., & Borman, L. (1976). Introduction to special issue on self-help groups. *Journal of Applied Behavioral Science, 12,* 261-264.

President's Commission on Mental Health. (1978). *Report to the President* (Vol. 1). Washington, DC: U.S. Government Printing Office.

Schulberg, H. C., & Killilea, M. (1982). Community mental health in transition. In H. C. Schulberg & M. Killilea (Eds.), *The modern practice of community mental health* (pp. 40-94). San Francisco: Jossey-Bass.

Silverman, P. R. (1982). People helping people: Beyond the professional model. In H. C. Schulberg & M. Killilea (Eds.), *The modern practice of community mental health* (pp. 611-632). San Francisco: Jossey-Bass.

Swenson, C. R. (1981). Using natural helping networks to promote competence. In A. N. Maluccio (Ed.), *Promoting competence in clients—a new/old approach to social work practice* (pp. 125-151). New York: Macmillan.

Torrey, E. F. (1983). *Surviving schizophrenia: A family manual.* New York: Harper & Row.

Tracy, G. S., & Gussow, Z. (1976). Self-help groups: A grass-roots response to needs for services. *Journal of Applied Behavioral Science, 12,* 310-316.

Uzoka, A. (1979). The myth of the nuclear family-historical background and clinical implications. *American Psychologists, 34,* 1095-1106.

Vattano, A. J. (1972). Power to the people: Self-help groups. *Social Work, 17,* 7-15.

Vine, P. (1982). *Families in pain: Children, siblings, spouses, and parents of the mentally ill speak out.* New York: Pantheon.

Wasow, M. (1982). *Coping with schizophrenia: A survival manual for parents, relatives and friends.* Palo Alto, CA: Science and Behavior Books.

Weiss, R. S. (1982). Relationships of social support and psychological well-being. In H. C. Schulberg & M. Killilea (Eds.), *The modern practice of community mental health* (pp. 148-162). San Francisco: Jossey-Bass.

Wellman, B. (1981). Applying network analysis to the study of support. In B. H. Gottlieb (Ed.), *Social networks and social support* (pp. 171-200). Beverly Hills, CA: Sage.

# Coping Strategies of Family Caregivers

*LeRoy Spaniol*

## INTRODUCTION

Families encounter many problems in living with a family member who has a severe psychiatric disability. The type and extent of problems encountered have been well documented (Creer & Wing, 1974; Hatfield, 1978, 1981; Jung, Spaniol, & Anthony, 1983; Thompson & Doll, 1982). The types of problems reported include difficulties in dealing with professionals, treatment options, medication, community resources, housing, disturbing behavior, and meeting the needs of other family members. The extent of problems reported ranges from minimally disruptive to extremely disruptive to family life. Although an increasing amount of information has become available on the needs of families, little information has become available on how families currently cope with these problems. Understanding how families cope can lead to the development of more successful intervention strategies for family members and for professionals who work with families.

The focus of the study to be described in this chapter was on personal coping styles of families. Because the problems families face in managing their lives and assisting their disabled family member often go beyond their own limited ability to make an impact, families have recognized their need to become involved in organizational, community, and legislative/policy changes if their family members are to

LeRoy Spaniol. Center for Rehabilitation Research and Training in Mental Health, Boston University, Boston, Massachusetts.

receive the services they require. Families want to deal directly with the social—political structures that affect their lives. Coping strategies for dealing with this larger arena have been developed by many families and family groups throughout the country. This larger arena was not the focus of the current study; however, the authors may refer to it at times where it seems appropriate.

Studies of the family as a reactor to mental illness have pointed to the burden placed on family members. While many studies have found that families will tolerate a great deal of deviance in their disabled relatives, they experience great emotional stress as they attempt to cope with psychiatric disability and the helping resources. Rather than blaming the family for the psychiatric disability, a "reactive" viewpoint sees the family as managing its problems as well as it can through coping strategies. Some strategies are experienced as more useful than others. This initial shift in attitude or viewpoint from "causative" to "reactive" opens up the possibility of approaching families more pragmatically. A nonblaming stance broadens the possibilities of working with families as partners. It also assists in understanding the family's role in relation to psychiatric disability.

## Coping and Family Attitudes

One of the factors affecting coping styles in families is the attitude held by family members toward their disabled relative. Attitudes are the "trigger" that determine our internal and external reactions to stressful events in our lives. Attitudes can affect interaction by predisposing family members to act in ways that indicate acceptance or rejection of their disabled relative. Surprisingly, the research on family attitudes, hospitalization rates, and role performance of the disabled relative has been mixed. Freeman and Simmons (1963) found that families of successfully discharged patients accepted their relatives as basically normal people, tended not to blame them, and held a positive attitude toward the hospital. Family members who reported that they were "very pleased" with having the psychiatrically disabled relative at home tended to refrain from using rehospitalization as a coping device (Barett, Kuriansky, & Gurland, 1972). Not all studies have found a positive correlation between acceptance and community tenure. Kelly (1964) found a nonsignificant difference in family acceptance and community tenure in a group of 65 discharged schizophrenic patients from a psychiatric evaluation project. Family acceptance was not related to exacerbation of symptoms. Other studies have also reported that family members' attitudes toward mental illness are not significantly related to outcome (Davis, Freeman, & Simmons, 1957; Lorei, 1964).

The results of a study by Brown, Birley, and Wing (1972) indicated that a return to certain types of "accepting" environments, especially an overinvolved and overprotective family, was not the best alternative for patient or family. This has been found to be particularly true for moderately to severely disturbed patients. Brown and his associates found a correlation between high "expressed emotion" (EE) and relapse. The concept of high EE is defined as frequent negative comments indicating criticism, hostility as inferred from nonverbal cues, and emotional overinvolvement. Of these factors, the first was the most predictive of relapse.

Several studies in the last decade have confirmed the relationship between EE and relapse (Falloon, Boyd, McGill, Strang, & Moss, 1981; Vaughn, et al., 1982). Because of these research results, and because the concept of EE comprises observable, measurable, and teachable behaviors, it is expected that this research area will be more extensively studied in the next decade. Unfortunately, calling families "high EE" maintains and reinforces an attitude of stigma toward families. It is another label that defines families in terms of a negative symptom. This further labeling of families does them a great disservice. The concept of high EE fails to adequately acknowledge the many positive aspects of a family's relationship to the ill member. It is a deficit model that doesn't even begin to tap the richness and complexity of the strengths, the caring, the concern, and the activities that families provide on behalf of their disabled member. Families express many positive attitudes toward their disabled family member—even when they are also intrusive and negative.

To date, research on families has failed to do justice to the range of positive attitudes expressed by many families of the severely mentally ill. In spite of the research evidence pointing to the mixed impact of positive attitudes and the likely detrimental impact of negative attitudes, families report many positive attitudes toward their disabled member (Spaniol, Jung, Zipple, & Fitzgerald, 1984). And in spite of multiple failures, frustrations, breakdowns, abuse, lack of resources, and limited community support, many families continue to invest themselves in helping their disabled member. Their approach is to work out their problems and to keep trying. The effort families exert is not simply a reaction to guilt. It comes from their genuine concern for their disabled member.

Families also express a profound sense of loss over what might have been if things had been different. Many cope with this loss and continued longing for a more normal life-style through acceptance and through building a life-style that is workable for them. Others cope in less useful ways. They may find it difficult, for example, to let go of a dream of what might have been, because there may be so little support for accepting the reality of what they have to live with. The reappraisal of their situation (i.e., attitudes, beliefs) is made acutely difficult by personal, professional, and community biases against psychiatrically disabled individuals and families. Family support and advocacy groups have become a resource for families in resymbolizing their current and past experiences with a disabled family member in more useful ways and in rebuilding family self-esteem.

The purpose of the study described in the following sections was to identify current stressful and unsuccessful coping strategies used by families. Successful strategies are those that families report to be useful to them. Other families can possibly use these strategies in dealing with their own family situations. Unsuccessful strategies are those that families have not found to be useful. Research efforts were begun at the Rehabilitation Research and Training Center at Boston University in 1979. The survey of coping strengths and deficits was part of a larger survey of the needs of families, their coping strengths and deficits, and professional perceptions of the needs of families. The survey of coping strengths and deficits included both rated and open-ended questions. This chapter will focus on the responses of the family members to the open-ended questions. Responses to the remaining parts of the survey, as well as information on sampling, design, and instrumentation, will be found in chapter 8. Family members were asked to respond to 9 open-ended questions. Each dealt with a particular problem area and how families currently coped or did not cope well with this problem area. In the following section, the author describes and discusses the family responses to these items.

## HOW FAMILY MEMBERS TAKE CARE OF THEMSELVES

Families have developed a wide variety of techniques to take care of themselves and to prevent exhausting themselves while caring for their family member with a disability. When families are subjected to continuous and, at times severe, stress, physiological and psychological dysfunctions increase (Adams, Hayes, & Hopson, 1977; Benson, 1975). Families' prolonged stress can lead to "burn-out," a depletion of personal resources to the point of loss of energy to fulfill necessary functions. Families of a person with a psychiatric disability have improved their coping by developing strategies to reduce and/or prevent the physical and psychological effects of sustained stress (Spaniol et al., 1984).

One of the most commonly reported strategies is for family members to involve themselves in activities and hobbies that have nothing to do with mental illness. These are activities and hobbies that family members find personally satisfying and enriching. Family members report involvement in physical activities such as tennis and other forms of exercise; they spend time with friends doing things that are fun; they read novels; they go fishing; they go to movies and the theater; and they take frequent walks.

Some family members find that meaningful work away from home helps them to achieve a better balance in their lives. Balance is a key concept. Since the sources of stress cannot always be eliminated, families frequently need to find ways to take care of themselves in situations that are not likely to change. When they are excessively focused on deficits and problems, families report being drained and worn out. Families who are coping well appear to have moved from the position of burn-out to one of greater balance in their lives. And meaningful work outside the home is one of the reported sources of this balance.

Another way in which family members report taking care of themselves is through a deliberate effort to maintain a normal family lifestyle and a life of their own. The experience of living with a person with a severe psychiatric disability can be very disruptive to regular patterns of living. The demands on time and the energy required are often a tremendous drain on a family member's personal resources. Families report that activities, interests, and daily routines that once were habitual are either no longer occurring or are no longer occurring in the same way. A conscious effort is required to maintain a familiar family life-style that is sensitive to the needs of the person with a disability and that respects the needs of other family members. Related to the issue of life-style is the need family members express to maintain a life of their own. To this end, spouses report being particularly sensitive to each other's needs and wants by making sure that each spends time alone, gets away on weekends, and spends time with old friends; and by maintaining other ways of putting energy into taking care of themselves and each other. Putting excessive energy into the family member with the disability drains the family and models to other family members and to the disabled member how not to succeed. Other family members need the example of parents who know how to take care of themselves.

Family support and advocacy groups are also a major source of the permission family members need at times to take better care of themselves. Many family members have found these groups to be a source of personal support. They report discovering that they are not alone in experiencing the effects of living with a person with a severe psychiatric disability. In addition, families model self-nurturing to one another.

Support and advocacy groups help family members to deal with many of the serious negative feelings and images, such as guilt, self-blame, and stigma, that frequently affect families of the severely psychiatrically disabled. Families help each other learn how to challenge the self-fulfilling prophecy of their own negative beliefs about themselves and their family life. (A self-fulfilling prophecy is a belief that is false, and when acted upon becomes true.) Once they have challenged their false beliefs, they can begin to shift toward more positive attitudes toward themselves and their family life.

Families also report that personal strategies such as accepting, distancing, and setting limits are ways in which they take good care of themselves. The various meanings that families have attached to these concepts are paraphrased below:

*Acceptance*
- acknowledging the reality of the disability and the likelihood that it will be around for a long time
- being able to move from a reactive toward a more responsive form of coping
- being able to work toward what is possible in their situation rather than maintaining unrealistic expectations for themselves or their disabled family member
- being able to feel the pain, move through it, and move on to other feelings and options
- becoming less intense
- knowing that whatever they are doing is the best they can do at that time
- knowing that they are not the only ones who can make a difference

*Distancing*
- separating themselves from behaviors that they cannot change or should not be trying to change
- tolerating behaviors that may be a little strange to them but that are not dangerous or harmful
- not assuming responsibility where it does not need to be assumed
- letting other family members' lives unfold more naturally
- letting go of what is not possible and focusing on what is possible
- being selective in their helping

*Setting Limits*
- being firm around behaviors they do not like
- being firm around behaviors they do like
- knowing their limits and not waiting until they are pushed over the edge
- living with the upset their limits cause and getting through it
- knowing that structure can communicate caring
- caring enough not to let their loved ones do something that is harmful to themselves or others and encouraging their loved ones to do things that are in their own best interests.

Family members who are religious also take care of themselves through prayer, Bible reading, and fellowship with other believers. Religious beliefs and activities can sustain family members in their caring. Acceptance is often fostered by deep religious beliefs. The ability to handle pain, suffering, and rejection, and the trauma of suicide, physical injury, and violence is sustained by religious beliefs. Religious beliefs imply that there is more to life than what we ordinarily see, and that there is a power and a force that supports us if we are open to acknowledging it and calling upon it. Family members report strong religious beliefs and regularly acknowledge that these beliefs sustain them in their daily lives.

Lastly, families report that living apart from the family member with the disability is another way in which they take care of themselves. Independent living, halfway houses, or other alternative living situations provide all family members, including the disabled member, with needed respite from the strains and stresses of continuous contact. It is also developmentally appropriate for parents and their offspring to separate after the age of adolescence. Living apart can help to normalize the experience of family members and help them to develop a personal life-style of their own.

## COPING STRATEGIES FOR MANAGING SPECIFIC PROBLEMS

*Medication Management Coping Strategies*

Medication management is a serious concern of families. A recent survey (Spaniol et al., 1984) identified medication management as one of the most important needs of families. Families currently cope with this issue in a variety of ways. One of the most commonly reported ways is through constantly reminding the family member with the disability to take the medication. Families report discussing the importance of the medication in reducing symptoms and staying in the community. They acknowledge how easy it is to forget and then remind the family member in a kind and caring way.

Other families report more confrontation. They tell their family member that he or she will deteriorate without the medication and will have to return to the hospital. Or, if the family member lives apart, families may refuse to allow a member to visit if he or she is not taking the medication. Others resort to more extreme forms of confrontation such as bribery, blackmail, or seeking a court order.

Some families enlist the help of others such as helping professionals. They report arranging family conferences around the issue of medication. Support and encouragement from someone outside the family has been found to be useful in medication management. Families also report many concerns and fears about the impact of the medication on their disabled member. They express frustration with inadequate medication options and the lack of medical management from the medical profession, especially the lack of monitoring the effects of the medication.

Some families report encouraging their family member with the disability to assume responsibility for taking the medication. They believe that he or she can act responsibly and also can live with the consequences of their own decisions. This can be very difficult for families, particularly if there are problems establishing a suitable and effective drug regime. It requires that the person with the disability be able to acknowlege the early signs of return of symptoms and to do something about it.

Families find that physical contact and touching can help to encourage their family member to take the medication. Physical contact is a basic human need. It helps us to feel connected and grounded in our relationships and in our environment. Physical contact often has a very calming effect particularly when it is available as a normal part of family life. It is also a major resource for handling the daily stresses that make the managing of psychiatric symptoms very difficult. Being held in a caring way can sometimes provide the disabled family member with the security and reassurance needed to think clearly and to feel valued and cherished.

*Bizarre and Abnormal Behavior Management*
*Coping Strategies*

The management of bizarre and abnormal behavior is another major concern of families. The most commonly reported strategy is to sit down and talk calmly with the disabled family member. Families report expressing their concerns in a caring way and listening to any questions or issues their family member has. This caring kind of communication has been found to help the family member manage his or her bizarre or abnormal behavior.

Another useful approach is to be firm, without relying on anger or threats, about what behaviors are not appropriate. This approach requires setting clear limits on what is allowed and what is not allowed and holding to these limits through verbal reminders. Setting limits can help clarify the reality of the environment. It can provide an anchor that may help in self-management. Limits imply caring and may foster a sense of belonging to a family. Limits also imply protection. They say that you will help to take care of the family member with the disability when he or she is out of control or has relinquished control for the moment. Limits remind the family member that self-control is possible if he or she wants to maintain it. They also may create an expectation of self-control that may help to shape the desired behavior in the family member with the disability.

Confrontation also has been used successfully by families to manage bizarre and abnormal behavior. Some families report confronting the unreality of the behavior by telling the family member that what he or she is experiencing is not real but a part of the illness. They may suggest that the family member needs extra medication or treatment. Confronting the reality of the behavior can provide the "mirror" some disabled family members need in order to distance themselves from the effects of their own illness. If they have already been able to acknowledge the lack of reality in some of their behavior, confrontation may help them develop the extremely useful self-management tool of being able to distinguish the real from the unreal.

At times other types of confrontation are used by families. Some report "really getting angry" at inappropriate behavior. Another approach is to directly or bluntly disagree with, for example, the paranoia, and to refuse to discuss it because it is unreal. Or they threaten the family member by saying that they will call the police if the behavior continues. Families report that these more extreme approaches can serve to shock the disabled person back into reality and help him or her to better manage symptoms. Confrontation can be difficult because our motivation for confronting often comes from our own frustration and is a way of taking care of ourselves in a difficult situation. It may or may not help the other person and can even make matters worse. When its source is our own genuine caring for the disabled person, and this caring is reinforced by our words, our behavior, and the general environment we create, then confrontation has a much better chance of working. It also has a better chance of working if it is not our only resource for dealing with bizarre and abnormal behavior.

Physical contact was again mentioned by family members as a useful resource in managing behavior. Touching, back rubs, and neck massage, for example have been found to be comforting, calming, and reassuring to the disabled family member. Physical contact is a resource for anchoring a family member in physical and emotional reality.

Finally, some families find they use other methods such as humor or reassurance to allay the disabled person's fears. Or, at times they learn to live with behaviors that are not personally dangerous. Some try to distract the person by taking him or her for a ride in the car. Some reach out to others, such as people in a crisis clinic or friends, for information and support. Some may find that hospitalization is their only reasonable resource.

### Antisocial and Aggressive Behavior Management Coping Strategies

Antisocial and aggressive behaviors are especially perplexing and frustrating for family members. Many report not knowing how to deal with these behaviors successfully. The most commonly reported strategy is to talk directly with the family member about his or her behavior. Families suggest keeping calm and speaking in a normal voice. Also they recommend being firm and clear about what they want the disabled person to do or not to do. Communicating the firmness and clearness of their position is a recurring theme in family responses to many of the coping situations. Some families report that they are able to tolerate some forms of asocial behavior, such as not wanting to be around guests or relatives. They are able to distance themselves from behaviors that are not too harmful. However, having limits and making these limits known in a firm and caring way appears to be a useful strategy for some families.

Another resource for families is calling outside help, such as a crisis clinic or even the police. Families often feel quite helpless, as well as personally frightened, around asocial and aggressive behavior. Letting the person know that they are frightened by the asocial/aggressive behavior can sometimes help. However, many families report needing to get some form of outside assistance if the behavior is excessive. In some cases, families report using hospitalization as a resource to manage these behaviors. The disabled person may need a period of medical supervision, therapy, or simply some respite from the stresses and strains of normal family life.

Other families report using humor and encouragement, rewarding the family member for good behavior, confronting the inappropriate behavior, and even considering moving the family member to a separate apartment because the management issues are too difficult for them to handle on a daily basis.

### Social Withdrawal and Isolation Management Coping Strategies

Family members cope with social withdrawal and isolation in a variety of ways. Many families report actively involving the person with the disability in family and social activities to be especially useful. Families acknowledge that their disabled member needs to be alone at times, but they find that actively involving him or her in family activities helps to reduce social withdrawal and isolation. Some families report initiating activities that are especially interesting or enjoyable to their disabled member, such as bowling or fishing. It appears from the responses that families are the major social resource for many psychiatrically disabled persons. Without active family involvement, their social withdrawal and isolation might very well be much greater.

Other families encourage their disabled family member to become involved in a social rehabilitation program. Unfortunately, social rehabilitation programs are not available to many families. Families identify this lack of programs as a major source of frustration in their efforts to assist their family member. Some families and groups of families have become actively involved in the development of social rehabilitation programs in their communities. They have either designed programs and solicited funds themselves or worked with mental health organizations in developing programs (Shifren-Levine & Spaniol, 1985). However, this important need continues to represent a major program gap for families and their disabled members.

Other strategies families report include actually intervening with their family member's friends by encouraging them to call or to do things with him or her. Or they may suggest activities for their family member and his or her friends to do. If the disabled family member has concerns about social activities, families provide reassurance and listen to the concerns. They either help the family member to work out the problems, or they let the member work them out alone until he or she asks for help. Some families have found purchasing a pet useful. The pet provides an opportunity for some people to get outside of themselves and develop their caring and nurturing skills.

Finally, some families suggest not pushing too hard on issues of withdrawal. They acknowledge the need their family member has for time and space by him- or herself. Slow, measurable growth is often the most successful with people with severe psychiatric disability. They often need "down time" for integration and sorting out their experiences. What may be unnecessary for other family members may be required for the family member with the disability. Although we all need a certain amount of "down time," a person with a severe mental illness may need a great deal more than most of us.

## Hygiene and Appearance Management Coping Strategies

Families report using many gentle reminders and encouragements to enhance their family member's personal hygiene and appearance. These constant reminders to "put on a clean shirt," "comb your hair," and "wear different clothes," for example, appear to be the most common strategy used.

Another strategy is to focus on what the family member with the disability is already doing well. Some families deliberately enhance and enrich the positive self-image of their family member. They compliment the family member on how well he or she looks or dresses. They offer suggestions for how to improve hygiene and appearances rather than simply rejecting or discounting what they feel is inappropriate. An individual's self-esteem is often fragile, particularly when he or she has to deal with the exigencies of a severe mental disability. Compliments and positive reinforcement can help an individual to shore up a weakened self-image and shape behavior in a direction that is more socially appropriate.

Some families also report buying new clothes, shampoo, and other items for their disabled family member. Some families will even lay out clean clothes at the beginning of each day, or they will make suggestions for matching clothes, coordinating colors, and choosing styles that are appropriate for an event such as a job interview or a social gathering.

Some families report having had to acknowledge the range of styles that are acceptable among their family member's peers. What may be unacceptable to family members may be quite acceptable to peer groups. Many families have learned to live with what is possible and to be sensitive to the values and styles of the family member's own peer group.

## Self-Destructive and Suicidal Behavior Management Coping Strategies

Self-destructive and suicidal behavior is especially distressing to families. It can generate profound feelings of anxiety, helplessness, anger, guilt, and concern. Families report that sympathetically listening to their member's concerns is a major coping strategy. Families reaffirm their love and acceptance of their family member through their caring communication. They reaffirm that their family member is a valuable part of the family and that he or she is needed by other family members. Families may tell their disabled member that life is not one's own to take; that it was given to be lived and enjoyed; and that if one is willing to deal with life's problems, one will find a way to make life workable. They may remind their family member that other people, even many of the disabled member's friends, have problems that have been dealt with successfully; that he or she is not alone in dealing with the effects of the problems; and that other family members and caring professionals are available to assist the family member with the disability.

If the threat of self-destructive behavior or suicide does not subside, families report talking to the disabled member about where to get immediate help. They may call a crisis center, or another family with a psychiatrically disabled member, for suggestions. This process may give them additional information or support to continue to deal with the problem at home.

If the family member has already acted on a threat, families may need to stop the self-destructive or suicidal behavior, even physically if necessary. The family member may need immediate medical attention such as hospitalization or stomach pumping. If medical attention is refused, some families report calling the police or taking legal action to force the issue of medical help.

## CONCLUSIONS

This brief discussion of current coping strategies of families highlights many of the problems families have to deal with on a daily basis. The overall impression that the authors' have tried to convey is one of empathy and respect for the courage, strength, and tenacity families exhibit in caring for their disabled loved ones. The ability and motivation to continue their investment in spite of the pervasive personal burden of the illness and the lack of support and understanding from the professional and legislative community is a glowing testimony to the depths of their love and commitment.

In many ways, the strategies used by the families that include a person with a psychiatric disability are not very different from the strategies used by families of the nondisabled. Communicating in a healthy and caring way, setting limits, seeking outside advice, and taking good care of oneself are some of the strategies used by most, if not all, types of families. The difference between families of the disabled and nondisabled lies in the intensity of the problems and their continuity over time. The problems encountered by families of the disabled are very difficult to manage and frequently don't ever go away. After many years of trying, these families wonder whether they have had any impact or whether their efforts have been worthwhile. Families struggle to put meaning into their efforts; to justify in their own minds what they have put themselves through; and to find some way to symbolize the years of investment of energy, particularly when their effect on the disabled member has been minimal. But in the final analysis, they usually remain emotionally involved with and supportive of their disabled member, and they keep trying.

One of the important developments in the lives of families that include a person with a psychiatric disability has been the recent availability of family support and advocacy groups. Families have found them to be a tremendous source of information, skills, support, and advocacy, and have come to rely on them as the one resource that often works for them and their disabled member. Families report that with these groups, they have exchanged useful ideas on strategies for managing the varieties of behaviors discussed in this chapter.

## ACKNOWLEDGMENT

This chapter is based, in part, on research supported by the National Institute of Handicapped Research and the National Institute of Mental Health.

## REFERENCES

Adams, J. D., Hayes, J., & Hopson, B. (1977). Transition: Understanding and managing personal change. New York: Universe Books.

Barett, J. E., Kuriansky, J., & Gurland, B. (1972). Community tenure following emergency discharge. American Journal of Psychiatry, 128, 958-964.

Benson, H. (1975). The relaxation response. New York: Morrow.

Brown, G. W., Birley, J. L. T., & Wing, J. K. (1972). Influence of family life on the course of schizophrenic disorders: A replication. British Journal of Psychiatry, 121, 241-258.

Creer, C., & Wing, J. K. (1974). Schizophrenia at home. London: Institute of Psychiatry.

Davis, J., Freeman, H. M., & Simmons, O. (1957). Rehospitalization and performance levels of former mental patients. Social Problems, 5, 37-44.

Falloon, I. R. H., Boyd, J. L., McGill, C. W., Strang, J. S., & Moss, H. B. (1981). Family management training in the community care of schizophrenia. In M. J. Goldstein (Ed.), New developments in interventions with families of schizophrenics. (New Directions for Mental Health Services, No. 12, (Vol. 32, pp. 61-77). San Francisco: Jossey-Bass.

Freeman, H. E., & Simmons, O. G. (1963). *The mental patient comes home.* New York: Wiley.

Hatfield, A. B. (1978). Psychological costs of schizophrenia to the family. *Social Work, 23,* 355-359.

Hatfield, A. B. (1981). Coping effectiveness in families of the mentally ill: An exploratory study. *Journal of Psychiatric Treatment and Evaluation, 3,* 11-19.

Kelly, F. (1964). Relatives' attitudes and outcome in schizophrenia. *Archives of General Psychiatry, 10,* 389-394.

Lorei, T. (1964). Prediction of length of stay out of hospital for released psychiatric patients. *Journal of Consulting Psychology, 28,* 358-363.

Shifren-Levine, I., & Spaniol, L. (1985). The role of families of the severely mentally ill in the development of community support services. *Psychosocial Rehabilitation Journal, 8*(4), 83-94.

Spaniol, L., Jung, H., Zipple, A. M., & FitzGerald, S. (1984). *Families as a central resource in the rehabilitation of the severely psychiatrically disabled: Report of a national survey (final report).* Boston: Boston University, Center for Rehabilitation Research and Training in Mental Health.

Thompson, E. H., & Doll, W. (1982). The burden of families coping with the mentally ill: An invisible crisis. *Family Relations, 31,* 379-388.

Vaughn, C. E., Snyder, K. S., Freeman, W., Jones, S., Falloon, I. R. H., & Liberman, R. P. (1982). Family factors in schizophrenic relapse: A replication. *Schizophrenia Bulletin, 8,* 425-426.

# III

## NEW PERSPECTIVES ON SERVICE PROVISION AND RESEARCH

# 11

# The Beat of a Different Drummer

*Evelyn M. McElroy*

## FAMILIES VERSUS MENTAL HEALTH PROFESSIONALS: A CLASH OF PERSPECTIVES

There is much to suggest that families of the seriously mentally ill and the professionals who treat them march to the beat of a different drummer. Findings from several studies indicate that each group holds different views about the needs of the families (Hatfield, 1982; McElroy, 1985; Spaniol, Jung, Zipple, & Fitzgerald, 1984). Furthermore, disparate perceptions about the quality of services rendered to families have also been reported (Hatfield, 1978; Holden & Lewine, 1982; McElroy, 1985; Spaniol et al., 1984). Since many of the programs are developed by professionals and are aimed at helping such families cope effectively with a catastrophic major mental illness in a relative, it is imperative that professionals be aware of the family perspective on the meaning of mental illness. Successful programs for these families must articulate the expressed needs and approaches deemed to have merit by the targeted population. This chapter explores differences in the perceptions of the needs of the families as viewed by professionals and by the families themselves. It also describes how a therapeutic alliance may be developed to benefit both the patient and the family through a change in the approaches utilized by professionals. A theme is developed for viewing the family as adult learners as opposed to unidentified patients.

Evelyn M. McElroy. School of Nursing, University of Maryland, Baltimore, Maryland.

Some professionals must change their negative or counterproductive perceptions about families and begin to regard them as a valuable source of social support for the mentally ill relative (Caplan, 1976, pp. 19-36). Families, in turn, must attempt to reinforce those effective sensitive and caring approaches of professionals who choose to work with such difficult populations as the seriously mentally ill. These collaborative efforts by families and professionals will make possible better treatment for the patient, greater readiness to learn from families, and improved use of professionals' efforts.

## FAMILIES ARE CAREGIVERS

Families who have relatives with a major mental illness such as the schizophrenias or the bipolar affective disorders have concerns that are important for professionals to consider when developing treatment plans for the mentally ill relative. Most families welcome and recognize the need for information and help from professionals who consider family members' observations and knowledge about the afflicted individual's developmental history, value systems, assets, problems, and responses to stress, including treatment. Families want information, not necessarily treatment, from professionals (Hatfield, 1978, 1979, 1981, 1984; National Alliance for the Mentally Ill, 1982; Spaniol et al., 1984).

The thrust of deinstitutionalization of the chronically mentally ill and the different but pressing problems of the young adult chronically ill population places the emphasis on care in the community, with the family members expected to assume primary responsibility for monitoring the treatment (Brown, Birley, & Wing, 1972; Falloon, Watt, & Shepherd, 1978; Vaughn, 1982; Vaughn & Leff, 1976, 1981), to assure compliance with rehabilitative objectives (Blackwell, 1976), and to prevent relapses. Families are often the primary caregivers (Doll, 1976; Falloon, Boyd, & McGill, 1984; Goldman, 1982, Hatfield, 1978, 1979, 1981; Holden & Lewine, 1982; Kreisman, Simmons, & Joy, 1979; Lamb & Oliphant, 1978; Wasow & Wikler, 1983). Studies estimate that between 49-66% of the patients return to the family following discharge from the hospital (Goldman, 1982). Research indicates that families maintain involvement with the relative even after long separations (Evans, Bullard, & Solomon, 1961). In fact, the rehabilitative program of the recovering relative is enhanced if families are involved in supportive and positive ways with the patient (Freeman & Simmons, 1963).

There are large numbers of families who need to be informed about mental illness. It is estimated that 4.5% of Americans are chronically mentally ill. This represents approximately 12,000,000 people who have a serious mental illness. Conservatively, this means that at least 24,000,000 family members are affected by a catastrophic mental illness (Talbott, 1984, p. 22).

## Discharge Planning

Families need to know about the illness of their relative if they are to be informed consumers and expected to help the recovering individual. Furthermore, family members need knowledge about initial methods to cope with the crises created by mental illness in the family that is accurate, timely, and delivered by informed and sensitive persons (Caplan, 1974; Katz & Bender, 1976). As Andreasen (1984, p. vii) has said, knowledge is power.

Since families often initiate health-seeking activities and purchase services for their ill relative, they need to know about reasonable and current treatment approaches so that they can select services based upon sound scientific principles. Despite federally mandated regulations for inpatient psychiatric facilities receiving Medicare reimbursement to develop discharge plans (Brands, 1980; Department of Health and Human Services, 1983), few mental health professionals seriously consider the family's educational needs in the discharge planning process in ways that are meaningful to the family. The provision of an aftercare plan that includes the family's recommendations, capabilities, and resources for their relative's rehabilitation program needs to be considered if the discharge plan is to be viable. Failure to include families in the discharge planning process in appropriate ways may suggest that professionals hold different perceptions of needs.

## FAMILY-STAFF DISSONANCE

Many experts in the psychiatric field have written about the need to respond to the families of the seriously mentally ill in a more helpful manner and to reduce dissonance (Anderson, Hogarty, & Reiss, 1980; Appleton, 1974; Bernheim, Lewine, & Beale, 1982; Hatfield, 1982; Robinson & Thorn, 1984; Torrey, 1979). Professionals who are also family members have indicated that some mental health professionals have actually increased the burden of the illness during their time of crisis through a variety of deleterious transactions that were psychologically distressing (Turnbull & Turnbull, 1978; Wasow, 1980, 1982; Wasow & Wikler, 1983). Hatfield has indicated that therapists and families are worlds apart in their perceptions of families, as evidenced by language used in the professional literature to describe families (Hatfield, 1982). Walsh (1985, pp. 154-179) elaborated on those observations and discussed the impact on families when negative stereotyping occurs and they are characterized as "psychovermin" by many of those charged with helping them. Lefley (1985) has reported on changes in perceptions that occur among practitioners when a relative becomes mentally ill. Some have claimed that a few professionals have regarded families as adversaries rather than allies (Raymond, Slaby, & Lieb, 1973) and some professionals' actions have suggested a lack of awareness of the grief experienced by the families (Wasow, 1982). The complexities faced by family members caring for a relative with a chronic mental disability are not always understood (Kreisman & Joy, 1974).

Diseases that drastically alter an individual's selfhood are different from any other form of chronic illness. Tremendous psychological loss and grief are experienced by families of the seriously mentally ill (Debuskey, 1970; Hatfield, 1981; McElroy, 1982; Travis, 1976). The cyclical nature of some of the psychiatric illnesses and the periodic reappearance of the "former self" creates prolonged periods of grieving. Appropriate forms of bereavement for persons who are living but appear to be "gone" or who periodically partially reappear have not been adequately recognized by society; yet, families of the mentally ill cope with this form of unsanctioned grief daily (Osterweis, Solomon, & Green, 1984). Recognition of the need for support systems for these families is crucial to understanding their perspective and dilemma (Caplan, 1976, pp. 19-36).

Not being understood by professionals can exacerbate the distress of families and unnecessarily increase their burden (Hatfield, 1978, 1982; McElroy, 1985; Spaniol et al., 1984). Hartocollis (1965) recognized that the disturbed families described by professionals were not abnormal and attributed their disturbance to the fact that they were not understood by professionals.

Other areas of perceptual differences between families and professionals are observed in their evaluation of services rendered (Creer & Wing, 1974; Hatfield, 1978; Holden & Lewine, 1982; McElroy, 1985; Spaniol et al., 1984).

Families often begin their relationships with professionals with the expectation that information and guidance will be forthcoming (Creer & Wing, 1974). Robinson and Thorn (1984) have characterized this stage of health-seeking behavior as naive trusting. Dissatisfaction expressed by families who received professional services has focused on the lack of information and guidance provided by service providers. The subjects in the Creer and Wing study (1974) cited the lack of practical advice from psychiatrists making it clear that professionals must be more aware of family needs. Such problems characterize the families' stage of disenchantment with the responses of professionals (Robinson & Thorne, 1984).

Hatfield's (1981) study of family members' perception of traditional psychiatric services revealed that standard treatment modalities such as individual and family therapy were reported to be of little help to families whereas psychopharmacological intervention given to the patient *was* perceived to be of benefit. Interestingly, drug therapy and practical forms of therapy were reported to be among the most effective forms of treatments for schizophrenia (May, Tuma, & Dixon, 1981). Parents who utilized mutual support groups for assistance were reported to cope better than those who turned toward professionals (Hatfield, 1981). This finding has been reported in other areas; for example, studies indicate that widows who receive assistance from other widows reported fewer health problems and a better sense of well-being than a comparison group without such a confidante (Madison & Walker, 1967). Similarly, findings of a controlled study of parents of abused children indicated that those who had access to a support group exhibited fewer subsequent episodes of abuse and viewed the parent "helper" as more effective than professionals (Baker, 1976). It seems that for some illnesses or conditions, support groups are beneficial for coping with the common situations experienced by the recipients of care (Caplan, 1976; Katz & Bender, 1976). Controlled studies on such benefits for the family members of the seriously mentally ill need to be carried out.

A study by Hatfield (1981) revealed disparities between the treatment goals held by families and those espoused by professionals. In a study of attitudes of staff members and families toward family involvement in treatment of hospitalized chronic mental patients, a lack of agreement between staff members and families on crucial treatment variables was considered to jeopardize family involvement, although two-thirds of the family members reported concern and willingness to be involved with professionals (Smets, 1982). Despite dissatisfaction with services rendered, families appear to acknowledge the importance of professional help (Holden & Lewine, 1982), an aspect of the relationship with providers that has been referred to as the stage of guarded alliance (Robinson & Thorne, 1984).

## FAMILY NEEDS

It is obvious that it is important to gain an understanding of what families want and need from professionals. Kreisman and Joy (1974) reviewed the literature to determine the burden placed on the family as a result of the relative's mental illness. They concluded that the needs of these families had been poorly assessed, and, consequently, that the mental health professionals were not effectively responding to their needs. Doll (1976) described families who had actively psychotic relatives as living under severe stress. Because of the demands of deinstitutionalism and the lack of community programs, many of these families had turned their homes into psychiatric hospitals without the benefit of adequate numbers of trained staff to manage the troubled relative. The families were fatigued and not prepared to handle that constant form of home-based psychiatric treatment. A later study by Hatfield revealed that families reported needing respite and "real" community support programs to relieve some of the burden placed on them. Predictably, the survey found that families need advice concerning appropriate expectations for patients; specific techniques for managing disturbed behavior; and information about the common forms of treatment of and practical management techniques for the major mental illnesses (Hatfield, 1979). Despite the failure of some professionals to meet their needs and to understand them, the families wanted assistance from professionals on management and coping strategies (Hatfield, 1979, 1981).

In addition, having access to brief hospitalization for the relative during a relapse may be perceived to lessen the families situational crisis and "burden." Herz, Endicott, and Gibbons's (1979) research revealed that patients were rehospitalized because of psychopathology and maladaptive functioning rather than because of perceived family burden. Similarly, community treatment and support services, when indicated, were perceived by families as helpful in relieving the sense of burden caused by the relative's mental illness (Holden & Lewine, 1982; Stein & Test, 1980).

A national survey comparing perceptions of families' needs among 140 family members who belonged to the National Alliance for the Mentally Ill (NAMI) and 93 mental health professionals (Spaniol et al., 1984) revealed that families and professionals do not view families in similar ways. Predictably, professionals perceive services rendered to families in a more favorable manner than do families. Family dissatisfaction with mental health services was high. The families were most satisfied with the professionals' attitudes toward the ill member and themselves, but were dissatisfied with treatment coordination, practical advice, information about the illness, emotional support, and referral assistance. These findings are consistent with Hatfield's earlier conclusions (1978, 1981).

Managing troubling behaviors exhibited by the ill relative continued to be cited as a need for these families (Spaniol et al., 1984). The lack of information about medication was especially important because most of the relatives had been prescribed medication and many of the family respondents had not been informed about the side effects. The study revealed that the majority of the family respondents perceived that professional assistance in helping them understand the relative's illness was inadequate. Advice from professionals was perceived to be vague, incomplete, impractical, contradictory or nonexistent. These findings were similar to Creer and Wing's results (1974).

Families who coped well were reported to have relatives who were effectively managed on medication that diminished their symptoms, making home management possible. This group also felt supported by the professionals and had been adequately prepared to respond to the specific tasks associated with home management of a recovering patient. Families who were described as not coping well reported dissatisfaction with many mental health practices and services. They reported a lack of information about the illness, possessed few resources, experienced little emotional support, and demonstrated few management techniques. Feelings of severe burden and a lack of support from professionals were reported by these families (Spaniol et al., 1984).

Hatfield (1981) also reported that families who appeared not to be coping well had relatives that were not responding to medication or had illnesses of a more recent onset than those described as coping well. It is unclear if the "non-copers" in Spaniol's study had relatives who were unresponsive to medication. Families with severely mentally ill relatives who do not respond to medication or who exhibit disruptive behavior would predictably be under more stress than others. These families may project dissatisfaction to professionals for failing to help their relatives. In turn, the professionals may withdraw from these families at a time of greatest need.

### Family Needs and Bothersome Behaviors of the Relative

McElroy (1985) conducted a descriptive study to identify the educational needs of families of the seriously mentally ill ($N = 52$) and to describe from their perspective behaviors of the mentally ill relative that bothered them. Since professionals are usually responsible for developing programs aimed at educating families about the mental illness of the relative in order to promote effective coping strategies, another purpose of the study was to compare the professionals' (60 nurses) perceptions on the same dimensions as the families. Congruency among the two groups would suggest that professionals were able to empathize with the families' perspective. Discrepancies between the two groups could suggest the failure of professionals to understand the family perspective. Dissonance could jeopardize collaborative efforts and its presence indicate areas of intervention that could be addressed. Additional objectives of the study were to identify demographic characteristics of the Alliance for the Mentally Ill (AMI) of Greater Baltimore and to assess the members' perceptions of services rendered to their mentally ill relative and other family members.

A survey of the 150 members of AMI of Greater Baltimore was conducted in April 1983. The forms were returned by 60 people, representing a 40% return rate, and 6 forms were eliminated because instructions were not followed or because 60% of the questionnaires were incomplete. Thus 52 persons, or 34.6% of the population, comprised the sample reported in this preliminary study. Generalization to other populations is obviously limited.

Of the respondents, 71% were mothers with a mentally ill offspring and 21% were fathers. The remaining respondents were two siblings and a husband.

Most of the family respondents were married (75%) and the remaining were widowed (8%), separated (8%), or divorced (10%).

Half of the sample was in the 50–59-year-old age bracket, while 21% were under 49 years of age and 29% were age 60 or over.

The mean educational level of the family members was 14.1 years $(SD = \pm 3.71)$.

Concerning finances, 49% of the respondents were helping to provide partial support for the mentally ill relative, 27% were assuming total support of the individual, and 24% were not responsible for any financial support to their relatives.

Interestingly, only 27% of mentally ill relatives were reported to receive Social Security Disability Insurance (SSDI).

Of the families responding, 47% ($n = 24$) reported that the illness of the relative was sudden and unexpected, while 51% indicated that the onset of the illness was gradual and had developed over a long period of time, 28% of the family respondents indicated that they had more than one seriously mentally ill relative.

Most of the relatives who had experienced a serious mental illness were reported to be male (69%) as compared to female (31%). The average age was 29 and the range of ages for the mentally ill relative was between 19 and 47.

The gender of the mentally ill relative and relationship to the family respondents were compared with Hatfield's (1978) study (see Table 1). Mothers of mentally ill sons were predominant in both studies.

The mean educational level of the mentally ill relative was 13.4 years $(SD = \pm 2.10)$. A comparison between the mean educational level of the mentally ill relative and the family member was computed.

Table 1.
Characteristics of Patients Provided by Family
Respondents in Two Studies

| | Hatfield ($n = 89$) | | McElroy ($n = 51$) | |
|---|---|---|---|---|
| | n | % | n | % |
| Male | 63 | 70.7 | 35 | 69 |
| Female | 26 | 29.2 | 16 | 31 |
| Son | 61 | 69 | 33 | 65 |
| Daughter | 16 | 18 | 14 | 27 |
| Other | 12 | 13 | 4 | 8 |

A paired $t$ test revealed a score of 1.73 with 48 df. This was significant at the .05 level. Families had more education than the mentally ill relative, thus suggesting the downward drift. Offspring failed to surpass the educational (economic) status of their parents.

Surveys were mailed to the 163 registered nurses comprising the total RN population of a publicly supported psychiatric hospital.[1] Sixty completed forms were returned, which represented a 36.8% return rate, and used in the analysis.

Of the nurses, 40% were diploma graduates ($n = 24$), 37% ($n = 22$) possessed associate degrees, 18% ($n = 11$) held bachelor's degrees, and 5% ($n = 3$) had earned master's degrees.

A comparison of the educational needs of families of the seriously mentally ill and nurses perceptions of the families needs, using the same questionnaire, revealed statistically significant differences on 23 of the 48 variables comprising the analysis according to two-tailed $t$ tests with separate estimates for each item.

The items that received the five highest and lowest means from both groups in response to information perceived to be of interest to families are listed in descending order in Table 2.

A comparison between the family group and the nurse group of the five areas of highest mean scores revealed differences in perceptions of educational priorities. Similar discrepancies between the two groups were noted in regard to perceptions of what families perceived to be the *least* important needs. In fact, the families cited obtaining current information and research on the major mental illnesses as among the five *most* important areas of concern, while the nurses perceived that area to be of little concern to families.

An analysis was completed on a comparison of behaviors dis-

1. Appreciation is given to Betty McDuffie, RN, MS.

*Table 2.*
Perceptions of the Educational Needs of Families

| Nurses (n = 60) | Families (n = 52) |
|---|---|
| **Of most concern** | |
| 1. Methods to handle suicidal behavior and ways to manage drinking among the mentally ill relative were perceived to be the two areas of information nurses felt families wanted.[a] | 1. Information on psychotropic drugs. |
| 2. Psychosocial techniques for managing physical aggression at home. | 2. Management techniques to promote independence and self-esteem in the ill relative. |
| 3. Techniques for managing confusion at home. | 3. An update on research on the major mental illness. |
| 4. Management techniques for motivating apathetic behavior at home. | 4. Housing—what are the options? |
| 5. Knowledge about the forms of treatment for the major mental illnesses. | 5. Information on how to handle "burn-out" among themselves. |
| **Of least concern** | |
| 1. The medical record—how to determine if active treatment was provided. | 1. Conducting a search for a missing relative (none was missing). |
| 2. Current court findings on the treatment of the mentally ill. | 2. The legal rights of minors. |
| 3. An update on research on major mental illnesses. | 3. Guilt associated with death wishes concerning the ill relative. |
| 4. How to handle mental health professionals. | 4. How to manage drinking behavior in the relative. |
| 5. Ethical/legal issues surrounding audio/videotaping of family sessions. | 5. Ways to improve personal hygiene of the relative. |

[a]These two items received the same scores among the respondent group.

played by the mentally ill relative that bothered families and the behaviors that the nurses thought bothered families. There were statistically significant differences on 23 of the 29 variables comprising the questionnaire using two-tailed $t$ tests with separate estimates for each item.

Of the 29 items, those that received the five highest and lowest means—that is, the areas perceived by both groups to be most and least bothersome to families—are listed in Table 3.

A comparison between the families' and the nurses' perceptions of which behaviors bothered family members most during the preceding 6 months also revealed discrepancies between the two groups based on the five highest mean scores.

*Table 3.*
Perceptions of Behaviors Displayed by the Mentally Ill Relative that Bother Families

| Families (n = 52) | Nurses (n = 60) |
|---|---|
| Most bothersome | |
| 1. Inability of the relative to achieve his or her potential. | 1. Suicidal behavior of the mentally ill relative. |
| 2. Lack of motivation. | 2. Homicidal behavior. |
| 3. Inability to prepare for a vocation. | 3. Verbal and physical aggression. |
| 4. Inability to work. | 4. Creating scenes in the neighborhood. |
| 5. Inability to adhere to or develop a predictable schedule. | 5. Creating unusual or strange behavior. |
| Least bothersome | |
| 1. Steals from others. | 1. Boredom. |
| 2. Homicidal behavior. | 2. Inability to complete school. |
| 3. Drug abuse. | 3. Lack of motivation. |
| 4. Problems with elimination. | 4. "Mooches" from others. |
| 5. "Mooches" from others. | 5. Elimination. |

Both groups indicated that "mooching" from others was of little concern to families. This may be related to the possibility that the mentally ill relatives of the respondents rarely displayed that behavior. The remaining four categories scored as *least* bothersome by the respective groups were also dissonant. Nurses perceived the family members to be bothered little about motivating the mentally ill relative, whereas families indicated that this lack of motivation bothered them a great deal.

Of the families reporting, 45% said that they had not been involved in discharge planning with the staff, while 55% reported that they had been included in the discharge plans. Following discharge, 52% of the patients returned to a family that was expected to enhance the recovering relative's rehabilitation program.

Sixty-one percent of the family respondents were favorably impressed with the quality of care rendered during the relative's last hospitalization, while 37% viewed the quality of care as poor, and 2% felt that quality of care was a compromise between "good" and "poor."

The incongruity between the families and the professionals perceptions of priorities suggest that some professionals may need to modify their approaches with families to include endeavors that they deem to have merit. Interestingly, both professional and family respondents in the national survey had concerns about the usefulness of family therapy to help families and, agreeing with Hatfield's (1979) earlier finding, revealed that the "one service they typically do not want from professionals is therapy for themselves" (Spaniol et al., 1984, p. 34). However, families do want to be educated by professionals (Hatfield, 1979, 1981; Holden & Lewine, 1982; Spaniol et al., 1984).

## FAMILY MEMBERS AS ADULT LEARNERS

Many families propose an educational perspective as an initial step to coping and adapting to the circumstances associated with caring for a relative who may become dysfunctional periodically (Hatfield, 1981; Spaniol et al., 1984). Educational approaches rely on multimodal strategies that consider the cognitive style of the learner and use principles of learning, rather than theories of family causation, as a framework. Such strategies enhance the potential for success of programs.

The educational approach views the adult learner as mature, self-directed, problem-focused, and practical. Furthermore, adult learners are described as managers and decision makers.

It is important to use accumulated life experiences as a resource for learning, to provide opportunity for immediate application of knowledge, and to use activities that are problem-centered and practical rather than theoretical (Knowles, 1970). It is also important to address relevant developmental tasks expressed by the learner and to consider the social roles of the recipients of the care when planning intervention programs (Knowles, 1970; Swezey & Swezey, 1976). Creating environments for change that foster openness, directness, and honesty is essential for attracting the learners, maintaining involvement, and establishing the credibility of the educator (Peterson, 1979; Redman, 1978). These factors are also conducive to the development of a therapeutic alliance between families and professionals aimed at supporting the treatment and rehabilitation efforts of the patient.

## THERAPEUTIC ALLIANCE

Therapeutic alliances with families require mutuality of goals among all concerned and sensitive approaches to families that address reciprocal interests. The following letter from a mother illustrates an effective therapeutic alliance between the family and professionals:

Dear Dr. X:
    The purpose of this letter is to acknowledge the effort and interest that you have demonstrated in treating our son, Eric, for his psychiat-

ric condition. We appreciate your persistence in engaging Eric in therapy by demonstrating interest in him as a worthy individual with many assets, and who has functioned as an advocate on his behalf when other patients were discounting him during ward meetings on one of his eight hospitalizations during the past year.

I am particularly appreciative of your ability to communicate to Eric that rehospitalizations are not necessarily a failure on his part (or ours) to control the symptoms of his illness. As you know, many mental health professionals relate relapse rate to maladaptive communication styles among the family. That approach tends to create an adversarial position between the family and the therapist with the possible result that the patient loses a network of support at a time when one is greatly needed. Your approach seriously challenges the psychosocial stress model as the primary explanation for relapses. We observed that after the correct medication was discovered, Eric could tolerate levels of "stress" that would have distressed most people and was able to progress in life.

Including our family in the deliberations of your treatment is to be commended, since it is likely to result in a therapeutic alliance which could maximize the achievement of treatment goals.[2]

Sincerely,


J. Doe
(personal communication, November 12, 1982)

The parents' concern for their son was recognized and the staff responded by treating them as dignified adults with valid reasons for distress and recognizing that this concern was an asset for the patient. The family was perceived as a valuable source of support for the youngster. In turn, the professional involvement with the family supported the family through their son's repeated and frequent relapses prior to the discovery of an effective medication. The staff created an atmosphere conducive to psychological growth and responded to the family as a "family" and not as patients. Goals were jointly developed.

On the other hand, unilateral treatment goals delineated by professionals without regard for family input (Korpell, 1984) are likely to lead to misalliance. Harbin (1982) has written about family–staff conflict in psychiatric facilities. If conflict is allowed to escalate, the tension may jeopardize treatment and create misalliance. Terkelsen (1983) has described some of the limits of using psychogenic–sociogenic theories to guide the clinical interventions with families of the seriously mentally ill.

Unfortunately, professionals do not always view families as collaborators dealing with the common goals of caring for the patient and

---

2. The psychiatrist was Dr. Robert Lessey of Wyman Park Hospital in Baltimore.

reducing distressing aspects of the illness among all members through dissemination of information or involvement in treatment. Too often, professionals view the family as unidentified patients needing treatment rather than as adult learners attempting to deal with a major mental illness (Terkelsen, 1983).

Professionals who utilize a theoretical framework for guiding their clinical practice and who embrace inaccurate assumptions about family causation in the etiology of mental illness can produce distress among the recipients of their services since such theories and assumptions often view families as stressors implicated in the symptomology of their mentally ill relative. Therapists who believe that disturbed family communication patterns are related to the manifestation of schizophrenia or the affective disorders and unilaterally develop treatment plans based upon those theories are especially likely to meet with resistance from families (Medical Record, #1178, 1981; B. Doe, personal communication, April 1983).

Many families reject the a priori assumption that they are implicated in the symptomology of their relatives and are in need of healing, particularly since little empirical evidence from replicated, well-controlled studies supports those theories. Others have described the deleterious effects of implementing interventions with families predicated on the sociogenic or psychogenic theories of mental illness (Terkelsen, 1983; Torrey, 1983).

The following example illustrates how interventions based on sociogenic models result in a misalliance:

> A mother had consented to discuss the possibility of her family therapy to augment the treatment rendered to her offspring. She met with the therapist and his supervisor to explore their methods, to gain information about confidentiality, and to learn of their orientation in treatment. Ten minutes after the interview had begun and she had revealed private, sensitive information, she was informed that three other persons were viewing the interview without her permission or knowledge. None of the "eavesdroppers" stopped the interview. They were a psychiatrist, a psychiatric nurse with a master's degree and a mental health worker.

Such practices constitute violations of families' constitutional rights. They permit unauthorized invasion of privacy and misrepresentation on the part of those involved and are unethical and often illegal because they are performed without providing information to families about the full implications of informed consent (D. Trazzi, personal communication, November 1983). The example also indicates the differences in perceptions among the mother and the professionals. The mother wanted to learn about the professionals' credentials and modus operandi in order to decide if she wanted to engage in family systems therapy. The professionals had a different agenda, which was never fully communicated to the mother. The family therapist had inappropriately assumed the son's relapses were caused by the family's communication. Such approaches are unethical and jeopardize therapeutic alliances. The example illustrates the failure of the professional to empathize with the family's perspective and how this failure can result in the violation of all principles of learning.

For professionals to gain understanding of the family perspective, as well as for the development of mutuality, regard, and viable collaborative treatment goals, examination of their own attitudes; of the validity of theories of practice espoused; of practice behaviors implemented, and of semantics used to describe families are essential. Carper (1978) had proposed a framework for evaluating theories used to direct clinical practice that included understanding the perspective of those affected by the care rendered. Personal knowledge includes understanding the impact of treatment plans and actions on consumers. Chinn (1985) has discussed the importance of examining the premises underlying many of the theories used to direct clinical interventions. She also claims that such personal examination and awareness among both the recipients and providers of care are crucial parts of their respective value systems that effect the care rendered. Such an analysis of the family-professional network can lead to understanding and reveal issues that are of concern and can be addressed and negotiated.

Robinson and Thorne (1984) described an example of how such an analysis resulted in reformulating family interference in the sick relative's health care. The interfering behavior became understandable when one looked at the families' disillusionment and dissatisfaction with previous health care relationships. The authors felt that the interfering behaviors displayed by the families were part of an evolving stage of helping relationships with providers which were described earlier: (1) naive trusting; (2) disenchantment; and (3) guarded alliance. As such, the interfering behaviors represented the family's methods for productively influencing their sick member's experience with illness. Since it seemed unlikely that the families would initiate new endeavors with professionals because previous experiences had been unsuccessful, it was proposed that professionals instigate the negotiation process. This could be done by actively soliciting input from families regarding care. Next, negotiating decisions that are mutually satisfying could occur. Family interference considered within the context of health care relationships could be understood and developed. Traditional hierarchial approaches to family involvement would likely be counterproductive. The authors concluded that professionals need to understand the family perspective and to value family involvement on a peer level that considers the social roles of the members. The special expertise that families have is relevant to quality care and the family's expressed needs must be given priority (Robinson & Thorne, 1984).

## CONCLUSION

It is clear that families of the seriously mentally ill and some professionals march to the beat of a different drummer. To bring these two groups into step, programs that meet the families' educational priorities should be developed. Since the success of the programs depends upon mutual goals, respect, and reciprocity among all involved, better perceptions among professionals who are to be the educators or therapists of families of the mentally ill also need to be established. Findings from these assessments could provide the foundation for successful family educational programs, mutually satisfying relations, and therapeutic alliances.

## REFERENCES

Anderson, C. M., Hogarty, G. E., & Reiss, D. J. (1980). Family treatment of adult schizophrenic patients: A psycho-educational approach. Schizophrenia Bulletin, 6, 490–505.

Andreasen, N. C. (1984). The broken brain. New York: Harper & Row.

Appleton, W. S. (1974). Mistreatment of patient's families by psychiatrists. American Journal of Psychiatry, 131(6), 655–657.

Baker, J. (1976). Parents anonymous self-help treatment for child abusing parents: A review and evaluation. Tuscon, AZ: Behavior Associates.

Bernheim, K. F., Lewine, R. R., & Beale, C. T. (1982). The caring family. New York: Random House.

Blackwell, B. (1976). Treatment adherence. British Journal of Psychiatry, 129, 513–531.

Brands, A. (Ed.). (1980). Assessing therapeutic environment for active psychiatric treatment settings (DHHS publication No. (ADM) 81-1109). Washington, DC: Department of Documents.

Brown, C. W., Birley, J. T. L., & Wing, J. K. (1972). Influence of family life on the course of schizophrenic disorders: A replication. British Journal of Psychiatry, 121, 241–258.

Caplan, G. (1974). Support systems and community mental health. New York: Behavioral Publications.

Caplan, G. (1976). The family as support system. In G. Caplan & M. Killilea, (Eds.), Support systems and mutual help: Multidisciplinary explorations. New York: Grune & Stratton.

Caplan, G., & Killilea, M. (Eds.). (1976). Support systems and mutual help. New York: Grune & Stratton.

Carper, B. A. (1978). Fundamental patterns of knowing in nursing. Advances in Nursing Science, 1(1), 13–86.

Chinn, P. L. (1985). Debunking myths in nursing theory and research. *Image, 17*(2), 45-49.

Creer, C., & Wing, J. (1974). *Schizophrenia at home.* London: Institute of Psychiatry.

Debuskey, M. (Ed.). (1970). *The chronically ill child and his family.* Springfield, IL: Charles C. Thomas.

Department of Health and Human Services, Health Care Financing Administration. (1983, January 4). Medicare and Medicaid programs: Conditions of participation. *Federal Register, 23,* 2.

Doll, W. (1976). Family coping with the mentally ill: An unanticipated problem of deinstitutionalization. *Hospital and Community Psychiatry, 27,* 183-185.

Evans, A. S., Bullard, D. M., & Solomon, M. H. (1961). The family as a potential resource in the rehabilitation of the chronic schizophrenic patient: A study of 60 patients and their families. *American Journal of Psychiatry, 117,* 1075-1083.

Falloon, I. R. H., Boyd, J. L., & McGill, G. W. (1984). *Family care of schizophrenia: A problem-solving approah to the treatment of mental illness.* New York: Guilford.

Falloon, I., Watt, D. C., & Shepherd, M. (1978). A comparative controlled trial of pimozide and fluphenazine decanoate in the continuation therapy of schizophrenia. *Psychological Medicine, 8,* 59-70.

Freeman, H. E., & Simmons, O. G. (1963). *The mental patient comes home.* New York: Wiley.

Goldman, H. H. (1982). Mental illness and family burden: A public health perspective. *Hospital and Community Psychiatry, 33,* 557-559.

Harbin, H. (1982). Family treatment of the psychiatric inpatient. In H. Harbin (Ed.), *The psychiatric hospital and the family.* New York: Spectrum.

Hartocollis, P. (1965). Our patients' anxious relatives: Overcoming interference with treatment. *Mental Hospitals, 16,* 180-183.

Hatfield, A. B. (1978). Psychological costs of schizophrenia in the family. *Social Work, 23,* pp. 355-359.

Hatfield, A. B. (1979). The family as a partner in the treatment of mental illness. *Hospital and Community Psychiatry, 30,* 338-340.

Hatfield, A. B. (1981). Coping effectiveness in families of the mentally ill: An exploratory study. *Journal of Psychiatric Treatment and Evaluation, 3,* 11-19.

Hatfield, A. B. (1982). Therapists and families: Worlds apart. *Hospital and Community Psychiatry, 33,* 513.

Hatfield, A. B. (1984). *Coping with mental illness in the family: The family guide.* Baltimore: Mental Hygiene Administration of Maryland.

Herz, M. I., Endicott, J., & Gibbon, M. (1979). Brief hospitalization. *Archives of General Psychiatry, 36,* 701-705.

Holden, D. F., & Lewine, R. R. J. (1982). How families evaluate mental health professionals, resources, and effects of illness. *Schizophrenia Bulletin, 8,* 626-633.

Katz, A. H., & Bender, E. I. (1976). Self-help groups in Western society. *Journal of Applied Behavioral Sciences, 12,* 265-282.

Killilea, M. (1976). Mutual help organizations: Interpretations in the literature. In G. Caplan & M. Killilea (Eds.), *Support systems and mutual help.* New York: Grune & Stratton.

Knowles, M. S. (1970). *The modern practice of adult education.* New York: Associated Press.

Korpell, H. (1984). *How you can help.* Washington, DC: American Psychiatric Association Press.

Kreisman, D., Simmons, S., & Joy, V. (1979). *Deinstitutionalization and the family's well-being.* New York: New York State Psychiatric Institute.

Kreisman, D. E., & Joy, V. D. (1974). Family response to the mental illness of a relative with schizophrenia. *Schizophrenia Bulletin, 10,* 34-57.

Lamb, R., & Oliphant, E. (1978). Schizophrenia through the eyes of the families. *Hospital and Community Psychiatry, 9,* 803-806.

Leff, J., & Vaughn, C. (1981). The role of maintenance therapy and relatives' expressed emotion in relapse of schizophrenia: A two-year follow-up. *British Journal of Psychiatry, 139,* 102-104.

Lefley, H. P. (1985). Etiological and prevention views of clinicians with mentally ill relatives. *American Journal of Orthopsychiatry, 55,* 363-370.

Madison, D., & Walker, W. L. (1967). Factors affecting the outcome of conjugal bereavement. *British Journal of Psychiatry, 1,* 1057-1076.

May, P., Tuma, A., & Dixon, W. J. (1981). Schizophrenia: A follow-up study of the results of five forms of treatment. *Archives of General Psychiatry, 38,* 776-784.

Medical record #1178. (1981, April 28). [Team meeting with family] Unpublished raw data.

McElroy, E. (1985). *A comparison of families' and nurses' perceptions of the educational needs of the families of the seriously mentally ill.* Paper presented at the 6th Annual Psychiatric Nursing Professional Day at the Brattleboro Retreat, Brattleboro, Vermont.

McElroy, E. (1982). *Coping with a mentally ill adolescent.* Unpublished manuscript.

National Alliance for the Mentally Ill. (1982). *Proceedings of the Annual Convention.* Washington, DC.

Osterweis, M., Solomon, F., & Green, M. (Eds.). (1984). *Bereavement.* Washington, DC: National Academy Press.

Peterson, G. G. (1979). Power: A perspective for the nurse administrator. *Journal of Nursing Administration, 2,* 7-9.

Health, Education & Welfare Task Force. *Report of the HEW Task Force on Implementation of the Report to the President,* DHEW (ADM) 79-848. (1979). Washington, DC: U.S. Government Printing Office.

Raymond, M., Slaby, A., & Lieb, J. (1973). *The healing alliance.* New York: Norton.

Redman, B. K. (1978). Curriculum in patient education. *American Journal of Nursing, 78,* 1363-1366.

Reynolds, I., & Hoult, J. E. (1984). The relatives of the mentally ill. *The Journal of Nervous and Mental Disease, 172,* 480-489.

Robinson, C. A., & Thorne, S. (1984). Strengthening family "interference." *Journal of Advanced Nursing, 9,* 597-602.

Smets, A. C. (1982). Family and staff attitudes toward family involvement in the treatment of hospitalized chronic patients. *Hospital and Community Psychiatry, 33,* 573-575.

Spaniol, L., Jung, H., Zipple, A. M., & Fitzgerald, S. (1984). *Families as a central resource in the rehabilitation of the severely psychiatrically disabled: Report of a national survey* (final report). Boston: Boston University Center for Rehabilitation Research and Training in Mental Health.

Stein, L. I., & Test, M. A. (1980). Alternative to mental hospital treatment: I. Conceptual model, treatment program and clinical evaluation. *Archives of General Psychiatry, 37,* 392-397.

Swezey, R. L., & Swezey, A. M. (1976). Educational theory as a basis for patient education. *Journal of Chronic Disease, 29,* 417-422.

Talbott, J. (Ed.). (1984). *The chronic mental patient: Five years later.* New York: Grune & Stratton.

Terkelsen, K. G. (1983). Schizophrenia and the family: II. Adverse effects of family therapy. *Family Process, 22,* 191-200.

Torrey, E. F. (1979). A fantasy trial about a real issue. *Psychology Today, 10,* 24.

Torrey, E. F. (1983). *Surviving schizophrenia: A family manual.* New York: Harper & Row.

Travis, G. (1976). *Chronic illness in children: Its impact on child and family.* Stanford, CA: Stanford University Press.

Turnbull, A. P., & Turnbull, H. R. (1978). *Parents speak out.* Columbus, OH: Charles H. Merrill.

Vaughn, C. E. (1982). Family factors in schizophrenic relapse: A replication. *Schizophrenia Bulletin, 8,* 425-426.

Vaughn, C. E., & Leff, J. (1976). The influence of family and social factors in the course of psychiatric illness. A comparison of schizophrenic and depressed neurotic patients. *British Journal of Psychiatry, 129,* 125-137.

Vaughn, C. E., & Leff, J. P. (1981). Patterns of emotional response in relatives of schizophrenic patients. *Schizophrenia Bulletin, 7*(1), 45-56.

Walsh, M. (1985). *Schizophrenia: Straight talk for families and friends.* New York: William Morrow.

Wasow, M. (1980). *Professionals have hurt us—parents of schizophrenics speak out.* Unpublished manuscript. (Available from M. Wasow, Mt. Sinai Medical Center, 950 N. 12th St., P.O. Box 342, Milwaukee, WI 53201.)

Wasow, M. (1982). *Coping with schizophrenia: A survival manual for parents, relatives and friends.* Palo Alto, CA: Science and Behavior Books.

Wasow, M., & Wikler, L. (1983). Reflections on professionals' attitudes toward the severely mentally retarded and the chronically mentally ill: Implications for parents. *Family Therapy, 10,* 229-307.

# Family Consumerism: Coping with the Winds of Change

*Kayla F. Bernheim*

For several decades prior to the 1950s, the chronically mentally ill had been housed and cared for in large, isolated state institutions. Since treatment was rarely successful, families with ill members typically became estranged from their relatives as time, distance, and lack of hope for discharge gradually eroded their emotional involvement. Professionals tended to see the family as part of the stressful or pathogenic environment from which patients needed asylum (Rothman, 1971). They interacted little with families (and, indeed, there was little reason to do so) except to counsel them to forget their ill relative and go on with their lives.

In the mid-1950s, several factors emerged to change this situation. First, the development of antipsychotic medications greatly ameliorated the symptoms of many patients, who were then able to return to the community, at least for variable periods of time between acute exacerbations of illness. Early enthusiasm has been dampened, however, by the recognition that, for most patients, long-term deficits in thinking, feeling, and relating remain long after the acute psychotic episode is brought under control. Moreover, uncomfortable side effects, lack of insight, and fear of stigmatization provoke many patients to take medication sporadically if at all. Thus, families found (and continue to find) that their relatives, while not in need of the constant high level of care that a hospital provides, nonetheless suffer long-term

Kayla F. Bernheim. Livingston County Counseling Services, Mt. Morris, New York.

occupational, social, and personal impairments, and are at risk for relapse and rehospitalization.

In the 1960s, perhaps spurred by advances in treatment, cognizant of the financial expense inherent in institutional care, and consistent with the dominant humanistic ideals of the decade, both federal and state governments began a process of deinstitutionalization, the goal of which was to treat patients in the community through transfer of monies from the institution to a wide array of community-based supportive services (as in Public Law 88-164, the Community Mental Health Centers Construction Act of 1963). The role of primary caretaker was thus further shifted from the institution to the family. However, as we now know, the promise of high quality, accessible, appropriate support services was, by and large, an empty one. Even now, such services are scarce and treatment of the chronically mentally ill has received low priority in community mental health centers (Hogarty, 1971; Kirk & Thenlen, 1975; Lamb & Edelson, 1976). Problems of financial reimbursement, inadequate transportation, and the patient's motivational deficits further complicate families' attempts to obtain access to whatever services are available.

In the 1970s, the issue of patients' rights began to have an impact on the delivery of mental health services. Both judicial decisions and legislative reforms made it quite difficult to hospitalize or treat the mentally ill involuntarily (Talbott, 1978). As a result, some families find themselves coping with dangerous, suicidal, and severely impaired relatives, often without benefit of institutional support. Further, interpretations of confidentiality regulations sometimes frustrate their efforts to get the information they need as caretakers, even when professionals are involved. The outcome of these converging trends has been to exacerbate the already substantial practical, emotional, and financial burden experienced by families of the chronically mentally ill (Hatfield, 1978; Arey & Warheit, 1980). Hatfield and Smith (in press) have noted:

> The success of the community care movement may be in jeopardy if the primary caregivers, the families of mentally ill persons, cannot sustain the burden placed upon them. Given present fiscal restraints, there is little likelihood that socially provided services will soon replace families. Logic, then, dictates that attention be given to appropriate ways of shoring up these families . . . [and] that we learn from them what it is they need to best equip them for the difficulties they face. (p. 1)

Professionals have generally failed to be responsive to families' needs, as evidenced by several recent surveys of family members

(Beels, 1978; Creer & Wing, 1974; Hatfield, 1979, 1983a; Holden & Lewine, 1982). A number of investigators have acknowledged that family burden has been underassessed (Doll, 1976, Goldman, 1982; Kreisman & Joy, 1947) and that families suffer hardships that include physical symptoms of stress, marital discord, financial strain, and collapse of the indigenous social support system, among others (Creer & Wing, 1974; Holden & Lewine, 1982; Kreisman, Simmons, & Joy, 1979; Lamb & Oliphant, 1978; Thompson, Doll, & Lefton, 1977). Families generally have been of interest to professionals only insofar as they are assumed to have had a pathogenic influence on the development of the illness (e.g., see Haley, 1980; Lidz, 1973; Madanes, 1981; Wynne, 1978) or on the maintenance of psychiatric disability in the patient (Brown, Birley, & Wing, 1972; Vaughn & Leff, 1981). Further, there has been a tendency among mental health professionals to eschew consumer satisfaction measures of outcome as too dependent on psychodynamic distortion (Schulberg, 1981). Descriptions of families of the chronically mentally ill in the professional literature have been ubiquitously negative (Hatfield, 1982) and family therapy, when it is attempted at all, is typically designed to elucidate and modify the noxious environment that is presumed to contribute to at least the maintenance, if not the cause, of the patient's psychiatric disability. The goals of the family are generally not those set by their therapists (Hatfield, 1983a). It is small wonder, then, that families overwhelmingly report their contact with professionals to be frustrating, guilt-inducing, and unhelpful. The professional-family relationship has ranged from nonexistent to adversarial, with few exceptions until recently.

The emerging consumerism, advocacy, and militancy of families reflects, at least in part, a profound dissatisfaction with the services proffered by the mental health professional community to date (Gartner & Riessman, 1977; Hornstra, Lubin, Lewis, & Willis, 1972; Hurvitz, 1976). Families object to being treated as "the patient;" they object to the imbalance of power in the professional-family relationship that is fostered by the withholding of information that would allow them to make informed decisions, not only about the patient's treatments but also about their own participation in therapy or other rehabilitative efforts; they object to the professional's exclusive focus on the patient's well-being and the neglect of attention paid to their own needs, values, and plans; they object to the lack of true citizen participation in the planning and delivery of community mental health services (Morrison, Holdridge-Crane, & Smith, 1978).

The primary outlet for families' dissatisfaction has been the development of mutual support groups that began as a way of getting and giving the emotional nurturance that had been missing in relationships with professionals, but that rapidly expanded to include the goals of consumerism and advocacy (Hatfield, 1981a). This development is not surprising in view of the American propensity for affiliation (Katz, 1961; Katz & Bender, 1976). Mutual support and self-help groups are endemic to the culture, with an estimated 15 million people belonging to a half million such groups (Gartner & Riessman, 1977). Thus, the movement is consistent with the populist trend that infuses our society (Gartner & Riessman, 1977, 1982; Vattano, 1972).

Consumerism can also be seen as an attempt at mastery—a way of overcoming feelings of powerlessness in the face of chronic illness and professional neglect (Hatfield, Chap. 3, this volume). It reflects resistance toward bureaucratic definition of problems, and insistence on problem definition by those who are directly involved. The support of the group enhances self-esteem and helps families to identify and affirm their rights. It also provides the power (in numbers) to affect service provision, and the knowledge about the mental health system that enables families to effect change (Lamb & Oliphant, 1979). Their need to be of help to their own relative, a need that is frustrated by the chronicity of the illness, is modified to include being of service to the mentally ill as a class (Katz, 1961). This is sublimation of the healthiest, most adaptive kind.

The consumer movement among families is represented by the National Alliance for the Mentally Ill (NAMI) and its over 430 state and local affiliates. Currently comprised of over 25,000 formal members, the rapidity of its growth and level of sophistication is nothing short of astonishing. The history of its formation has been documented elsewhere (Hatfield, 1981b). Its membership can be characterized as predominantly white, middle-class parents of a mentally ill adult child, although spouses, siblings, and children with mentally ill parents are also represented. Among its goals, the one relevant to the current discussion is education of the professional community about the needs and perspectives of family members. Activities oriented to achieving this goal have already had a substantial impact on the field and can be expected to profoundly influence the future of the professional–family relationship at the level of the individual practitioner as well as at the institutional level. The remainder of this chapter will explore the ways in which this relationship will change, and the various ways in which professionals can respond to the newly articulate, well-informed family consumer.

## AVENUES TO POWER

In an attempt to rectify the perceived imbalance of power between the family consumer and the mental health professional (Hollander, 1980; Lenrow & Burch, 1981), NAMI groups have taken several steps. First among these has been accessing and disseminating information about chronic mental illnesses (primarily schizophrenia and bipolar disorder). National, statewide, and local conferences feature professional speakers willing to share with families what is known about the etiology, treatment, and management of these disorders. In addition, the past decade has produced a body of literature written for the layperson about these illnesses. The best of these books, pamphlets, and articles are publicized and sold through NAMI (see, e.g., Bernheim & Lewine, 1979; Bernheim, Lewine, & Beale, 1982; Hatfield, 1983b; Kantor, 1982; Torrey, 1983; Walsh, 1985; Woesner, 1983). Thus, armed with a vocabulary in which to converse with professionals and a newfound understanding of the variety of theoretical models and practical applications that characterize the field, the new consumer is in a better position to ask the right questions and competently evaluate the answers received (Hornstra et al., 1972). Willett (1977) has pointed out that consumer education is a tool that enhances effective use of resources, reduces the risk of marketplace exploitation, and "equips the individual to understand and use, and thereby enforce, the laws of the land" (p. 2).

Having access to this information allows family consumers to gain power in several related ways. First, they are now in a position to demand and to exercise institutional grievance procedures that provide a forum for their concerns. If their ill relative is not receiving what they believe to be appropriate services, or if they themselves are being treated insensitively by the treatment team, they are able to articulate their objections cogently and forcefully. Many institutions have responded by codifying the necessity for family members to be involved in treatment and discharge planning.

In addition, NAMI groups in many areas have developed lay referral networks (Gottlieb, 1976) through which families that are new to the mental health system are informally directed to professionals and agencies sympathetic to families' perspectives. This may prove to be a powerful influence on professional behavior in the future, particularly in the private arena, as clinicians who hold to a "family as etiological agent" model will be avoided, while those who work collaboratively with families will be used extensively.

To the extent that individual families are in control of payment for services, they will exert power in the marketplace (Hatfield, 1984; Klerman, 1979). To the extent that family support groups can use this power to influence the reimbursement models through third-party payers, they will be in a position to change the present system, which encourages "traditional, ineffective and inefficient patterns of mental health care" (Mechanic, 1978, p. 483) and discourages outpatient rehabilitation services that may be more therapeutic as well as more cost-effective for the chronically mentally ill.

With increasing sophistication, families' consumer groups have begun to exert influence by placing members on institutional advisory and overseeing boards. In this capacity, they serve a watchdog function, ensuring that service provision is as close to "state of the art" as possible, and that families' needs for information and inclusion in discharge planning are taken into account (Willett, 1977). At least some professionals (e.g., Chu & Trotter, 1974; Hollander, 1980) have challenged the view that service providers are in a better position than consumers to know what is needed. Hollander (1980) has noted that "uncritical acceptance of expert direction is an important factor in the intransigence of many problems and . . . expert intervention often creates its own set of iatrogenic difficulties, often leading to cycles of 'disabling help' " (p. 563). While community mental health centers have been required to have citizen participation since the 1975 amendments to the Community Mental Health Centers Act, often this requirement has been inadequately implemented. The consumer-advocacy organizations will give members the kind of backing they need to insist on meaningful participation (Hatfield & Smith, in press; Wilder, 1975).

A model program at Northampton State Hospital in Massachusetts (Reiter & Plotkin, 1985) uses family members to monitor ward activities and provide feedback to administrative staff. This program was developed as a cooperative effort of the hospital administration, the state Department of Mental Hygiene, and the local NAMI affiliate. As such, it represents a concrete example of the ability of professionals and families to work together to strengthen the power of advocacy. Why professionals might be motivated to do so, we shall discuss shortly.

As members of governmental advisory boards at state and local levels, families have begun to influence the allocation of funds so as to ensure that the needs of the chronically mentally ill are addressed. At the national level, NAMI has a full-time lobbyist, while many of the statewide affiliates grow daily more adept at using lobbying and other political strategies to achieve their goals. In 1984, for example, NAMI's political effort was instrumental in restoring funds for the Community Support Services program nationally.

In addition, patients' rights groups (as well as advocates for the mentally retarded) have set a model for the use of class action suits and related legal remedies that family advocacy groups can be expected to follow. Court-ordered remedies on issues like the right to refuse treatment, the right to treatment, and the right to the least restrictive setting have had far-reaching, unpredictable, and mixed results in the past. However, they have been valuable in drawing attention to the need for change and have set precedents that pushed other jurisdictions to address important issues. In California, for example, public law now mandates notification of family when a patient is psychiatrically hospitalized, released, transferred, ill, injured, or dead, unless the patient expressly requests that this information not be provided. The California affiliate of NAMI (CAMI) was responsible for the change in the statute (CAMI staff, personal communication, May 1985).

Finally, public relations efforts by family consumer groups can be expected to change the public's perception of the chronically mentally ill and their families. Monitoring of media presentations of the mentally ill, public education efforts, letters to the editor, and similar strategies will change the public's perception of the mentally ill as dangerous, hopeless people, as well as the notion that mental illness is the result of faulty parenting.

The winds of change are upon us. The emerging consumer movement will change the way families behave as collateral clients with respect to treatment of individual patients. This will necessitate a change in the way clinicians behave in return. It will also change what is expected of the mental health delivery system as a whole and will stimulate major modifications in training and programming.

## THE NEW CONSUMER AS "CLIENT"

Increased knowledgeability and assertiveness will change the nature of the professional-family relationship. Families can be expected to become more selective users of services. They will be less willing to passively accept treatment plans unless they understand the reasons for decisions that are made. They will request information about treatment outcome and cost-effectiveness. They will become more insistent that their own needs are taken into account in the discharge and planning process. They will expect staff to be available to them, to answer questions, and to provide advice.

For professionals who have had little contact with the families of their patients, the emotional impact will be profound. It will be tempting to view such families as aggressive or intrusive. It will be tempting to stand more firmly upon the bulwark of "confidentiality" as a self-protective maneuver (forgetting that the privilege rests with the patient, not with the professional). It is easy to see why this is so. Time constraints on busy, already overburdened clinicians make working with families difficult. There are always other tasks that seem more pressing. Many of us have been ill prepared for this approach by our training and orientation, which may lead us to view the family as pathogenic, or which may simply have offered few models for working collaboratively with families. Our own uncertainties and lack of confidence in what we know and can do for the chronically mentally ill may be stimulated through family contact. We may be threatened by the notion of sharing our fragile power and authority with family members. How will they view us when they find out how little we actually know?

Nonetheless, there are good reasons for changing the way we operate. Informed, educated family members are invariably easier to work with in the long run. They develop more realistic expectations, can be taught to develop the structured, low-key environment that we now know is optimally conducive to recovery (e.g., Falloon & Liberman, 1983), and can take on a meaningful role as the "eyes and ears" of the treatment team. As institutional care becomes a smaller and smaller part of treatment, and families play a larger role, successful rehabilitation will depend more heavily on helping families cope with residual symptoms of the illness.

In addition, as Hare-Mustin, Maracek, Kaplan, and Liss-Levenson (1979) and others (Coyne, 1976; Levant, 1978; Winborn, 1977) have pointed out, we have an ethical obligation to provide for informed consent to treatment. When patients, due to their mental condition, are unable to give informed consent, it falls to family members to do so. In these cases we are duty-bound to make available to them information about the benefits and risks of various treatment options. We should also alert them to the available alternatives to treatment, which may include self-help groups, religious activities, nursing services, crisis centers, and rehabilitation services among others. Further, when the family is being asked to participate (in family therapy, for example) the same holds true. We can not assume that family members are never harmed by therapy (Graziano & Fink, 1973; Hare-Mustin, 1980; Terkelsen, 1983). Hidden agendas, paradoxical instructions, and the possibility of deterioration in the patient's condition (due to overload of emotional stimuli) are examples of issues that, at the very least, present ethical dilemmas to the family therapist. Hare-Mustin has suggested the use of contracts to define the therapeutic relationship. They would specify the methods, goals, and duration of therapy; the length and frequency of sessions; cost and the method of payment; the degree of confidentiality; and would enumerate any techniques that might be at odds with the client's values. Further, we should consider our moral obligation to families to whom we discharge impaired patients. Only a very narrow view would overlook the burden the patient's presence imposes on the family. Supportive professional contact (Bernheim, 1982) is essential to minimizing the deleterious effects on the family system and the individuals within it.

Not only should we be encouraging responsible, informed consumerism in individual families with whom we work, but we should also be cognizant of the fact that working constructively with families is politically inevitable from a systems point of view (Beels, 1978). Families represent a constituency whose goals are in many ways synonymous with those of professionals. Both groups wish for expanded rehabilitation services, an array of community living options, more sensible reimbursement models, and allocation of funds for basic research and professional training. Both groups have an investment in ensuring that a reasonable proportion of tax monies be allocated to the needs of the chronically mentally ill. The professional community can not advocate alone for these ideals without appearing self-serving (Arbuckle, 1977; Torrey, 1978). In partnership with family consumers, much more could be accomplished.

The family–professional relationship is further complicated by the pressure brought to bear by ex-patients' groups that have their own issues and agendas. The patients' rights movement has goals that are sometimes consistent with and sometimes opposed to those of the family consumer movement. While both groups advocate for a wider range of services and oppose discrimination against the mentally ill, they diverge sharply on issues of enforced treatment and legal responsibility of persons with mental illness. Indeed, they often diverge on the issue of whether disordered behavior should be considered representative of an illness at all, with some militant ex-patients' groups adhering to the "mental illness is myth" model put forth by Szasz (1976) and others (Chamberlain, 1978). To a certain extent, this posture of denial has been solidified by the mystification of mental illness to which patients as well as families have been subjected. While the tension between these consumer groups will never be wholly resolved, increased communication, wider dissemination of knowledge, and efforts to reduce stigma can help to make the conflict creative rather than destructive. In the meantime, professionals are often truly on the horns of a dilemma as they struggle to meet the needs of families for information and assistance while protecting patients' rights to privacy and autonomy.

## EMERGING PROFESSIONAL RESPONSES

It is clear that the typical clinic model of individual, confidential one-on-one psychotherapy is ineffective and inappropriate for the rehabilitation of the chronically mentally ill. Nor is family therapy, as it is traditionally practiced, the treatment of choice (Bernheim, 1982). Family surveys consistently report that families have fairly clear and consistent goals for their work with professionals. They want information about the illness, advice about handling residual symptoms and other practical problems posed by living with a mentally ill relative, availability and assistance during times of crisis, and the opportunity for contact with other family members (Hatfield, 1983a; Yess, 1981). Programs that address these goals have begun to appear with increasing frequency (Falloon, Boyd, McGill, Strang, & Moss, 1981; McFarlane, 1983). It is ironic that most of these programs have developed, not in direct response to family requests, but rather out of interest in the literature on "expressed emotion," which indicates that family behavior can have an impact on patient relapse (Brown, et al., 1972; Vaughn & Leff, 1981). While family members have voiced the concern that this concept is yet another way of pointing an accusatory finger at the family, the resultant "psychoeducational" approach is, in fact, much more consistent with their needs. This is not surprising if we acknowledge that the chronically mentally ill (at least schizophrenics) experience deficits in the ability to modulate, filter out, and organize sensations and perceptions. Given this deficit they need a specialized kind of environment, one that is low in stimulation and high in clarity and organization. Within the range of normal family environments, some fit this characterization more closely than others. Further, some families have learned, through trial and error, how to produce such an environment while others have not. Psychoeducational programs teach families just these skills through grounding practical advice and skill training in a conceptual understanding of the illness.

While these programs vary in length, location (home or clinic), intensity, whether or not the patient is present, and whether or not single or multiple families are targeted, they have in common an educational, problem-solving focus. They each involve reducing the knowledge discrepancy between professional and family members, mutual goal-setting and exchange of information, ongoing feedback and collaboration, and empowerment of the family. They provide an array of models from which institutions and agencies could draw in developing their own family support program. Ideally, one could envision that each geographic region, through collaboration between various service providers, would have available a menu of offerings including short-term educational seminars; long- and short-term multifamily groups; workshops in problem solving, communication skills, and stress management strategies; individual supportive family counseling; and networking with local NAMI affiliates. Family members could then choose, aided by the advice of their ill relative's therapist, those services that would best meet their needs.

In areas where such a system of services is not feasible, much could still be done. Written orientations to procedures and policies of inpatient and residential settings, along with the name of an ombudsman or contact person for families would be most valuable. Regular family coffee hours with treatment staff could be held. Office hours for telephone contact with families could be set aside. Brief psychoeducational seminars could be offered on a repeating basis. Referrals to local NAMI affiliates could be made (with face-to-face introduction arranged) by intake workers. Notification of families upon patient transfer or when there is a significant change in the treatment plan could be mandated. A service plan for families could be included as part of the patient's treatment plan to ensure that the families' needs are at least considered.

While possible co-optation of self-help groups by professionals is a real risk, professionals could provide assistance to individuals who wish to start a self-help group or who need help in relating to groups that already exist by teaching group development and process skills, conveying public-relations techniques, and helping the group develop resources and linkages. Professional participation should generally be time limited so as to discourage member dependence, reduce the risk of professionalizing a nonprofessional movement, and prevent usurpation of power by providers (Gartner & Riessman, 1982). Additional institutional responses might include promulgation of clear grievance procedures should families feel inadequately served, and development of a standing committee composed of volunteer family members and professional staff to monitor and suggest responses to family concerns.

## ISSUES IN PROFESSIONAL TRAINING

In order to respond to the changing consumer, professionals will have to adjust their attitudes and bring their knowledge and skills up-to-date. In-service training programs for current staff as well as changes in the training of new professionals must be put into place. These will incorporate the following:

1. Sensitization to the plight, burden, and tasks of families. This can be accomplished through reading what family members have written (see, e.g., Vine, 1982; Wasow, 1982; Wilson, 1968; Woesner, 1983), and familiarization with the professional literature on family burden. However, readings can not substitute for face-to-face contact with families, which can be achieved through attendance at local NAMI meetings or educational seminars designed for this purpose. Family members could be invited to speak to graduate classes in psychology, psychiatry, social work, and nursing. Lewine (1983) has suggested that

trainees be assigned to patients (and families) rather than to agencies so that they can better understand how the system works for (or against) the consumer.

2. Development of a critical orientation to the "family as etiological agent" model of psychopathology. Current research that points to a biochemical basis for schizophrenia and major affective disorders should be a major focus of graduate curricula, which should also include available methodological and theoretical critiques of alternate environmental causation models (Fontana, 1966; Goldstein, 1981; Liem, 1980; Reiss, 1980; Terkelsen & Cole, unpublished manuscript).

3. Training in didactic skills. The role of educator is more appropriate than the role of therapist when working with families of the chronically mentally ill (Guerney, Stollak, & Guerney, 1971). While some of the requisite skills overlap (for example, clarity of communication and accurate listening), professionals will need to learn how best to organize presented material, how to develop and use visual aids, how to assess what is being learned, how to balance experiential and intellectual approaches, and how to tailor the material to the intellectual capabilities and interests of the learner. These skills are not currently taught in most clinical graduate programs. To do so might require linkages with graduate schools of education wherein the appropriate expertise resides.

4. Training in related areas. The application of problem-solving training and the building of communication skills in families have both been found to be useful in lowering recidivism rates in schizophrenic patients (Falloon & Liberman, 1983). Presumably, these skills are useful to the well family members also. While stress-management training has not been formally incorporated into psychoeducational programs to date, it would appear that this would also be useful to families of the chronically mentally ill (as well as to patients themselves). Professionals will need to learn how to conduct training in these areas, through in-service training or graduate courses.

5. Supervised practicum experiences. Curricula in graduate programs should include supervised experiences in psychoeducational groups and supportive family counseling (Atwood & Williams, 1978; Bernheim, 1982; Bernheim & Lehman, 1985). These programs are often weak in preparing new clinicians to work with the chronically mentally ill in general, and often provide few, if any, opportunities to interact collaboratively with family members. Observing videotapes of senior clinicians engaging in psychoeducational counseling could be followed by practicing these skills under observation. Family members would, no doubt, be willing to provide corrective feedback to trainees that might prove even more valuable than that offered by the supervisor.

## EFFECT OF FAMILY CONSUMERISM ON
## MENTAL HEALTH SERVICES

We mental health professionals can expect to be held more closely accountable for what we do for and to the chronically mentally ill and their families than we have ever been before. This will be true at the level of the individual clinician, as well as at the system level. In an era of dwindling resources, families will be looking for cost-effectiveness data as they decide which programs to support and which to oppose. It will ultimately become politically impossible to develop programs without input from respresentative family members, as families of the mentally ill follow the course charted a decade ago by families of retarded persons (Katz, 1961; Wolfenberger, 1972). We will see a continuation of the developing trend to allocate a more appropriate proportion of mental health funds to the needs of the chronically mentally ill. We will see a weeding out of practitioners who are insensitive to the needs of these patients and their families and a gradual change in the etiological models espoused by professionals as families publicize and support research into the biological bases of these illnesses (Hatfield, 1981a). While there is no doubt that the period of transition will be stormy at times, and fraught with conflict, change, and compromise, the final result will be a system of services developed through a partnership of professionals, researchers, families, and patients, that is more flexible and responsive to the needs of those whom it is meant to serve.

## REFERENCES

Arbuckle, D. (1977). Consumers make mistakes too: An invited response. *Personnel and Guidance Journal, 56,* 226-228.

Arey, S., & Warheit, G. (1980). Psychological costs of living with psychologically disturbed family members. In L. Robins, P. Clayton, & J. K. Wing (Eds.), *The social consequences of psychiatric illnesses.* New York: Brunner/Mazel.

Atwood, N., & Williams, E. O. (1978). Group support for families of the mentally ill. *Schizophrenia Bulletin, 4,* 415-425.

Beels, C. (1978). Social networks, the family, and the schizophrenic patient. *Schizophrenia Bulletin, 4,* 512-520.

Bernheim, K. F. (1982). Supportive family counseling. *Schizophrenia Bulletin, 8,* 634-641.

Bernheim, K., & Lehman, A. F. (1985). Teaching mental health trainees to work with families of the chronic mentally ill. *Hospital and Community Psychiatry, 36,* 1109-1110.

Bernheim, K. F., & Lewine, R. R. J. (1979). *Schizophrenia: Symptoms, causes, treatments.* New York: Norton.

Bernheim, K. F., Lewine, R. R. J., & Beale, C. T. (1982). *The caring family: Living with chronic mental illness.* New York: Random House.

Brown, G. W., Birley, J. L. T., & Wing, J. K. (1972). Influence of family life on the course of schizophrenic disorders: A replication. *British Journal of Psychiatry, 121*, 241-258.

Chamberlain, J. (1978). *On our own: Patient controlled alternatives to the mental health system.* New York: Hawthorne.

Chu, R. D., & Trotter, S. (1974). *The madness establishment.* New York: Grossman.

Coyne, J. C. (1976). The place of informed consent in ethical dilemmas. *Journal of Consulting and Clinical Psychology, 44*, 1015-1016.

Creer, C., & Wing, J. K. (1974). *Schizophrenia at home.* London: Institute of Psychiatry.

Doll, W. (1976). Family coping with the mentally ill: An unanticipated problem of deinstitutionalization. *Hospital and Community Psychiatry, 27*, 183-185.

Falloon, I. R. H., Boyd, J. L., McGill, C. W., Strang, J. S., & Moss, H. B. (1981). Family management training in the community care of schizophrenia. In M. J. Goldstein (Ed.), *New developments in interventions with families of schizophrenics* (New Directions for Mental Health Services No. 12). San Francisco: Jossey-Bass.

Falloon, I. R. H., & Liberman, R. P. (1983). Behavioral family interventions in the management of chronic patient. In W. R. McFarlane (Ed.), *Family therapy in schizophrenia.* New York: Guilford.

Fontana, A. F. (1966). Familial etiology of schizophrenia: Is it a scientific methodology? *Psychological Bulletin, 66*, 214-227.

Gartner, A. J., & Riessman, F. (1977). *Self-help in the human services.* San Francisco: Jossey-Bass.

Gartner, A. J., & Riessman, F. (1982). Self-help and mental health. *Hospital and Community Psychiatry, 33*, 631-635.

Goldman, H. H. (1982). Mental illness and family burden: A public health perspective. *Hospital and Community Psychiatry, 33*, 557-559.

Goldstein, M. D. (Ed.). (1981). *New developments in interventions with families of schizophrenics* (New Directions for Mental Health Services, No. 12). San Francisco: Jossey-Bass.

Gottlieb, B. (1976). Lay influences on the utilization and provision of health services: A review. *Canadian Psychological Review, 17*, 126-136.

Graziano, A. M., & Fink, F. S. (1973). Second-order effects in mental health treatment. *Journal of Consulting and Clinical Psychology, 40*, 356-364.

Guerney, B., Stollak, G., & Guerney, L. (1971). The practicing psychologist as educator—an alternative to the medical practitioners model. *Professional Psychology, 3*, 276-282.

Haley, J. (1980). *Leaving home: The therapy of disturbed young people.* New York: McGraw-Hill.

Hare-Mustin, R. T. (1980). Family therapy may be dangerous to your health. *Professional Psychology, 11*, 935-938.

Hare-Mustin, R. T., Marecek, J., Kaplan, A. G., & Liss-Levenson, N. (1979). Rights of clients, responsibilities of theapists. *American Psychologist, 34*, 3-16.

Hatfield, A. B. (1978). Psychological costs of schizophrenia to the family. *Social Work, 23*, 355-359.

Hatfield, A. B. (1979). Help-seeking behavior in families of schizophrenics. *American Journal of Community Psychology, 7*, 563-569.

Hatfield, A. B. (1981a). Families as advocates for the mentally ill: A growing movement. *Hospital and Community Psychiatry, 32*, 641-642.

Hatfield, A. B. (1981b). Self-help groups for families of the mentally ill. *Social Work, 26*, 408-413.

Hatfield, A. B. (1982). Therapists and families: Worlds apart. *Hospital and Community Psychiatry, 33*, 513.

Hatfield, A. B. (1983a). What families want of family therapists. In W. R. McFarlane (Ed.), *Family therapy in schizophrenia*. New York: Guilford.

Hatfield, A. B. (1983b). Coping with mental illness in the family: The family guide and the leader's guide. College Park, MD: University of Maryland.

Hatfield, A. B. (1984). The family consumer movement: A new force in service delivery. In B. Pepper & H. Ryglewicz (Eds.), *Advances in treating the young adult chronic patient* (New Directions for Mental Health Services, No. 21).

Hatfield, A. B., & Smith, H. B. (in press). The role of the consumer in quality assurance. In G. Stricker & A. Rodriquez (Eds.), *Quality assurance in mental health: A comprehensive handbook*.

Hogarty, G. (1971). The plight of schizophrenics in modern treatment programs. *Hospital and Community Psychiatry, 22,* 197-203.

Holden, D. F., & Lewine, R. R. J. (1982). How families evaluate mental health professionals, resources, and effects of illness. *Schizophrenia Bulletin, 8,* 626-633.

Hollander, R. (1980). A new service ideology: The third mental health revolution. *Professional Psychology, 11,* 561-566.

Hornstra, R., Lubin, R., Lewis, R., & Willis, B. (1972). Worlds apart: Patients and professionals. *Archives of General Psychiatry, 27,* 872-883.

Hurvitz, N. (1976). The origins of peer-self-help psychotherapy group movement. *Journal of Applied Behavioral Science, 12,* 283-294.

Kantor, J. (1982). Coping strategies for relatives of the mentally ill. Bethesda, MD: Alliance for the Mentally Ill.

Katz, A. (1961). *Parents of the handicapped: Self-organized parents' and relatives' groups for treatment of ill and handicapped children.* Springfield, IL: Thomas.

Katz, A., & Bender, E. (1976a). Self-help groups in Western society. *Journal of Applied Behavioral Science, 12,* 265-302.

Katz, A. H., & Bender, E. I. (Eds.). (1976b). *The strength in us: Self-help groups in the modern world.* New York: New Viewpoints.

Kirk, S. A., & Thenlen, M. F. (1975). Community mental health myths and the fate of former hospitalized patients. *Psychiatry, 38,* 209-217.

Klerman challenges professions to prove therapy works. (1979). *American Psychological Association Monitor, 11,* 1.

Kreisman, D., & Joy, V. (1974). Family response to the mental illness of a relative: A review of the literature. *Schizophrenia Bulletin, 1*(10), 34-57.

Kreisman, D., Simmons, S., & Joy, V. (1979). *Deinstitutionalization and the family's well-being.* New York: New York State Psychiatric Institute.

Lamb, H., & Edelson, M. B. (1976). The carrot and the stick: Inducing local programs to serve long-term patients. *Community Mental Health Journal, 12,* 137-144.

Lamb, H., & Oliphant, E. (1978). Schizophrenia through the eyes of families. *Hospital and Community Psychiatry, 9,* 803-806.

Lamb, H., & Oliphant, E. (1979). Parents of schizophrenics: Advocates for the mentally ill. In L. Stein (Ed.), *Community support systems for the long-term patient* (New Directions for Mental Health Services, No. 2). San Francisco: Jossey-Bass.

Lenrow, P. B., & Burch, R. W. (1981). Mutual aid and professional services—opposing or complementary? In B. H. Gottlieb (Ed.), *Social networks and social support*. Beverly Hills, CA: Sage.

Levant, R. (1978). Family therapy: A client-centered approach. *Journal of Marriage and Family Counseling, 4,* 35-42.

Lewine, R. R. J. (1983). Parents: Mental health professionals' scapegoats. In E. Sigel & L. M. Laosa (Eds.), *Changing families*. New York: Plenum Press.

Lidz, T. (1973). *The origin and treatment of schizophrenic disorders.* New York: Basic Books.

Liem, J. H. (1980). Family studies of schizophrenia: An update and commentary. *Schizophrenia Bulletin, 6,* 429-455.

Madanes, C. (1981). *Strategic family therapy.* San Francisco: Jossey-Bass.

McFarlane, W. R. (Ed.). (1983). *Family therapy in schizophrenia.* New York: Guilford.

Mechanic, D. (1978). Considerations in the design of mental health benefits under national health insurance. *American Journal of Public Health, 68,* 482-488.

Morrison, J., Holdridge-Crane, S., & Smith, J. (1978). Citizen participation in community mental health. *Community Mental Health Review, 3,* 1-9.

Reiss, D. (1980). Pathways to assessing the family: Some choice points and a sample route. In C. K. Hofling & J. M. Lewis (Eds.), *The family: Evaluation and treatment.* New York: Brunner & Mazel.

Reiter, M. S., & Plotkin, A. (1985). Family members as monitors in a state mental hospital. *Hospital and Community Psychiatry, 36,* 393-395.

Rothman, D. J. (1971). *The discovery of the asylum, social order and disorder in the new republic.* Boston: Little, Brown.

Schulberg, H. C. (1981). Outcome evaluations in the mental health field. *Community Mental Health Journal, 17,* 132-142.

Szasz, T. S. (1976). *Schizophrenia: The sacred symbol of psychiatry.* New York: Basic Books.

Talbott, J. D. (Ed.). (1978). *The chronic mental patient: Problems, solutions, and recommendations for a public policy.* Washington, DC: American Psychiatric Association.

Terkelsen, K. G. (1983). Schizophrenia and the family: II. Adverse effects of family therapy. *Family Process, 22,* 191-200.

Terkelsen, K. G., & Cole, S. A. (1984). *Methodological flaws in the schizophrenic hypothesis: Implications for psychiatric education.* Unpublished manuscript.

Thompson, E., Doll, W., & Lefton, M. (1977, April 13-17). *Some affective dimensions of familial coping with the mentally ill.* Paper presented at the 54th Annual Meeting of the American Orthopsychiatric Association, New York.

Torrey, E. F. (1978, September). The mental health lobby: Providers vs. consumers. *Psychology Today,* pp. 17-18.

Torrey, E. F. (1983). *Surviving schizophrenia: A family manual.* New York: Harper & Row.

Vattano, A. J. (1972). Power to the people: Self-help groups. *Social Work, 17,* 7-15.

Vaughn, C. E., & Leff, J. P. (1981). The influence of family and social factors in the course of psychiatric illness. *British Journal of Psychiatry, 139,* 102-104.

Vine, P. (1982). *Families in pain: Children, siblings, spouses, and parents of the mentally ill speak out.* New York: Pantheon.

Walsh, M. (1985). *Schizophrenia: Straight talk for families and friends.* New York: William Morrow.

Wasow, M. (1982). *Coping with schizophrenia: A survival manual for parents, relatives, and friends.* Palo Alto, CA: Science and Behavior Books.

Wilder, J. F. (1975). Strengths of the community mental health movement in urban areas. In W. E. Barton and J. Sanborn (Eds.), *An assessment of the community mental health movement.* Lexington, MA: Lexington Books.

Willett, S. (1977). Consumer education or advocacy—or both? *Social Policy, 8,* 2-8.

Wilson, L. (1968). *This stranger, my son: A mother's story.* New York: Putnam.

Winborn, B. (1977). Honest labeling and other procedures for the protection of consumers of counseling. *Personnel and Guidance Journal, 56,* 206-209.

Woesner, M. E. (1983). A professional's guide to books for families of the mentally ill. *Hospital and Community Psychiatry, 34,* 925-933.

Wolfensberger, W. (1972). *The third stage in the evolution of voluntary associations for the mentally retarded.* Toronto: International League of Societies for the Mentally Handicapped and the National Institute on Mental Retardation.

Wynne, L. C. (1978). Family relationships and communications: Concluding comments. In L. C. Wynne, R. M. Cromwell, & S. Matthysse (Eds.), *The nature of schizophrenia.* New York: Wiley.

Yess, J. P. (1981). What families of the mentally ill want. *Community Support Service Journal, 2*(1), 1-3.

# Current Educational and Supportive Models of Family Intervention

*Anthony M. Zipple*
*LeRoy Spaniol*

Families who have psychiatrically disabled relatives often need assistance from mental health professionals. One of the most important groups of innovations in the attempts to provide assistance to families has been the development of educational and supportive approaches (Beels & McFarlane, 1982). Such approaches are useful and important for two reasons. First, it appears that families with psychiatrically disabled relatives often prefer support and education to more traditional interventions such as family therapy (Hatfield, 1979, 1981). Second, there is a growing body of evidence that these approaches result in significantly improved outcomes for the disabled family member (Anderson, Hogarty, & Reiss, 1981; Byalin, Jed, & Lehman, 1982; Falloon, *et al.*, 1982).

Existing approaches will be divided into four general categories: (1) informational approaches that are designed primarily to provide information, (2) skill-training approaches that are designed primarily to develop skills, (3) supportive approaches that are designed primarily to enhance the family's emotional capacity to cope with stress, and (4) comprehensive approaches that incorporate information, skill training, and support in a single intervention. It should be noted that most models use elements of more than one of these approaches. However, these conceptual divisions are useful in that they provide a clear image of the central goal of the intervention.

Anthony M. Zipple and LeRoy Spaniol. Center for Rehabilitation Research and Training in Mental Health, Boston University, Boston, Massachusetts.

## INFORMATIONAL APPROACHES

Informational approaches are those interventions that are designed to provide knowledge about psychiatric disability and its management. The goal of information models is to increase the family members' understanding of their disabled relative's disorders and of the interventions that may be helpful in treating the disorder. Typically, family members learn about the etiology, symptoms, and course of disabling psychiatric disorders. In addition, they learn about various treatments, such as medications, therapy, and psychosocial rehabilitation programs. While many informational approaches offer practical advice about caring for a disabled relative, they do not generally teach specific skills to participants. That is, they do not focus on skill demonstration, skill practice, feedback, or skill-based homework assignments. While other informational approaches have been described in the professional literature (Bernheim, 1982; McLean, Greer, Scott, & Beck, 1982; Plummer, Thornton, Seeman, & Littman, 1981), the following three are a representative sample of such approaches.

The most comprehensive informational model currently being used with families of the psychiatrically disabled is the model developed by Anderson, Hogarty, and their associates (Anderson, 1983; Anderson, Hogarty, & Reiss, 1980, 1981). The model has two central goals. First, it attempts to decrease patient vulnerability to environmental stimulation through a program of maintenance chemotherapy. Second, it attempts to increase the level of stability and predictability of the family environment by decreasing family anxiety about the patient, increasing their knowledge about the disorder, and increasing their confidence in their ability to be effective caregivers.

There are four parts to the intervention. First, the clinician must establish a relationship with the family. This process, which is referred to as "connecting," consists of eliciting the family's experience with their disabled relative, mobilizing family concern, establishing the clinician as the family's ombudsman, and developing a treatment contract.

The second phase of the process is a 1-day, multifamily workshop referred to as a "survival skills workshop." It should be noted, however, that the primary goal of the day's activities is to provide information rather than skill training. Information about the disorder and medications are always included. In addition, family members are encouraged to be concerned about their own lives and stress levels and are given permission to maintain a relatively normalized life-style in spite of their disabled relative.

The third part of the intervention consists of family sessions, held every 2 to 3 weeks for 6 months to a year, in which application of the information supplied during the 1-day workshop is monitored. Special attention is paid to developing respect for interpersonal boundaries and enhancing the personal responsibility of the disabled family member.

The final part of the intervention is a decision to continue the family sessions, modify the arrangement, or terminate the intervention. There is no specific time limit on the length of the intervention. Most families spend at least 2 years in treatment (Anderson, 1983).

The results of this approach are encouraging. The rate of relapse of disabled individuals whose families participate in the model is less than 10% compared to a relapse rate of 34% in the control group. This low relapse rate is achieved in spite of the fact that most patients continue to experience some severe level of disability (Anderson et al., 1981).

A second information model was developed by Dincin, Selleck, and Streicker (1978) at Thresholds, a well-established psychosocial rehabilitation center. The primary goal of the model is to restructure parental attitudes towards their psychiatrically disabled adult children by providing them with information about the disorder and its management. Specifically, the program is designed to help parents allow and encourage their adult children to separate from the parental home.

During the time that family members are in the program (usually 12 weeks), they are given information about the etiology and management of the disorder and encouraged not to feel guilty or responsible. Instead, it is suggested that emancipation of their adult children is best for both the family and the child.

The results of the program are encouraging. Of the parents who participated, 60% reported that the group helped them to make significant gains. In addition, significantly more adult children of participants left the parental home during the course of the group as compared to the adult children of nonparticipants. This is important in that having the disabled relative in the home has been found to correlate with both decreased levels of satisfaction for the nondisabled family member (Spaniol, Jung, Zipple, & Fitzgerald, 1984) and an increased sense of burden (O'Connor, 1983).

A final example of an informational approach to working with families with psychiatrically disabled relatives is provided by Hatfield (1982). Hatfield's program entails six 2-hour seminars that families attend weekly. Each week a different subject is discussed. Topics include (1) the meaning of mental illness to the family, (2) understanding chronic mental illness, (3) the treatment for mental illness, (4) creating a low-stress environment, (5) managing disturbing behavior, and (6) promoting growth and rehabilitation. The emphasis is on cognitive mastery of the material. Participants are encouraged to share relevant personal experiences and insights. The atmosphere is kept informal but task-oriented. A wide range of reading material, including the training manual, is utilized. While the model seems promising, no data on participant satisfaction or patient outcome has yet been provided.

These three models and other similar approaches share three strengths. First, they provide specific information relevant to each of the five major areas of need reported by families in existing surveys of family needs (Hatfield, 1979; Spaniol, Jung, et al., 1984; Wasow, 1980). Since these models provide some of what families seem to want, it is likely that families would experience them as useful and satisfying. Second, all of the models explicitly state that their emphasis is on teaching rather than treating families. This tends to limit the possibility of families feeling blamed by professionals for their relatives' disorders and, in turn, enhances the willingness of families to participate in the intervention (Wasow, 1980). In addition, there is less stigma attached to informational approaches than to therapy (Hatfield, 1983). Again, this enhances the willingness of families to participate. Third, in each of these models, the professional functions as a consultant to the family and displays a willingness to share control over interventions with other family members. This willingness to include the family as a partner is both satisfying for families (Hatfield, 1979) and liberating for professionals, since they are able to utilize other family members as valuable resources in caring for the disabled individuals whom they serve (Spaniol, Zipple, & Fitzgerald, 1984).

In spite of these important strengths, informational models share a similar limitation. Although these models provide families with some skills, none of the models is designed to provide structured skill training. Recent surveys of family needs suggest that families need both information and specific skills related to being effective caregivers for their disabled relatives (Hatfield, 1979; Spaniol, Jung, et al., 1984; Wasow, 1980). While psychoeducational programs seem to recognize the importance of both information and skills, they provide primarily information to participants. These information-based interventions can be effective, but they may not be powerful enough if the family wants and needs skills as well. An additional limitation is that the content of these informational approaches is narrowly focused on the interactions between families and their ill family members. Often families need information about "out of family" activities such as advocacy and resource management. Failure to include such content in current informational approaches means that some of the information needs of some families go unmet.

## SKILL-TRAINING APPROACHES

Skill-training approaches are those interventions that attempt to directly and systematically teach specific behaviors that will enhance the caregiving abilities of individuals with psychiatrically disabled relatives. The goal is to increase the family members' ability to be helpful to the disabled family member and manage that member's psychiatric disorder more effectively. Typically, individuals are taught a range of communication skills; problem-solving skills; limit-setting techniques; and basic behavioral interventions, such as how to use rewards, develop contracts, and define problem behaviors. Most skill-training programs offer information to trainees but the primary emphasis is on the acquisition and application of skills.

The group that has developed one of the most comprehensive skill-training approaches for families with psychiatrically disabled relatives is the Mental Health Clinical Research Center for the Study of Schizophrenia (Falloon, Liberman, Lillie, & Vaughn, 1981; Liberman, Wallace, Vaughn, & Snyder, 1979). This group has developed and evaluated a 10-week series of 2-hour training sessions for family members and their disabled relatives (Liberman, Aitchison, & Falloon, 1979). The goals of the program are to strengthen the problem-solving skills of the disabled family member and to improve the emotional climate in the home by training all family members in communication skills. The program draws heavily from the work on "expressed emotion" in the family (Brown, Birley, & Wing, 1972; Leff & Vaughn, 1981). This research suggests that relapse is related to the level of negative emotion expressed toward the disabled individual by other family members and that teaching relatives to moderate the expression of such emotions will lead to improved outcome.

Weeks 1 and 2 of the program are informational and discuss the nature of schizophrenia and medications. Weeks 3-8 are designed to teach a series of problem-solving and communication skills to family members. Skills such as listening, expressing positive and negative feelings, and aftercare planning are covered. Week 9 is a review and good-bye session. Week 10, which occurs 3 months after the ninth session, is a follow-up to the problem-solving skill session and an opportunity to collect outcome data. During this same period, all disabled relatives of the trainees receive similar training in problem-solving and communication skills in separate training meetings. Each skill-training session contains behavioral descriptions of the skill, practice exercises, and related homework assignments. The disabled individuals who participated in this program with their relatives had a significantly lower relapse rate at a 12-month follow-up than the control group subjects who received holistic interventions including insight-oriented family therapy. Successful refinements, expansions, and further evaluation of this approach have also been reported (Falloon et al., 1982; Falloon, Boyd, & McGill, 1984), and the Center is continuing its efforts in this area.

Another example of a skill-training approach is provided by Goldstein and Kopeikin (1981). They report on the impact of a short-term treatment program combined with chemotherapy. While the program is described as "crisis oriented therapy" (Kopeikin, Marshall, & Goldstein, 1983), the therapy appears to consist largely of skill training. The program is a series of 6 weekly family sessions following the discharge of the patient from a hospital setting. The model emphasizes the importance of stress management and has four specific goals. First, it helps the family members to learn how to identify situations that are stressful for the patient. Second, it attempts to teach strategies for avoiding and/or coping with stress. Third, it teaches family members to evaluate and refine their stress-management techniques. Finally, the program teaches families to anticipate stressful situations and to plan proactive responses to them.

Results of this approach are encouraging. None of the 25 patients who participated in these sessions with their families and received relatively high doses of medication experienced a relapse during a 6-month follow-up. This compares to a 48% relapse rate for a control group.

These skill-training approaches to helping families with disabled relatives all share similar strengths. First, each is clearly designed to provide family members with specific behaviors that may be useful in their attempts to be effective caregivers. For families who want and need an intervention that is more powerful than information and/or support alone, skill training may be the approach of choice. Second, each is relatively nonstigmatizing in that the professional's role is more like that of a teacher than of a traditional therapist. The less like therapy the intervention appears, the more likely it is that families will experience it as a helpful intervention (Hatfield, 1979; Wasow, 1980).

Skill-training approaches also share three significant limitations. First, each model assumes the importance of a set of skills and then attempts to teach families what it has to offer. The trainer comes to the session with a training curriculum and a belief that the families attending want and need to learn communication skills, problem-solving skills, stress-management skills, and so on. The skill-training approach is only as useful as this belief is valid. If some families do not want and need these skills, these approaches may not be helpful or satisfying to them. Second, there is an unnecessary tendency to describe some of these interventions as "therapy" rather than "training"

(Falloon, *et al.*, 1981; Kopeikin, *et al.*, 1983). This may be the result of insurance reimbursement pressures, professional status issues, or professional training models. Whatever the reasons, this poses a risk. The more therapy-like the intervention appears to families, the more likely it is that families may feel blamed for their relative's disorder by the professional leading the training (Spaniol, Jung, *et al.*, 1984). Given how sensitive families are to implications of blame (Hatfield, 1979; Wasow, 1980), pure skill training approaches that are described as therapies may be limited in that some families will refuse to participate because they will feel blamed and stigmatized by the approach. Third, as is the case with psychoeducational approaches, skill-training approaches tend to be narrowly focused on interactions between families and their ill family member and fail to address the need that families have for training in "out of family" activities such as advocacy.

## SUPPORTIVE APPROACHES

Supportive approaches are those interventions that are primarily designed to enhance the emotional capacity of the family to cope with the stresses of caring for a psychiatrically disabled relative. Typically, the family engages in a process of sharing their feelings and experiences regarding caring for the disabled relative. In return, the family is reassured that such caregiving is difficult, that they are doing the best they can, and that they do not need to feel guilty. While provision of information and skill training may occur at times, the central goal of support approaches is to alter the emotional state of the participants.

The more widely used support model is the one developed by the National Alliance for the Mentally Ill (NAMI) (Hatfield, 1981; Straw & Young, 1982; Wasow, 1982). NAMI is not an approach that was developed by professionals in response to the needs of families. Instead, NAMI was developed by individuals with psychiatrically disabled relatives as a self-help and advocacy group (Hatfield, 1981). NAMI has grown dramatically since its official founding in 1979 and currently is composed of hundreds of local chapters representing more than 40,000 members.

NAMI seems to be able to meet many of the needs of the families more successfully than many professionals (Spaniol, Jung *et al.*, 1984). It also provides families with a powerful vehicle for advocating for changes in the mental health system. Family members also discovered that there was a great deal of comfort to be found in mutual support (Hatfield, 1981). Joining together to share experiences with a common problem is a useful experience for many individuals and is the basis for other types of self-help groups (Killilea, 1976, 1982).

NAMI appears to be a successful group that meets an important need, as indicated by its large and growing size. Hatfield (1979) surveyed 79 NAMI and NAMI-like support groups and found that the large majority of the members were satisfied with their groups. Many chapters have become actively involved in political advocacy (Straw & Young, 1982), and some chapters are beginning to provide direct services to psychiatrically disabled individuals (Shifren-Levine & Spaniol, 1985). The core of most groups, however, remains the support/ advocacy function that it provides for its members. Spaniol, Jung et al. (1984) reported that families with mentally ill members have a variety of needs met by support groups such as NAMI. In the national survey taken by Spaniol and associates, 75% of the respondents reported that self-help groups were helpful and 33% reported that self-help groups were the *most* important source of support. Further, 31% reported that self-help groups such as NAMI were the *best* source of information about mental illness. Clearly, self-help groups are able to meet many information and support needs for a significant number of families.

Mental health professionals also attempt to provide support to families. One such supportive model is reported by Byalin, Jed, and Lehman (1982) whose goal was to "enhance the capacity of families of these patients to cope with the stresses of caring for a severely and chronically ill member without overtly attempting to change behavior" (p. 2). In this model, the professional visits the family home as a guest and makes no attempt to provide therapy. Instead, two themes are emphasized. First, the family is told that they are cosufferers in a family tragedy rather than the people who caused the tragedy. Second, the family is told that mental health professionals have failed to provide significant aid. The family maintains control over the interaction and decides on the scheduling and the duration of the visit. The results of this approach are encouraging. Not only do families feel comfortable with the model, but a small pilot study using the model found that it significantly reduced the hospitalization time of disabled family members.

Supportive approaches share two strengths. First, they meet a need expressed by families. Wasow (1980) found that the most frequently voiced need of families was to not be blamed for their relative's disorder. Supportive approaches, whether provided by professionals or by family members themselves, seem to share the ability to relieve some of the guilt, anger, and frustration experienced by families. Second, supportive approaches are nonstigmatizing and relatively unintrusive. For family members who want and need an opportunity to share their experiences with other individuals in similar situations but who do not want or need skill training or structured educational sessions, a supportive approach provides a nonthreatening alternative. In addition, at least one supportive approach (NAMI) has an overt interest in advocacy.

Supportive approaches also have a serious limitation. If a family wants or needs skills or information that will help them to be more effective caregivers, supportive approaches will probably not provide a powerful enough intervention to meet their needs. Since most family members want and need specific skills and information at some time during the course of their caregiving efforts, supportive approaches by themselves may not be enough.

## COMPREHENSIVE APPROACHES

At least one model developed by professionals is intended to provide information, skills, and support as parts of a structured and comprehensive intervention (Leff, Kuipers, Berkowitz, Eberbein-Vries, & Sturgeon, 1982). This approach, termed "social intervention," is a three-part model. First, families receive four lectures on etiology, symptoms, and prognosis of schizophrenia in an attempt to provide them with basic information. Second, families participate in a multifamily support group that is designed to provide an opportunity to share experiences, problems, and solutions. Finally, families receive 1–25 individual sessions with a mental health professional. These sessions provide families with a combination of dynamic insights and the teaching of behavioral interventions. The results of this approach are encouraging. The relapse rate of disabled individuals whose families participated in this group was only 9% over a 9-month period compared to 50% for a control group receiving traditional outpatient treatment.

This approach has the combined strengths (and limitations) of the informational, skills-training, and supportive approaches. It is important to note that in spite of its comprehensiveness, the client outcome data is not significantly better than other less comprehensive approaches. The relapse rate of patients whose families participated in Anderson's (1983) informational model was also less than 10%. Goldstein and Kopeikin's (1981) skill-training approach resulted in an even lower rate of relapse. Although the relapse rates are not provided by Byalin, Jed, and Lehman (1982) for their support-alone approach, the mean rate of hospitalization for their group over a 12-month period was only 10.3 days compared to a mean rate of 56.3 days per year for these same individuals during the preceding 4 years.

## SUGGESTIONS FOR ENHANCING
## EDUCATIONAL AND SUPPORTIVE APPROACHES

There are two possible explanations for the similarity in the effectiveness of these models. First, it may be that global outcome indicators such as relapse or recidivism rates are too broad to capture significant differences between the approaches. Utilization of outcome measures of family satisfaction, client satisfaction, client level of functioning, family level of functioning, and stress level may demonstrate some differences between the models in terms of outcome.

An alternative and perhaps more plausable explanation for the similarities in outcome is that all of the approaches share a core group of common features. Each of the approaches attempts to engage the family in a partnership and gives the family some control over the intervention. Each of them attempts to *not* blame the family for the disability of the mentally ill member. Each of the approaches provides either skills, information, or support, or some combination of these services designed to help families to cope more effectively with their mentally ill relative. The comparable outcomes of all of these models may be explained by arguing that each of them employs a range of strategies that may actually be independent of a specific causal model of family distress or patient relapse, but that somehow relate directly to what families have been saying they want or need from professionals. Identifying these key features and incorporating them into professional practice is of critical importance to practitioners working with families with mentally ill members. In reviewing the literature on educational and supportive interventions and after spending many hours discussing this topic with families, we suggest that there are at least 15 professional activities that enhance a practitioner's ability to develop and implement educational and supportive approaches.

### Learn Educational Approaches

Professionals should utilize educational approaches as the treatment of choice. Educational approaches do not assume sickness but rather a lack of knowledge and skills (Anthony, Cohen, & Cohen, 1983). Therefore, less stigma is attached to educational approaches. Within this conceptual framework, the primary role designated for the professional vis-à-vis the family might be that of teacher. Families tend to support a teaching role for professionals. They want assistance and practical advice. Rehabilitation/educational models require different skills and attitudes from professionals. Becoming familiar with these models, being open to learning new skills, and challenging current attitudes will help professionals to work more effectively with families.

## Clarify Mutual Goals

One clear lesson learned from our research is to be open to negotiating and clarifying the goals of teaching with families. What professionals believe families want and what families want is often different. Assuming what families need without adequately checking out underlying assumptions usually leads to families feeling discounted, devalued, and disenfranchised by professional intervention. Professionals should be reluctant to teach without a clear statement from family members regarding what they want. Being open and honest, listening and responding to their concerns will more likely result in a useful and helpful interaction.

## Don't Force Families to Fit a Specific Model

Family educational approaches are often independent of theoretical explanations of causes for problems families may identify. Rigid adherence to models of family functioning, causality, and therapy can seriously limit a professionals' ability to hear and experience what families are trying to tell them.

## Acknowledge Your Own Limitations

Professionals should be clear with families about the complexity of the disability and the limitations of current knowledge of how to treat it. Families need to hear that professionals also are struggling to determine how best to help their disabled family member. This awareness will help families to come to terms with their own hopes, fears, and limitations. Awareness will also prepare them to be partners in working out a more realistic medical and rehabilitation plan for their disabled family member (Yess, 1981).

## Work as a Team

Professionals should develop a team approach to teaching, regularly utilizing families as co-trainers. It is important to note that with the exception of NAMI and Hatfield's approaches, none of the current educational or supportive models use family members as teachers. Involvement of family members in the development, implementation, and evaluation of training increases the likelihood that the training will be helpful to families. Families of the mentally ill have a wealth of information on coping with the problems created by caring for their ill family member.

## Point Out Family Strengths

It is important to focus on family strengths as well as areas in need of change. Professionals should give ample time to acknowledging what families are doing that is effective and help them to acknowledge it to themselves. Self-esteem and feelings of competence are greatly enhanced by acknowledgment of strengths. In fact, many families report coping very well with their own lives and the problems of their disabled member (Spaniol, Jung et al., 1984). Acknowledgement of family strengths on a regular basis as well as dealing with the families' need for information and assistance will provide the balance needed to build a truly helpful relationship with families (Wasow, 1982).

## Learn to Respond to Intense Feelings

Professionals need to learn how to deal with the intense feelings of family members. Some families report a long history of frustration and abuse by the mental health system. Their feelings may be deeply felt and strongly expressed. It is necessary for professionals to learn how to listen to what they are saying. If professionals are able to respond with clear understanding and compassion rather than defensiveness, they will be in a better position to respond to family's requests for information or assistance.

## Encourage Family Enrichment

Families may need permission to put greater time and energy into themselves. Professionals can encourage families to create a greater balance within their own lives. This balance can be encouraged by helping families to refocus their energies on their own needs and wants. As their stresses increase, family members need to take care of themselves so that they have the energy to take good care of others around them. Families can learn to get beyond stress management by refocusing their energies into more creative and enriching directions. Creating positive options in their life can increase their feelings of competence, their sense of self-esteem, and confidence that they can make their life work for them on a daily basis. Positive options can include activities such as spending time with old friends, going to the theater, reinvolving themselves in activities that have nothing to do with mental illness, and doing other things that they enjoy individually and as a family.

## Provide Information about Psychiatric Illness and Medications

Families report that their need for information about mental illness and concerns about problems associated with drug management are very high priorities (Spaniol, Jung et al., 1984). Lack of information in these two areas is a frequent complaint of family members. Professionals need to be able to teach family members about mental illness. Educational approaches should include information on types of diagnosis and likely prognosis, the reasons for treatment and rehabilitation plans, and how to deal with common problems of behavioral and drug management.

## Provide Practical Advice

A large body of literature has developed on the needs and practical problems of families of the mentally ill. Professionals should familiarize themselves with this literature and find out what families are saying they need. It is important to give special attention to the practical management strategies families say they need and how to teach them. One way to enhance these strategies is to include experienced family members as co-trainers. Many families have learned useful coping skills and can teach professionals and other family members what they have learned.

## Provide Information About Community Resources

Professionals should provide information about the resources in the community. It is important for professionals to become familiar with the quantity as well as the quality of these resources and to learn to link resources together for the benefit of their clients and their clients' families. Professionals need to visit these resources and find out how families can best use them. It is also useful for professionals to get to know the people who provide the services. A local resource guide can be developed with very little effort. Inviting some family members to work with you in its development will lighten the work load and provide a valuable opportunity for substantive family-professional interaction.

## Encourage Involvement in Local Family Support and Advocacy Groups

It is essential that professionals get to know the family groups in their area by attending some of their meetings and finding out what their concerns are. Professional assistance, while useful, may not be enough for families in the long term. In order for families to fully adjust and cope with their disabled family member, peer support, peer modeling, and peer advocacy are essential and it is helpful to refer families to these support groups for these services. Some professionals have made up lists of family support groups in their area, which they distribute to family members so that new families can locate a family group. Some agencies have found it useful to assign a specific agency staff member to be the liaison person to the family groups. This person can help to update other professionals in the agency and at the same time serve as a resource to a local family group. Professionals should also volunteer to share their information with these groups through formal presentations or group discussion. Professionals should also ask family members in to talk to their staff members and to serve as co-trainers. Practitioners might invite group members' comments on mental health programs and ask how they might better serve the needs of families. Join the National Alliance for the Mentally Ill (1901 Ft. Myer Dr., Suite 500, Arlington, VA).

## Make a Personal Commitment

Professionals need to make a commitment to the most severely disabled. Even if only a portion of a professional's time and practice is involved in this commitment, they will find themselves welcomed by families who are looking for sympathetic and skilled professionals. The investment of a caring professional in their disabled family member will go a long way toward alleviating the anxiety, worry, guilt, and stress that families may be experiencing. A professional can be a spokesperson and advocate for this commitment within his or her agency and community. It also is important to find ways to educate professional peers, funding sources, and legislatures about the wants and needs of families with psychiatrically disabled members.

## Acknowledge Diverse Beliefs

Professionals should acknowledge the variety of beliefs and needs that exist among families, former patients, professionals, and administrators of mental health programs. For example, they might want to discuss how professionals can work more cooperatively with families without compromising their relationship with the disabled family member, or, why the family may prefer that the major portion of the professional's energy be directed toward the disabled person rather than toward other family members. The professional's learned assumptions, allegiances, and loyalties may be regularly challenged as he or she begins to get more involved and includes more of the participants in this process of healing.

## Develop Your Own Supports

Because of the new stresses and challenges professionals will likely encounter, it is important for them to develop their own support network. Educational approaches with families may not come easily because of professional resistances and the new demands that these commitments entail. Professionals will also need their own support resources to help them to understand and cope with their experiences, share successes and failures, gain new knowledge, and learn new skills (Spaniol, Zipple et al., 1984).

## CONCLUSIONS

The increased use of educational and supportive approaches to meeting the needs of families with mentally ill members is an exciting and long overdue development. It is a recognition that families with mentally ill members usually want and need skills, information, and support rather than therapy and that mental health professionals can be instrumental in meeting these wants and needs.

However, the current state of the art could be improved. This new and developing set of approaches is in need of expansion and refinement. Currently the content of these approaches is rather limited and there have been limited efforts to disseminate and utilize them. Finally, families with mentally ill members have generally not been included in the development and implementation of these approaches. The authors suggest that when these three limitations are successfully addressed, educational and supportive approaches will become the interventions of choice, rather than an innovation, for families with mentally ill members.

## REFERENCES

Anderson, C. M. (1983). A psychoeducational program for families of patients with schizophrenia. In W. R. McFarlane (Ed.), Family therapy in schizophrenia. New York: Guilford.

Anderson, C. M., Hogarty, G., & Reiss, D. J. (1980). Family treatment of adult schizophrenia patients: A psychoeducational approach. Schizophrenia Bulletin, 6, 490-505.

Anderson, C. M., Hogarty, G., & Reiss, D. J. (1981). The psychoeducational family treatment of schizophrenia. In M. Goldstein (Ed.), New developments in interventions with families of schizophrenics (New Directions for Mental Health Services, No. 12). San Francisco: Jossey-Bass.

Anthony, W., Cohn, M., & Cohn, B. (1983). The philosophy, treatment process, and principles of the psychiatric rehabilitation approach. In L. Bachrach (Ed.), Deinstitutionalization. New Directions for Mental Health Services, No. 17. San Francisco: Jossey-Bass.

Beels, C. C., & McFarlane, W. R. (1982). Family treatment of schizophrenia: Background and state of the art. Hospital and Community Psychiatry, 33, 541-550.

Bernheim, K. F. (1982). Supportive family counseling. Schizophrenia Bulletin, 8, 634-641.

Brown, G. W., Birley, J. L. T., & Wing, J. K. (1972). Influence of family life on the course of schizophrenic disorders: A replication. British Journal of Psychiatry, 121, 241-258.

Byalin, K., Jed, J., & Lehman, S. (1982). Family intervention with treatment-refractory chronic schizophrenics. Paper presented at 20th International Congress of Applied Psychology, Edinburgh, Scotland.

Dincin, J., Selleck, V., & Streicker, S. (1978). Restructuring parental attitudes: Working with parents of the adult mentally ill. Schizophrenia Bulletin, 4, 597-608.

Falloon, I. R. H., Boyd, J. L., & McGill, C. W. (1984). Family care of schizophrenia, New York: Guilford.

Falloon, I. R. H., Boyd, J. L., McGill, C. W., Razani, J., Moss, H. B., & Gilderman, A. M. (1982). Family management in the prevention of exacerbations of schizophrenia: A controlled study. New England Journal of Medicine, 306, 1437-1440.

Falloon, I. R. H., Liberman, R. P., Lillie, F. J., & Vaughn, C. E. (1981). Family therapy of schizophrenics with high risk of relapse. Family Process, 20, 211-221.

Goldstein, M. J., & Kopeikin, H. S. (1981). Short- and long-term effects of combining drug and family therapy. In M. J. Goldstein (Ed.), New developments in interventions with families of schizophrenics (New Directions for Mental Health Services, No. 12). San Francisco: Jossey-Bass.

Hatfield, A. B. (1979). The family as a partner in the treatment of mental illness. Hospital and Community Psychiatry, 30, 338-340.

Hatfield, A. B. (1981). Self-help groups for families of the mentally ill. Social Work, 26, 408-413.

Hatfield, A. B. (1983). What families want of family therapists. In W. McFarlane (Ed.), Family therapy in schizophrenia. New York: Guilford.

Hatfield, A. B. (1982). Coping with mental illness in the family: The family guide. Baltimore, MD: Maryland Department of Health and Mental Hygiene.

Killilea, M. (1976). Mutual help organizations: Interpretations in the literature. In G. Kaplan & M. Killilea (Eds.), Support systems and mutual help. New York: Grune & Stratton.

Killilea, M. (1982). Interaction of crisis theory, coping strategies, and social support systems. In H. C. Schulberg & M. Killilea (Eds.), The modern practice of community mental health. San Francisco: Jossey-Bass.

Kopeikin, H. S., Marshall, V., & Goldstein, M. J. (1983). Stages and impact of crisis oriented family therapy in the aftercare of acute schizophrenia. In W. McFarlane (Ed.), Family therapy in schizophrenia. New York: Guilford.

Leff, J., Kuipers, L., Berkowitz, R., Eberbein-Vries, R., & Sturgeon, D. (1982). A controlled trial of social intervention in the families of schizophrenic patients. British Journal of Psychiatry, 141, 121-134.

Leff, J., & Vaughn, C. (1981). The role of maintenance therapy and relatives' expressed emotion in relapse of schizophrenia: A two-year follow-up. *British Journal of Psychiatry, 139,* 102–104.

Liberman, R. P., Aitchison, R. A., & Falloon, J. (1979). *Family therapy in schizophrenia: Syllabus for therapist.* Unpublished manuscript. (Available from Mental Health Clinical Research Center for the Study of Schizophrenia, Camarillo/UCLA Research Program, Box A, Camarillo, CA 93010).

Liberman, R. P., Wallace, C. J., Vaughn, C. E., & Snyder, K. L. (1979, April). *Social and family factors in the course of schizophrenia: Towards an interpersonal problem-solving therapy for schizophrenics and their families.* Paper presented at the Conference on Psychotherapy of Schizophrenia: Current Status and New Directions, Yale School of Medicine, New Haven, CT.

McLean, C., Greer, K., Scott, J., & Beck, J. (1982). Group treatment for parents of the adult mentally ill. *Hospital and Community Psychiatry, 33,* 564–568.

O'Connor, M. P. (1983). *An investigation of family burden in the parents of schizophrenic patients.* Unpublished masters thesis, Boston University School of Nursing, Boston.

Plummer, E., Thornton, J., Seeman, M., & Littman, S. (1981). Coping with schizophrenia: A group approach with relatives. *Journal of Psychiatry Treatment and Evaluation, 3,* 257–262.

Shifren-Levine, I., & Spaniol, L. (1985). The role of families of the severely mentally ill in the development of community support services. *Psychosocial Rehabilitation Journal, 8*(4), 83–84.

Spaniol, L., Jung, H., Zipple, A. M., & Fitzgerald, S. (1984). *Families as a central resource in the rehabilitation of the severely psychiatrically disabled: Report of a national survey* (final report). Boston: Boston University, Center for Rehabilitation and Training in Mental Health.

Spaniol, L., Zipple, A. M., & Fitzgerald, S. (1984). *How professionals can share power with families: A new approach to working with families of the mentally ill.* Manuscript submitted for publication.

Straw, P., & Young, B. (1982). *Awakenings: A self-help group organization kit.* Washington, DC: National Alliance for the Mentally Ill.

Wasow, M. (1980). *Professionals have hurt us—parents of schizophrenics speak out.* Unpublished manuscript. (Available from M. Wasow, Mt. Sinai Medical Center, 950 N. 12th St., PO Box 342, Milwaukee, WI 53201.)

Wasow, M. (1982). *Coping with schizophrenia: A survival manual for parents, relatives, and friends.* Palo Alto, CA: Science and Behavior Books.

Yess, J. P. (1981). What families of the mentally ill want. *Community Support Service Journal, 2*(1), 1–3.

# Professionals Who Work with Families of the Chronic Mentally Ill: Current Status and Suggestions for Clinical Training

*Stephen A. Cole*
*with Dalen S. Cole*

## PROLOGUE

Schizophrenia not only alters the mental perspectives of the patients and their families, but also affects the outlook of practitioners who deal with this puzzling disease. Since my first interest in schizophrenia as a medical student, I have studied with, read about, and been exposed to "experts" in this field. But equally important in this education has been my exposure to those suffering from schizophrenia and their families. It is this duality, listening to both voices, that informs the following. One's own training must necessarily be a vital part of the presumption to discuss the concepts of training others in this important field (see epilogue).

In this chapter, a review of the recent literature, I attempt to describe the problems faced by persons with severe and chronic schizophrenic disorders, the families of these patients, and the health care system treating them. I will frame the "solutions" to these problems as new directions in the training of mental health professionals. I have focused on the schizophrenic disorders not only because of the richness of research in this field but also because of my own greater familiarity with the treatment of this problem.

Stephen A. Cole. Family Support Project, New York Veterans Administration, New York University, New York, New York.
With: Dalen S. Cole, M.A., Writer

## THE PROBLEMS

### The Patients

The mass exodus of patients from mental hospitals over the past 30 years has brought with it a host of unanticipated problems for patients, their families, and the community at large. The more than 1 million persons with severe mental disability currently living in the community (Goldman, Gattozzi, & Taube, 1981) pose a formidable challenge to our health care system. Minkoff (1978) has predicted that by 1985, more than 1 million persons will be eligible for community care. Because of the nature of their disorder, schizophrenics are particularly vulnerable.

Persons with schizophrenic disorders suffer from severe adaptive difficulties, which Wing (1978) and Strauss and Carpenter (1981) have described using a "multidimensional view." To fully understand the problems faced by these persons, it is necessary to take into account the severity of the disease process; the patient's prior personality; the extent of the afflicted's "secondary handicaps" (through lowered self-esteem, diminished expectations, altered personal habits); the social or family context within which it occurs; and the social consequences resulting from deficits in education, occupational skills, and social supports. Cohen (1984) has written that chronic schizophrenics have no useful social roles, since the socioeconomic system does not provide them with job opportunities adjusted to their reduced level of functioning. Thus, they are forced to rely on external supports, and, as a result, often assume attitudes of apathy and dependency.

Astrachan (1985) has written that the cost to society is measured through lost productivity, welfare and disability payments, the drain on family resources, and the anguish of other family members. Of the 30–50% of discharged mental patients able to find employment within 6 months of leaving the hospital, nearly 50% lose their jobs within a half year of beginning work (Minkoff, 1978). Many of these patients lack adequate food and shelter (Lamb, 1981) and still more are deprived of sufficient health care and rehabilitation services (Talbott, 1978b).

Even when appropriate treatment and supportive services are available, many chronic patients do not avail themselves of such. Minkoff (1978) estimates that less than 25% of chronic mental patients participate in regular aftercare programs, while 30–60% do not adhere to their prescribed regimens of medication and psychosocial rehabilitation. It recently has been estimated that 40% of persons suffering from psychosis never have received treatment of any kind (Richman & Barry, 1985). A further challenge to the health care system is posed by the "young ult chronics" who appear particularly unmotivated for treatment. Bachrach (1982) and Pepper, Kirschner, and Ryglewicz (1981) have described these people as alienated from the social system and abusers of drugs and alcohol who behave destructively towards themselves and aggressively toward those who try to help them.

## The Families

Arnhoff (1975) and Goldman (1982) have called attention to the heavy burden assumed by family members living with the 70% of mental patients who return to their homes. Family members must cope with irrational patients at times beset with hallucinations, delusions, and paranoia, who may commit violent acts. Even in periods of remission, these patients appear too lethargic and unmotivated to begin taking the first steps toward becoming self-sufficient. Grad and Sainsbury (1963, 1968) have described the objective family burdens of decreased earning power of those members who sacrifice themselves to the care of the patient, the deprivations of "normal" siblings whose needs must take second place, and the disruption to important household routines that maintain the symbolic integrity of the family unit.

Creer and Wing (1975) and Doll (1976) have further described the emotional costs of families trying to cope with patients who present severe management problems. These family members fell anxious over the uncertainty of the course of the illness, depression over the loss of their child's premorbid personality, guilt for their imagined role in causing the illness and for not being able to prevent relapse, and anger and frustration at the failure of treatment to bring about a cure. High rates of marital disharmony and psychiatric disturbance in parents are often a result (Hirsch & Leff, 1975). Beels, Gutwirth, Berkeley, and Struening (1984) have described how such families become overinvolved with one another and isolated from formal and informal sources of social support in the community.

Hatfield (1984) and Lefley (Chapter 2, this volume) have also detailed the family's response to the patient's disorder as an attempt to adapt to a crisis situation. When the strain of having to cope exceeds the family's knowledge, skills, and resources, relatives become emotionally exhausted. Rose (1959) and Kreisman and Joy (1975) have recounted the process of estrangement and rejection that results from the patient's worsening condition as well as from repeated hospital admissions.

Studies undertaken by Hatfield (1979) and Holden and Lewine (1982) and reviewed by Platman (1983) reveal that family members are eager for professional assistance and feedback from members of other families coping with mental illness. They want more information about the nature, course, and treatment of schizophrenia so they can set realistic expectations, and about specific management techniques that will better motivate the patient to take medication and cooperate with treatment programs. Accurate maps of community resources and supportive services are also desired. There has been a ground swell in the growth of self-help organizations, which, under the leadership of the National Alliance for the Mentally Ill (NAMI), have provided families with the opportunity to discuss their experiences and act as a pressure group to influence policymakers at the local, state, and national level to improve the health care system. However, neither the health care system nor health care professionals heretofore have been especially sympathetic to the problems of patients with chronic mental illnesses and their families.

## The Health Care System

The majority of severely ill mental patients are treated in the community through an often disorganized potpourri of "public sector" facilities that include the federal Veterans Administration (VA), public health, and armed forces hospitals and clinics; state hospitals and aftercare clinics; community mental health centers (CMHCs); county and city hospitals; and freestanding clinics and psychosocial rehabilitation centers (Pepper and Ryglewicz, 1982; Talbott, 1985). Problems generic to the effective care of the chronic mentally ill include inadequate funding; lack of comprehensive services; too great an emphasis on arbitrary rules, regulations, and policies (rather than meeting the needs of individual patients); and lack of continuity of care (Mollica, 1983; Talbott, 1984b).

State hospitals, CMHCs, and federal facilities continue to face difficulties attracting quality clinical and administrative staff, especially for those programs designed to meet the needs of the chronic mentally ill (Fink & Weinstein, 1979; Nielson et al., 1981; Okin, 1982). Professionals are discouraged by burdensome paperwork; a lack of academic and professional recognition; too little time to write, teach, or conduct research; isolation from colleagues; lack of training of allied staff; misunderstanding and devaluation of their work by the wider society; constant public scrutiny; and heavy caseloads. A combination of the above may even lead concerned caretakers to "burn-out" (Donovan, 1982; Miller, 1984; Mirabi, Weinman, Magnetti, & Keppler, 1985; Pines & Maslach, 1978; Talbott, 1984a; Winslow, 1979).

While state hospitals continue to provide essential services for the chronic mentally ill, CMHCs, with a few notable exceptions, primarily offer psychotherapy for persons with acute disorders and "problems-in-living" (Sharfstein, 1978). Winslow (1982) has reported that the decreasing proportion of CMHC patients with diagnoses of schizophrenia or major depression may reflect both a shift away from "medical model" diagnosis and treatment and an increased tendency to treat the less severely ill. Mollica (1983) has attributed this to a decline in the ethic of social responsibility and to a tendency of clinicians to shy away from chronic, lower-class patients for fear that others will view them as "lower-class therapists." Another reason for this trend may lie with frustrations of therapists who fail to achieve overly ambitious treatment goals and come to doubt their healing abilities (Eichler, 1982; Lamb & Peele, 1984).

Attributing dependent and passive attitudes to character defects, rather than to an effect of the disorder or society's failure to provide social roles for disabled people, is a common response (Menninger, 1984; Meyerson, 1978; Paul, 1978; Pines & Maslach, 1978). The attitude that persons with schizophrenic disorders are hopeless, lazy, and unresponsive to treatment is passed on to trainees by their supervisors, and often has the effect of discouraging the best young professionals from choosing to work for the chronic mentally ill. Instead, more and more clinicians compete in the private sector for the few "good patients" who are less ill, and respond more readily to psychotherapy and to professionals' own needs for personal gratification (Richman & Barry, 1985).

Both state hospitals and CMHCs have witnessed a reduction in the quality of their psychiatric staffing. Reasons for the reluctance of American-trained psychiatrists to work in the public sector include inadequate salaries, prescription writing and other purely mechanical tasks that only physicians are allowed to do, infighting between professional groups, and the sometime antimedical, antipsychiatric bias (Borus, 1978; Fink & Weinstein, 1979; Nielson, et al., 1981).

The Community Support Program (CSP), created in 1980 through the National Plan for the Chronic Mentally Ill and the Mental Health Systems Act, was an attempt to encourage states to provide a "network of caring" for the most seriously ill chronic mental patients through federal contracts (Morrissey & Goldman, 1984; Tessler & Goldman, 1982). This plan was the result of cooperation between mental health professionals and NAMI representing an emerging network of consumers (Hatfield, 1981). The CSP was to have provided comprehensive crisis care, psychosocial rehabilitation, supportive living arrangements, medical and mental health care—all coordinated through case management. This bold initiative, however, was repealed by the Reagan Administration's use of limitations on federal spending, the cap on Medicaid funds, termination of patients from the Social Security Insurance (SSI) and Social Security Disability Insurance (SSDI) rolls, and the institution of Diagnosis Related Groups (DRGs) for Medicare and VA patients.

Tantam (1985) has recently written that although controlled studies demonstrate the greater cost-effectiveness of outpatient services for the chronically mentally ill, their care is being compromised by a combination of vested interests channeling patients and funds to the hospitals. Reasons cited for this are: the greater third-party reimbursements for patients receiving hospital care; the public desire for patients to be out of sight; and a closer alliance of psychiatry with other medical professions.

The current trend in ambulatory mental health care reflects the granting of private contracts from industry and government to provider groups (including CMHCs). This new system, which also accepts patients with private insurance, will inevitably slight both the indigent and the seriously mentally ill. Astrachan (1985) and Mollica (1983) have written that lower-class patients with chronic mental disorders will become even more dependent on state and county aftercare clinics and on private practitioners willing to take on "charity cases." Such a system may further compromise essential supportive rehabilitation and residential services, as well as patient transport programs, staff training, quality assurance, and outcome research.

## Families and Family Therapists

Deinstitutionalization occurred during the era of "radical environmentalism," when the majority of mental health professionals believed that "functional" psychotic disorders were caused not by biological events but by faulty upbringing sustained by family transactional processes that continued to drive patients "crazy" (Beels & McFarlane, 1982). Family therapists used certain "buzz" words to describe these pathological processes: "schizophrenogenic mother," "undifferentiated family ego mass," "schism and skew," "double bind," "mystification," "pseudomutuality," and "perverse triangle" (Cole, 1982). Each of these models was originally presented as a hypothesis that would explain how the families of schizophrenics were different from other families, and how their differences damaged the psychological development of the patient. These constructs, once reified by therapists, served as a perceptual filter through which the reality of family life became distorted. However, there exists little evidence to document the validity of these concepts.

Goldstein and Rodnick (1975) reported no substantive evidence for the double-bind hypothesis, and noted that families of schizophrenics did not differ from "normals" in the degree of dominance, conflict, or expression of emotion. Updating this review, Liem (1980) concluded that no consistent evidence linked the occurrence of schizophrenic disorder in families with power relations, symbiotic relatedness, or eroticized parent–child relations. A similar, sobering view of these hypotheses was presented by Goldstein and Doane in 1982.

The enthusiasm expressed by family therapists for currently fashionable models of the family etiology of schizophrenia does not reflect the dearth of supporting research results. Nonetheless, this "naive" translation of tentatively posed research concepts into dogmatic principles of clinical practice (Reiss & Wyatt, 1975) has provided family therapists with sufficient ammunition to cause some distress. Many therapists have either submitted family members to guilt-inducing reviews of early life events, presented them with a confusing array of directives and injunctions designed to liberate the patient from having to be the "symptom bearer," or attempted to extricate the patient altogether from a "damaging environment." Whether through assertion or innuendo, certain practitioners appeared to be blaming families, and thereby increasing a previously felt burden of guilt (Appleton, 1974; Hatfield, 1984; Torrey, 1983). Furthermore, some therapists failed to give the patient's diagnosis and did not help the family to understand how the victim's life would be affected by the disease (Holden & Lewine, 1982; Terkelsen, 1983).

Family members tended to retreat from such encounters with an attitude of distrust, withholding important information and refusing further collaboration with the treatment team. In Chapter 9 of this book, Hatfield argues that a sense of mutual alienation has resulted, as families believed that professionals were mainly interested in financial gain and in exploiting them for research purposes, while professionals believed that the families were irrational and in need of regulation and control.

The preceding does not bode well for patients, their families, or for the health care system. Patients continue to suffer from relapse and social breakdown, relying on an often poorly planned and disorganized system of treatment. Patients frequently lack close medication follow-up, psychosocial rehabilitation, and residential services. Professionals working in the public sector can be made to feel alienated and unmotivated to work with the chronic mentally ill. Families feel burdened by having to cope with difficult patients and seemingly unsympathetic professionals.

The following section will develop a model of illness that adheres closely to recent findings concerning the nature of schizophrenic disorder and will present suggestions for the improvement of treatment and services for the chronically mentally ill. The final section will explore how these suggestions can be incorporated into clinical training programs.

## A MODEL FOR UNDERSTANDING SCHIZOPHRENIC DISORDERS AND THEIR TREATMENT

### The Illness Model

While the nature of the disease process in schizophrenia is still unknown, it is possible to conceptualize its onset and course through a "biopsychosocial model" (Neuchterlein & Dawson, 1984). The basic deficit appears to consist of an inability to handle complex information, a concommitant breakdown in attention-focusing mechanisms associated with hyperarousal of the autonomic nervous system (ANS), and subsequent deterioration in interpersonal functioning (Ciompi, 1983; Hogarty, 1984). A genetic vulnerability may "allow the individual to develop the syndrome in the face of certain environmental triggers" (Cancro, 1982, p. 96), stressful life events, or tension-laden relationships with significant others that overwhelm the vulnerable person's defenses and coping mechanisms (Zubin, 1980; Zubin, Magaziner, & Steinhauer, 1983). This leads to an overload of information-processing capacity, further ANS arousal, and an impairment in both cognitive processing and the integration of social stimuli. The tendency of persons with schizophrenic disorders to resort to social withdrawal is thus seen as one way to cope with an unremitting barrage of environmental stimulation.

The patient's experience of acute psychosis may be said to evolve gradually from a sense of feeling overwhelmed to a restriction in range of thought, a disinhibition of impulses, disorganization of the external world, and fragmentation of self, to a psychotic resolution with the development of delusional explanations (Docherty, van Kammen, Siris, & Marder, 1978). The "positive symptoms"—hallucinations, paranoia, incoherent speech, uncontrollable behavior—are often observed in the acute state of the disorder. The decision to admit a patient to the hospital usually follows such socially intolerable behavior (Falloon, Marshall, Boyd, Razani, & Wood-Siverio, 1983). This condition dies down during times of remission, but reappears during times of relapse.

The long-term course of this disorder is often marked by residual or deficit states with such "negative symptoms" as lethargy, withdrawal, and lack of motivation. Patients with the most severe residual symptoms become chronically dependent and are often unable to work or make close social contacts outside the home. Crow (Crow, Cross, Johnstone, & Owen, 1982) believes that positive symptoms result from an overactivity of brain cells akin to a ferbrile state, while negative symptoms are the expression of an underactivity or dying out of neurons. Brain-imaging techniques suggest that we may soon be able to estimate the extent of a given patient's biological impairment, and thus determine with greater accuracy his or her particular therapeutic requirements (Brown & Kneeland, 1985).

Yet the long-term outlook in schizophrenia is more favorable than was once thought, and the disease need not always result in severe residual states. In Bleuler's (1978) 25-year study of over 200 cases, two thirds to three quarters followed a benign course, with one fourth to one third experiencing complete recoveries and less than one third going on to states of mental and social deterioration. Harrow, Carare and Westermeyer (1985) described three typical courses of illness: (1) permanent reduction in or elimination of "positive symptoms" during hospitalization; (2) persistent psychosis of reduced intensity for many years; and (3) episodic psychosis with intermorbid periods of remission. While a majority of patients begin to show improvement 5 years after the onset of the first psychotic break Strauss and Carpenter (1977) (drawing from International Pilot Study data), suggested that the patient's future life course can be predicted from a knowledge of three variables: (1) the number and duration of hospitalizations; (2) the quality and quantity of social contacts; (3) the patient's work record.

Cobb (1976), Mechanic (1980), and White (1974) have discussed how patients' own coping and defense mechanisms serve to solve problems posed by threatening life events. When one's own resources fail, members of a support system are called upon to render assistance. However, before enlisting the help of others, one must see oneself as worthy of being helped and perceive others as caring persons willing to be of assistance. Since persons with schizophrenic disorders in varying degrees of decompensation often feel little self-worth and have difficulty processing interpersonal cues, they may be unable to seek out social support. With severe attention-focusing difficulties, they are easily shaken by situations with conflict and ambiguity, and have nowhere to go but to their own close family (Beels, 1981; Cohen & Sokolovsky, 1978; Hammer, Makiesky-Barrow, & Gutwirth, 1978). To compound the problem, these family members themselves often have less contact than "normals" with sources of social support outside the family system.

Patients who experience frequent relapses report a clustering of stressful life events (SLEs) in the preceding 3 weeks (Birley & Brown, 1970; Leff, Hirsch, Gaind, Rohde, & Stevens, 1973; Lukoff, Snyder,

Ventura, & Neuchterlein, 1984). Schizophrenics also relapse more frequently in the presence of family members with high expressed emotion (EE) (Brown, Birley, & Wing, 1972; Brown, Monck, Carstairs, & Wing, 1962; Vaughn & Leff, 1976; Vaughn, Snyder, Jones, Freeman, & Falloon, 1984). High-EE relatives are said to be intrusive, overprotective, and self-sacrificing (referred to as emotional overinvolvement or EOI), hostile (H), or make critical comments (CC) to the patient, and have unrealistically high expectations that pressure the patient to behave more like a "normal" person (Vaughn & Leff, 1981). Vaughn and Leff have also found that parents' critical remarks which more often refer to patients' residual symptoms (such as lack of motivation, which they may interpret as laziness) may respond to a cognitive and educational approach. Intrusive, overprotective, and self-sacrificing behavior (EOI), however, appear to be the products of long-term adaptation, and so are less responsive to therapeutic intervention (J. P. Leff, personal communication, 1985).

It has been suggested that patients are sensitive to two sources of environmental stress, acute (via SLE) and chronic (via high-EE) (Leff, Kuipers, Berkowitz, Vaughn, & Sturgeon, 1983). Antipsychotic medication can protect patients from an overload of one kind of stress, but not from a simultaneous overload of both. Similarly, if one could teach high-EE relatives to deal with the patient in a low-EE manner (by recognizing the limitations posed by the disease process, setting realistic expectations, allowing the patient to be alone if desired, and dealing with problems in a calm and collected manner), it might be possible to afford a greater degree of protection against relapse.

Treatment of this situation demands attention to both the patient and the family. All need to be assured that the patient is suffering from a disease process whose origins are undetermined and for which no one is held responsible. The patient requires antipsychotic medication to counteract the neurochemical processes contributing to symptom expression and needs help learning survival, social, and problem-solving skills. Family members with high EE need to learn less emotionally intense ways of dealing directly with the patient and must be helped to appreciate the benefits of forming social ties outside the family system.

## The Treatment Model

It is essential to adjust the mode and intensity of intervention to the particular phase of the illness process and the developmental stage of the family (Wynne, 1983). Strauss, Hafez, Lieberman, and Harding (1985) have described typical stages in the life course of schizophrenic illness as a series of cybernetically controlled recursive processes of interaction between the patient, environmental challenges, and the social environment. Thus, interventions must be gauged by an accurate understanding of the phase of illness (acute, remission, or residual), the mode of adaptation of the patient (moratorium, change point, or ceiling) and type of response in the patient's social environment (undemanding or overdemanding). Identification of sequences of recursive behaviors will help therapists predict whether to apply negative corrections to patterns of escalation or positive corrections to patterns of overcontrol.

MEDICATION

Antipsychotic medication has proved effective in controlled trials for dissolving or dampening the positive symptoms of acute schizophrenia and for preventing, avoiding, or delaying relapse (e.g., Hogarty et al., 1979). Two main difficulties posed by neuroleptic drugs are side effects, which may exacerbate "negative symptoms" and produce tardive dyskinesia (TD) in susceptible individuals, and patient noncompliance with prescribed regimens. Schooler (1984) has written that one must arrive at the patient's optimal dosage level, which prevents the expression of "positive symptoms" but does not exacerbate "negative symptoms" or cause TD. Kane (1983) has reported that lower dose strategies (e.g., one fifth the normal dose) are associated with a significant decrease in abnormal movements and a greater level of patient psychosocial adjustment.

In the "targeted strategy," patients are followed in a drug-free state and only prescribed neuroleptic medication when experiencing the onset of the "prodromal symptoms" of relapse (Herz & Melville, 1980). Carpenter and Heinrichs (1983) combined case management, medication, stress reduction, and six sessions of patient and family education on the recognition of prodromal symptoms. Compared to patients receiving continuous, standard-dose medication, patients in the experimental group took less total medication, spent fewer weeks on the drug, and did not differ in psychiatric or social status. Herz (1984) reported similarly encouraging results and has isolated three groups of medication responders: those who remain symptom-free off medication; those who require continuous medication to remain symptom-free; and those who are able to follow a "targeted strategy."

Noncompliance with medication, once thought solely a manifestation of patient intransigence, is now considered a result of several factors, some attributable to the patient and others to the treatment situation. In his study of 85 chronic schizophrenics, van Putten (1974) found that 46% were "drug reluctant" because of unpleasant side effects, especially akathisia, the "syndrome of impatience." Blackwell (1976) believed that in many cases nonadherence is a manifestation of the patient's effort to reduce the side effects. Blackwell (1976) and Falloon (1984) discussed the effect of the patient's health belief system: Some patients fear that taking medication will lead to addiction and a state of dependency; others believe that only individuals of weak character need drugs; yet another group refuse to believe they are sick and stop pills to confirm the notion there is nothing terribly wrong with them. Soskis and Jaffe (1979) as well as Blackwell and Falloon have pointed out the iatrogenic factors often responsible for noncompliance. These include a lack of clear instructions and understandable rationale for the use of medication, the perception that the doctor really isn't interested in them, crowded waiting rooms, long waits to see the doctor, and *en masse* appointments. In addition, many doctors view medication as a patient-physician issue and fail to enlist the aid of the family.

Patient adherence to medication regimens can be improved by (1) showing genuine interest in and concern for the patient; (2) providing patients and family members with an understanding of schizophrenic disorders and the rationale for medical treatment; (3) explaining and predicting side effects; (4) offering patients positive incentives (praise, privileges, etc.) for complying; (5) reinforcing what has been learned with "cognitive restructuring"; and (6) having family members monitor the patient's drug-taking behavior and provide necessary positive reinforcement.

## INDIVIDUAL PSYCHOTHERAPY

Hogarty et al. (1979) reported that Major Role Therapy (MRT), a form of pragmatic, behaviorally oriented individual therapy, helped to protect patients on maintenance medication from the effects of environmental stress and enhanced social functioning. However, those patients on placebo relapsed faster on MRT than the less intensive treatment-as-usual (TAU), which consisted of supportive psychotherapy. In a 10-year study at McLean, Gunderson and co-workers (Gunderson et al., 1984) have reported that in a controlled investigation, Reality-Adaptive-Supportive (RAS) psychotherapy was superior to Exploratory-Insight-Oriented (EIO) psychotherapy for the long-term treatment of chronic schizophrenia. RAS-treated patients scored higher in occupational functioning and social adaptation and spent fewer days in the hospital, whereas the psychodynamically oriented approach resulted in only mild enhancement of ego functioning (insight) and cognition (organization of thinking). Thus, pragmatic, behaviorally oriented supportive psychotherapy is effective, but only for patients on adequate medication dosages; for patients uncontrolled on medication, supportive psychotherapy may cause early relapse.

GROUP THERAPY

Liberman and associates (Liberman, 1982; Liberman, Massell, Mosk, & Wing, 1985) and Keith and Matthews (1982) have reported that behaviorally oriented group therapy for chronic patients is effective when it focuses on the acquisition of survival, social, and coping skills through a structured, didactic approach that emphasizes modeling, role playing, task assignment, and the judicious use of positive reinforcement.

FAMILY THERAPY

Goldstein and co-workers (Goldstein, Rodnick, Evans, May & Steinberg, 1978) have shown that a course of brief family crisis treatment (FCT) immediately after hospital discharge is highly effective for preventing relapse when combined with a moderate dosage of medication. The goals of FCT were to have the patient and family understand that the patient suffered from an illness, that the illness was exacerbated by SLEs, and that by altering the family's coping style, the impact of these events could be moderated and a relapse avoided.

Several recently concluded demonstration projects (Anderson, Hogarty, & Reiss, 1980, 1981; Falloon, Boyd, McGill, Razanni, Moss, & Gilderman, 1982; Falloon, Boyd, McGill, 1984; Falloon, Boyd, McGill et al., 1985; Leff, Kuipers, Berkowitz, Eberlein-Vries, & Sturgeon, 1982) have shown that "psychoeducational" family-oriented treatment is effective in preventing relapse. These studies compared family-oriented treatment to a control or comparison group receiving supportive individual psychotherapy or TAU, with all groups stabilized on medication.

The approaches have two principal elements in common. First, relatives (and in one project, patients as well) are told the patient's diagnosis and provided with full scientific explanations of our current knowledge about schizophrenia and the course of illness, and a full rationale for the importance of medication. Second, relatives are taught behavioral management skills, including how to handle difficult patient behavior while preserving a tolerant, low-key attitude. Two projects bring the relatives of different families together, in one for a periodic all-day "psychoeducational workshop," and in another for twice monthly relatives' groups meetings. The third project conducts individual family therapy in the home. The interventions succeed in diminishing EE, reducing 9-month relapse rate, and enhancing the patient's level of social functioning.

## MULTIPLE FAMILY GROUPS

While no outcome research has yet been published documenting the effectiveness of the use of multiple family groups, several writers have presented cogent arguments for its probable utility (Barter, Quierlo & Ekstrom, 1984; Cole, 1983; Kanter & Lin, 1980; McFarlane, 1983). Here, patients and family members are brought together with other similarly situated families. Meeting among others in the same condition fosters an atmosphere of trust in which experiences and feelings can be shared openly and members can learn to give and receive instrumental assistance. In this setting, professionals serve as teachers of scientific knowledge and facilitators of the mutual-aid process, while family members contribute the experiential knowledge and advice they have learned from actually living with the patients.

## PSYCHOSOCIAL REHABILITATION

Anthony and Nemec (1984) have written that the goals of rehabilitation are to teach patients the knowledge and skills needed to deal with stressful life situations in their private, social, working lives, and to help them make better use of existing environmental resources and supportive services. Patients should be encouraged to enter psychosocial rehabilitation programs once they have demonstrated they are capable of dealing with pressure, usually 6 months to a year after recovering from a relapse.

## COMMUNITY OUTREACH

Comprehensive programs of community outreach, such as that undertaken by Stein and Test (Stein & Test, 1980; Test, 1984) have resulted in greatly reduced hospital readmission rates, increased rates of patient employment, more contact with friends, greater life satisfaction, and reduced family burden. The Wisconsin Program of Stein and Test provided patients and families with material assistance (aid in obtaining welfare and disability); taught patients *in vivo* coping skills; helped to strengthen social and family support systems through family and network therapy; encouraged greater patient involvement with supportive services; and provided patients and families with information about the patient's disorder, prognosis, and the importance of taking medication. Unfortunately, the effects of all such projects appear to wear off once they are terminated: 1 year later, no differences could be found between patients receiving the project services and those receiving TAU.

## DAY TREATMENT

In his review of outcome studies, Luber (1984) concluded that programs of partial hospitalization are effective alternatives to inpatient treatment for patients undergoing psychotic decompensation. Furthermore, day treatment reduces the social stigma of mental hospitalization and helps to minimize disruption of the patient's social life. Linn and co-workers (Linn, Caffrey, Klett, Hogarty, & Lamb, 1979) found that chronic schizophrenics attending VA day treatment centers relapsed at a lower rate when the programs were of low pressure and were open-ended, with a pragmatic, rehabilitation orientation. Patients relapsed at a much higher rate when they attended day programs requiring participation in intensive individual and group psychotherapy and the attainment of goals at preset deadlines. Again, overstimulation appears to lead to early patient relapse.

## INPATIENT HOSPITALIZATION

Inpatient services are necessary during periods of severe psychosis, for brief stays and stabilization on medication, to protect the patient and others from the patient's potentially harmful behavior, to investigate the possible underlying medical causes of psychosis, and to prepare some unmotivated patients for engagement in treatment (Schnitzer, 1984; Stein & Test, 1980). Ciompi (1983) and Keith and Matthews (1982) reported that the optimal inpatient setting for patients with schizophrenic disorders is a small, quiet, nonhierarchical unit with easy intermingling of staff and patients, that pursues a problem-oriented, behavioral approach to treatment that allows for interdisciplinary collaboration.

## TREATMENT PHILOSOPHY

Heinrichs and Carpenter (1983) have classified therapeutic interventions according to whether they reduce or increase the patient's level of arousal. High intensity, overly ambitious modes of psychotherapy, such as insight-oriented individual therapy, process-oriented group therapy, and forms of family therapy that employ confrontation and escalation of buried conflicts, all risk overstimulating the patient. And we have seen that day programs that set deadlines for the completion of patient goals and that provide activating forms of psychotherapy are associated with higher rates of patient relapse. Even low-intensity, pragmatic-supportive therapy is risky for patients not controlled on medication. Thus, neuroleptic medication is the most powerful activation-reducing agent, producing this effect at the level of the brain synapse. Once stabilized on medication, the patient's level of activation may be further reduced through forms of individual, group, and family therapy that explicitly attribute illness to biological factors extrinsic to the individual and family-of-origin; that teach more effective coping skills for dealing with life stress and problematic relationships; and that model tolerance and emotional neutrality (Wing, 1978).

*Summary*

In this section, we have learned that the following advances have been made in our knowledge of chronic schizophrenia and its treatment:

1. It appears that the schizophrenic syndrome may be the manifestation of an underlying brain disease.
2. Therefore, the occurrence of schizophrenia may not be attributed either to faulty upbringing or to poor character.
3. The majority of patients eventually get better.
4. Overstimulation of the patient may result in early relapse.
5. Neuroleptic medication is the most effective deterrent to relapse.
6. Tardive dyskinesia and certain severe residual states can be prevented through programs of controlled medication reduction.
7. Patients can reduce overstimulation through the acquisition of more effective techniques for coping with life stress.
8. If provided with information and helpful suggestions, family members can become essential components of the treatment team.
9. Relatives and members of the treatment team can be taught to reduce patient overstimulation.
10. Psychosocial treatment is only effective for patients receiving carefully titrated medication.
11. The best treatment programs provide continuity of care within a comprehensive network of supportive services coordinated through case management.
12. Programs providing aggressive community outreach and *in vivo* patient and family contact are more effective than office- or facility-based programs.
13. Patients and their families may benefit considerably by joining self-help groups composed of other patients with schizophrenia and their families.

## IMPLICATIONS FOR THE TRAINING OF CLINICIANS

*Impediments to Be Overcome*

Now that we have developed a set of principles and guidelines for improving the treatment of chronic schizophrenic illness, we come to the more difficult task of implementation. Leaving the higher realms of speculation, basic science, and demonstration projects, we return to the reality of the health care system and training programs as they are today. Let us first review the highlights of the first section, in which we discussed the problems facing persons with chronic schizophrenic disorders, their families, and the system of care.

1. The mental health treatment system is not comprehensive enough to meet the needs of chronic schizophrenics.
2. The large majority of public-sector mental health facilities are not satisfactory places to work.
3. Most mental health professionals would rather not work with chronic schizophrenics.
4. Many mental health professionals do not fully understand the problems of family members.
5. Many mental health workers do not believe that schizophrenics suffer from a disease process that should be treated in the same manner as any other disabling illness.
6. Certain highly stimulating forms of psychosocial treatment may be harmful to persons with schizophrenic disorders.

Reviewing the literature critical of professional training programs, Nielson *et al.*, (1981) deplore the attitude of therapeutic pessimism held by clinical supervisors who view the chronic mentally ill as dull, trivial, or useless. Talbott (1984a) criticizes medical schools for their overemphasis of acute disorders amenable to cure and underemphasis of chronic disorders and for the evaluation of levels of disability and their remediation through programs of rehabilitation. Nonmedical students graduate with an insufficient appreciation for the biological aspects of mental disorders, and have little understanding of the neurosciences of psychopharmacology (Hogarty, 1984).

Trainees of all disciplines in public facilities are burdened down with heavy caseloads and high turnover rates, and have little opportunity for the intensive treatment and study of patients and their families coping through time with a complex illness. In fact, some trainees may never even meet patients' families, visit their homes, or travel to community agencies or residences. Trainees with creative ideas find them stifled by rigid rules and regulations, and learn that those who make waves are soon washed ashore.

Survey research indicates that a lack of interest in public-sector mental health care is widespread among professionals at all levels. Knesper (1981) has conducted a 15-year follow-up study of 900 psychiatrists from 1961 to 1976, and has found that those who graduated from U.S. medical schools spent an increasing proportion of their time treating outpatients in private practice. A poll of 86 psychiatry residents in the Washington, DC, area in the mid-1970s showed strong support for psychoanalysis and for the practice of psychotherapy and only minimal interest in somatic treatment (Greden & Casariego, 1975). Coryell (1982) has reported that in a series of nationwide polls of psychiatric residents in 1976, 1978, and 1980, nearly 60% still preferred the psychoanalytic perspective; in 1980 only 15% planned to enter public service, and only 4% viewed research as essential to their training. Fisher and Weinstein (1979) surveyed the "value priorities" of 114 psychiatrists at University of California at San Francisco in the late 1970s and found a strong preference for psychoanalysis and social approaches and a low level of interest in biological and neurobiological concepts. A more recent poll of 541 medical students (276 responded) who were selected for psychiatric residency programs indicated a decline in the popularity of psychoanalysis—only 12% chose this as a career interest—with an even smaller percentage choosing community psychiatry (2.2%), public health (2.6%) and full-time research (2%) (Weissman & Bashook, 1984).

The findings of these studies help to explain why graduates of clinical training programs in the mental health professions choose not to work with the chronically mentally ill. They are confirmed by Schnitzer (1984) and Alpert (1984) who lament the trend of clinical psychology graduates preferring to work with "neurotic" patients. According to Hogarty (1984), a recent report to the Council of Social Work Education states that 80% of social work students hope to enter private practice!

## Model Training Programs

In a series of major policy statements, the American Psychiatric Association (Ad Hoc Committee on the Chronic Mental Patient, 1979; Talbott, 1978a, 1979) called for an expansion of services for the chronically mentally ill and the overhaul of training programs to meet anticipated staffing requirements. Several demonstration programs responded to this call. The Massachusetts Mental Health Center (White & Bennett, 1981) has established a comprehensive system of psychosocial rehabilitation and residential care that residents rotate through at every stage of their training. The University of Oregon (Cutler, Bloom, & Shore, 1981; Faulkner, Rankin, Eaton, & Kinzie, 1983) places residents in an integrated system of state hospitals and CMHCs. St. Vincent's Hospital in New York City (Mayo, Gabel, & Carvalho, 1982) trains residents within a coordinated system of inpatient, outpatient, and day treatment centers that assure continuity of care. The San Francisco Veteran's Administration Medical Center (Rankin & McKinnon, 1984) rotates (PGY-2) residents through two continuing care clinics. The University of Maryland (Harbin, 1982) boasts that over two thirds of its graduates have taken jobs within the Maryland state hospital system; Harbin attributes recruitment success to administrative leadership that provides high-quality training and encourages clinical and programmatic creativity.

The New York University postdoctoral fellowship program in clinical psychology seeks out "retreads" who have already learned their clinical skills and are not afraid to disturb regulation-minded administrators in setting up new programs for the chronically ill (Alpert, 1984). The University of Pennsylvania (Worley & Lowery, 1984) conducts a program in administrative nursing for the chronically mentally ill. Yale's graduate nursing program is oriented towards "milieu management" and health teaching (Krause, 1984).

Innovations in the training of mental health clinicians common to these model programs will be presented in the following pages. The suggestions offered here have been drawn from the sources cited and from the writer's clinical experience. It is hoped that they will not surprise the attentive reader, since they are meant to flow from the exegesis developed up to this point in the chapter.

## Components of a Model Training Program

### THE TREATMENT MODEL (Hogarty, 1984)

Trainees will be taught the diathesis–stress model of schizophrenia and understand those variables that positively affect treatment response, course, and outcome.

### INFORMATION AND KNOWLEDGE (Bloom, 1984; Schnitzer, 1984; Talbott, 1984a)

Trainees will be given a thorough grounding in the neurosciences, psychophysiology, psychopharmacology, human genetics, cognitive and behavioral psychology, social psychology, general and family systems theory, community psychology and sociology, and cultural and social anthropology. Graduates should be able to understand the interrelationships among individual psychopathology and diagnosis, individual vulnerability, environmental and social stress, survival and coping skills, insight capacity, support systems and social networks, economic and vocational requirements, and leisure and cultural needs.

TREATMENT SKILLS (Guze, 1977; Hogarty, 1984)

With particular emphasis depending upon disciplinary specialty, trainees will learn how to (1) make accurate diagnostic and functional assessments, (2) prescribe medication, (3) conduct psychoeducation, (4) act as case managers, (5) strengthen patient cognitive and behavioral skills, and (6) assist family members and significant others to modify their attitudes, to improve their management skills, and to learn from one another.

VALUES AND ATTITUDES

1. Patients are viewed as fellow human beings stricken with a disease causing significant cognitive impairments. Given the right conditions and encouragement, patients can learn new skills and recover from their illness.

2. Patient passivity and dependency are seen not as negative character traits but as residual symptoms of the disease process, which can be ameliorated through a judicious manipulation of medication, mobilization of coping skills, enlistment of social support, and provision of long-term care.

3. Families are seen not as pathogens or adversaries but as valuable partners in the care process who are trying their best to cope with chronic illness, and who require accurate information about the disease and practical suggestions for its management in order to render greater assistance towards the patient's recovery.

4. The goal of treatment is not cure but recovery through the mitigation of disease, the reduction of disability, and the improvement of the quality of life (Adler, 1981).

5. Regardless of specialty, professionals should respect not only one another's particular expertise, but also the person's viewpoint and the totality of what they have to offer.

CLINICAL EXPOSURE

1. Trainees will be rotated through model programs (Meyerson, 1978).

2. Trainees will have continuous contact with patients in many phases of remission and relapse over a long period of time (throughout the length of training) to better appreciate the "terrain" of recovery (Kubie, 1968).

3. Trainees will be assigned caseloads light enough to permit the intensive study of a few patients.

4. Trainees will be required to include members of the patient's family and close support network in the treatment process.

5. Case conferences and supervision will be conducted by senior faculty dedicated to the treatment of chronic mental patients.

6. Trainees will be required to make home visits, meet with agency staff, and visit community residences.

7. Trainees will be required to attend meetings of community self-help groups and serve as advisers or visiting "experts."

8. Trainees will have experience working on multidisciplinary teams, both in the hospital or clinic and in the community.

9. The service will encourage a sharing of the work load, the taking of necessary "time-outs," and the holding of frequent informal staff meetings to discuss issues of common concern and provide one another with mutual support.

10. Seminars will be held bringing trainees up-to-date on the results of demonstration programs and outcome research.

11. Clinical research will be encouraged.

## CLINICAL SUPERVISION (Grinker, 1975; Krause, 1984; Talbott, 1984a)

Teachers and supervisors who are dedicated to the treatment of the chronic mentally ill, will be employed—as therapists, researchers, or clinical theorists, and to help trainees to see beyond the superficial frustrations of working with chronic patients to the challenging complexity of understanding and helping people to recover from schizophrenic illness.

## ACADEMIC AFFILIATIONS (Knesper & Hirtle, 1981; Nielson, et al., 1981)

Academic affiliation with general hospitals or medical school departments of psychiatry will help to encourage a more careful and scholarly clinical approach to patient care and provide opportunities for clinical teaching and research. Academic appointments should be given to enourage young faculty to opt for further work in the field.

## RECRUITMENT (Hogarty, 1984)

To recruit quality personnel, the administrative leadership should (1) present a clear model of illness and consistent treatment philosophy, (2) encourage creativity, intellectual curiosity, collegial respect, and a sharing of responsibilities between the disciplines; and (3) provide opportunities for further training and growth.

HEALTH POLICY

None of these changes will be brought about unless the funding sources (e.g., third-party insurers and local, state, and federal governments) allocate more money for comprehensive treatment programs for the chronically mentally ill. In addition, greater financial incentives must be provided in the form of higher salaries and increased funding for demonstration projects and clinical and basic research.

At a time of retrenchment in the public funding of the human services, the prospects for accomplishing the goals outlined here may seem dim indeed. Perhaps their attainment will come about through a massive campaign of public education and consumer activism spearheaded by a "citizen-professional alliance" (Sharfstein, 1984).

## EPILOGUE

I first became interested in schizophrenia and the family while writing a medical school paper on the epidemiology of schizophrenia for Bruce Dohrenwend's course in social psychiatry at Columbia University. I went on to do an internship that included studies with systems theorist, Harley Shands, followed by a psychoanalytically oriented residency at the Albert Einstein College of Medicine (AECOM) in the Bronx. AECOM developed two residency programs in the early 1970s that were community based and devoted to the care of the chronic mentally ill. Attracted by their sense of mission and enthusiasm, I decided to do an elective and then a fellowship under their aegis at the family service at the Bronx State Hospital. Beels (1975) has described the pioneering spirit that infused this program, whose philosophical base derived from family systems theory.

During my 2 years working with a family crisis team, I witnessed a dramatic change in our approach, that evolved from viewing the psychotic patient as the "symptom bearer" of a dysfunctional family system to recognizing that some schizophrenic patients may have brain disorders similar to epilepsy. We began our work holding families responsible for causing and perpetuating the problem and were unable to bring about a cure of the patient or a change in the family structure through the mere manipulation of family communication and transactional processes. We became more helpful to these families when we realized that their anguish resulted not from family system pathology but from struggling for many years with a highly disturbed relative. Seeing how isolated from the wider community these families had become, we brought them together in multiple family groups where they were able to relieve their pain by sharing stories, learning from one another, and providing one another with support and assistance. This experience has contributed strongly to the subsequent direction of my career, especially to an interest in developing family-oriented psychoeducational programs for the chronic mentally ill.

## REFERENCES

Ad Hoc Committee on the Chronic Mental Patient. (1979). Position statement: A call to action for the chronic mental patient. *American Journal of Psychiatry, 136*, 748-752.

Adler, D. A. (1981). The medical model and psychiatry's tasks. *Hospital and Community Psychiatry, 32*, 387-392

Alpert, M. (1984, July). *Breaking the mold: Post doctoral training in clinical psychology as the route toward improving the care of the chronic patient.* Paper presented at the NIMH Workshop on the Chronic Mentally Ill, Rockville, MD.

Anderson, C. M., Hogarty, G. E., & Reiss, D. J. (1980). Family treatment of adult schizophrenic patients: A psychoeducational approach. *Schizophrenia Bulletin, 6*, 490-505.

Anderson, C. M., Hogarty, G. E., & Reiss, D. J. (1981). The psychoeducational treatment of schizophrenia. In M. J. Goldstein (Ed.), *New developments in interventions with families of schizophrenics (New Directions for Mental Health Services, No. 12, pp. 79-94)*. San Francisco: Jossey-Bass.

Anthony, W. A., & Nemec, P. B. (1984). Psychiatric rehabilitation. In A. S. Bellack (Ed.), *Schizophrenia: Treatment, management, and rehabilitation* (pp. 375-413). New York: Grune & Stratton.

Appleton, W. S. (1974). Mistreatment of patients' families by psychiatrists. *American Journal of Psychiatry, 131*, 655-657.

Arnhoff, F. N. (1975). Social consequences of policy toward mental illness. *Science, 188*, 1277-1281.

Astrachan, B. M. (1985). Costs of practice, barriers to psychiatric service and research expenditures: Failures of policy. *Archives of General Psychiatry, 42*, 625-626.

Bachrach, L. L. (1982). Young adult chronic patients: An analytical review of the literature. *Hospital and Community Psychiatry, 33*, 189-197.

Barter, J. T., Quierlo, J. F., & Ekstrom, S. P. (1984). A psychoeducational approach to educating chornic mental patients for community living. *Hospital and Community Psychiatry, 35*, 793-797.

Beels, C. C. (1975). Family and social management of schizophrenia. *Schizophrenia Bulletin, 1*(13), 97-118.

Beels, C. C. (1981). Social support and schizophrenia. *Schizophrenia Bulletin, 7*(1), 58-72.

Beels, C. C., & McFarlane, W. R. (1982). Family treatments of schizophrenia: Background and state of the art. *Hospital and Community Psychiatry, 33*, 541-549.

Beels, C. C., Gutwirth, L., Berkeley, J., & Struening, E. (1984). Measurements of social support in schizophrenia. *Schizophrenia Bulletin, 10*, 399-411.

Birley, J. L. T., & Brown, G. W. (1970). Crises and life changes preceding the onset or relapse of acute schizophrenia: Clinical aspects. *British Journal of Psychiatry, 116*, 327-333.

Blackwell, B. (1976). Treatment adherence. *British Journal of Psychiatry, 129*, 513-531.

Bleuler, M. (1978). *The schizophrenic disorders: Long-term patient and family studies* (S. M. Clemens, Trans.). New Haven: Yale University Press.

Bloom, B. L. (1984). Community mental health training: A personal view. *American Journal of Community Psychology, 12,* 217-226.

Borus, J. F. (1978). Issues critical to the survival of community mental health. *American Journal of Psychiatry, 135,* 1029-1035.

Brown, G. W., Birley, J. L., & Wing, J. K. (1972). Influence of family life on the course of schizophrenic disorder: A replication. *British Journal of Psychiatry, 121,* 241-258.

Brown, R. P., & Kneeland, B. (1985). Visual imaging in psychiatry. *Hospital and Community Psychiatry, 36,* 489-496.

Brown, G. W., Monck, E. M., Carstairs, G. M., & Wing, J. K. (1962). Influence of family life on the course of schizophrenic illness. *British Journal of Preventive and Social Medicine, 16,* 55-68.

Cancro, R. (1982). The role of genetic factors in the etiology of the schizophrenic disorders. In L. Grinspoon (Ed.), *Psychiatry 1982: Annual review* (pp. 92-97). Washington, DC: American Psychiatric Press.

Carpenter, W. T., & Heinrichs, D. W. (1983). Early intervention, time-limited, targeted pharmacotherapy of schizophrenia. *Schizophrenia Bulletin, 9,* 533-542.

Ciompi, L. (1983). How to improve the treatment of schizophrenia: A multicausal concept and its therapeutic components. In H. Stierlin, L. C. Wynne & M. Wirschung (Eds.), *Psychosocial intervention in schizophrenia: An international view* (pp. 53-66). New York: Springer-Verlag.

Cobb, S. (1976). Social support as a moderator of life stress. *Psychosomatic Medicine, 38,* 300-314.

Cohen, C. I. (1984). Schizophrenia and work. *Hospital and Community Psychiatry, 35,* 1040-1042.

Cohen, C. I., & Sokolovsky, J. (1978). Schizophrenia social networks: Ex-patients in the inner city. *Schizophrenia Bulletin, 4,* 522-545.

Cole, S. A. (1982). Problem-focused family therapy: Principles and practical applications. In J. R. Lachenmeyer & M. S. Gibbs (Eds.), *Psychopathology in Childhood* (pp. 341-374). New York: Gardner Press.

Cole, S. A. (1983). Self-help groups. In H. I. Kaplan & B. J. Sadock (Eds.), *Comprehensive group psychotherapy* (2nd ed.) (pp. 144-150). Baltimore, Williams & Wilkins.

Coryell, W. (1982). The organic-dynamic continuum in psychiatry: Trends in attitudes among third-year residents. *American Journal of Psychiatry, 139*(1), 89-91.

Creer, C., & Wing, J. K. (1975, July). Living with a schizophrenic patient. *British Journal of Hospital Medicine,* pp. 73-82.

Crow, T. J., Cross, A. J., Johnstone, E. C., & Owen, F. (1982). Two syndromes in schizophrenia and their pathogenesis. In F. A. Henn & H. A. Nasrallah (Eds.), *Schizophrenia as a brain disease* (pp. 196-234). New York, Oxford University Press.

Cutler, D. L., Bloom, J. D., & Shore, J. H. (1981). Training psychiatrists to work with community support systems for chronically mentally ill persons. *American Journal of Psychiatry, 138*(1), 98-101.

Docherty, J. P., van Kammen, D. P., Siris, S. G., & Marder, S. F. (1978). Stages of onset of schizophrenic psychosis. *American Journal of Psychiatry, 135,* 420-426.

Doll, W. (1976). Family coping with the mentally ill: An unanticipated problem of deinstitutionalization. *Hospital and Community Psychiatry, 27,* 183-185.

Donovan, C. M. (1982). Problems of psychiatric practice in community mental health centers. *American Journal of Psychiatry, 139,* 456-460.

Eichler, S. (1982). Why young psychiatrists choose not to work with chronic patients. *Hospital and Community Psychiatry, 33,* 1023-1024.

Falloon, I. R. H. (1984). Developing and maintaining adherence to long-term drug-taking regimens. *Schizophrenia Bulletin, 10,* 412-417.

Falloon, I. R. H., Boyd, J. L., & McGill, C. W. (1984). *Family care of schizophrenia: A problem-solving approach to the treatment of mental illness.* New York: Guilford.

Falloon, I. R. H., Boyd, J. L., McGill, C. W., Razani, J., Moss, H. B., & Gilderman, A. M. (1982). Family management in the prevention of acute exacerbation of schizophrenia: A controlled study. *New England Journal of Medicine, 306,* 1437-1440.

Falloon, I. R. H., Marshall, G. N., Boyd, J. L., Razani, J., & Wood-Siverio, C. (1983). Relapse in schizophrenia: A review of the concept and its definitions. *Psychological Medicine, 13,* 469-477.

Falloon, I. R. H., Boyd, J. L., McGill, C. W. (1985). Family management in the prevention of morbidity of schizophrenia. *Archives of General Psychiatry, 42,* 887-896.

Faulkner, L. R., Rankin, R. M., Eaton, J. S., & Kinzie, J. D. (1983). The state hospital as a setting for residency education. *Journal of Psychiatric Education, 7,* 153-166.

Fink, P. J., & Weinstein, S. P. (1979). Whatever happened to psychiatry? The deprofessionalization of Community Mental Health Clinics. *American Journal of Psychiatry, 136,* 406-409.

Fisher, J., & Weinstein, M. R. (1979). Present as prologue? Psychiatry in the 1980s. *Comprehensive Psychiatry, 20,* 435-448.

Goldman, H. H. (1982). Mental illness and family burden: A public health perspective. *Hospital and Community Psychiatry, 33,* 557-560.

Goldman, H. H., Gattozzi, A. A., & Taube, C. A. (1981). Defining and counting the chronically mentally ill. *Hospital and Community Psychiatry, 32*(1), 20-22.

Goldstein, M. J., & Doane, J. A. (1982). Family factors in the onset, course and treatment of schizophrenia sepctrum disorders. *Journal of Nervous and Mental Disease, 170,* 692-700.

Goldstein, M. J., & Rodnick, E. H. (1975). The family's contribution to the etiology of schizophrenia: Current status. *Schizophrenia Bulletin, 14,* 48-63.

Goldstein, M. J., Rodnick, E., Evans, J. R., May, P. R. A., & Steinberg, M. R. (1978). Drug and family therapy in the aftercare of acute schizophrenics. *Archives of General Psychiatry, 35,* 1169-1177.

Grad, J., & Sainsbury, P. (1963). Mental illness and the family. *Lancet, 1,* 544-547.

Grad, J., & Sainsbury, P. (1968). The effects that patients have on their families in a community care and a control psychiatry service—a two-year follow-up. *British Journal of Psychiatry, 114,* 265-278.

Greden, J. F., & Casariego, J. I. (1975). Controversies in psychiatric education: A survey of residents' attitudes. *American Journal of Psychiatry, 132,* 270-274.

Grinker, R. R. (1975). The future educational needs of psychiatrists. *American Journal of Psychiatry, 132,* 259-262.

Gunderson, J. G., Frank, A. F., Katz, H. M., Vannicelli, M. L., Frosch, J. P., & Knapp, P. H. (1984). Effects of psychotherapy in schizophrenia: II. Comparative outcome of two forms of treatment. *Schizophrenia Bulletin, 10,* 564-598.

Guze, S. B. (1977). The future of psychiatry: Medicine or social science? *Journal of Nervous and Mental Disease, 165,* 225-230.

Hammer, M., Makiesky-Barrow, S., & Gutwirth, L. (1978). Social networks and schizophrenia. *Schizophrenia Bulletin, 4,* 522-545.

Harbin, H. T. (1982). Psychiatric manpower and public health: Maryland's experience. *Hospital and Community Psychiatry, 33,* 277-281.

Harrow, M., Carare, B. J., & Westermeyer, J. F. (1985). The course of psychosis in early phases of schizophrenia. *American Journal of Psychiatry, 142,* 702-707.

Hatfield, A. (1979). Help-seeking behavior in families of schizophrenics. *American Journal of Community Psychology, 7*, 563-569.

Hatfield, A. B. (1981). Self-help groups for families of the mentally ill. *Social Work, 26*, 409-413.

Hatfield, A. B. (1984). The family. In J. A. Talbott (Ed.), *The chronic mental patient: Five years later* (pp. 307-323). New York: Grune & Stratton.

Heinrichs, D. W., & Carpenter, W. T. (1983). The coordination of family treatment with other treatment modalities. In W. R. McFarlane (Ed.), *Family therapy in schizophrenia* (pp. 267-287). New York: Guilford.

Herz, M. I. (1984). Intermittent medication and schizophrenia. In J. M. Kane (Ed.), *Drug maintenance strategies in schizophrenia* (pp. 52-67). Washington, DC: American Psychiatric Association Press.

Herz, M. I., & Melville, C. (1980). Relapse in schizophrenia. *American Journal of Psychiatry, 137*, 801-805.

Hirsch, S. R., & Leff, J. P. (1975). *Abnormalities in parents of schizophrenics* (Maudsley Monographs No. 22, pp. 99-101). London: Oxford University Press.

Hogarty, G. E. (1984, July). *Curricula and administrative issues addressed to the needs of the (chronic) mentally ill.* Paper presented at the NIMH Human Resources Workshop, Rockville, MD.

Hogarty, G. E., Schooler, N. R., Ulrich, R., Mussare, F., Ferro, P., & Herron, E. (1979). Fluphenazine and social therapy in the aftercare of schizophrenic patients. *Archives of General Psyciatry, 36*, 1283-1294.

Holden, D. F., & Lewine, R. R. J. (1982). How families evaluate mental health professionals, resources and effects of illness. *Schizophrenia Bulletin, 8*, 626-633.

Kane, J. M. (1983). Low dose medication strategies in the maintenance treatment of schizophrenia. *Schizophrenia Bulletin, 9*, 528-532.

Kanter, J., & Lin, A. (1980). Facilitating a therapeutic milieu in the families of schizophrenics. *Psychiatry, 43*, 106-119.

Keith, S. J., & Matthews, S. M. (1982). Group, family and milieu therapies and psychosocial rehabilitation in the treatment of the schizophrenic disorders. In L. Grinspoon (Ed.), *Psychiatry, 1982: Annual review* (pp. 166-178). Washington, DC: American Psychiatric Press.

Knesper, D. J. (1981). How psychiatrists allocate their professional time: Implications for educational and manpower planning. *Hospital and Community Psychiatry, 32*, 620-624.

Knesper, D. J., & Hirtle, S. C. (1981). Strategies to attract psychiatrists to state mental hospital work. *Archives of General Psychiatry, 38*, 1135-1140.

Krause, J. (1984, July). *The health professions, mental health services delivery and the chronic mentally ill: Research, service and training priorities for the next decade.* Paper presented at the NIMH Workshop on the Chronic Mentally Ill, Rockville, MD.

Kreisman, D. E., & Joy, V. D. (1975). The family as reactor to the mental illness of a relative. In E. Struening & M. Guttentag (Eds.), *Handbook of evaluation research* (Vol. 2, pp. 483-518). Beverley Hills, CA: Sage.

Kubie, L. S. (1968). Pitfalls of community psychiatry. *Archives of General Psyciatry, 18*, 257-266.

Lamb, H. R. (1981). What did we really expect from deinstitutionalization? *Hospital and Community Psychiatry, 32*, 105-109.

Lamb, H. R., & Peele, R. (1984). The need for continuing asylum and sanctuary. *Hospital and Community Psychiatry, 35*, 798-802.

Leff, J. P., Hirsch, S. R., Gaind, R., Rohde, P. D., & Stevens, B. C. (1973). Life events and maintenance therapy in schizophrenic relapse. *British Journal of Psychiatry, 123,* 659-660.

Leff, J., Kuipers, L, Berkowitz, R., Eberlein-Vries, R., & Sturgeon, D. (1982). A controlled trial of social intervention in the families of schizophrenic patients. *British Journal of Psychiatry, 141,* 121-134.

Leff, J., Kuipers, L., Berkowitz, R., Vaughn, C., & Sturgeon, D. (1983). Life events, relatives' Expressed Emotion and maintenance neuroleptics in schizophrenic relapse. *Psychological Medicine, 13,* 799-806.

Liberman, R. P. (1982). Social factors in the etiology of the schizophrenic disorders. In R. Grinspoon (Ed.), *Psychiatry 1982: Annual review* (pp. 97-112). Washington, DC: American Psychiatric Press.

Liberman, R. P., Massell, H. K., Mosk, M. D., & Wong, S. (1985). Social skills training for chronic mental patients. *Hospital and Community Psychiatry, 36,* 396-403.

Liem, J. H. (1980). Family studies of schizophrenia: An update and commentary. *Schizophrenia Bulletin, 6,* 429-455.

Linn, M. W., Caffrey, E. M., Klett, C. J., Hogarty, G. E., & Lamb, H. R. (1979). Day treatment and psychotropic drugs in the aftercare of schizophrenic patients. *Archives of General Psychiatry, 36,* 1055-1066.

Luber, R. F. (1984). Partial hospitalization. In A. S. Bellack (Ed.), *Schizophrenia: Treatment, management, and rehabilitation* (pp. 219-246). New York: Grune & Stratton.

Lukoff, D., Snyder, K., Ventura, J., & Neuchterlein, K. H. (1984). Life events, familial stress, and coping in the developmental course of schizophrenia. *Schizophrenia Bulletin, 10,* 258-292.

McFarlane, W. F. (1983). Multiple family therapy in schizophrenia. In W. F. McFarlane (Ed.), *Family therapy in schizophrenia* (pp. 141-172). New York: Guilford.

Mayo, J., Gabel, R., & Carvalho, R. (1982). Planning for the future in psychiatric training: The place of the chronic care program. *Comprehensive Psychiatry, 23*(1), 1-8.

Mechanic, D. (1980). *Mental health and social policy* (2nd ed., pp. 107-117). Englewood Cliffs, NJ: Prentice-Hall.

Menninger, W. (1984). Dealing with staff reactions to perceived lack of progress by chronic mental patients. *Hospital and Community Psychiatry, 35,* 805-808.

Meyerson, A. T. (1978). What are the barriers or obstacles to treatment and care of the chronically disabled mentally ill? In J. A. Talbott (Ed.), *The chronic mental patient* (pp. 129-134, 240-242). Washington, DC: American Psychiatric Press.

Miller, R. D. (1984). Public mental health work: Pros and cons for psychiatrists. *Hospital and Community Psychiatry, 35,* 928-933.

Minkoff, K. (1978). A map of chronic mental patients. In J. A. Talbott (Ed.), *The chronic mental patient* (pp. 11-37). Washington, DC: American Psychiatric Association.

Mirabi, M., Weinmen, M. L., Magnetti, S., & Keppler, K. N. (1985). Professional attitudes toward the chronic mentally ill. *Hospital and Community Psychiatry, 36,* 404-405.

Mollica, R. F. (1983). From asylum to community: The threatened disintegration of public psychiatry. *New England Journal of Medicine, 308,* 367-373.

Morrissey, J. P., & Goldman, H. H. (1984). Cycles of reform in the care of the chronic mentally ill. *Hospital and Community Psychiatry, 35,* 785-793.

Neuchterlein, K. H., & Dawson, M. E. (1984). A heuristic vulnerability/stress model of schizophrenic episodes. *Schizophrenia Bulletin, 10,* 300-312.

Nielson, A. C., Stein, L. I., Talbott, J. A., Lamb, H. R., Osser, D. N., & Glazer, W. M. (1981). Encouraging psychiatrists to work with chronic patients: Opportunities and limitations of residency education. *Hospital and Community Psychiatry, 32,* 767-775.

Okin, R. L. (1982). State hospitals in the 1980s. *Hospital and Community Psychiatry, 33,* 717-721.

Paul, G. L. (1978). The implementation of effective treatment programs for chronic mental patients: Obstacles and recommendations. In J. A. Talbott (Ed.), *The chronic mental patient* (pp. 99-127). Washington, DC: American Psychiatric Press.

Pepper, B., Kirschner, M. C., & Ryglewicz, H. (1981). The young adult chronic patient: Overview of a population. *Hospital and Community Psychiatry, 32,* 463-469.

Pepper, B., & Ryglewicz, H. (1982). Unified services: Concept and practice. *Hospital and Community Psychiatry, 33,* 762-765.

Pines, A., & Maslach, C. (1978). Characteristics of staff burnout in mental health settings. *Hospital and Community Psychiatry, 29,* 233-237.

Platman, S. R. (1983). Family caretaking and Expressed Emotion: An evaluation. *Hospital and Community Psychiatry, 34,* 921-925.

Rankin, R. M., & McKinnon, J. A. (1984, July) *Teaching psychiatric residents to work with the chronic mentally ill: The CCD experience.* Paper presented at the NIMH Workshop on the Chronic Mentally Ill, Rockville, MD.

Reiss, D., & Wyatt, R. J. (1975). Family and biologic variables in the same etiologic studies of schizophrenia: A proposal. *Schizophrenia Bulletin, 14,* 64-81.

Richman, A., & Barry, A. (1985). More and more is less and less: The myth of massive psychiatric need. *British Journal of Psychiatry, 146,* 164-168.

Rose, C. L. (1959). Relatives' attitudes and mental hospitalization. *Mental Hygiene, 43,* 194.

Schnitzer, R. D. (1984, July). *Some fundamentals for the care of the chronically mentally ill: Their educational and delivery implications.* Paper presented at the NIMH Workshop on the Chronic Mentally Ill, Rockville, MD.

Schooler, N. R. (1984). Discussion: Alternative drug treatment strategies in schizophrenia. In J. M. Kane (Ed.), *Drug maintenance strategies in schizophrenia* (pp. 84-90). Washington, DC: American Psychiatric Press.

Sharfstein, S. (1978). Will community mental health survive the 1980's? *American Journal of Psychiatry, 135,* 1363-1365.

Sharfstein, S. (1984). Sociopolitical issues affecting patients with chronic schizophrenia. In A. S. Bellack (Ed.), *Schizophrenia: Treatment, management, and rehabilitation* (pp. 113-132). New York: Grune & Stratton.

Soskis, D. A., & Jaffe, R. L. (1979). Communicating with patients about antipsychotic drugs. *Comprehensive Psychiatry, 20,* 126-131.

Stein, L. I., & Test, M. A. (1980). Alternative to mental hospital treatment: I. Conceptual model, treatment program and clinical evaluation. *Archives of General Psychiatry, 37,* 392-397. II., 400-405. III., 409-412.

Strauss, J. S., & Carpenter, W. T. (1977). Prediction of outcome in schizophrenia: III. Five-year outcome and its predictors. *Archives of General Psychiatry, 34,* 159-163

Strauss, J. S., & Carpenter, W. T. (1981). *Schizophrenia.* New York: Plenum Medical.

Strauss, J. S., Hafez, H., Liberman, P., & Harding, C. M. (1985). The course of psychiatric disorder: III. Longitudinal principles. *American Journal of Psychiatry, 142,* 289-296.

Talbott, J. A. (1978a). Policy statement and recommendations. In J. A. Talbott (Ed.), *The chronic mental patient* (pp. 211-220), Washington, DC: American Psychiatric Association.

Talbott, J. A. (1978b). What are the problems of chronic mental patients? A report of a survey of psychiatrists' concerns. In J. A. Talbott (Ed.), *The chronic mental patient* (pp. 1-7), Washington, DC: American Psychiatric Association.

Talbott, J. A. (1979). Care of the chronic mentally ill—still a national disgrace. *American Journal of Psychiatry, 136,* 688-689.

Talbott, J. A. (1984a). Education and training for treatment and care. In J. A. Talbott (Ed.), *The chronic mental patient: Five years later* (pp. 91-101), New York: Grune & Stratton.

Talbott, J. A. (1984b). The patient: First or last? Hospital and Community Psychiatry, 35, 341-344.

Talbott, J. A. (1985). The fate of the public psychiatric system. Hospital and Community Psychiatry, 36(1), 46-50.

Tantam, D. (1985). Alternatives to psychiatric hospitalization. British Journal of Psychiatry, 146, 1-4

Terkelsen, K. G. (1983). Schizophrenia and the family: II. Adverse effects of family therapy. Family Process, 22(2), 191-200.

Tessler, R. C., & Goldman, H. H. (1982). The chronic mentally ill: Assessing community support programs (pp. 3-20). Cambridge, MA: Ballinger.

Test, M. A. (1984). Community support programs. In A. S. Bellack (Ed.), Schizophrenia: Treatment, management, and rehabilitation (pp. 347-373). New York: Grune & Stratton.

Torrey, E. F. (1983). Surviving schizophrenia: A family manual (p. 94). New York: Harper & Row.

van Putten, T. (1974). Why do schizophrenic patients refuse to take their drugs? Archives of General Psychiatry, 31, 67-72.

Vaughn, C. E., & Leff, J. P. (1976). The influence of family and social factors on the course of psychiatric illness: A comparison of schizophrenic and depressed neurotic patients. British Journal of Psychiatry, 129, 125-137.

Vaughn, C. E., & Leff, J. P. (1981). Patterns of emotional response in relatives of schizophrenic patients. Schizophrenia Bulletin, 7(1), 43-44

Vaughn, C. E., Snyder, K. S., Jones, S., Freeman, W. B., & Falloon, I. R. H. (1984). Family factors in schizophrenic relapse. Archives of General Psychiatry, 41, 1169-1177.

Weissman, S. H., & Bashook, P. G. (1984). The 1982 first-year resident in psychiatry. American Journal of Psychiatry, 141, 1240-1243.

White, H. S., & Bennett, M. B. (1981). Training psychiatric residents in chronic care. Hospital and Community Psychiatry, 132, 339-343.

White, R. W. (1974). Strategies of adaptation: An attempt at systematic description. In G. V. Coelho, D. A. Hamburg, & J. E. Adams (Eds.), Coping and adaptation. New York: Basic Books.

Winslow, W. W. (1979). The changing role of psychiatrists in community mental health centers. American Journal of Psychiatry, 136, 24-27.

Winslow, W. W. (1982). Changing trends in community mental health centers: Keys to survival in the eighties. Hospital and Community Psychiatry, 33, 273-277.

Wing, J. K. (1978). Social influences on the course of schizophrenia. In L. C. Wynne, R. L. Cromwell, & S. Matthysse (Eds.), The nature of schizophrenia: New approaches to research and treatment (p. 606). New York: Wiley.

Worley, N., & Lowery, R. N. (1984, July). Chronic mental illness: The context and education of professionals. Paper presented at the NIMH Workshop on the Chronic Mentally Ill, Rockville, MD.

Wynne, L. C. (1983). A phase-oriented approach to treatment. In W. R. McFarlane (Ed.), Family therapy in schizophrenia (pp. 251-265). New York: Guilford.

Zubin, J. (1980). Chronic schizophrenia from the standpoint of vulnerability. In C. Baxter & T. Melnechuk (Eds.), Perspectives in schizophrenia research (pp. 269-294). New York: Raven Press.

Zubin, J., Magaziner, J., & Steinhauer, S. R. (1983). The metamorphosis of schizophrenia: From chronicity to vulnerability. British Journal of Psychiatry, 143, 551-571.

# An Adaptation Framework: Its Meaning for Research and Practice

*Harriet P. Lefley*

In this book, the contributors have attempted to provide a new theoretical paradigm for considering the lives, behaviors, and capabilities of families of the severely disabled mentally ill. In using an adaptation framework, the aim of the book has been to reframe conceptualizations of families from a model of psychopathology to one of coping mechanisms and strengths in the face of persistent and often overwhelming stress.

One of the foci of this book has been on the social psychology of the attitudes of mental health professionals toward families, and particularly on the cultural need to find a human causative agent for the major mental illnesses. With our major value orientation of mastery over the unknown, the frustrations of inadequately understood disorders and therapeutic failures require an explanatory paradigm that has been filled by a model of familial deficit. Yet this may be a culture-bound phenomenon, and if so, transitory and subject to change. In an article on transcultural psychiatry and family therapy, DiNicola (1985), commenting on the early expressed emotion (EE) researchers, pointed out that "Brown et al. [Brown, Birley, & Wing, 1972], in the more individually-oriented British society emphasize the negative aspects of family involvement, while Third World researchers in Qatar and India highlight instead the positive aspects of family-centredness and concern, chanelling it into patient care" (p. 99). This is partly what we have

Harriet P. Lefley. Office of Transcultural Education and Research, Department of Psychiatry, University of Miami, Miami, Florida.

tried to do in this book; to refocus the image of families from one of adversaries to support systems; from interferers with patients' treatment to facilitators of patients' recovery; from pathogens to caregivers.

In this final chapter, I will attempt to integrate the observations of the contributors into some basic questions involving research, practice, and social policy. Some of the major issues include: social consequences of etiological and family systems therapy; appropriate roles of families in caregiving; commonalities with other disorders; stressors specific to families of the mentally ill; and various coping strategies that families have developed in dealing with major mental illness. In the latter section, I will deal with some alternative hypotheses for explanatory models commonly found in the literature. Finally, there is an emphasis on demonstrated strengths of families of the mentally ill, and research and policy directions indicated for exploring and enhancing healthy models of adaptation to these devastating life stressors.

## KNOWLEDGE AND SOCIAL CONTEXT: CLINICAL AND RESEARCH EXPECTANCY EFFECTS

To what extent does general cultural "knowledge" affect coping capabilities of families? Despite a rapidly growing literature on schizophrenia as a biogenic disorder that is affected rather than produced by environmental phenomena, family causation concepts and terminology continue to be found in the pages of contemporary books. For example, in a list entitled "Common Terms in Family Therapy Literature," we find the term "schizophrenogenic" defined as "that process, be it mother-child, father-child or general family interaction, that can foster paralogic ideation, untenable emotional needs, contradictory models of identification or failure to provide models, *leading to a schizophrenic reaction in a child*" (Luber & Anderson, 1983, p. 146; italics mine). Reynolds and Farberow (1981) state that "in addition to genetic factors, there seem to be at least five characteristics attributable to schizophrenic families: (1) excessively closed family systems, (2) shared family myths or delusions, (3) paralogic modes of thinking in all the family members, (4) lack of individuation and self-identity of members from the family 'ego mass' . . , and (5) intense, pathological symbiotic attachments of the child to parents and of parents to grandparents" (p. 126). Categorical statements like this are quite astounding, since there is no evidence in any scientifically controlled studies that any of these conditions is even modally the case. Even the communication deviance literature makes no claim of "paralogic modes of thinking in all the family members." Thus, although respected researchers maintain that there is no empirical evidence that familial factors are either a necessary or sufficient cause for the schizophrenic syndrome (Group for the Advancement of Psychiatry, 1984; Howells & Guirguis, 1985; Stone, 1978; Tsuang, 1982; and many others), family theorists blithely continue operating on this assumption in clinical training and practice.

Liem (1980) has raised the issue of the relevance of the social context to psychiatric outcome in families, pointing out that family characteristics have been treated on a level analogous to the treatment of personality from a trait theory perspective. This strategy, she points out, can have such consequences as (1) "masking a relationship between a family variable such as communication deviance and schizophrenia which is quite substantial for some populations and not for others," promoting the unwarranted generalization of this relationship to all families, and (2) "inadvertently portraying the family as a closed system of relations" (p. 103).

The point Liem has made is that observed relationships between familial variables and psychopathology in a member may wax and wane according to social context. Terkelsen (1983) has specifically addressed the social context of the clinical and experimental situation as a factor in these correlations, suggesting that much of what is observed may be produced by the observer's own behavior. An example of this may be derived from Schuman's (1983) discussion of the application of Bowenian therapy to families of hospitalized schizophrenic patients. He divides these families into two categories. There is the "schizophrenic family," in which all members of the family function at a very low level, and the "family with a schizophrenic member," which has members with a higher level of functioning. In the latter system, "there may be high levels of social or vocational achievement; on an emotional level, however, significant members possess low levels of self. They function with what Bowen has described as "pseudo-self" rather than solid self. . . . These are the families who are quite cooperative when the identified patient is hospitalized; but, when the patient is discharged they fail to continue in treatment" (p. 43).

Consider the self-fulfilling prophetic effects of this statement, which categorically assigns a "pseudo-self" label to admittedly functional members of the family of a schizophrenic patient, and then assigns a symptomatic value to their failure to continue in treatment with those who a priori do not consider them whole people. The tacit communication rules in family relationships presumably do not obtain in the interactions of families and therapists, who are permitted to say things they do not believe and to behave in inauthentic ways without having their message discovered (see Maranhao, 1984).

Family systems theory deals with interlocking relationships and the functional values of behaviors and roles within intersecting social fields. Yet the intrusion of the interveners' belief system, its mode of expression, and the behaviors evoked by these beliefs are subjects almost never recognized as worthy of consideration. The extent to which family theory has changed the dymanics of the social field in which all actors move has seldom if ever been acknowledged, let alone researched. Yet the best explanatory model for familial behavior (in vivo as well as in vitro) may well be the powerful social impact of the epistemology of the professional community at any given time and place.

A suggested hypothesis is that our research findings on communication deviance and related variables are derived from a culture-bound constellation of events, in which researchers and families tacitly agree on their respective behaviors and roles because they share the same cultural epistemology. This is an issue of overwhelming importance. There is a whole literature in social psychology on expectancy effects, effects of the experimental situation, and the impact of social context on stimulus perception and response style. To what extent are the social-class linked differences found in research discrepancies (see Hirsch & Leff, 1975) an artifact not of class communication styles, but of knowledge of researchers' expectancies? Do middle-class subjects (whose classification is heavily dependent on education) feel stigmatized and defensive in these studies in ways that less educated people do not? If so, does this defensiveness take the form of reinforcing the researcher's hypothesis, whether through expiation of guilt or identification with the professional helpers? What kind of families agree to be involved in research, and for what reasons? How many of them are aware of family causation theories? (Current surveys of the National Alliance for the Mentally Ill [NAMI] indicate that a great many are indeed aware.) What happens when a person who already feels indicted (and perhaps guilty) of making her child crazy is exposed to testing conditions that she is sure will reveal her pathology? Hirsch and Leff (1975) discussed situational effects in a number of studies and pointed out that "our unplanned experiment shows that parents are very susceptible to the conditions of testing and confirms that altering the Rorschach technique can lead subjects to respond more fully and thus increase their deviance scores" (pp. 154, 156).

The questions raised here are based on a hypothesis that requires testing: that is, are research differences found primarily in cultures where the family subjects fear or expect revelation of guilt through the experimental or clinical situation? Will naive subjects in less sophisticated cultures respond differently? If we control for level of pathology in the schizophrenic members, as all of these studies purport to do, a simple cross-cultural paradigm would seem to offer a first step toward assessing the panhuman consistency of these relationships. Following this, of course, more complex cross-domain research is needed—particularly the interaction of research expectancy effects and variables in the social context, such as family structure, belief systems, and systems supports for the chronically mentally ill.

## RESEARCH ON PSYCHOGENESIS: SHOULD IT BE CONTINUED?

Current trends indicate a movement away from etiological questions in schizophrenia (at least in the psychosocial area) and more concentration on environmental factors that exacerbate symptoms, including the intrafamilial climate as one of many stressors. Yet, the nagging questions of psychosocial etiology remain. On the one hand, one would like to dispense with investing dollars in this type of research altogether, and on the other, to dispense with the question itself through unambiguous findings. Even those who still hold to the notion of unidirectional family psychopathology have critically cited the fuzziness and nonspecificity of the data, as well as the contrasting experiences of different clinicians who seem to have different opinions of familial behavior. In this connection, Goldstein and Rodnick (1975) have stated: "Perhaps most lacking currently are large-scale epidemiological studies on the incidence of disordered family relations in broad representative samples of schizophrenic patients as contrasted to normally developing comparison groups. Most family studies have worked with small and probably nonrepresentative samples so that the generality of the statistical correlations found is still unknown" (p. 60).

The basic question in this notion of family etiology is, of course, that of prevention. Thus, the above authors state the intensive research on populations at risk for schizophrenia will serve the following objectives: "First, it will indicate whether disordered family relationships are predictive of subsequent schizophrenia, and if predictive, the degree of specificity for this particular form of psychopathology. Second, it opens the way for another critical type of evidence based on the effects of different types of early interventions on populations varying in risk for schizophrenia" (Goldstein & Rodnick, 1975, p. 60).

Although more recent reports of the University of California, Los Angeles (UCLA) Family Project (Rodnick, Goldstein, Doane, & Lewis, 1982) have suggested that parental communication and affective styles can, to some extent, predict schizophrenia spectrum disorders in preschizophrenic offspring, the two variables independently do not seem to be significantly related to outcome. It is particularly interesting that of 8 adolescent index cases with families high in communication deviance but benign in affective style, 7 turned out to be nonschizophrenic. The inference here, as in the EE literature, is that arousing environmental stimuli, rather than the bewildering communication styles of parents, may be precursors of psychotic episodes. But these stimuli may, of course, come from any source.

Communication deviance and affective styles are trait markers of the individuals assumed to produce schizophrenic offspring. The reason these parental characteristics do not inflict such massive damage on siblings of the index case is, presumably, because (1) the siblings lack equivalent vulnerability, and/or (2) their total environment, from conception on, has been different, and/or (3) they have been differentially treated by their parents. Obviously, all three sets of conditions are interrelated, and the latter two are contingent on (1). Yet surely the law of parsimony holds that we first investigate the parameters of vulnerability—as is currently being done in biological psychiatry—without invoking the specter of parental culpability, with all the devastating social consequences that these theories have provoked.

In the same National Institute of Mental Health (NIMH) volume on preventive intervention in schizophrenia, Watt, Shay, Grubb, and Riddle (1982) have pointed out that "85-95 percent of adult schizophrenics do *not* have schizophrenic parents, and perhaps 60-70 percent of them do not have schizophrenic relatives . . . which means that broad-based intervention to prevent schizophrenia must ultimately define 'risk' in terms of characteristics of children rather than of parents or relatives" (p. 252). The authors suggest that the most obvious locus for intervention is in the schools, particularly in building self-esteem and social skills. In the longitudinal Mauritius Project, nursery school experience focusing on promoting positive social interactions for identified high-risk children has been the preventive intervention (Mednick, Venables, Schulsinger, & Cudeck, 1982).

Is further research warranted on family schizophrenogenesis? In their critical overview of the schools of thought that have linked schizophrenia to defective family functioning, Howells and Guirguis (1985) maintain that five criteria must be satisfied to establish a causal relationship.

- *Time sequence*. It should be established that the family psychopathology predates rather than postdates the onset of the schizophrenia.

- *Consistency of replication.* The work should be capable of easy replication by others.
- *Strength of association.* There should be a direct and strong association between family psychopathology and schizophrenia in one family member. It should be possible to explain why other family members have excaped schizophrenia.
- *Specificity of association.* The psychopathology should be unique to the families of the schizophrenics.
- *Coherence of explanation.* The research should explain the known features of schizophrenia, such as its onset in adolescence and its clinical course. (p. 330)

It is clear that all research to date has failed to satisfy these reasonable conditions for establishing a premise of family etiology. The question we now turn to is research on the resolution of some issues in family theory that continue to inform therapeutic approaches. These issues vitually affect the coping capacities of families, who are often advised that their loved one cannot receive treatment unless they agree to participate in family therapy. If this modality is, in turn, based on unproven or incorrect theory, its long-term potential to damage the family or to strip it of resources without benefit, are readily apparent.

## RESEARCHING THE SOCIAL CONTEXT
## OF PSYCHOTIC EPISODES

Dell (1980) has stated, "The active psychotic state that causes people to be hospitalized is considered by family theory to be the outcome of an escalating interactional process between patient and family. Through this process, the patient is defined as incompetent and maintained in that role by the manner in which patient and family provoke each other to react. . . . The process that keeps the patient in the role of incompetent is considered to periodically escalate into the disordered state of active psychosis" (p. 332).

This interactional theory of psychotic episodes, social labeling, and reaffirmation of the psychotic role through hospitalization suggests that the family acts as a catalyst for the psychotic behavior, which then provides the behavioral basis for the labeling and subsequent identity of the labeled person. There is no controversy regarding labeling and social identification. However, the initial familial role as an "interactional" one in precipitating the psychotic episode can easily be studied. There are many adolescents who have their first psychotic episode after or *because* they have left the protective family setting for an independent life in school or at work. An investigation of the number of college students who have their first episode in a lonely dormitory, away from familial supports, is in order. Cases of dual disability—young people whose first psychotic episode is precipitated by drugs, in a peer environment, is another case in point. The epidemiology of first reported psychotic episodes would certainly seem to offer a feasible area of research that could easily demonstrate the correctness of the statement by Dell that "the active psychotic state that causes people to be hospitalized is . . . an outcome of an escalating interactional process between patient and family" (p. 332). To our knowledge, this has not been demonstrated empirically. On the contrary, it would seem that the majority of patients brought into the crisis centers of urban hospitals are people who have decompensated precisely because they have no interaction with significant others who are concerned enough to make sure that they take their medication or have adequate nutrition or shelter. Again, in order to avoid a more basic confusion, we must be very specific about the patients we are talking about. Are we talking about a population of young people having their first psychotic episode regardless of diagnostic category? about clearly diagnosed patients living at home with their parents? about clearly diagnosed patients living outside of the family setting with a quantified range of interactions with significant others? At this point we have no large-scale data base on living arrangements of the severely mentally ill at time of relapse. Despite the patterns found in the EE research, the actual incidence of psychotic episodes and their situational and contextual precipitants is an area little researched and as yet dimly understood. This is an area that lends itself well to investigation, and its resolution would do much to confirm or reject some of these basic postulates of family theory. In this connection, explorations of variables that precipitate relapse and psychotic episodes in schizophrenics in low EE cultures would certainly seem to offer a profitable avenue of research. Here, if by definition the family cannot be singled out as the toxic agent, it will become possible to reveal other and perhaps more significant triggers of aversive psychophysiological arousal.

While this section has focused on contextual aspects for the patient, we must focus on the incidence and meaning of such episodes for the families. Regardless of where the psychotic episode occurs, the family responds with anguish, confusion, and now, during a period of deinstitutionalization, often lack of an appropriate resource to which to turn. The incidence of catastrophic life events in families of the mentally ill, and their mode of coping, are areas that have been grossly underinvestigated.

## RESEARCH ON LIFE EVENTS AMONG FAMILIES OF THE MENTALLY ILL

The lack of awareness of many professionals regarding the traumatic impact of mental illness on the family (see Lamb, 1983) is in a pattern with the indifference of researchers, who have failed to mention this unique category in most of the literature on families and life stressors. Dohrenwend and Dohrenwend's (1974) book on stressful life events discusses life stresses only in relation to psychiatric disorder, not in relation to living with psychiatric disorder in the household. A two-volume work on stress and the family (Figley & McCubbin, 1983; McCubbin & Figley, 1983) allots only one chapter to family stress and coping with chronic illness, focusing on a 14-year-old girl with cystic fibrosis. In the book on family stress, coping, and social support by McCubbin, Cauble, and Patterson (1982), there is only one chapter that bears on the issue of familial coping with prolonged illness—a study of 217 families that had a child with cerebral palsy. The commonalities of life with severe chronic illness are apparent. The authors list the following: *altered relationships with friends and neighbors* along with parental and sibling embarrassment; *major changes in family activities*, such as reduced options for family vacations, tightening work schedules, reduced flexibility for use of leisure time; *medical concerns* related to side effects with medications and home treatment responsibilities; *intrafamily strains* "including overprotectiveness, rejection of child, denial of disabilities, ongoing worry about the CP's child's safety and care, concerns about the extended parenthood, increase in the amount of time focused on the CP child at the possible expense of other family members, as well as discrepancies between children as a result of uneven physical, emotional, social, and intellectual development"; *medical expenses; specialized child care needs* and difficulties related to limited community resources and difficulties in finding the best care and services; *time commitments* that disrupt family routines, and the predictable although disruptive situation of extra demands on family life; and *medical commitments* "which call for repeated efforts to clarify and verify medical information . . . and frustrations with the general quality of medical care, which does not match parent's expectations" (McCubbin, et al., 1982, pp. 170–171).

All of these stressors, of course, are highly familiar to families of the mentally ill. However, we must add still more to this core situation. While the trauma of living with cerebral palsy cannot be overestimated, there are factors present in living with severe mental illness, particularly in an adult child, that would seem to render the latter situation potentially more stressful for families. First is the patient's deterioration from a previous level of functioning and the loss of aspirations that previously seemed realizable. Thus, there is very real mourning for the loss of what was and is no more. Second is the pain inherent in empathizing with the agony of the mentally ill family member, and the fear of suicide or other self-destructive acts. Finally, there is an ongoing potentially explosive situation, rife with threatening, annoying, abusive, or bizarre behaviors that can result in family stigmatization and self-isolation well beyond that imposed on families with physically ill children. In a recent study of the experiences of 84 mental health professionals with family members suffering from long-term psychotic disorders, I found that illness-related stressful life events appeared to be an ongoing concomitant of the disorder. As an example of normative family burden, in a representative year of the patient's illness, 75% of the sample reported regular emergency calls to the psychiatrist or primary therapist. Over 73% had needed to hospitalize their family member during the year. Almost 51% reported calling the police at least once, and 38% had to obtain a court order for involuntary commitment at least once. With respect to other stressors, over and above the patients' difficult behaviors, more than 50% of the practitioner group perceived failure on the part of their colleagues to interact compassionately and/or informatively with families (Lefley, 1984).

When we consider the relative salience of normative transitions as stressors (Holmes & Rahe, 1967; McCubbin & Figley, 1983), the enormity of the problems faced by families with mentally ill members becomes readily apparent. The closest analogue is with families of substance abusers; however, in the latter case we are dealing with patients who have a higher level of functioning and presumably more volitional control over the precipitants of their disordered behavior.

There have been some attempts at comparative studies of families with patients with different types of disorder, for example, schizophrenia and Alzheimer's disease (Wasow, 1985). More are needed to target the specific coping strategies that are relevant to each, as well as the commonalities previously discussed. Of particular concern is the impact of these continuous life stressors induced by the illness of the patient on the emotional and physical health of family members. This is an area that presumably will see increasing research investment as

Alzheimer's disease becomes a significant social problem in the years ahead.

## RECONCEPTUALIZING FAMILIAL BEHAVIORS: ALTERNATIVE HYPOTHESES

Humans develop a variety of coping strategies in dealing with life, and, in particular, in dealing with the types of lives that involve the permanent and periodically intolerable stress described in these pages. It is evident that some of these strategies are adaptive and some maladaptive, and even that the quality of their usefulness to the organism varies according to context and condition.

We have not heretofore looked at families of the mentally ill in this perspective. It is evident, however, that many of the old paradigms of the "deficit model" have not been demonstrated as empirical verities or as useful constructs for therapy. New directions are therefore called for in conceptualization and in research. The following issues are discussed in a framework of coping and adaptation.

### Relational "Deficits": State, Trait, or Coping Mechanism?

Leff and Vaughn (1985) stated that their clinical experience with families of schizophrenics indicated that such concepts as marital "skew" and "schism," "double-bind," and "communication deviance" were encountered in some, but by no means all, families of schizophrenics. Moreover, they were also found in families of other psychiatric groups. These characteristics are not considered by Leff and Vaughn to play any etiological role in schizophrenia, although they may exacerbate symptoms. The authors stated, however, that the concepts should not be discarded but investigated further to determine if there is overlap with relatives' EE.

Family theory has represented these constructs, however, as antecedent characteristics of specific family systems, and has used them as a rationale for the development of a specific type of psychiatric disorder. The assumptions of the adaptation framework are that these types of behaviors, when observed, are maladaptive modes of responding to life situations that may be overwhelming. It has frequently been suggested that as a population, relatives of schizophrenics are likely to demonstrate a small but disproportionate degree of subclinical manifestations of schizophrenia-spectrum disorders because of the common genetic vulnerability (see McFarlane & Beels, 1983). If the small subset with communication deviance or relational aberrations indeed reflects this vulnerability, we would seem to have characteristics that, parsimoniously, must be considered correlative without any particular etiological significance. Moreover, the aberrant mode may be a far more common maladaptive response to stress than has yet been demonstrated. The ubiquitous nature of "marital schism" as an adaptive mechanism is well demonstrated in the over 50% divorce rate in the United States. Because of the serious social consequences of etiological explanatory models, these alternative hypotheses merit further exploration.

## Defense Mechanisms

Like all human beings, relatives of the mentally ill use a variety of defensive strategies in dealing with stress. Some of these may be maladaptive for both themselves and the patient, particularly emotional overinvolvement, overprotection, and focusing on the patient to the exclusion of their own needs and those of other family members. However, some defensive maneuvers typically considered unhealthy may, in these circumstances, be adaptive for all considered. Instructing high-EE individuals in low-EE techniques involves, necessarily, a purposeful suppression of affect in the face of situations that would normally provoke justifiable anger or irritation. Denial and repression are typically considered maladaptive, particularly if the family is unwilling to take action when apparent symptoms of decompensation occur. We have a whole "prevention" technology teaching symptom recognition and urging early psychiatric intervention, despite the constant caveats in the literature against the dangers of labeling, the perils of hospitalization, and nonefficacy of many psychotherapies (Howells & Guirguis, 1985; Klerman, 1984; Torrey, 1983). We have no data on how many first-break or incipient schizophrenics may have been treated with neuroleptics by family physicians and saved from premature hospitalization, identity change, and stigmatization because their families "denied" that these were psychogenic disorders. To what extent does the resistance of families reflect a prescient wisdom that will protect patients from theories and treatment modalities that will, later in history, ultimately be discredited?

An important defensive maneuver that requires investigation is the movement of some families away from the patient, whether through active extrusion or passive absence. This is related to the social policy issue of who shall be the caregivers, and it is as important for families as it is for patients. Physical and sometimes psychological separation from the patient is often the only means a family can use to maintain its own integrity, because it cannot continue to be buffeted by the patients' abnormal behaviors and their social sequelae. Psychoeducational family therapy is not the answer here, because the assumption of constant patient-family interaction cannot be sustained nor can the latter be considered healthy for all concerned. Additionally, we have not yet begun to investigate the potentially salutary effects of schizophrenics' self-imposed isolation, although the literature on hyperarousal suggests that this may be adaptive on their part. The parameters of optimal interaction between families and patients is at issue here, quantitatively as well as qualitatively, and there is a need to continue studying this question rather than focusing on the nature of the interaction alone.

## Reactions to Therapeutic Interventions

In many programs, family therapies have become the treatment of choice. Although psychoeducational interventions are more concordant with expressed family needs for information and support, we do not know the extent to which these modalities have supplanted older family therapy approaches, nor their impact on professional thinking. As indicated earlier in this chapter, the professional literature continues to be filled with generalizations about families' psychodynamics and functional needs for patients' symptoms to hold the dysfunctional unit together; these theoretical formulations, of course, demand systems rather than educational interventions.

We do not yet have hard data on (1) comparisons of families receiving information and support in informal (self-help) as opposed to formal (professional) context, and (2) long-term effects of various models of family therapy. Some clinicians have specifically stated that conjoint family therapy is contraindicated for psychotic young adults and their parents (Guttman, 1973). The long-term outcome study of over 1,000 families done by an important family therapy program, the Eastern Pennsylvania Psychiatric Institute, indicated a 63% nonimprovement rate (57% no change, 6% deteriorated) during an 8-year period (Bernal, Deegan, & Konjevich, 1983). This was a general population study, not limited to families of the severely mentally ill. The latter, however, give consistently low ratings to the usefulness and efficacy of family therapy (Hatfield, 1983; Holden & Lewine, 1982; Lefley, 1984). Since monies and energies are being invested in these modalities, it is important to investigate in depth their cost-effectiveness and the specific ways in which they may help or hinder coping capabilities of families.

## COPING WITH DEINSTITUTIONALIZATION:
## SOCIAL POLICY ISSUES

One of the major social policy issues of the family movement is the societal expectancy that deinstitutionalized patients will return to live with their families. The tacit premises of EE research, the psychoeducational family interventions derived from this research, and the current five-center collaborative research project on treatment strategies in schizophrenia have been criticized for precisely this reason; they seem to assume that the most important psychosocial influences in the lives of deinstitutionalized patients will be the families. The research paradigm thus seems to ignore the realities of patients living in boarding homes, foster homes, residential treatment facilities, and the like, and the behavioral impact of their caregivers and therapists in other settings. Indeed, if the issue is patients' psychophysiological arousal to aversive stimuli, a range of other individuals, rather than families alone, must be given psychoeducational training. To ignore this area of training is to reinforce the implicit social policy of family care.

A research area barely touched, but just now coming to the fore with the trauma of Alzheimer's disease, is the short- and long-term social effects of forcing family members into an unbearable caregiving situation. Until now, endorsements of patients' separation from families have largely been based on (1) the putative toxic effects of living with families, or (2) the need for patients to attain autonomy by relinquishing their symbiotic dependency on others. More enlightened commentaries have suggested the need for patients to live in structured therapeutic environments that will permit them to assume responsibilities and learn skills and socialization techniques that are not easily acquired when they are living as adults in the parental home (Dincin, Selleck, & Streikers, 1978).

Above all, members of the family movement have maintained that families must not be considered as primary caregivers and providers of housing. As James Howe, president of NAMI, pointed out in an article on this subject (Howe, 1985), there are enormous tensions in caring for a mentally ill member, including a heavy toll on well children living at home; the parental home is never the best milieu for the growth of independence; and, finally, aging parents will die before their adult children have developed sufficient necessary skills for living on their own. Above all, residential caregiving is scarcely an appropriate role for older people at a time in life when they have the least energy to invest in this type of physically and emotionally draining effort, and the most right to enjoy their surviving years free of pressure and pain.

The particular pain of continuing to live with and nurture difficult adult children, as opposed to the obligations of taking care of Alzheimer's patients, is another area of comparative investigation. Here, the notion of instrumental rewards and reciprocity for past services may well be investigated using an anthropological pardigm, as suggested by Lefley in Chapter 5 of this volume. Since the Alzheimer's families issue will become a very important one in the years ahead, this is a social policy issue that clearly warrants investigation.

A related area of social policy involves the relations of families and the provider system. Families have generally viewed themselves in an adjunctive role rather than as primary providers themselves. Yet, with deinstitutionalization, families have indicated that they are often called upon by providers when a patient is acting out and they may be required to remove a psychotic patient from the treatment system (see Lefley, 1985b). Exclusionary policies of community support programs, and selective admission criteria that screen out those who are less functional also provide problems for families. In areas with inadequate resources, many families have become the primary day treatment system, even if the patients do not share their homes. NAMI families have increasingly banded together for resource development when community support programs and residential facilities are lacking. These developments involve very serious issues of public policy, that is, the role of government and the locus of responsibility for care of the disabled. The issue is compounded in the case of the mentally ill, since epidemiological data indicate that a disproportionate number of those who are most likely to require hospitalization are from lower socioeconomic strata (Dohrenwend et al., 1980). These are the patients whose families are least likely to be able to afford or develop community alternatives.

The third vital issue in social policy involves the interrelations of patients, families, and legal advocates. Legal changes focusing on patients' rights and least restrictive settings have, of course, affected many patients and families adversely. Homelessness, repeated visits to crisis emergency units, misdemeanors that lead to the criminal justice system, and the like are stressors for all concerned. Legal restrictions on police intervention unless criminal behavior is personally observed have led to many crises for families, whose assaultive, property-destroying relative may suddenly turn quiet when the police arrive. In this type of familiar case, the legal system often forces the family to use up its only option for mental health treatment, leaving jail for assault as the only alternative. The adversarial posture into which families are placed in involuntary commitment proceedings is another stress point. For many families, it almost seems as if the legal system is focused on driving a wedge between patients who reject necessary treatment and families who want them to have it.

These themes are quite common in NAMI conferences and discussion groups, but there is almost no research on how the social policy of deinstitutionalization is affecting the coping strength of families, and very little on effects on patients. The need for long-range studies on the social consequences of these policies, and recommendations for improving present procedures, is quite apparent.

## COPING STRENGTHS OF FAMILIES

Much of this book has focused on the experiential impact of mental illness on the family and the parameters of family burden. The research on family burden has been sparse, but at least some attention has been paid to this area of study. Almost nowhere, however, do we find any substantial evidence of research on adaptive strategies used by families that reflect strength in the face of adversity.

Taylor (1983) has proposed that adjustment to threatening events centers around three themes: "A search for meaning in the experience; an attempt to regain mastery over the event in particular and over one's life generally; and an effort to restore self-esteem through self-enhancing operations" (p. 1161). In Chapter 3 of this work, Hatfield has emphasized White's (1974) concept of mastery, entailing competence, action, and changing the environment, as key components of adaptation. Many of these variables are involved in the following manifestations of coping strength by families of the mentally ill.

### Self-Help and Advocacy Groups

A rather remarkable coping mechanism is exemplified in the development of NAMI, a grass-roots organization largely composed of families of the severely and chronically mentally ill. Founded just a few years ago (1979), NAMI has grown at a prodigious rate and today boasts affiliates in every state of the union, an expanding national office, a respected lobbying capability in Washington, and a growth rate of at least 10 new local groups per month. Among its many functions, the organization provides mutual support groups; education for members, the public, and mental health professionals; information and referral resources; evaluation and monitoring of mental health services; vigorous advocacy at all legislative levels; and resource development.

In the same way that the discovery of low EE or calm, rational, and accepting behavior in over 50% of the families of schizophrenics (Leff & Vaughn, 1985) gives the lie to stereotypes of schizophrenogenesis, the phenomenal growth of the family movement invalidates generalizations about inadequacies in families of schizophrenics. Prior "encapsulation" rapidly disappears in the supportive environment of the mutual support group. Energies are mobilized for advocacy rather than invested in futile despair. It is difficult to reconcile notions of dysfunctional individuals manifesting confused communication styles and paralogic ideation with the image of vigorous lobbyists and successful negotiators for services. We now have a national phenomenon of families advocating for service funds to pay the salaries of some of the very professionals who have categorically questioned their functional capabilities.

The emergence, functions, political infuence, and rapid growth of the family movement well merits sociological investigation, particularly because the mentally ill have lacked a constituency for such a long period of time. Why did families of the mentally ill take so long to "catch up" with families of the developmentally disabled? One hypothesis has been that it required a particular conjunction of historical events, including deinstitutionalization, the discharge of large numbers of patients to their families, the need for family advocacy, and a particular developmental stage of knowledge to bring this about. In connection with the latter, some have postulated iatrogenic deterrents to the emergence of family strength—particular the vision of families as inadequate and pathogenic. The appearance of compelling research findings from genetic and biological psychiatry, confirming diathesis, and a small but powerful literature on family burden, set the stage for more enlightened attitudes from professionals and a basis for provider-family alliances.

## Productivity of Other Family Members

The organization of families for mutual support, education, advocacy, and resource development indicates remarkable coping strengths in persons who have undergone inordinate stress. The strengths of other family members—siblings and "invulnerable" children—is another area that merits further exploration. Samuels and Chase's (1979) study of the well siblings of schizophrenics showed a high level of adjustment, despite a predominant emotion of guilt. In an overview of other studies of siblings, Samuels found minimal functional impairment. In a study of well-established mental health professionals with mentally ill relatives, Lefley (1985a) found that among those whose relatives' psychosis was manifested before they entered training (primarily siblings), two thirds reported that the illness influenced them to become helping professionals. The author has been present at a number of case conferences during which the talents and high productivity of siblings of the patient has been a matter of comment. The afflicted relatives of NAMI members frequently have siblings with characteristics that may well be investigated for health-producing rather than pathogenic influences in the family system. Of particular interest are the compensatory mechanisms selected and the number who manifest the "urge toward mastery" by entering the mental health professions.

*Family Strategies for Averting Patient Relapse:*
*Alternatives to EE Research*

As we have indicated, many in the family movement have become understandably concerned about two perceived implications of the EE research and its subsequent applications: (1) that family factors are the major issue in patients' decompensation, and (2) that families will be the primary caregivers and therefore are the best target group for psychoeducational interventions.

Because there has been so much emphasis on EE, there is a danger of masking more critical precipitants of decompensation. By definition, patients have already decompensated before their families are assessed on the EE dimension. The Camberwell Family Interview is typically administered when the patient is hospitalized. Yet, in the large body of research in the United Kingdom, the majority of families have been characterized as low EE (Leff & Vaughn, 1985). Accordingly, it was apparently other, nonfamilial factors that triggered the psychotic breakdowns that resulted in the initial hospitalization or relapse of the patients under investigation. What can families do, beyond regulating their own behavior, to prevent these from occurring?

Herz (1984) has found that relatives can usually recognize early signs of decompensation and has stated that this "is extremely important to the therapeutic management of the patient" (p. 346). At NAMI conferences, families are often asked by professionals to describe their perception of the behavioral precursors of relapse, and the coping strategies used to prevent the decline (e.g., Strauss, 1985). A range of strategies have been verbally described. Some families and patients are acutely aware of the diurnal rhythms and peak periods for hallucinatory or delusional activities, and of a range of stressors to be avoided in their individual cases. This would seem a more fertile field of investigation than simply continuing to replicate the EE studies.

On the EE dimension itself, however, it would be profitable to go well beyond the crude correlations between criticalness and relapse. (Vaughn, Snyder, Jones, Freeman, & Falloon, 1984, have now indicated that most parents do not score highly on emotional overinvolvement regardless of cultural origin.) If criticalness is a trait of a specific subset of family members, it appears to be readily amenable to change through educational interventions. Of greater interest to the field are the *positive* elements of expressed emotions—the calm, benign, understanding behaviors depicted by Jenkins (1981) in her description of families of Mexican-American schizophrenics. The widespread prevalence of low EE, of course, violates the stereotypes of intrusive, overcontrolling, or hostile families. As Spaniol, Jung, Zipple, and Fitzgerald (1984) have suggested, however, low EE may not be uniformly desirable. Purposeful and perhaps unhealthy suppression of affect, disengagement, or indifference may be correlates of low EE. Certainly more research that focuses on a continuum of total acceptance to total disengagement, rather than on the dichotomizing of a complex set of behaviors is required.

## OTHER COPING STRATEGIES

Hatfield (1981) has posed a series of research questions to identify ways in which families cope with mental illness and to distinguish effective and ineffective strategies. These include (1) inner strengths or life events associated with the capacity to accept the fact of mental illness in the family, with a specific focus on meaning of illness, resources, and passage of time as relevant variables; (2) personal factors that may explain differences in problem-solving skills; (3) psychological defenses that reduce emotional stress and permit better cognitive functioning; (4) identification of patient behaviors that produce most stress reactions; (5) roles of natural support systems of relatives and friends in easing lives of caregivers; and (6) the model of therapeutic relationship that will result in enhanced coping of families. In this connection, there are an ever increasing number of advocates for a cognitive approach focusing on knowledge and management skills as an alternative to psychogenic or family systems models.

Research is clearly needed to identify the specific behavioral correlates of these various coping mechanisms, the situations in which they are applied, and their effectiveness in (1) regulating the emotional status of the principals involved, and/or (2) changing the reality situation so that the stressor is minimized or eliminated.

## ENHANCING THE COPING STRENGTHS OF FAMILIES

Families of the mentally ill have always been faced with tremendous emotional, financial, and logistical pressures. With the increasing erosion of hospital resources, and the failure of community programs to fully fill the gap, families will be faced with increasing stressors in coping with the realities of chronic disability in a loved one. Remedies to enhance, rather than erode the coping capabilities of families must come from the professional and public sectors. New research, training, and service directions must be explored. Several areas that clearly need to be developed are indicated here, linking public and provider policies with their impact on the coping capabilities of families.

1. *To alleviate anxiety about adequate treatment for a loved one:* Mechanisms for assuring continuing and expanded (rather than reduced) public aid for community support programs, treatment facilities, and residential resources for the chronically mentally ill.

2. *To minimize adversarial situations with the patient:* Legislative clarity with respect to the "least restrictive setting" versus "right to treatment" issues that presently divide many patients and families.

3. *To relieve forebodings about the patient's survival "when I am gone":* State and federal policies that will provide incentives for development of guardianship and trust programs without jeopardizing financial entitlements for the mentally disabled.

4. *To assume mastery and control over decisions affecting one's life:* A mandated role for family representation on mental health planning boards and in monitoring and evaluating tax-supported mental health services.

5. *To eliminate frustration, futility, and anger, at being excluded from the treatment process:* Administrative regulations assuring clear lines of communication between families and the provider system.

6. *To strengthen families' understanding of and commitment to therapeutic objectives:* Provider policies that encourage collaborative involvement of patients and families in treatment and discharge planning.

7. *To assure state-of-the-art expertise on the part of professionals treating the family member:* Funding resources, research initiatives, and other incentives for clinical training programs to prepare and enourage professionals to work with the chronically mentally ill.

8. *To find meaning in adversity by seeking to eliminate mental illness:* Legislative advocacy and private initiatives for large-scale funding resources for etiological research.

9. *To change relationships between families and mental health professionals:* Incentives for research and training that will update the

knowledge base in clinical education and foster a coping and adaptation model for conceptualizing families of the mentally ill.

## REFERENCES

Bernal, G., Deegan, E., & Konjevich, C. (1983). The EPPI Family Therapy Outcome Study. *International Journal of Family Therapy, 5*(1), 3-21.

Brown, G. W., Birley, J. L. T., & Wing, J. K. (1972). Influence of family life on the course of schizophrenic disorders: A replication. *British Journal of Psychiatry, 121,* 241-258.

Dell, P. F. (1980). Researching the family theories of schizophrenia: An exercise in epistemological confusion. *Family Process, 19,* 321-335.

Dincin, J., Selleck, V., & Streiker, S. (1978). Restructuring parental attitudes—working with parents of the adult mentally ill. *Schizophrenia Bulletin, 4,* 597-608.

DiNicola, V. F. (1985). Family therapy and transcultural psychiatry: An emerging synthesis: I. The conceptual basis. *Transcultural Psychiatric Research Review, 22,* 81-113.

Dohrenwend, B. P., Dohrenwend, B. S., Gould, M. S., Link, B., Neugebauer, R., & Wunsch-Hitzig, R. (1980). *Mental illness in the United States: Epidemiological estimates.* New York: Praeger.

Dohrenwend, B. S., Dohrenwend, B. P. (Eds.). (1974). *Stressful life events.* New York: Wiley.

Figley, C. R., & McCubbin, H. I. (Eds.). (1983). *Stress and the family* (Vol. 2, *Coping with catastrophe*). New York: Brunner/Mazel.

Goldstein, M. J., & Rodnick, E. H. (1975). The family's contribution to the etiology of schizophrenia: Current status. *Schizophrenia Bulletin, 14,* 48-63.

Group for the Advancement of Psychiatry. (1984). *Research and the complex causality of the schizophrenias.* New York: Brunner/Mazel.

Guttman, H. A. (1973). A contraindication for family therapy. *Archives of General Psychiatry, 29,* 352-355.

Hatfield, A. B. (1981). Coping effectiveness in families of the mentally ill: An exploratory study. *Journal of Psychiatric Treatment and Evaluation, 3,* 11-19.

Hatfield, A. B. (1983). What families want of family therapists. In W. R. McFarlane (Ed.), *Family therapy in schizophrenia* (pp. 41-65). New York: Guilford.

Herz, M. I. (1984). Recognizing and preventing relapse in patients with schizophrenia. *Hospital and Community Psychiatry, 35,* 344-349.

Hirsch, S. R., & Leff, J. P. (1975). *Abnormalities in parents of schizophrenics* (Maudsley Monographs No. 22). London: Oxford University Press.

Holden, D. F., & Lewine, R. R. J. (1982). How families evaluate mental health professionals, resources, and effects of illness. *Schizophrenia Bulletin, 8,* 626-633.

Holmes, T. H., & Rahe, R. H. (1967). The Social Readjustment Rating Scale. *Journal of Psychosomatic Research, 11,* 213-218.

Howe, J. W. (1985, January). What do families of citizens with mental illness want from clinicians? *Tie-Lines,* pp. 8-9.

Howells, J. G., & Guirguis, W. R. (1985). *The family and schizophrenia.* New York: International Universities Press.

Jenkins, J. A. (1981, December). *The course of schizophrenia among Mexican Americans.* Paper presented at the annual meeting of the American Anthropological Association, Los Angeles, California.

Klerman, G. L. (1984). Ideology and science in the individual psychotherapy of schizophrenia. *Schizophrenia Bulletin, 10,* 608-612.

Lamb, H. R. (1983). Families: Practical help replaces blame. *Hospital and Community Psychiatry, 34*, 893.

Leff, J., & Vaughn, C. (1985). *Expressed emotion in families.* New York: Guilford.

Lefley, H. P. (1984, August). *Practitioners with mentally ill relatives: A view from the bridge.* Paper presented at the annual meeting of the American Psychological Association, Toronto, Canada.

Lefley, H. P. (1985a). Etiological and prevention views of clinicians with mentally ill relatives. *American Journal of Orthopsychiatry, 55*, 363-370.

Lefley, H. P. (1985b, April-May). *The role of family groups in community support systems.* Issue paper for the Seventh NIMH Community Support Program Learning Community Conference, Rockville, Maryland.

Liem, J. H. (1980). Family studies of schizophrenia: An update and commentary. *Schizophrenia Bulletin, 6*, 429-455.

Luber, R. F., & Anderson, C. M. (1983). *Family interventions with psychiatric patients.* New York: Human Sciences Press.

Maranhao, T. (1984). Family therapy and anthropology. *Culture, Medicine, and Psychiatry, 8*, 255-279.

McCubbin, H. I., Cauble, A. E., & Patterson, J. M. (1982). *Family stress, coping, and social support.* Springfield, IL: Charles C Thomas.

McCubbin, H. I., & Figley, C. R. (Eds.). (1983). *Stress and the family* (Vol. 1, *Coping with normative transitions*). New York: Brunner/Mazel.

McCubbin, H. I., Nevin, R. S., Cauble, A. E., Larsen, A., Comeau, J. K., & Patterson, J. M. (1982). Family coping with chronic illness: The case of cerebral palsy. In H. I. McCubbin, A. E. Cauble, & J. M. Patterson (Eds.), *Family stress, coping, and social support* (pp. 169-188). Springfield, IL: Charles C Thomas.

McFarlane, W. R., & Beels, C. C. (1983). Family research in schizophrenia: A review and integration for clinicians. In W. R. McFarlane (Ed.), *Family therapy in schizophrenia* (pp. 311-323). New York: Guilford.

Mednick, S. A., Venables, P. H., Schulsinger, F., & Cudeck, R. (1982). The Mauritius Project: An experiment in primary prevention. In M. J. Goldstein (Ed.), *Preventive intervention in schizophrenia: Are we ready?* (pp. 287-296). Rockville, MD: National Institute of Mental Health.

Reynolds, D., & Farberow, N. L. (1981). *The family shadow: Sources of suicide and schizophrenia.* Berkeley, CA: University of California Press.

Rodnick, E. H., Goldstein, M. J., Doane, J. A., & Lewis, J. M. (1982). Association between parent-child transactions and risk for schizophrenia: Implications for early intervention. In M. J. Goldstein (Ed.), *Preventive intervention in schizophrenia: Are we ready?* (pp. 156-172). Rockville, MD: National Institute of Mental Health.

Samuels, L., & Chase, L. (1979). The well siblings of schizophrenics. *American Journal of Family Therapy, 7*(2), 24-35.

Schuman, M. (1983). The Bowen theory and the hospitalized patient. In R. F. Luber & C. M. Anderson (Eds.), *Family interventions with psychiatric patients* (pp. 29-47). New York: Human Sciences Press.

Spaniol, L., Jung, H., Zipple, A., & Fitzgerald, S. (1984). *Some comments on expressed emotion research.* Unpublished manuscript, Boston University, Center for Rehabilitation Research and Training in Mental Health.

Stone, M. H. (1978). Etiological factors in schizophrenia: A reevaluation in the light of contemporary research. *Psychiatric Quarterly, 50*(2), 83-119.

Strauss, J. (1985, June 29). *More sides to making it: Reclaiming life after psychosis.* Workshop with J. Strauss, C. Harding, C. Howe, & K. Terkelsen, seventh annual conference of the National Alliance for the Mentally Ill, New Orleans.

Taylor, S. E. (1983). Adjustment to threatening events: A theory of cognitive adaptation. *American Psychologist, 38,* 1161-1173.

Terkelsen, K. G. (1983). Schizophrenia and the family: II. Adverse effects of family therapy. *Family Process, 22,* 191-200.

Torrey, E. F. (1983). *Surviving schizophrenia: A family manual.* New York: Harper & Row.

Tsuang, M. T. (1982). *Schizophrenia: The facts.* Oxford: Oxford University Press.

Vaughn, C. E., Snyder, K. S., Jones, S., Freeman, W., & Falloon, I. R. H. (1984). Family factors in schizophrenic relapse. *Archives of General Psychiatry, 41,* 1169-1177.

Wasow, M. (1985). Chronic schizophrenia and Alzheimer's disease: The losses for parents, spouses, and children compared. *Journal of Chronic Diseases, 38,* 711-716.

Watt, N. F., Shay, J. J., Grubb, T. W., & Riddle, M. (1982). Early identification and intervention with emotionally vulnerable children through the public schools. In M. J. Goldstein (Ed.), *Preventive intervention in schizophrenia: Are we ready?* (pp. 242-258). Rockville, MD: National Institute of Mental Health.

White, R. W. (1974). Strategies of adaptation: An attempt at systematic description. In C. V. Coelho, D. A. Hamburg, & J. E. Adams (Eds.), *Coping and adaptation.* New York: Basic Books.

# Index